THE BROKEN WAVE

HARVARD EAST ASIAN SERIES 90

The East Asian Research Center at Harvard University administers research projects designed to further scholarly understanding of China, Japan, Korea, Vietnam, Inner Asia, and adjacent areas.

The Broken Wave

---◆---

THE CHINESE COMMUNIST
PEASANT MOVEMENT, 1922-1928

ROY HOFHEINZ, JR.

HARVARD UNIVERSITY PRESS
CAMBRIDGE, MASSACHUSETTS
AND LONDON, ENGLAND   1977

Library of Congress Cataloging in Publication Data

Hofheinz, Roy, 1935-
    The broken wave.

    (Harvard East Asian series; 90)
    Bibliography: p.
    Includes index.
    1. China—Politics and government—1912-1937.
2. Communism—China.   3. Peasant uprisings—China.
I. Title.   II. Series
DS777.47.H65   1977   951.04'1   76-56097
ISBN 0-674-08391-1

PREFACE

This book is about a peasant revolution that failed. It is also about men with an idea of revolution that ultimately succeeded. These two concerns, rather than fascination with a voluminously documented historical tragedy, have led me to retell the story of the Chinese Revolution of the 1920s. Contemporary events compel us to consider the conditions that produce revolutions—especially rural ones—as well as the quality of the men who continue to rule the world's most populous nation.

Two theses emerge from this retelling. The first is historical: that the practice of rural revolution later propounded by Mao Tse-tung and others had its origins before the Red Army, the rural soviets, or the anti-Japanese liberated areas were even conceived of. A corollary of this thesis is that the characteristic attitudes of Peking's present-day leaders bear the stamp of this early failure as much as of later success. The second thesis is analytical: that the Chinese Communists failed to win their rural revolution in the 1920s because they had not laid the proper political foundation for it. By showing that revolutionary politics, like any other kind, requires a proper mixture of persuasion, compromise, and coercion, this thesis challenges those who would define revolutionary potential in other than political terms. The conditions for revolution, as well as for successful counterrevolution, are essentially artifacts of human effort rather than immutable givens of social structure, economics, or demography.

These theses point to no conclusions about the desirability of revolution or the moral worth of men who seek it. I remain persuaded that human warfare of whatever kind is inane. The real tragedy of the Chinese Revolution, to use Harold Isaacs's famous title, was not so much that one side failed to win as that the goals of national unity and broader political participation for the mass of villagers could not be achieved without great bloodshed. It is relevant to our concerns in the 1970s to learn why this was so.

This work could not have been done without help. I owe a great debt to many people who shared with me their knowledge of China. Etō Shinkichi, Ichiko Chūzō, Ishikawa Tadaō, and Eugene Wu pointed me to new materials and guided me through the maze of Chinese and Japanese documentation. Edward C. M. Chan, Frances Hsieh, June Mei, and Marcia Reed Yee helped me interpret the raw materials at our command. Donald W. Klein, Joseph S. Nye, Jr., Michel Oksenberg, Harold Zvi Schiffrin, and Ezra F. Vogel offered valuable observations on earlier drafts. Suzanne Berger and John D. Powell shared insights into other kinds of peasant politics than I treat here. My intellectual debt to my predecessors in the study of China in the twenties—Conrad Brandt, Robert North, Harold Isaacs, Jean Chesneaux, and C. Martin Wilbur—will be obvious to those who know of their seminal work. To John K. Fairbank, Benjamin I. Schwartz, and John M. H. Lindbeck, teachers and colleagues, I owe a special personal debt. Without their support and that of the East Asian Research Center at Harvard, where we worked together, this book would not have been written. Finally, Harriet Parker Hofheinz has contributed the hope and good cheer without which sustained scholarly effort is impossible.

The title of *The Broken Wave* carries a double meaning. Explicitly it promises to explore the wave of peasant revolution in south China that crested and crashed between 1922 and 1928, a task undertaken in Parts One and Two. Less evidently, it points to the father of Chinese rural communism, P'eng P'ai, whose chosen name mimicked the booming sound of breaking waves. Until he receives the recognition he deserves in China, Part Three will have to serve as a partial tribute to his seminal role in modern Chinese politics.

CONTENTS

TABLES

PART ONE

———◆———

Strategy

Does agrarian revolution
descend from heaven?

Stalin, May 1927

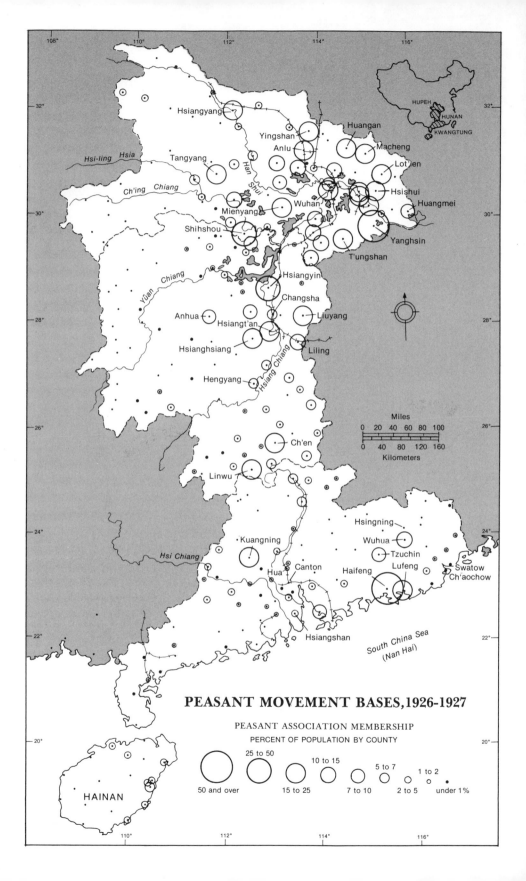

PEASANT MOVEMENT BASES, 1926-1927

PEASANT ASSOCIATION MEMBERSHIP
PERCENT OF POPULATION BY COUNTY

25 to 50   10 to 15   5 to 7   1 to 2

50 and over   15 to 25   7 to 10   2 to 5   under 1%

1

THE BIRTH
OF THE RURAL
STRATEGY

Not many realize today that the consciously articulated idea of peasant revolution is only a few decades old. Our perspective is distorted by the recent past. Just as a century ago Europe cowered at the thought of urban insurrection, we have been haunted throughout the 1950s and 1960s by the specter of peasant uprisings. The Malayan emergency of 1947-1953, the Philippine Huk insurgency, and the Viet Minh movement were Asian examples of what appeared to be a worldwide pattern of rural turmoil. The threat posed by a boldly stated strategy of rural revolution was one consideration that drove several American presidents to intervene in the Indochinese civil war.

Yet fifty years ago virtually no one would have argued that the place to start a revolution was in the countryside. In part the previous century's Marxist tradition, a tradition that regarded progress as an urban phenomenon closely linked to industrialism and demanding intellectual skills and leadership, inhibited the emergence of such a concept. Before 1920 there was also little empirical evidence of what we now so easily think of as the revolutionary potential of the peasantry. It is safe to say that China was the country where the present-day concept of peasant revolution was born. The Chinese model of revolution, with its emphasis on united fronts, rural bases, and politically sophisticated armies, remains in the quieter 1970s the major conceptual basis for theorists of rural revolution.

The rural strategy adopted successfully by Mao Tse-tung and other Chinese Communists in the 1930s and 1940s and by certain Chinese-oriented Communist parties in the 1950s and 1960s emerged from peculiarly Chinese circumstances of the 1920s. Between 1923 and 1927 both Russian and Chinese Communists argued heatedly among themselves and with the Chinese Nationalists, whom they supported, about how much help the dominant warlords could expect from the massive Chinese peasantry, already nearly four hundred million strong. Out of this argument and out of the crushing defeat of the Communists' rural strategy in 1927-1928 emerged a small group of Chinese Communist leaders determined to continue the revolution in the countryside. Their view of the nature of revolution, as well as of the role of the countryside in political affairs the world over, has been deeply affected by the arguments over tactics and strategy in south China a half-century ago.

We must put ourselves in the position of the radical politicians of the early 1920s to see what a new idea the rural strategy was. China was ruled, if that is a proper word for the control of military and financial power in the provincial capitals, by the degenerate successors of regional military governors of the last imperial dynasty. The so-called revolution of 1911, which produced the first Chinese republic, hardly altered the chain of command in the capital city of Peking, much less in the provinces. The leader of the Nationalist party (the Kuomintang), the missionary-trained revolutionary, Dr. Sun Yat-sen, was the sole exception. Sun's new party, based on his own ideology of opposition to the palace, on the support of China's extensive secret societies, and on money from wealthy overseas Chinese in Southeast Asia and America, grew rapidly in the early teens in south China and elsewhere, only to be declared illegal and driven underground by the resurgent former protectors of the monarchy. By the early 1920s the size of China's standing armies had grown by a factor of ten as military figures, having put down the tentative parliaments of the teens, sought to resolve the struggle for control of China by military buildup and struggle. Sun Yat-sen's own Kuomintang force, which captured the southern city of Canton in autumn of 1922 and declared the city liberated from the warlords, was itself simply one of these warlord armies.

The founders of the Chinese Communist party (CCP) in 1921 were themselves children of the declining new republic. The views of Ch'en Tu-hsiu and Li Ta-chao, the two cofounders, represented minor variations on the major theme of dissatisfaction with the performance of the postdynastic rulers. Their new party consisted exclusively of parlor intellectuals and student dissidents who at their birth might have been expected to become prominent members of China's mandarin class. Ch'en, Li, and other early Communists entered political life during the turmoil of the late teens, when waves of protest spread across the land against the high-handed disdain of the world powers for China's claims during the peace negotions at the end of the First World War. They, along with young Mao Tse-tung, a Hunanese provincial serving as Li Ta-chao's librarian at Peking University, were Nationalists before they were Communists, intellectuals before they were politicians, students of the Chinese classics before the Marxist classics.

It is commonplace to remark on the tardiness of Marxism-Leninism's arrival in China. None of the Communist party's founders had read much of Marx or Lenin before the Russian Revolution of October 1917. The claims of theoretical communism needed the practical proof of a capacity to transform a nation as large as Russia before they could sway young Chinese Nationalists. In the same way, the early Communists after their conversion paid little attention to the writings of Lenin on the role of agriculture and the peasantry in revolutions. When Lenin wrote in 1911 that the Chinese Revolution resembled the Russian events of 1905 in employing an alliance between town and country, few Chinese could see the parallel. In China there was no Narodnik populist movement to precede Communist workers into villages; there were no radical aristocrats prepared as in Russia to build rural democracy. Even young Marxists like Li Ta-chao and Mao Tse-tung learned as schoolboys that peasants (*nung-min,* or tilling people) were simple-minded beings easily dominated by the gentry class. Proponents of a rural Communist effort would have to demonstrate its efficacy before it would become an accepted part of the Communist program.

Little wonder then that the early history of the Chinese Communist party suggests no precocious commitment to rural work. The

earliest CCP programs did mention land-rent controls and food-
grain tax ceilings, but the first official CCP manifesto to the peasantry did not appear until October 1925.[1] Chinese Communists
moved individually into rural work well before their Central Committee gave its public blessing. This is not to say, however, that the
leaders of the party actively discouraged rural work. Their commitment to urban labor organization and to the anti-imperialist struggle simply crowded their concern with China's rural conditions into
the background. Ch'en Tu-hsiu publicly expressed his skepticism in
August 1923 in a note to a young supporter who urged large scale
rural and local Communist movements. Ch'en chided the enthusiast
for being too romantic and described China as a nation of small
peasants with an unwavering consciousness of private property.
"How could the Communist movement possibly expand in a rural
China of many land-owning peasants?" he asked.[2]

Ch'en could not have been encouraged by the results achieved
before 1924 in peasant organization. Not that he actively dissuaded
Communists from participating in rural movements, present-day
Maoist historians notwithstanding. In fact, in a little-known article
of late 1923 he called for Communist leadership in agitation
designed to bring the peasantry into the national revolutionary
movement. His suggestions on this occasion read like a tactical
handbook to the peasant movement of the future: work during slack
agricultural periods; use many visual aids; keep your slogans simple;
set up rural peasant associations designed to appeal to all strata in a
China lacking any clear class distinctions. But the essence of Ch'en's
attitude toward rural work was that it had to be a part of Communist efforts to support the national revolution. He pointed to the
failure of the first Communist peasant movement, that of P'eng P'ai
in Haifeng, which by late 1923 had collapsed in a wave of conservative local opposition.[3]

By 1924 the Chinese Communist Party was only four hundred
strong. While Ch'en carefully steered away from committing mea-
ger Communist forces to rural struggle, Moscow's message to China
throughout the twenties maintained a persistent, if sometimes
ambiguous, hint of agrarianism. As early as the Comintern's Second
Congress in July 1920 Moscow urged each Communist party to
become the party of the villages as well as of the towns. The Fourth
Congress, in November 1922, published the first agrarian action

program for the world Communist parties. This document showed the influence of the Indian Communist, M. N. Roy, who had begun to develop his view that revolutions in the countries of the East would have to rely on the broad peasant masses. Karl Radek rose at this congress to demand specifically that the Chinese Communists turn to the peasant masses as well as to the workers. By mid-1924, as the Chinese Communists began to engage in village work around Canton, the Comintern was encouraging them to "demonstrate that the Communist party is the *only* organization acceptable to the peasantry."[4]

It is tempting to argue that the Russians forced China's gradual turn toward village work after 1924. For three years between 1924 and 1927 the Comintern toyed with the inherent ambiguity of its position on revolution in the East. It jumped eagerly to support strikes and working-class movements in the cities whenever they appeared, such as during the May Thirtieth movement of 1925 or the 1925-1926 Hong Kong-Canton strike. But it also waxed eloquent about the rural potential. The high point of Moscow's romantic interest in the peasantry came with Nikolai Bukharin's speech to the Fifth Plenum of the Comintern in March 1925. Bukharin hinted that under certain conditions colonial and semicolonial societies might be able to move into socialism without going through the capitalist phase of development. He claimed to see such conditions already emerging in China, where the peasantry was becoming a self-conscious, ideologically motivated group whose numbers alone made its direct assistance in the socialist revolution indispensable. He divided the world into developed metropoles and backward colonies and compared the developed nations to defenseless cities surrounded by a hostile countryside. He employed a vivid image in his argument: "These conflicts amount to no less in the economic life of the world than clashes between the world city—the present industrial centers and the world village—the colonial periphery." It was a remarkable metaphor, one picked up again forty years later in an equally famous speech by Lin Piao, who doubtless had read Bukharin's report while a student at the Whampoa Academy in Canton. It pointed to the conclusion that the rural strategy was as inevitable in world revolution as Marx's or Lenin's proletarian one was for the developed countries.[5]

But convincing as the evidence of Moscow's explicit urging of the rural strategy on the Chinese Communists is, there is yet another element in the situation that hastened the Chinese Communist turn to the countryside and shaped the strategy to meet Chinese circumstances of the twenties. That factor was the Communist alliance with Sun Yat-sen's Kuomintang. The Communists turned to the countryside first in south China, in the neighborhood of Canton where Sun's party held sway after 1922. Without the Kuomintang, the Communists would have had little chance of gaining peasant support.

The circumstances suggest that the move was more an accident than a conscious product of the alliance between the two parties. Prior to the First Congress of the newly reorganized Kuomintang (KMT) in January 1924 the Nationalists had shown no interest in the countryside. Sun,who had begun to appoint Communists to committees to recommend reorganization procedures along Leninist lines in September 1922, turned to them in earnest only in 1924 in the expectation that they would help him expand his party's mass base. The Kuomintang in Kwangtung in 1924 was essentially an urban party, composed largely of members of well-entrenched craft unions such as the economically conservative Machinists' Union or the traditional base for Sun's overseas party, the Seamen's Union. The Communist party members in Canton were under strict orders from their Central Committee to maximize the growth rate not of their own party but of the Kuomintang.[6] Communist talents poured into building KMT strength where it had not previously existed. In the Canton area that meant in the rural towns and in the countryside. After a few weeks of organizational work in Canton in early 1924, for example, Communist organizers such as T'an P'ing-shan and Feng Chü-p'o moved to the surrounding counties to build KMT cells along the Canton model.[7] This seemingly natural and commonplace political activity was in fact unheard of in China at that time. It resulted less from a belief in the power of peasant organization than from the fact that the countryside was still a political vacuum for the Kuomintang as well as for the Communist party.

In a sense the very disinterest of Sun Yat-sen and the older revolutionary politicians in his entourage encouraged the Communists to make this plunge into rural work. Sun had from the beginning of the collaboration employed the Communists to draft manifestos and propaganda outlines to extend his party's appeal. These early tracts are strikingly devoid of any class analysis. Practically the only reference to the countryside is in the form of praise for the indigenous militia (Min-t'uan or Popular Corps). Curiously, the Communist-ghosted tracts of 1923 recommend arming the militia to shape it into a province-wide force of self-defense for the new Kuomintang government.[8] These naïve proposals, which made no provision for ensuring that the corps so formed would not fall into the hands of the counterrevolutionary opposition, suggest that neither Sun nor the Communists had thought much about the implications of the idea of a rural base for their revolution.

Sun Yat-sen's favorable attitude toward the countryside was a direct result of his ignorance of it. Sun's connections before the early 1920s had been with the power holders and revolutionary leaders of his time. Long periods of exile and travel to the West had kept him away even from China's treaty ports. He had made his last visit to his native village in Hsiangshan county near Canton in 1912. His writings before 1924 contain virtually nothing on the countryside apart from the occasional reference to county self-government. His speeches at the time of the First Congress of the (reorganized) Kuomintang in January 1924 show little grasp of the Leninist teachings his adviser, Borodin, supposedly had offered. He failed to understand that a Leninist party would be composed of only an elite fraction of the population. His notion of the division of the Chinese into the four categories of gentry, farmer, worker, and merchant allowed little potential for the class conflict that Marxist theory suggested.[9]

Despite these obvious divergences from the Communist line, Sun did begin to think about the problem of peasant organization in the last year of his life. Particularly in two speeches in midsummer 1924 Sun staked out a claim to being the uncle, if not the father, of the rural strategy for the KMT-CCP alliance. The speech of August 20 was given at the first public meeting of the newly formed KMT central peasant bureau. Sun himself called it the first encounter between the revolutionary party and the peasants. He began with his usual message about the wickedness of the Manchu dynasty and the cruel rule imposed by the foreign powers on Chinese soil. But he soon moved on to the question of the peasantry. The peasants toil and suffer to sow and reap the grain, he said. And yet if one day they refused to sell their grain, all of China would go begging. He took issue with those who argued that China's small holders were inherently better off than the Russian serfs because they owned their own land. The Russian lords possessed large and productive lands and could afford to be generous to their minions. The Chinese petty landlords by contrast "squeeze a pint from every peck, a coin from every string of cash." Under such conditions, Sun urged the peasants of Kwangtung to join the new revolutionary government and to form a Peasant Corps Army (Nung-t'uan-chün), promising government weapons that would turn it into the most powerful master of China. But Sun also warned against premature claims for peasant political power. He warned against moving prematurely and stressed the importance of the balanced development of the new mass organizations. He admitted his new government's continued need for the income from agricultural taxes and for support from all classes, including the landlord class. The peasantry must be brought to consciousness, he said, and consciousness meant willingness to accept the claims of his party over their own interests. In the peasant flag that he designed around this time, the brown plough of traditional agriculture is prominently superimposed on the red background of radicalism; but the masthead corner is dominated by the white-sun-blue-sky symbol of his Kuomintang party.[10]

It is hard to escape the conclusion that the Chinese Communists turned to the countryside neither to obey orders nor to follow a natural bent but rather in pursuit of potential opportunity. The origins of what we have called the strategy of rural revolution thus must be sought in the peculiar circumstances of Chinese politics of the 1920s—circumstances in which political questions were inevitably translated into military ones, in which the Communist party was not the dominant revolutionary party, and in which the rural population had not yet been touched by any modern political force. Moscow's encouragements, Ch'en Tu-hsiu's cautious interest, the rural successes of Cantonese Communists, and Sun Yat-sen's warm, if qualified, welcome to peasant agitators all beckoned the Chinese Communist party into the countryside around Canton and then elsewhere. But the very circumstances that generated the rural strategy bore the seeds of its defeat in 1927-1928.

Turning to village politics has its costs. Villages are scattered and rustic, their inhabitants poor and diffident. In seeking the villagers' support, one risks losing that of more influential, wealthy, or powerful persons because the needs of the former may conflict with those of important city people or with the elders of their own villages. Where circumstances force a decision between rural and urban constituencies, the countryside is at a disadvantage unless it can capitalize on its strengths: a large population and open space. And even where the countryside is still considered a valuable constituency, there may be far quicker ways to political power than relying on the rural strategy.

Reluctance to adopt a rural strategy was thus a result of much more than simple ignorance of rural potentials. It was easy to mouth phrases about a twenty-four-million-man Peasant Army of Kwangtung but not so easy to organize one. It was easy to propose that farmers stop paying rent but not so easy to enforce the proposal. The task of the Communists who proposed the rural strategy to their Kuomintang allies was to convince them that peasant support was relevant to their common revolutionary goals. These efforts continued unabated until the first split in 1927 broke the alliance. But it is fair to say that within the first year of the collaboration they had already failed to be convincing.

In 1924-1925 the Communist leaders of the Kuomintang peasant movement announced important contributions to the greater cause under the rubric of political struggle. On four separate occasions before Sun Yat-sen's death in March 1925, it was claimed, the newly formed peasant associations and their associated Peasant Self-Defense Army played decisive roles in what was called political struggle.

On one of these occasions, Sun proposed establishing a province-wide corps of militiamen in Kwangtung, a Popular Corps in which workers, merchants, and peasants would all have their own units. It was a shining example of Sun's irrepressible naïveté: of the three great classes in the corps, only the merchants had the means to arm their own militia. Canton's greatest crisis of 1924 erupted in August when Sun discovered that the merchants had purchased enough weapons in Hong Kong to equip a force that rivaled his own army. On August 10 Sun seized a boatload of arms consigned to the great Hong Kong banker, Ch'en Lien-po, in Canton. By the twenty-sixth Sun had closed down all commerce, received a rebuke from England's foreign minister, and witnessed open combat in the streets of his revolutionary capital.

The crisis was ultimately resolved by compromise, but the terms of the compromise insulted the new leaders of the peasant cause by denying the Canton Suburban Peasant Association the right to vote in new elections for mayor of the city. Thus the inaugural meeting of the Canton Suburban Peasant Association devoted itself entirely to demonstrations in favor of a vote for farmers. The handful of associations in other counties sent telegrams of protest. Well-organized, nonviolent, and unfortunately nonproductive, the new peasant movement's initial participation in a political movement was more like a Chartist rally than a peasant insurrection.

The second occasion for political struggle came less than a month later when Sun Yat-sen embarked on the short train ride to Shaokuan to begin his abortive Northern Expedition. Sun took along with him several thousand members of the Kwangtung Peasant Army. The expedition marked the first instance of what was already called armed propaganda. "We intend," declared the Peasant Army officers, "to cause the peasants in every village through which the Revolutionary Army passes . . . to rise up and give approval and assistance to the revolutionary government, to rise up and resist the aggression of the warlords."[11] A noble task, which when it could be translated into actual practice twenty-odd years later would bring a different peasant movement and revolutionary army to victory over other warlords. But this time it was merely empty exhortation. The corps did travel on Sun's train, fanning out at whistle stops to spread handbills, but they did little more than enjoy the ride.

A few days later the peasant officers had their third chance to play a politically important role when Sun canceled his expedition to return in force to Canton. The Merchants' Corps had in his absence breached the August agreement. Sun and his Communist advisers planned a large rally down the main street of Canton to demonstrate their revolutionary power to the insolent bourgeoisie. The bourgeoisie responded by surrounding the parade and opening fire.

In the shooting the peasant associations and peasant institute students lost eleven killed and eighty captured—enough to demonstrate peasant willingness to sacrifice for Sun's cause. Sun took the survivors into his residence to be his personal bodyguards for the duration of the incident. But the peasant contingent marched at the rear of the retreating procession, as befitted their second-class status as revolutionaries, so they suffered fewer losses than did the cadets of the Whampoa Academy. When the next day Sun moved his headquarters to the Whampoa campus, again the farmers took a back seat to the soldiers. Chiang Kai-shek, the young principal officer returned from Russia, refused to permit the unarmed country boys a bivouac on his academy grounds. And on October 14 and 15 Chiang finally put down the "paper tigers" of the Merchants' Corps in the brief house-to-house campaign that first brought him to prominence. He owed no debt whatever to the motley peasant crew. With two thousand crack troops and sound Russian military advice, who needed a few hundred men from the surrounding countryside? The associations tried feebly to claim some of the victory, but their participation, while clearly relevant, had not been decisive.

The fourth putative contribution claimed in 1924 owed far more to Sun's personal largesse than to any real movement strengths. Sun, his hope of conquering China by a quick military march dashed, considered seeking diplomatic support from the politicians in Peking. He volunteered to visit the old capital and join in a national assembly. Communist leaders convinced Sun that he would demonstrate his power over the masses by appearing with ordinary peasants in his delegation. In fact, the four or five Kwangtung leaders he took with him were the only self-styled peasants to attend the meeting, and Sun was favorably impressed by the publicity he got. Back in Canton, peasant organizers made the expected claims; but Sun fell ill, weakened, and died in Peking by early March 1925, leaving Canton in the hands of men less easily impressed with tokenism.[12]

The striking fact about all four of these 1924 instances of political struggle is that they took place in cities. It might be argued that so long as the proponents of the rural strategy have to produce immediate urban results to win their case, they will be unlikely to succeed. The year 1925 should have given them a better opportunity to demonstrate the strength of the organized peasantry, for that was the year the Kuomintang moved beyond the Canton delta into the hinterland of the province. Surely during the great campaigns of that year to unify the province the peasant movement had an opportunity to demonstrate its great value. The peasant associations and their organizers participated in three major ground-taking operations in 1925 and once again made impressive claims for peasant efficacy. But again the details are instructive.

Chiang Kai-shek's decision to launch an Eastern Expedition into the coastal counties between Canton and Swatow brought his new Party Army, composed largely of Whampoa graduates and politically loyal recruits, into contact with the countryside for the first time. The expedition set out on January 20 and by early March had moved in three routes all the way to the Han River valley and Ch'aochow Bay on the east, bringing dozens of county seats under Canton's rule for the first time in several years. Peasant movement leaders, helping plan the expedition with Chiang and his Russian advisers, had obtained promises from Chiang's chief aide, Hsu Ch'ungchih, that he would not forage for grain en route, that he would not commandeer private homes for quartering, and that he would not impress coolies. These three promises, the first crude form of the "Eight Rules and Three Disciplines" that in various versions became the official code of conduct of later Chinese Communist armies, were indeed kept and doubtless contributed to the army's favorable reception along its route. Once again peasant organizers, this time assisted by a number of Communist political representatives fresh from the Whampoa Academy, gave out handbills along the way. They distributed a half-million proclamations to enemy troops, fifty thousand scores of revolutionary songs, and a hundred thousand posters with proclamations to the peasantry. This time the peasant organizers took advantage of their training and stayed several days in selected villages, organizing associations and laying the base for future movement growth. Eyewitness accounts of the expedition published in the Communist party's official organ spoke convincingly of the warm welcome villagers gave the Party Army.[13]

The young Whampoa cadets certainly appreciated the receptions that were carefully prepared for them in some localities. The entry into Haifeng county seat on this expedition was indeed spectacular. P'eng P'ai, the native peasant leader, had preceded the army by four or five days. By the time Chiang Kai-shek's lead division arrived P'eng had staged a coup d'état and assembled a crowd estimated at thirty thousand, all of whom he claimed were loyal supporters of the peasant association he had created three years earlier.

Despite the achievements of Kwangtung peasant movement figures during the expedition, there were a number of signs that Chiang Kai-shek's military officers were not overwhelmed. The armies were interested far less in the reception than in the victory. They moved quickly from point to point, dwelling only long enough to wipe out pockets of armed resistance. Army propaganda men, although prominent at the first meetings held after a town or village was captured, soon moved on with their units. The ordinary foot soldier obviously enjoyed having a friendly population to fight for; but it was abundantly clear that *he,* and not the hustling political activists, was doing the fighting. It was one thing to strike a successful bargain with commander Hsu Ch'ung-chih, but Hsu could and did remain unconvinced that the matter of discipline had made the crucial difference in his campaign.

The second military operation of 1925 indicates that peasant movement leaders had begun to recognize their dilemma, if not to provide an answer to it. Peasant associations claimed they gave substantial military assistance in the operation to rescue the provincial capital of Canton from the Kwangsi militarists who seized it in Chiang Kai-shek's absence. Operatives from the Kwangtung Provincial Peasant Association staffed the reconnaissance office of the Party Army and drew upon their contacts among the suburban population for intelligence. At the climax of the struggle for the city (June 8-12, 1925) as the KMT armies converged on Canton, peasant associations supplied porters and sentries. Chiang Kai-shek entered the city accompanied by a farmers' brigade. Despite their efforts, the peasant movement leaders had begun to harbor doubts about their own effectiveness. A number of comrades, one Communist peasant committee admitted that summer, were complaining that the peasantry gained nothing from the defeat of the Kwangsi mutineers. The more militarily useful the movement's contributions were, the less it could claim that political work among farmers possessed a peculiar efficacy.

The third major military campaign of 1925 added a final reason why the rural appeal remained unpersuasive. The welcome given the Second Eastern Expedition, following the first by only six months, was by all accounts not as strong as the first. There were several other important differences between the two eastern campaigns. By late 1925 the Nationalist military had finally been forged into a coordinated force. This second expedition moved with a ruthless unified efficiency that left little time or need for public relations activity. Furthermore, by late 1925 the province of Kwangtung had been given an administrative backbone it had earlier lacked. Each of five new regions, one of which was being established in the expedition, was expected to supply its quota of funds to the provincial government, each region receiving in return its share of military appropriations. When the expeditions ended, the focus of revolutionary work shifted from military control and expansion to the consolidation of territory. Six months earlier only the peasant movement organizers had spoken for vast portions of the province's thirty million inhabitants, but now a party had to be staffed, the peace had to be kept, and the administration had to be established. All these were jobs for which the peasant associations (except perhaps in Haifeng) were little suited.

The peasant movement attempted through the rest of the year and a half to make the utmost of its participation in revolutionary struggle up to the point of the unification of Kwangtung at the end of 1925. There was hardly a document that failed to observe the ritual mention of the Canton mayoral election, the aborted Northern Expedition, and the two successful eastern ones. But no one seemed to notice that the nature of participation in these events had changed with the shifting of political forces. The promise of peasant support may have been very appealing to Sun Yat-sen, in a quandary over the future of his latest revolutionary adventure, but it would be quite another thing to his successors. In December 1925 the Kwangtung Provincial Peasant Association spoke out against the widespread view of what it called "some unenlightened men" that there was no longer a need for peasant association organization now that the province was under control. During 1925 they had tried to convince skeptics that a rural strategy was necessary by claiming victories that were not truly theirs. Now critics arose to ask whether the associations had any political use at all.[14]

The lesson that might have been drawn, but was not, was the following: so long as political struggle could be directed at the outside enemy of the revolutionary coalition, it would be welcome. And insofar as it was truly effective against that enemy and not simply a pleasant surprise, it would be impressive. In 1925 the Kuomintang generals appeared to be still convinced that no popular army could be defeated, nor an unpopular one win. But how many more swift expeditions, accomplished by a trained, disciplined, and well-armed military force, would really require mass support and the lofty motivation of the peasant organizers? The tragedy was that some of the military commanders—those few who after 1927 joined the Red

Armies—required the crushing of the peasant movement to convince them of the need to work in the countryside. By then a strategy of working in step with non-Communist politicians, with urban labor organizations, and with the new military elite had become impossible.

THE RESTRAINT OF THE PEASANTRY

Nineteen twenty-six was the fateful year for the peasant strategy in China. It began with the striking rise in Communist party influence over the Kuomintang Central Committee evidenced in the Second Kuomintang Congress in January. Sharp setbacks to the Communist cause came in the wake of Chiang Kai-shek's masterful March 20 coup. Then sweeping military victories in the Northern Expedition from July to October opened up vast areas of central China to new rural political activity. By the end of the year, strong signs appeared that the Communist party intended to radicalize itself and to place virtually all its hopes on the peasant movement.

One group of revolutionaries did not consistently represent the rural view in discussions within the KMT-CCP alliance. By 1926 at least three groups formed conceptions of the peasant movement's role in the national revolution. The first group, the non-Communist KMT politicians, continued to support mass activity; this group was loosely referred to as the KMT Left. Men like Ch'en Kung-po and Kan Nai-kuang continued throughout 1926 to welcome the efforts of Communists and peasant activists to build the mass base. But their support assumed that the peasant organizations would be willing to accept discipline and to shoulder burdens of taxation and administration. The second group was composed of active, would-be peasant politicians who were largely members of the Communist party. In early 1926 they were almost exclusively from Kwangtung, where peasant organizations were already half a million strong. This group by 1926 became an entrenched interest group devoted to preserving its hard-won gains in the countryside against myriad enemies both within and without the revolutionary movement. The third group consisted of the handful of Communist leaders who had brought their party into the alliance, sponsored, at least privately, Communist participation in rural work, and worried about the future of the national Kuomintang revolution after it succeeded.

This third group, dominated by Ch'en Tu-hsiu, ultimately decided the fate of the Communist-controlled peasant movement. When peasant movement leaders found at the end of 1925 that they could not convince the KMT military of the need to build a mass party, they and the Communist Central Committee turned to Ch'en for support. As it turned out, that support was late and, until the last moment, only half-hearted. The reasons are worth examining.

First, the Communist party had hesitated even during the period of rapid growth of the peasant associations in Kwangtung in 1925 to give unequivocal support to rural work. At its Fourth Congress held secretly in Shanghai in January 1925 the Central Committee had passed a separate resolution on the peasant movement that put it on record as opposing bad gentry, high taxes, and advance rents. But the communique of the congress linked the word peasant each time with a hyphen to the word worker and failed to provide a political program for the peasantry. Furthermore, Ch'en Tu-hsiu's Central Committee openly criticized the Kwangtung peasant movement for its radicalism in the matter of rent reduction. This was obviously a reference to the Kwangning county crisis of 1924-1925, which was still in full swing. The inclination to restrain the excesses of village agitators thus dated from early 1925 and sprang from a fear of disrupting the delicate balance between Communists and non-Communists in the Kuomintang. In early 1925 peasant organizers were effectively warned to keep Communist needs at the forefront.[15]

Secondly, in mid-1925 the Communist Central Committee became entranced once again with the potential for urban unrest. An incident in the foreign concessions of Shanghai in late May spread in a matter of days into a nationwide antiforeign agitation. This May Thirtieth movement, patterned in organizational style as well as in name after the earlier May Fourth movement of 1919, gave an enormous boost to the CCP fortunes: from a party of a thousand at the Fourth Congress, it grew during the summer to one of over ten thousand members. The very success of the summer's urban movement cast a shadow on the party's commitment to the peasantry. In November a poll showed that less than 5 percent of the newly expanded Communist party was of rural origin.[16]

The third element in Ch'en's thinking emerged logically from the second. The party's nationwide growth confirmed Ch'en's suspicions that Communists in Kwangtung were wrong to place so much faith in the Kuomintang-run peasant movement. There would be other opportunities in other provinces. If the Communists were to continue peasant work, they ought to be willing to claim the rewards. Although early in the year Ch'en had urged peasant organizers not to antagonize the Kuomintang, in late 1925 he struck a new note of independence. The most important allies of the peasantry, Ch'en argued in the party's first full-blown "Letter to the Peasantry" in October, are not the bourgeoisie but the working class. The peasant associations should demand full financial and political independence for themselves, as did labor unions. The peasant movement could no longer rely on the Kuomintang to protect it as had the Kwangtung comrades, who Ch'en said should stop behaving like mere delegates of their movement to the Communist party.[17]

These three elements — fear of breaking up the revolutionary alliance, a longing for urban influence, and the desire to maintain disciplined control of the peasant movement for specifically Communist ends — shaped Ch'en Tu-hsui's peasant strategy in 1926. The effect of the year's crises and opportunities was simply to alter Ch'en's emphasis. For example, in October 1925 he had noted that the peasant movement should develop independently of the national government but remain within the Kuomintang; in July 1926 he argued that the time had come to keep the associations organizationally independent of even the allied party. In 1925 he suggested the Communists expand their own party organization in the countryside, but in July 1926 he demanded that they seize the hegemony of the peasant movement. At the same time, his fear of antagonizing the bourgeois KMT supporters led him to recommend that landlords, even fairly well-to-do ones, ought to be accepted into the associations so long as they qualified as virtuous gentry. The potential contradictions in these recommendations revealed how much Ch'en was out of touch with the practical scene of rural work. How could Communists openly seize power within the associations and still win over the wealthy landowners?[18]

Two events of mid-1926 obscured the inherent contradictions in the Communist party policy. The first was Chiang's cleverly executed démarche against his Russian and Communist advisers in mid-March. In one stroke the supposedly leftist general removed the Communist deputy commander of his navy, demoted the Soviet and Communist advisers in his army, and disarmed the Communist

Picket Corps, which had spearheaded the recent anti-British strikes in Canton. But in the next several months Chiang backed off from the confrontation with the Communists and appeared satisfied with a mild set of resolutions limiting CCP influence in Kuomintang central offices. The ambiguity of Chiang's personal position made Chen Tu-hsiu's response difficult. Some voices urged an immediate insurrection to get back powers Chiang had stolen; others, largely Russian, blamed the adversity on excessively ambitious Chinese Communists. Ch'en simply drew the conclusion that the new right wing under Chiang Kai-shek was too powerful to confront directly at the moment.

He was saved from the confrontation by the second event: the launching of the Northern Expedition in early July. Before March 20 Ch'en might have welcomed an expansion of Kuomintang influence in the central and northern part of the country, but now he saw that it seemed more likely to produce an expansion of the new militarist influence than of the Communist influence. Yet his desire to keep the alliance alive and the strong recommendations of the Comintern adviser, Michael Borodin, led him to offer weak public support for the planned campaign. The irony was that the spectacular military successes of the expedition by mid-September opened up such rich new territories for Communist organization that even Ch'en was forced to applaud.[19]

The standard interpretation of the Great Revolution of 1925-1927 has been that local peasant movement Communists were uniformly more radical than Ch'en Tu-hsiu and had demanded early on that he come out for nationalization of the land and local insurrections. The reality was quite different, though it was obscured in the disciplined unanimity of public meetings and documents. In fact, by 1925 the Kwangtung rural Communist operatives had developed a powerful interest in their own movement, which Ch'en Tu-hsiu seemed at times cavalierly to dismiss. The Kwangtung Communists resented Ch'en's denigration of the importance of their work. Working within the Kuomintang but remaining thoroughly Communist, they had produced a bureaucracy with a sizable, if not yet powerful following. Ch'en's insistence that they yield control of their associations to what he called the KMT village Left, if it could be interpreted in their context at all, implied surrender to their most virulent enemies. Nowhere could the clash of their interests with his be seen more clearly than in his recommendations that the Popular Corps, which by 1926 was the most potent anti-Communist force in Kwangtung, be embraced and turned over to virtuous gentry—an expression they reacted to with hilarity.

At the same time, there is no evidence that Kwangtung peasant leaders in 1926 demanded a solution to the land question. That they did was asserted most recently in Chang Kuo-t'ao's memoir.[20] But Chang's remarks as well as those of Chu Ch'i-hua (Li Ang), who supported him, appear to be based upon the views not of the peasant movement groups but of the Kwangtung Regional Committee of the Communist party, an urban body led by former student organizers such as Chang T'ai-lei and then Ch'en Tu-hsiu's son, Yen-nien. That the urban Communists might favor introducing radical slogans so they could more easily distinguish the Left from the Right in the confused village scene is understandable. But the concerns of rural operatives in Kwangtung were less with sharpening struggle than with self-protection. Having urged the rural strategy, or rather, unlike other Communists, having practiced it, they naturally sought to carry it through to a favorable conclusion. Communist party discipline did not allow them to express their true demands openly. They did so only indirectly, as for example at an important conference of the Kwangtung Provincial Peasant Association (attended by Ch'en Tu-hsiu) in August 1926.[21] Their demands were rooted in local conditions. Only two of the five regions of Kwangtung, it appears, were demanding so much as a reduction in rent. All regarded the Popular Corps as their greatest difficulty. What they needed and demanded most were weapons to defend themselves. Only the Nationalist armies in Canton could have supplied them. Neither Ch'en Tu-hsiu in Canton nor Stalin in Moscow could do so. The charge that Ch'en Tu-hsiu restrained an impetuous, radical Kwangtung peasantry was not only vacuous, it openly expressed the failure of the peasant strategy as practiced in the Great Revolution.

BY MID-1927 most leftist politicians regarded the peasantry as the key to their revolutionary strategy. A complex interplay between ideology and reality, hope, and exigency drove Moscow, Ch'en Tu-hsiu, a vociferous minority of radical Communists, and a remnant of the Kuomintang Left to embrace peasant organization as the last hope of the national revolution.

Controversy raged after 1927 over the positions taken by the major actors. Ch'en Tu-hsiu's detractors insisted that he never relished the unleashing of an aroused peasantry. Stalin's enemies suggested that he sold out a real possibility of rural revolution to a handful of unreliable militarists. Borodin's critics chided the Russian-born former Chicago schoolteacher for courting first Chiang Kai-shek, then Chiang's rival Wang Ching-wei for too long and neglecting an eager, willing, and available partner: the armed and organized peasant. Few have suggested that political factors had already shaped the outcome.

The odds against the success of a strategy of open class warfare in Kwangtung were great indeed. Already in 1926 the Kwangtung peasant movement leaders had hinted at their private skepticism about the value of escalated violence in the villages. The striking fact about the last year of the Great Revolution is that the rebellious leadership in Hupeh and Hunan chose to sharpen the struggle and throw their still infantile organizations into the thick of civil warfare rather than scale down the demands and ambitions of the peasant movement in order to consolidate its not inconsiderable gains.

In order to understand the psychology of revolution in early 1927, it is important to review happenings in Wuhan. Wuhan was the collective name of the tri-city megalopolis (Hankow, Wuch'ang, and Hanyang) set astride the Yangtze as it passed through the flood plains of central Hupeh. Wuhan's population of more than a million had fallen to the Nationalist armies on October 10, 1926. The armies that had taken Hupeh, and before it central Hunan, were spearheaded by three of the eight corps Chiang Kai-shek had put together in July at the start of the expedition. One of the three was the Iron Army of Cantonese under Chang Fa-k'uei, which before its departure had defended the peasant movement in Kwangtung perhaps more than Chiang's own First Army. The third division of this army had rescued P'eng P'ai and other Communist peasant organizers from a near-disaster in Kwangning county in 1924. Beneath the Iron Army was an independent division (actually only a regiment in size) led by the Whampoa Academy Communist, Yeh T'ing, the highest ranking Communist officer in China. The breach of Wuch'ang was produced in no small part by the efforts of a Communist underground agent named Yü Shai-tu, a Whampoa graduate who later figured prominently in the Autumn Harvest Insurrection.

The rest of the Nationalist armies in the expedition did not stop their march across China with the taking of Wuhan. Chiang's First Army and the other two, now supplemented by literally dozens of ragtag units, marched northeastward through Kiangsi and by January and February 1927 were well on their way to Shanghai on the east coast of China. These units were the precursors of the *tsa-parh* (variegated armies) over which Chiang Kai-shek was to exercise such masterly sway in the next two decades. Their movement eastward marked the origin of the split between the Communist and Nationalist forces.

Wuhan soon became a Communist capital in all but fact. The Communist Chang Kuo-t'ao was assigned as plenipotentiary of the Central Committee and set up his offices in an ancient temple in Wuch'ang.[22] In December Borodin arrived, bringing with him the greater portion of the Canton national government officers (though not peasant bureau chief Kan Nai-kuang). Ch'en Tu-hsiu for some time resisted moving to Wuhan because he considered Shanghai to be the axis on which modern China revolved.[23] Then as Borodin arrived, so did Ch'en. The *Hsiang-tao chou-pao* (Guide weekly), heretofore a Shanghai organ, was published out of Hankow from December 5, 1926.

The mass organizations had preceded the party leaders in the provincial capitals of Ch'angsha and Wuhan. By April 1927 there were ten separate addresses in Hankow housing bureaus of the peasant movement alone; they included the Communist and the KMT bureaus and committees, the provincial associations, and the Hankow City Peasant Association. The drab walls of the ancient town were quickly covered and recovered with multicolored posters of the latest slogans and mobilization orders. Conferences, congresses, and mass meetings filled the calendar. By early spring, the young American reporter, Anna Louise Strong, eager to seek out the romance of the revolution, found Wuhan "the most exciting place on earth."[24]

It could not in fact be a Communist capital, however, because behind the gaudy red trappings stood the harsh facts of military and political power. To be sure, compromise with Chiang Kai-shek did not long remain necessary. Borodin, by insisting that the national government be established in Hankow, by forming a joint conference of the Kuomintang and national government officials to run that government, and by dictating these terms to Chiang Kai-shek, rid himself momentarily of Chiang's threat. On January 18, 1927, the split between Wuhan and Nanch'ang—where Chiang quickly set up a rival Central Committee—became irrevocable, and Borodin lost Chiang's support. Chiang was free thereafter of the Communist party, but the Communists would still remain unable to force their branch of the Kuomintang to declare Chiang a traitor.

Behind Borodin in Wuhan stood the new Kuomintang Left, united only in an unwillingness to submit themselves to Chiang, but otherwise a motley congeries of old T'ung meng hui revolutionaries, Western-educated overseas Chinese, and a tiny handful of intellectual politicians. And behind this group, which included Borodin and which dominated the Wuhan national government, stood the armies: the Fourth of Chang Fa-k'uei and the Sixth, larger and more powerful, of the Hunanese Buddhist general, T'ang Sheng-chih. The relation between these forces was doubtless best characterized by Borodin: the civil was to the military as the rabbit was to the anaconda.[25]

Before making the move to Wuhan, Ch'en Tu-hsiu took time to reconsider his July views of the peasant strategy. In the summer, after the March to May rollback in Communist influence in Kwangtung, it seemed clear that an escalation of demands for the peasant movement would be tantamount to suicide. But in November there were new pressures building up and new opportunities being offered. The Comintern seemed more eager than ever to sell the idea of agrarian revolution. Borodin, if we can believe Chu Ch'i-hua, was pushing all within his considerable influence to study the land question and think about solving it.[26] A radical delegation from the Comintern was in Shanghai urging Ch'en leftward.

By November 1926, Ch'en Tu-hsiu thought he could detect a turning tide in peasant movement fortunes all across China. Though the Kwangtung peasant movement leaders remained as gloomy as they had been in the summer, Ch'en felt able to assert that their province had reached a new stage. In a report to the Politburo sometime in mid-November, Ch'en claimed that many of the problems after March 20 had been caused by sloppy work by the Kwangtung Communist Peasant Movement Committee and they had already been corrected. He was doubtless referring to the enor-

mous effort that had been put into training peasant cadres and
shoring up the Communist organization. But more important,
Ch'en declared, the Kuomintang in Kwangtung now seemed more
receptive to peasant work. He noted several recent resolutions reaf-
firming support for the peasantry and gladly announced the resignation of the staunch anti-Communit chief of civil administration.
He referred admiringly to a Kuomintang local-national joint conference of October 15 that passed a new political program for the
peasantry far more satisfying than the ones drafted at the preceding
KMT national congresses.[27]

Ch'en, of course, did not realize that Borodin's manipulation
behind the scenes to obtain this platform from the conference was a
major source of irritation to a number of Cantonese politicians and
may have caused the defection of the central peasant bureau chief,
Kan Nai-kuang, a fortnight later. Articles submitted to his own
Guide weekly continued to warn of impending disaster in the
Kwangtung countryside.[28] He noted only that there were rumors
that provincial military governor Li Chi-shen had privately threatened to put controls on the Kwangtung movement. Overall, he
remained hopeful about the new stage of development.

Other provinces gave Ch'en even better grounds for optimism.
Not only were those central Yangtze cities under the control of
Nationalist forces under strong Communist influence, but the expedition passing up the center of Hunan (though not that passing
through Kiangsi to the east) had reportedly received an enthusiastic
welcome from the peasantry. The peasant movement in Hunan was
growing rapidly; three-quarters of the counties in Hunan with an
active peasant movement were, he believed, under Communist control. The newly established KMT officialdom of Hunan was supplying money to the movement to build training schools and finance
their operations.[29]

These sentiments along with pressure from the Comintern and
from his son Yen-nien, who headed the radical Kwangtung Regional Committee, are doubtless the reasons why Ch'en began to
prepare a move to the left in his agrarian policy before moving to
Wuhan. On November 4 and 5 he met with a delegation of the Communist International in Shanghai and drew up a nationwide propaganda program for the peasant movement.[30] This program was as
radical as most of the documents produced several months later dur-

ing the height of the Wuhan euphoria. It included a clause favoring the confiscation of land belonging to large landlords, militarists, bad gentry, monasteries, and temples. Although earlier KMT and Communist programs had often mentioned rent relief and some had suggested distributing uncultivated or state-owned land to poorer farmers, none had mentioned the taking of land by confiscation. Ch'en's draft recommended setting up political regimes of the common people in villages that would completely control all armed force in their area. Ch'en even approved a resolution on preparations for insurrection in the countryside that stressed the need for peasant armed forces.[31]

Despite these indications that Ch'en was prepared to move to positions on land, local power, and armed force that his party would wait six months to endorse, this draft became a dead letter. The Trotskyists later blamed the disappearance of this draft on the rightist opportunism of Ch'en and Borodin. They claimed the two had suppressed the document for three or four months and that only in January had it been circulated to local party organizations. Presumably it would then have been available to Mao's Hunan party organization in January, even if he had not known about it while in Shanghai in November. To the Trotskyists, this was clear proof of Ch'en's duplicity.

But there is no reason to look further than Moscow to explain why Ch'en failed to circulate this program more widely. The fate of T'an P'ing-shan at the Seventh Plenum of the Comintern demonstrated this painfully. T'an was the delegate who bore Ch'en's draft to the Comintern Plenum in late November and who ought to have spoken for it in the sessions. But Stalin and Bukharin would not permit him to present the Communist draft and instead persuaded him to substitute the October 15 Kuomintang program.[32] The Seventh Plenum resolution that T'an carried back with him did mention confiscation,[33] but limited the targets of that measure to those (including large landlords) who were fighting against the Kuomintang.[34] This introduction of a political consideration in the determination of whose land was to be confiscated would make a great deal of difference.

The Hunan delegation, later famous for its radicalism, produced a strategy of compromise at this November Plenum. They urged more concessions to the Kuomintang, compromise with the less reactionary rightists, and restraints on the "infantile disorders" of peasant Communists. The Hunanese views sounded suspiciously like Ch'en's own conservative July prescriptions for the Kwangtung movement. But Ch'en had shifted his ground in the intervening four months. He agreed with the Hunanese criticism of infantilism but criticized them for proposing to compromise with the KMT Right. The task was to create a broad peasant left wing within the Kuomintang. Although in July Ch'en urged the peasant movement to build a strong and independent Communist party to control the peasant movement, he now urged the Hunanese to put their energies instead into building the Kuomintang's basic-level organizations, the branches and party offices that could absorb true peasant elements.

He was almost back in 1924, when Communists were the first into the Kwangtung countryside to organize for the Kuomintang. Was it that doing KMT work went much easier in Hunan or that the Comintern had criticized his July stress on Communist work or that the Kwangtung restraint-and-self-strengthening program had shown severe weaknesses? We do not know. Whatever the reason, Ch'en, as secretary, to the end of his days would stick by his hapless line of building a village KMT Left.

Shortly after this exchange with the Hunanese, Ch'en moved to Hankow and received Moscow's Seventh Plenum directives. In a CCP plenum called on December 12, he explained the new directives and insisted that there was no need to raise the land question. We have no full text, but if the Trotskyists are to be believed, Ch'en reported that the greatest danger of the moment was the move to the left of the mass movement, which might easily attract the wrath of the Right. The disease of infantile leftism was his target, and its symptoms, he said, were "exorbitant demands" and "seizure of land by peasants."[35] After receiving the Comintern's response to his draft program, Ch'en must have decided to postpone introducing it to the party until the next party congress. New radical ideas would have to come from another quarter.

Rather than a puppet of the Russians or a pro-Kuomintang rightist, Ch'en Tu-hsiu thus appears in late 1926 as a Communist politician whipsawed by conflicting forces. Discouraged by attacks on the peasant movement in Kwangtung, he urged the movement not to provoke its own destruction. Encouraged by Northern Expedition successes, he urged the Communist party to maximize its gains in newly captured territories. But always the loyal Communist, by the end of the year Ch'en was persuaded by Stalin and Borodin to delay his plans for radicalizing the rural strategy. His silence became the cue for another Communist politician, Mao Tse-tung of Hunan, to enter the drama of rural strategy.

2

MAO TSE-TUNG
AS A RURAL
STRATEGIST

No name is more closely associated with the rise of the rural strategy of Communist revolution than that of the Hunanese Mao Tse-tung. From the jungles of Africa to the parlors of urban America, his name is invoked instead of Bukharin's or Ch'en Tu-hsiu's or P'eng P'ai's by those who appeal to the Chinese model of revolution. Considering that he led the Chinese Communist party to its victory in 1949 and that his followers have little to gain by belittling his historical role, this is entirely understandable. But if we are to appreciate the forces that produced the Chinese Communist victory and the attitudes produced by that victory, we must put the man in his proper place.

In early 1927 Mao Tse-tung was thirty, the veteran of three years' effort at organizing for the Kuomintang. Little, if any, of that effort went into the countryside. Rather, Mao concentrated on whipping up enthusiasm for the alliance with the Kuomintang among his fellow Hunanese, on perfecting the propaganda apparatus of the Nationalist party, and on educating young Communist recruits to the peasant movement in comfortable Canton. On his one brief trip to his native village in mid-1925, he worked to drum up support for anti-imperialist rallies in the provincial capital of Ch'angsha. Unlike

P'eng P'ai, the true founder of the peasant movement, Mao was a late convert to the rural strategy who arrived at it largely through calculating observation rather than the practice of rural campaigning.

Mao's biographers often trace his interest in the peasantry to his boyhood experiences in Shaoshan, Hunan, where he was the eldest son of a well-to-do farmer. Alternatively, they note his familiarity with the classical novels in which unlettered peasants wage dynastic warfare against the imperial forces. They often describe Mao as the loyal follower of Li Ta-chao, with Ch'en Tu-hsiu cofounder of the Chinese Communist party, who himself wrote in glowing terms of the peasant rebellions of Chinese history. But Mao's first written statements on the importance of the peasantry to the Chinese Revolution come after his introduction to the successes of the peasant movement in Kwangtung as the principal of the Peasant Movement Institute.

The origin of Mao's radical transformation in 1927 should be dated, therefore, not from the Seventh Plenum of the comintern or from the writings of Lenin on the peasant question, but from his own work at the institute in 1926. In a little-known article that he signed on September 1, 1926, as the preface to a large compendium of peasant movement articles, he struck a distinctive note; heard in retrospect, it was a prelude to his more famous Hunan report.[1]

Mao introduced his collection of readings with the standard remark about the peasant question's being the central problem of the national revolution. Already in 1926 the notion that that problem would have to be solved in some way had widespread currency, and Mao made that point. He went further to single out some people even in the revolutionary parties for criticism for having failed to understand this truth. He stated that any person who did not regard seriously or who tried to suppress the peasant movement was by definition a sympathizer with the corrupt officials and the evil gentry. The idea of restraining revolutionary activity was especially repugnant in the countryside. Although the political struggle in the cities had to be limited to a battle for the right to assemble and speak freely, in the countryside the peasantry had already progressed to the point where they were actively engaged in the struggle for political power. His evidence for this statement was the events in P'eng P'ai's Haifeng county, which his class of the Peasant Movement

Institute had just returned from visiting. There the baleful influence of Ch'en Chiung-ming had been successfully eliminated by the massive body of peasants who joined the peasant associations. If only every county in China could be made like Haifeng, Mao said, they could be considered to have won a revolutionary victory. Revolutionary leaders who failed to give the peasants in the countryside the special privilege of rising up were neglecting the central question. "Some people hold," he sneered, "that the insane behavior of the comprador class in the cities is exactly like that of the landlord class in the countryside, and that the two should be discussed in the same breath." In fact it was Mao Tse-tung himself who had spoken of them in the same breath — in the article on classes in the Chinese Revolution he had published in the peasant movement journal in January 1926. Now Mao was prepared to offer the peasants the special privilege of rising against their oppressors at a time when the workers were being restrained. His reasoning: the compradores and the rest of the urban enemy were concentrated in the major cities — Hong Kong, Canton, Shanghai, Hankow, Tientsin, Dairen, and other places next to the sea. These places were totally unlike the provinces, the counties, and the villages under the control of the landlord class all across China. Mao's personal feeling was that the workers should rise up to strike their oppressors in the city, too, but that without granting the peasants their privilege, success would be unlikely.

Far better known than Mao Tse-tung's early gropings toward the rural strategy is his Report on the Hunan Peasant Movement, written in February 1927 and widely circulated throughout the Communist world by early summer of that year. It was this report more than Mao's more conservative activities as an administrator in Wuhan that created his early reputation as a rural radical and laid the groundwork for his later elevation outside China to spiritual leader of all peasant revolutionaries. The document is worth a close examination.[2]

Mao's report was not written as an intraparty document — either for the Kuomintang or the Communist party. It lacks all the elements of a party report — references to organized effort, accounts of party activity, recommendations about policy. We know Mao to have been capable of writing a party document because both before and after this report he addressed himself to party policy questions for internal consumption. In those instances he was consistently a more conservative man, a fact that perhaps has given rise to the charge that he was an opportunist in 1927.[3] It was a piece of propaganda rather like an article he had already written about the peasant movement in Chekiang and Kiangsu.[4]

Yet there could be no doubt that this was no ordinary writer's view. Mao had become the chief of the Communist party's peasant movement committee in November 1926 just as he was collecting the material for the Kiangsu-Chekiang article and he must have been called upon by Ch'en Tu-hsiu for some guidance on the peasant question. At the time Mao was writing that article, the CCP Central Committee was considering its future policy toward Kiangsu and Chekiang and had in fact drafted a proposal on the support of armed insurrection in those provinces.[5]

Mao's report did not break any new ground for policy, at least in the sense in which the word was used in Communist circles at the time. It avoided the tough issues of the period. There was no reference anywhere to the problem of the Kuomintang Left, which preoccupied Stalin, Ch'en Tu-hsiu, and Borodin. Mao refers to the political parties only twice in the article and in neither case does he enter into their class content or the question of hegemony. There is no mention whatever of the matter of land ownership or confiscation — Mao's points on the importance of rent resistance neatly skirt the issue.

Mao Tse-tung's contribution to the discussions of peasant movement strategy lay rather in the area of psychology. His target was the attitude, not the policy, toward the peasant movement, just as in the September preface he had been concerned about the attitudes of some of the revolutionary leaders of that time. Again and again he referred to the erroneous views of so-called revolutionaries in the cities. These men had failed to take a revolutionary attitude; they thought that the Hunanese countryside was in dire straits. They failed to do their homework properly and did not investigate the situation in the villages and county seats outside the capital.

His message had three parts. First he stressed the emergence of a new revolutionary situation that had not been properly recognized in Ch'angsha and Hankow. County after county in Hunan, he asserted, had approached and exceeded the standard set by Haifeng in Kwangtung. There had been economic struggle on a large scale;

political struggle had produced new organs of rural administration. A massive armed peasantry had come into existence. There were challenges to every form of traditional authority, from that of clan elders and the clergy of various religions to that of male heads of households. Asking his readers to count these challenges he asserted that "none but local bullies and evil gentry will think them bad."[6]

Second, Mao singled out a new vanguard of the peasant movement, which he sought to make the cynosure of movement plans. He had recently keynoted a conference in Ch'angsha that had declared that the economic and political vanguard of the peasantry was the rural youth, a group that included young farmhands, shepherd boys, and the offspring of peasant families.[7] It was in fact the youth who had spearheaded the first penetration of the movement into Hunan during the Northern Expedition. But Mao's argument was that only the poorest people, the bottom rung of village society, were truly capable of leading the revolution. Revolution was a process of turning things upside down, and this meant that those who used to be considered the dregs of society would have to become the leaders. Mao brought as background to his argument his own theories of the Chinese rural class structure, which he had earlier elaborated in an article he wrote in March 1926. Here he simply offered a long statistical table showing how many members of each class had joined the associations.[8] Not surprisingly, tenants and hired hands made up the bulk of the membership, in Mao's view.

The new vanguard was not comprised simply of the poorer peasants but also included as its very best elements what had up to this point been called the riffraff (*p'i-tzu*) of Hunanese society. Mao defined the *p'i-tzu* as completely dispossessed people with neither land nor money, forced to leave home and become mercanaries or hired laborers or beggars. A good 20 percent of Hunanese rural society fell into this category, he claimed, and these had, particularly during the first phases of the peasant movement, assumed positions of leadership in the associations. It may well be that some of these people had some bad habits (in typical mock precision he offered a figure of 15 percent of all the poor peasants) but the important thing was to regard this class as the vanguard from which a few undesirables might be excluded.

Mao's third contribution was a changed attitude toward violence. Much of the criticism of peasant movement excesses, he argued, was

consciously or unconsciously pandering to ruling class interests. It
was the evil gentry who sponsored the charge that the peasants were
going too far. In a revolution people at the top of society are going
to be hurt. "A revolution is an uprising, an act of violence whereby
one class overthrows another." A rural revolution is a revolution by
which the peasantry overthrows the authority of the feudal landlord
class.[9] Violence is not to be deplored; it is to be celebrated. Mao
openly embraced the lynchings of persons declared to be evil gentry
as well as indignities to their female kin because he said it was necessary to have a brief reign of terror in every rural area. Had this
action not been taken, there would have been no way for the peasants to establish their absolute authority.

Mao's report was a masterful stroke of propaganda. It had just
enough local color to give the impression of authority. It stood in
blinding contrast to the shabby hackwork articles that were standard fare to readers of Guide weekly. Unlike them, it was full of
punch, drive, and style, even more readable than P'eng P'ai's or Lo
Ch'i-yuan's best efforts because it was well organized and had a clear
point. It cleared the air of depression which clouded the local
reports of movement work. These reports, like the once-a-month
articles on the Kwangtung movement in Guide weekly since October, were full of forebodings about the future. The difference was
striking: for the first time in the history of the peasant movement an
author had showered praises upon the common peasants instead of
invective upon their presumed enemies.

Although it is true that Mao carefully avoided making recommendations that would conflict with current KMT or CCP movement policy, the implications of his work were profound in the debate on peasant strategy. With one blow he released the inhibitions
of peasant leaders all across China. Why worry any longer about
the question of organization, of where the cadres are coming from
(the question Mao himself had raised in his September article on the
Kwangtung peasant movement)? Just unleash the new vanguard and
poor peasants would emerge to perform the cadres' tasks for them.
Why worry about relations between peasant associations and county
magistrates, the Kuomintang, or the financial authorities? In the
counties he visited, all political power was exercised by a new committee world, the world of county party committees, peasant associations, and county citizens' conferences. These committees were
all interlocking directorates of the same people, the revolutionary

vanguard, so how could they come into conflict? Why worry about the precise wording of slogans designed to appeal to the peasantry? The peasants have already told you what they want, so why bother to spell it out? Finally, why worry any longer about the possibility of retaliation by people who might not enjoy being made the brunt of peasant movement attacks? Were not the gentry in full disarray in central Hunan before the transformed peasantry? Was not the peasant movement likely in a very short time to "rise like a tornado or a tempest" and become "a force so extraordinarily swift and violent that no power, however great, will be able to suppress it"?[10]

The Hunan report was an utter fantasy, as much as were Mao's other widely touted visions — the Great Leap Forward of the 1950s or the Great Proletarian Cultural Revolution of the 1960s. Not that fantasy does not contain certain elements of reality. This one certainly did. But it was the uncanny perception of a powerful psychological need to believe his story that gave Mao's interpretation an influence far stronger than might have been supported by the factual base of his account.

While artfully avoiding the thorny political issues of the epoch, Mao radicalized the peasant movement in the fullest sense of the word. He expanded the targets of attack, gave highest sanction to the use of violence, and tried to turn the revolutionary movement against members of its own kind who failed to appreciate the new situation. His new radicalism encouraged the movement to reject the cautious and pragmatic path of movement building that had produced many of the results he purported to approve.

Mao thus offered a convenient and persuasive answer to those who had agonized over how the peasant movement could be justified to the rest of the political leadership. His answer to the question of what use is the peasant movement was that the very question was in error. The leaders of the peasant movement, Mao seemed to suggest, had been looking in the wrong place for political relevance. They should have looked to the countryside. The peasant movement *was* the revolution.

THE LAND QUESTION

The animus the land confiscation issue generated in the next five months and the next decade for the Communists is difficult to capture now, let alone to understand. While Chiang Kai-shek allowed the Shanghai workers to be massacred as he waited outside the city gates, while Li Chi-shen lined up members of the Kwangtung Provincial Peasant Association on the public execution grounds in Canton, while Hunanese village revolutionaries, given a signal, moved even more boldly to assert their new-found might, the Communist and Kuomintang Left sat in Wuhan and debated abstract theories of land ownership.

In part the fascination with the land question was a Russian import; the Chinese knew that Lenin in 1917 had used the offer of land to soldiers to end the war with Germany and then consolidate the support of the rural soviets. In part it was the heritage of Sun Yat-sen's own unrealized commitment to the platform of land to the tiller. Wang Ching-wei, who was invited back from abroad to resume his post as chairman of the KMT central executive in November 1926 and arrived in Wuhan in March, had urged the Kuomintang to proclaim Sun's proposal shortly after the founder died.[11] Even Chiang Kai-shek, as late as December 1926, was in favor of a rapid solution of the land question, though the expression he used in his diary to record his view privately was not standard peasant movement idiom.[12] But we may presume that the land issue was popular mainly because it touched sensitive nerves in many segments of the Wuhan body politic.

The Wuhan Central Land Committee held meetings that brought this issue to a head in early April 1927. Differences of opinion within the committee were apparently so great that it became necessary to gather data from the provinces and solicit opinions from many sides. Five separate expanded sessions were held, and then the committee broke up into four subcommittees to draft resolutions. In all, the committee and its offspring met over a dozen times from April 19 to May 6. All the members of the original committee were participants: various KMT central executive committeemen, people from the provincial and district party offices, various provincial and district peasant movement leaders, and responsible military comrades. The provinces represented included Hunan, Hupeh, Kwangtung, Honan, Chihli, Shantung, Anhwei, Kiangsu, Chekiang, Fukien, Jehol, Fengtien, Chahar, Kirin, and Shansi. The land committee meetings were the last attempt at a truly comprehensive overview of peasant movement possibilities and needs that included non-communist Kuomintang and military leaders.

One of the critical obstacles in the discussion of the land problem in Hankow was ignorance. No one, least of all the peasant leaders in Canton or Wuhan, had done any extensive study of landholding patterns. The massive studies of rural economists and sociologists we are now familiar with are a product of the 1930s and have no significant ancestry. The Russian advisers, Borodin in particular, noted the lack of information and set up a small research team to tackle the problem. A trio of Russian agrarian experts, Iolk, Volin, and Tarkhanov, produced a large tome entitled "Agrarian Relations in Kwangtung Province," which was destroyed in an anti-Communist bookburning in April 1927.[13] While his book was being demolished Comrade Tarkhanov was given another task: to write a report summarizing the distribution of land in all of China. Working with Mao Tse-tung, Tarkhanov produced a table that represented his best guess.[14]

His new-found knowledge stood him in good stead in the land committee's discussions. When one non-Communist suggested that the amount of land required to sustain an average standard of living was twenty Chinese *mou* (3.3 acres), Tarkhanov was able to point out that in Fukien that would make him a rich peasant. The line between poor and middle peasant in that province was drawn at ten *mou,* his researches showed.[15] Another point that might have been made is that Mao Tse-tung's estimates on landholding showed a bias that overstated the percentage of landless peasants. Mao's method of distribution allotted land to only 32 percent of the farm population, where the Russians were willing to offer 44. It is conceivable that Mao's estimate reflected the distribution of Kwangtung and Hunan correctly and Tarkhanov simply adjusted for a wider geographic base. But it seems more likely that he simply (and correctly) distrusted his Chinese comrade's estimate that more than a third of the rural population was in the category below the tenant farmer in landed status.

Perhaps the most important contribution of the Tarkhanov study was the interjection of a note about the complexity of China's landholding patterns. "The basic problem of the land," the Russian testified in the meetings, "would be easy to solve if only the majority of peasants were tenants and the minority were large landlords, and if the situation in each province were more or less the same as in others." In fact he showed that 85 percent of Kwangtung land was rented, but in Shantung, one of the target provinces for the touted expedition, the figure was more like 5 percent. "These facts indicate the presence of a number of small landlords, and hence the land problem will not be easy to solve."[16] But there is little evidence that the Russian's observations were given much thought.

The discussions centered around a draft resolution on the land question that had been commissioned by the left Kuomintang Third Plenum in mid-March. It fell to Mao Tse-tung, his Hunanese comrade I Li-jung, Lu Shen of Hupeh, and Tarkhanov's associate Iolk to write the paper. They produced an eight-sentence document that Mao later called "my thesis which carried recommendations for the widespread distribution of the land."[17] Mao recommended that land be confiscated by land committees set up by self-government organs led by the peasantry. Tarkhanov's problem of the skewness of land distribution would be handled by limiting the distribution of land to the village area or at the largest the district (*ch'ü*). The new landowners would not be absolved from paying rent but would be assessed an equitable fee that would go directly into government coffers. Already we see Mao Tse-tung thinking about the details of an agrarian law, a type of document that he would produce in many forms in the coming thirty years.[18] But the thesis contained only one simple sentence about whose land was to be confiscated: "the land of local bullies, evil gentry, corrupt officials and wicked bureaucrats, warlords, and all counterrevolutionaries in the villages." Not a word about landlords.[19] Thus Mao's proposal, although going far to spread the distribution of land, placed strict limits on how much was to be taken. The realities of the Hankow regime were beginning to recall him from his flight of Hunanese fancy.

The reasons given for the need to come up with a concrete land proposal were as disparate as the interests of the members of the Wuhan coalition. There were the ideologues whose opinions seemed based on not much more than the firm faith in the abolition of private property as a placebo for all social ills. The most prominent representatives of this group were the Hunanese Communists I Li-jung and P'eng Tse-hsiang, the men who had presumably opened Mao's eyes to the new vision of the peasantry in Hunan. They held that the ownership of land was the foundation of the feudal system that must be destroyed if the peasantry was to be fully liberated. Land confiscation was, along with killing of all evil gentry, one of the most effective means of producing the terror of a great rural revolution. This group found it difficult to tolerate Mao Tse-tung's new hesitation in supporting the comintern's land plank or his failure to mention the amuletic phrases about destruction of the system that he had popularized.

Hsia Hsi, Mao's close comrade-in-arms from the early 1920s, launched the attack. Hsia was the Hunanese who startled the Second Kuomintang Congress in January 1926 with his demand that the Popular Corps be abolished forthwith. Now he pointed out that Mao's proposals, since they would confiscate only a part of the land, would produce two classes in the countryside: one paying rent to the landlords and one to the state. The only way out of this contradiction was to take all the land and redistribute it. P'eng Tse-hsiang, another of Mao's Hunan colleagues, like I Li-jung destined to be a close associate in the uprisings of late 1927, seconded Hsia.

But Mao and other Communists in more responsible positions also had to contend with other opinions. The non-Communist military was present and voting on his proposed draft. Their issues were military morale and relations with the civilian population. A poorly fed or underpaid army was not a loyal one, so any step that increased funds for the armies would be desirable. Any attempt to confiscate the lands of either officers or men while they were fighting for the revolution would lessen the military's solidarity. Of course, many soldiers and even some officers were bankrupt peasants from the countryside who would benefit from land distribution, but this distribution should not be made until after the war was over, lest it tempt them to leave the ranks. This last point was not made by the military officers at the meeting, though they doubtless would have agreed with it.

A third opinion was represented by the bureaucrats responsible for the weakening Wuhan government and party. To them the critical question was not the satisfaction of peasant private interest or the safeguarding of military loyalty but the very future of the national revolution. Land to the peasants was a valuable idea, considering its parentage. But the question was whether nationalization of the land would backfire and hurt the revolutionary regime more than it helped. Publication of a bold confiscation program or even the promise of one might introduce a panic among the small landholders that could undermine the authority of the Kuomintang at home in Hupeh and Hunan and provide the soldiers of T'an Yen-k'ai and T'ang Sheng-chih with a chance to turn on the revolution. Prominent spokesmen of this opinion were the KMT left politicians such as Hsu Ch'ien and Wang Ching-wei. Hsu issued a stern warning that to use the methods now being tried in Hunan while "throwing a flaming brand at the enemy" might result in "burning our own hands."[20] Wang Ching-wei, still intrigued by the political value of the land plank in winning support for his government, reminded Hsu that if some kind of clear principle were not enunciated, "the flame itself might go out." T'an P'ing-shan, who had brought the Seventh Plenum directives back dutifully from Moscow, saw the land program as critically important in keeping the revolution alive, for without a much larger army than the present one (five hundred thousand — he was counting even that of Chiang Kai-shek), there was little hope of conquering all of China. But, in addition and closer to home, the financial crisis in Wuhan would have to be solved; a land tax that replaced landlord rent would be an enormous help. "A gigantic army of five million," T'an dreamed, "will require massive provisions. How can this livelihood problem be solved except by a solution to the land problem? Furthermore, only when peasants arm themselves and join in the fighting will the quality of our soldiers be improved."[21] Again the land was the answer.

Mao Tse-tung was one of those who used the financial argument to support a land tactic. He pointed out that the provincial government in Hunan in 1927 was bringing in around half what it had two years earlier under Chao Heng-t'i.[22] Mao doubtless shared this worry with those who knew anything about the provincial budgets. He pointed out that the land-registration tax had become impossible to collect in Hunan, not to mention the various supernumerary taxes whose disappearance he had cheered two months earlier. "If there is no escape from this difficulty," he warned, "the revolution will inevitably be defeated . . . There is no alternative to a solution to the land question."[23]

The clash of these conflicting concerns produced some curious exchanges and interesting compromises. The radical Hsia Hsi, for example, recommended that the nationalization idea not be made public so that the outside enemy — the warlords and imperialists — could not use it against them. He was answered by T'ang Sheng-chih, the militarist, who argued that the enemy would not cease to slander them just because they stopped solving the land question. But by and large the direction of the debate was predictable from the start. The major issues were the standards for confiscation and distribution, how to deal with the soldier question, and how to implement the proposals. Mao's proposal gave no definition of the enemy whose lands he wished to confiscate and thus attracted some criticism on that count from his own comrade, Hsia Hsi.[24] Wang Ching-wei was curious whether there was any difference in fact between the slogan of political confiscation and the old idea, dating from January, of confiscation of traitor's property.[25] In the end he accepted the slogan as less likely to induce panic among the small landlords in Hunan and Hupeh.

On April 22 Mao delivered a long and disorganized speech on the confiscation question. It demonstrated how much he sought to bestride the diverging positions of Hunanese radical and national leaders. Following the terminology Wang Ching-wei had recommended, Mao explained that the type of confiscation he had in mind in the draft was political confiscation in that it was aimed at the political enemies of the Wuhan regime and not at the economic enemies of the worker-peasant class. When the land of these persons was taken and distributed, it would be time to move to the second phase, the phase of economic confiscation wherein the land of every person who does not till it himself would become state property. During this phase, which had already been reached in Hunan, the land of the owner-cultivator and the middle peasant should not be confiscated, only that of the rich peasant. Here he went beyond the Central Committee's recommendations of the previous November in moving below the large landlords to include the rich peasants. He stressed that he was not talking about a tiny fraction of the peasantry—nothing like Tarkhanov's 13 percent. Even if half the families in a village rank in the rich category, they should have their property spread out among the other half, he declared.

Challenged by his radical friends, Mao excused himself for being so moderate. He said he agreed with land nationalization as a long-term goal but was concerned only with the present in these theses. He had two arguments: first, it was likely that demanding confiscation across all classes for all China would have an adverse effect in those provinces where peasants were not yet demanding the land.

Only in Hunan at present were the peasants demanding the land. When another four or five provinces reached that point, they should consider this question again. He further argued that meanwhile there was no reason Hunan could not just proceed as though complete confiscation were already in effect. He declared that refusing to pay rent was spontaneous confiscation, but only Hunan had reached that stage. Imagining that the entire country was in that stage was a fantasy.

The argument about land and the soldiery raised a fundamental issue that had never been faced before. Peasant movement propaganda from 1924 on had made striking claims for the support that their organizations had given the revolutionary army. The leaders of the movement had not considered the political quality of the soldiery. Such questions were the province of other sections of the revolutionary elite: the political workers, the Whampoa Academy teachers, the politician-generals, and the Communists who served on their staffs. In fact by the spring of 1927 there was only one officer of division rank who was a Communist (Yeh T'ing) in the entire National Revolutionary Army.[26] T'ang Sheng-chih had carefully prevented Communists from assuming even staff positions in his army.[27] Now peasant movement figures were forced to contemplate the results of their policies on armies whose loyalty to them was anything but assured. Some remained fixated on recent Russian history. The Hunanese radical, Leng Ping, argued that the Russian use of land to win the revolution was relevant to China. He surmised that confiscating land in China and distributing it to the soldiers would make them realize that the government supported their interests. Leng thought the problem of wealthy landowning officers was caused by the small landholders who would be dissatisfied because they have no concept of what a revolutionary government is all about. Unfortunately, they had all too clear a concept. T'ang Sheng-chih was quick to point out that the vast majority of the soldiers in the revolutionary army were from Leng's Hunan province. If they did not already know, it would not take long for them to find out what was going on at home. Justice Minister Hsu Ch'ien, in the same vein, ridiculed the idea that the offer of land would attract a powerful army to the ranks. "Our peasants are armed only with their hands and feet. There is little advantage," he argued, "to increasing the number of weaponless men."[28]

Mao Tse-tung's views on the army did not help solve the dilemma, which nevertheless he saw quite clearly. There had been much progress in the revolution to date, but the threat of a new crisis loomed. As soon as the crisis occurred they would need a potent army (*sheng-li-chün*) to avoid defeat. But the land problem needed to be solved for such an army to come into being, he said. With such a policy the peasants would fight bravely to protect their own land. But who were the peasants? Did Mao mean the officers in T'ang Sheng-chih's army? Or did he mean that the soldiers might rise up and overthrow T'ang if they were promised his land and that of other large Hunanese landholders? Or did he have in mind already another kind of armed peasant? We do not know the answer.

The third argument that raged at the land committee meetings in April brings us back to the central issue of peasant movement work in the Wuhan period: what the relationship was to be between peasant associations and the Wuhan regime. There was little sense in the left-wing government promulgating regulations on what was to be done in Hunan or Hupeh unless it could exercise some control over what was done. Ku Meng-yü, the propagandist and editor of the *Central Daily News,* spoke to this point. Ku was a maverick politician and publicist, rather like Kan Nai-kuang in his penchant for Marxist concepts, but in April 1927 not yet like Kan in passing over to the Chiang Kai-shek side. His point was that detailed discussions of the land problem made no sense without solving what he called the prior question. He said that when they reached the stage of putting their recommendations into practice, they would face the question of whether the peasants could carry on in the required slow, orderly fashion. Ku feared that when the time came, the peasants would grab for themselves as much as they could. The prior question, then, was who would have the power to enforce compliance with their resolutions and proceed in step-by-step fashion. It could be the party office, the peasant association, or the self-government organs, but in any case the main problem would be to keep the peasantry disciplined. Ku pointed his finger at the small Hunanese delegation and demanded to know whether the peasantry could be expected to observe the limits of discipline.

Wang Ching-wei quickly stepped in and declared Ku's worries unfounded since a portion of Mao's draft already referred to local self-government organs. A few minutes later Hsia Hsi rose to

attempt a more convincing response. What was needed was a clear
guideline, he assured Ku Meng-yü, that the peasants could follow.
With the line properly drawn the peasants would obey the party and
the government's leadership. But the question obviously remained
open.

The land committee remained deadlocked on these issues for a
week. During that time Ch'en Tu-hsiu apparently changed his mind
a number of times on the confiscation question.[29] We have evidence
that Ch'en and Borodin intervened only once. Borodin's suggested
solution was characteristically pragmatic and bureaucratic: make a
clear distinction between areas under their control and those they
are trying to win. In the latter, a clear land confiscation slogan was
essential. But in the former, confiscation must be orderly and carried out by local governments under revolutionary control. He did
not regard the existing county governments as legitimate bodies for
confiscation since they had not been set up according to the self-government law he was in the process of drafting. These self-government organs would be needed to preserve local order, carry on rural
education, and collect taxes for the government. Without them, he
implied, only disorder would result from beginning widespread confiscation and distribution.

If Borodin's advice had been heeded, it would have had the effect
of postponing any implementation of the land program until local
government could be completely reorganized. He seemed to be
siding with those who held that Hunan ought to wait half a year before stepping up the struggle. Ch'en Tu-hsiu, whose entrance into
the discussions coincided with Borodin's, agreed with his Russian
adviser about the differences between enemy and friendly territory.
But on the question of waiting for self-government, Ch'en favored
giving agrarian powers to already existing peasant associations and
party offices.[30] His tendency, already seen in the November draft, to
be to the left of his Russian superiors on the land question was still in
evidence.

The output of these land committee deliberations was less interesting than the interplay of ideas. On May 6 the committee passed a
resolution on solving the land question that compromised most of
the issues. Borodin won the last point with Ch'en and the future
self-government organs were to handle the land problem. The soldiers were assured that their landholdings would be protected and if

landless that they would receive land at the end of revolutionary hostilities. Tarkhanov won his point about the need for further investigation before arriving at a standard for the small freeholder, though the maximum size of a holding was set at no more than fifty *mou* of good land or a hundred of bad. It was this last very large limit that much later attracted Mao Tse-tung's sharp criticism. Mao Tse-tung, however, lost out on his issue of political confiscation. All large landlords who fell within the established criteria and who were not also revolutionary soldiers would have their lands confiscated.[31] Ch'en Tu-hsiu, of course, had taken a position perilously close to this one in his remarks to the Hunanese in November.

The Fifth Congress of the Chinese Communist party, convening in Hankow three days after the completion of this land resolution, followed it almost to the letter. But as though to give Mao and other Communists who were working closely with the Kuomintang on the land platform a slap on the hand, the congress criticized the mechanistic theory that the Kuomintang had charge of the peasantry while the Communist party was left only the proletariat.[32] Mao's plank on confiscating political enemies' lands was dropped from the Communist platform, which recommended simply the confiscation of large landlords' land. The text of the resolution went even beyond the land committee's platform in defining a radical solution to the land problem that included the fundamental redistribution of land based on the equalization principle. Nationalization would be required for this task, but the party was not yet prepared to make that demand. Ch'en Tu-hsiu was now under considerable pressure from his comintern advisers to prove that he was not afraid of the peasants in order to refute the charge laid against him by Trotskyists in China and Russia. He therefore acquiesced in the statement, made several times in the congress's resolutions, that the reason Kwangtung had been lost was his own failure to encourage heightened class struggle in the villages, a struggle that, he now declared, might have weakened the position of the reactionary classes.

But by this time the issue of the land program had become irrelevant to the future of the revolution. Neither party's program was put into effect, since within a fortnight of their passage the military underpinnings of the Wuhan regime collapsed. On May 18 Hsia Tou-yin, whose regiment occupied the Ch'angsha-Hankow section of the north-south railway, mutinied and marched on the capital of the revolutionary government. Though he was defeated through the valiant efforts of the one high-ranking Communist soldier in Wuhan (Yeh T'ing),[33] his move was a signal to the commander of the troops in Ch'angsha to move against the Communist party.[34]

At ten o'clock on the evening of May 21, 1927, Hsu K'o-hsiang, commander of the largest army garrisoned in Ch'angsha, raided the mass organization headquarters in the city and killed the chief of the student association, the KMT provincial youth secretary, a Communist delegate to the provincial assembly, and dozens of others. On the same day, called the Day of the Horse[35] in recent accounts, his troops searched over twenty offices in the city for evidence of Communist activity, demolished the special court and released all its political prisoners, raided the people's grain preservation association for its large sums of money, and arrested nearly a hundred men, Communists and leftists, who were soon put to death. There is some controversy about what produced the coup. Hsu K'o-hsiang in a recent brief memoir claims he obtained secret intelligence of an impending Communist coup. His wife, a close friend of the wife of a top Communist, reported overhearing plans scheduled for around May 25. We know that peasant self-defense armies were attempting to collect as many weapons as they could, sometimes by disarming police and soldiers of uncertain connections, in the week before the coup.[36] Whatever Hsu's motivation, his intentions became obvious. Hsu K'o-hsiang quickly obtained Chiang Kai-shek's approval and appointed a committee to reorganize and purge the Kuomintang of Communist and left-wing elements. The vaunted Hunanese peasant movement collapsed overnight as anti-Communist elements in county after county made their long-awaited moves. Within a matter of days, the peasant movement in Hunan and Hupeh had been crushed in a massive bloodbath.

The defection of the left-wing politicians did not take long. The arguments they used to justify their turn away from the Communists can be surmised from positions taken in the land committee discussions: disruption of finances, the impossibility of running a government, the failure of agricultural produce to reach Wuhan or Ch'angsha, a major inflation in the cost of rice, the destruction of tea production in Hunan by arbitrary orders from the peasant association. Wang Ching-wei could now afford to let his frustrations be known: "This kind of idiocy," he railed on June 1, "has brought down Hunan. Hunan is finished. It brought down Kiangsi. Kiangsi is finished. It brought down Honan. Honan is finished. Now all the KMT Central can do is close its doors . . . I dare now to speak out: The Peasant Association is an unprecedented mistake . . . Backed into such a blind alley, little wonder that Hsu and his lot have risen up to resist."[37]

Sun Yat-sen's son, Sun Fo, was even more vitriolic. The Communists have been "ranting and raving" about the rising up of two million Hunanese peasants. "Well, they did," he said. "They rose up and were pushed down by the army." The united front has been wrecked, and the biggest chaos ever reigns in Hupeh and Hunan. "Now not only is there no 'new political and economic organization,' even the old organization has been smashed to smithereens . . . The next time they open their traps and yell 'millions and tens of millions of peasants' we will know it is not the truth."[38]

But the next time, two decades later, it was the truth because the Communist party learned the folly of baseless radicalism.

WAS THERE a real hope for the left Kuomintang in Hupeh and Hunan? In the villages there clearly was little. There was no old Kuomintang out there, outside the county seats and the major market towns. Party offices outside the towns were creations of 1926 and thus more likely to be composed of Communist intellectuals than old-line KMT types. At the county level a large number of party offices in Hunan and Hupeh apparently had Communist majorities, but in these cases what sense was there in speaking of the KMT Left? The true meaning of Ch'en Tu-hsiu's notion of a village KMT Left was that the Communist party should absorb existing non-Communist organizations into the Kuomintang and call them Left. But usually wherever this policy was followed, disaster came shortly after. In Huangkang, Hupeh, the one non-Communist association, far from being easily absorbed, declared itself to be the holy peasant association and had to be suppressed violently.

The real hope, as in Kwangtung, was that all movement organization and work would be protected by a sympathetic provincial and county party bureaucracy. The Communists needed the Kuomintang desperately in Hunan, perhaps more than in Kwangtung. Ch'en Tu-hsiu's prediction of sharp polarization without the Kuomintang was correct. Where he erred was in not realizing the importance of the provincial Nationalist politicians. The Hunan Left Society was an intriguing case in point. Kan Nai-kuang, while still chief of the KMT central peasant bureau early in the winter of 1926, joined a group of politicians and scholars who hoped to counter the proto-Fascist influence of the Society for the Study of Sun Yat-senism in Canton and Ch'angsha. The leader of this left society (*tso-she*) in Hunan was Liu Yueh-ch'ih, who was at the time director of the KMT peasant bureau in Hunan. There were rumors that Ku Meng-yü, who played a constructive role in the land and other commissions in Hankow, was an associate. Liu was a rarity: a pre-1924 KMT member in Hunan. He disbursed the funds to the rapidly growing association and bore the burdens on provincial finance caused by the decline in tax revenues. Communist historians claim he was a large landlord and a member of the Property Preservation party. They also accuse him of the more serious crime of being a reformist and gradual reconstructionist.[39] He has no defenders.

The issue that brought him to his knees is worth our interest, however. On February 12, 1927, a few days after Mao Tse-tung completed his researches in the villages around Ch'angsha, Liu Yueh-ch'ih published in the Ch'angsha papers a plan for the peasant movement that his detractor claimed openly opposed rural class struggle, called peasant association members local ruffians and hooligans (*ti-p'i-liu-mang*—an elegant term for Mao's *p'i-tzu*), requested that peasants and landlords be friendly with each other and work to increase production and improve agriculture. Liu proposed tighter KMT control of peasant associations under threat of reorganization. This plan, we are told, earned the support of counterrevolutionaries and middle-of-the-roaders.

Such an obvious plot to disarm the revolution could not go unpunished, of course. The Hunanese Communist journal (The Militant) on March 5, 1927, published an article entitled "What kind of monster is the Left Society?" It was the same issue of the journal (number 35) that first published Mao Tse-tung's Hunan report. A third article singled out Liu Yueh-ch'ih for personal attack: "Your daily rice comes from rent. Your kind can always fall back on your long sleeves [gentry life] if you lose high office. Your kinsmen have from ancient times been middle and petty landowners. You joined the revolution only because Chao Heng-t'i [the former governor of

Hunan under warlord Wu P'ei-fu] drove you to it. Now you are much better off. All you need to worry about is that your family's three hundred *tan* of rent each year continues to get paid. Naturally you wish to use your own tricks to protect your and your family's ancient privileges."

The Communists commanded enough support in the provincial party office to suspend Liu and seven of his closest associates, though they did not dare to arrest him. The decision to put him under house surveillance was announced on February 27, the day before Mao submitted his report to the Central Committee. Three Ch'angsha private schools where presumably he or some associates taught were closed at the same time. The Hunan Left Society was banned.[40] We next hear of Liu Yueh-ch'ih (and three of his colleagues in the Hunan Left Society) as a member of the party purge committee appointed on May 28 by Hsu K'o-hsiang with Chiang Kai-shek's approval. Liu had gone the route of Kan Nai-kuang. Had he remained on the Left with Teng Yen-ta, would the history of the Hunan peasant movement have been any different?

How excessive were the peasant associations in fact? The Communist Liu Chih-sun, who has no reason to hide the dispensation of revolutionary justice, estimates that at most twenty people were put to death by the provincial special court after its establishment on January 4 and there were only "two or three actually brought to justice" by the people themselves.[41] One historical account of the county in Hupeh considered the best organized mentions somewhat over a dozen executions during the period of association control. Of these only five were persons shot in what was considered economic struggle. The rest were persons connected with armed groups presumably captured in open rebellion. One was the top leader of the Red Spears Society.[42] His early defection demonstrated the Russian folly of wooing this particlar peasant association.

Two of the biggest perpetrators of economic crimes were killed after a huge mass meeting in the county seat called for an anti-British rally sometime in April. They had been arrested in December, but their trial awaited the passage of regulations for the punishment of evil gentry in the provincial capital in March.[43] A similar chronology was followed in Hunan, where the provincial special court planned in January,[44] began operation in earnest only four months later.[45] But what little detail we have about association

activity does not suggest that even at the peak of the drive against
the rich and powerful did the Hunanese or the Hupehnese engage in
a major bloodbath. Anna Louise Strong was probably not far from
wrong when, in her first journalistic article after arriving in Hankow, she described the excesses of the Hunanese soldiery as far
greater than those of the peasants.[46]

The excesses of the Hupeh-Hunan associations appear to have
been, unlike those of Haifeng the following winter, largely confined
to the sphere of politics, discipline, and propriety. To begin with,
the language of the revolution was uncompromising. In press
reports no quarter was given. The Hunan KMT newspaper, *Min
Pao* (The people), was replete with stories of executions by peasant
associations.[47] Though the total probably ran to only a few dozen,
the publicity given to the death penalty for political crimes left a
widespread impression of terror. The generation of terror (*k'ung-
pu*) was in fact a conscious aim of some Hunanese Communists.[48]

But more offensive to members of the KMT camp in Wuhan was
the undeniable insubordination of some of the associations. The
Hunan Provincial Peasant Association sought a number of times to
put a stop to the rice export embargo.[49] Part of the problem was
that these embargoes had been encouraged at the First Hunan Peasant Congress in December, so local associations felt they had good
cause to continue. Once movement officials adopted the policy,
there was no way back without seeming to reverse the tide. The
Hunan radicals, while admitting that the embargo hurt commerce,
agricultural production, and government finances, declared that
this too could only be solved by a solution to the land problem.

The issue of spontaneous killings by associations had already been
raised by December. The Hunan finance minister reported to
Wuhan that evil gentry were being shot despite requests by the army
garrison that the government be consulted first. Borodin in January
personally disapproved of illegal executions done without the permission of superior organs. So long as the party and the government
had not issued a decision on a case, the masses should not spontaneously take direct action.[50] He proposed a complaint office that
individuals and groups could use to request the county and higher
offices to punish the enemy. But Borodin's attempt to regularize
revolutionary justice was openly attacked and privately subverted by
Hunanese Communist leaders. Mao Tse-tung, three days after his

article was published in the Guide weekly, made a speech at the KMT Third Plenum meetings in which he argued that dealing with evil gentry would require revolutionary methods. A court "suitable to the revolutionary situation" was desirable, Mao declared, but "the best thing is the direct action of the peasantry. Peaceful procedures are unlikely to overthrow the landed bullies and bad gentry."[51] The remark would be his best known public commendation of what he later admitted were peasant excesses. By June 13, Mao was trying to blame direct action on Ko-lao-hui secret society members who had infiltrated into the movement.[52]

The left politicians of the Wuhan government waited until after the coups of Hsu K'o-hsiang and Hsia Tou-yin before revealing their true feelings about peasant excesses. At a heated meeting on May 30 Wang Ching-wei and Hsu Ch'ien lashed out at the Communist party proponents of rural terror. Wang had just heard a report of the punishment of an evil gentry in Mienyang, Hupeh, at the hands of the county party office, which the Communist Liu Fen had proudly reported. "The party office strung up a sexagenarian doddler and then took turns lashing him with a leather whip. Is this the behavior of humans? Yet this is the report of Liu Fen, who never lies." Hsu Ch'ien, the minister of justice, complained about the lack of standards in arrests and asserted that punishment was more a matter of personal revenge than an administration of justice.[53]

Could the military have been held back? Or was it only a matter of time before the large landlords among the Hunanese officer corps would stage their reaction? Much was made of the economic interest of the officers in suppression of the peasant movement, including the petty bourgeois interest of the common soldier in a small strip to farm on his retirement. The cry of the Wuhan Land Committee to protect the interest of the revolutionary soldier has been translated in historical treatments into the major, if not the sole, sustaining prop of the Wuhan regime after Chiang Kai-shek's April 12 Shanghai coup.

We have no way of examining this proposition in detail because there is no information about either the real estate holdings or the true feelings of any of the military in Hunan. But there is at least reason to suspect that there were many other factors besides the threat to their holdings that made the Hunanese officers and foot-soldiers deeply suspicious of the peasant movement. Many, even officers, were as landless as the poorest peasant or city dweller. We surmise that the soldier was more concerned about at least three other things: his life, his rations, and his status. The radical peasant movement threatened him directly or indirectly on all three counts. First, there was the obvious possibility of an armed clash with peasant irregulars or with self-defense groups. Trained soldiers are experts in the control and use of weapons and do not like to see firepower in the control of other groups. The self-defense armies in Hunan, though by no means a match for the professional military, could put up a tough battle in some counties. On May 21 there were three thousand armed peasants and workers in Ch'angsha, who, though armed mostly with sticks and spears, did have enough firearms to inflict serious casualties. The demand of the Left to turn over a portion of the output of the Wuhan arsenal to the peasants, which was finally agreed to by Wang Ching-wei after the land committee deliberations, was flatly refused by T'ang Sheng-chih's ordnance master, who declared honestly that his men needed all the weapons they could get. For an army susceptible to epidemics of defection and the sale of weapons to share guns with rival groups was folly.

Second, the soldiers needed provisions. The Chinese army of the 1920s was unable to draw upon regular tax-based government revenues for its week-to-week supply of rice and vegetables, not to mention spending money. Foraging areas were battle prizes and were tapped as directly as possible: by moving from village to village to consume the available produce. Rice embargoes may have helped soldiers in Hunan, but they hurt them outside the province. Associations would further refuse garrison armies the right to tap tax funds for salary payments. In Huangkang, Hupeh, a KMT army moved into the county for foraging and was driven out by the Peasant Self-Defense Army.

Third, the military needed status. The potential humiliation or mistreatment of relatives was perhaps a greater threat than that to the land or to property. Liu Chih-sun admitted that Hsiung Chen, Hsu K'o-hsiang's predecessor as garrison chief of Ch'angsha, was very left until on traveling to Yochow to visit his family he learned his wife's father had been paraded through his village in a dunce cap. T'an Yen-k'ai, who spoke so well for a rational land policy in the Wuhan meeting, was embarrassed when his cousin near Ch'angsha was fined by a peasant court and sent a string of telegrams demanding an apology.[54] Lesser figures were threatened by other possibilities: the money sent home in packages might be confiscated by the peasant associations. Such incidents happened often enough to make the rumor plausible, though the Communists could always claim that the association was a phoney.

These were issues that were to affect the morale and efficiency of soldiers in China well past 1949.[55] Mao Tse-tung, soon after becoming a mountain guerrilla at the end of the year, worked on techniques to protect the dependents of his Red Army men. The mistake of failing to think them through before unleashing the peasant revolution was a fatal one.

THE AUTUMN HARVEST INSURRECTION

The anti-Communist turn of the Kuomintang leftists transformed the discussions of the rural strategy in the summer of 1927. No longer represented even by token ministers in the Wuhan government, the Communist party leaders could not pretend that they represented the wider revolutionary coalition. Their fabled mass organizations, with all the impressive flags and offices in the central cities, now rested solely on untested local branches. The military forces under Wuhan had to be divided clearly into those who would attack the mass organizations and those who would defend the Communists. The issue of mid-1927 was not whether to fight the Kuomintang, but how. The Wuhan split led inexorably to the Autumn Harvest Insurrection.

Our views of the Autumn Harvest events are largely distorted by hindsight. To many in China today the rural uprisings of late 1927 mark the beginning of the Maoist strategy of peasant revolution. Mao's comrades have praised him for having discovered in the course of the uprising the correct revolutionary strategy of relying on the countryside to carry on persistent guerrilla warfare.[56] Late 1927 was the first time Chinese Communists sought to transform their rural influence into political power, to deploy peasant-based armies against the ruling elites, and to build independent areas in the countryside insulated from government influence. But these activities, far from the products of one man's imagination, were inexorable results of the failure of the peasant movement strategy.

Mao's claims to originality during the year 1927 derive in part from the need to repudiate Ch'en Tu-hsiu's policy of collaboration with the Kuomintang, a policy in which Mao was personally implicated. Although a clear doctrine of insurrection appeared only after the hastily called August 7 conference, which dismissed and censured Ch'en, the Politburo had been actively considering armed uprising for some months. Tu-hsiu had recommended preparing for insurrection in Kiangsu and Chekiang before he moved to Wuhan in December. Only at Borodin's urging had he blocked the Hunan Provincial Committee's orders throwing poorly armed peasants against the city of Ch'angsha on the Day of the Horse.[57] He authorized the drafting by Ts'ai Ho-shen, the Hunanese militant, of a plan for insurrection in the two provinces of Hunan and Hupeh based on a secret telegram from Stalin. It was this draft, which emerged in late June or early July, not the documents of the August 7 conference, that marked the first turn toward a strategy of armed struggle.

There were significant differences between the plans written under Ch'en Tu-hsiu's leadership and those that finally were executed at the end of August. Ch'en's plans assumed that the insurrection would be carried out in the name of his left Kuomintang; the new Communist party Central Committee under Ch'ü Ch'iu-pai was prepared to overthrow the Wuhan government. Ch'en's plans were limited in scope to the two provinces controlled by Wuhan in July: Hunan and Hupeh. Ch'ü's extended to the southern provinces of Kwangtung and Kiangsi as well. The new plans were far more explicit in assigning geographic areas for operations and in specifying a sequence of expected events. Where Ch'en continued to rely on lower-level KMT cadres, the new leaders insisted that the main force of the insurrection be what they called peasant revolutionary armies. Where Ch'en and Ts'ai Ho-shen hoped for a simple transition from isolated terrorism to widespread insurrection, Ch'ü Ch'iu-pai and his Russian adviser, Lominadze, saw the need to coordinate an attack on the main cities of central China. Since for the first time the Chinese Communist leadership articulated the desire to seize the cities from the countryside on their own, the August 7 plans for insurrection do indeed mark the beginning of a new rural strategy.

But Mao's claim to originality does not rest solely on the new departures of the August 7 plans. Mao boasted to Edgar Snow in 1936 that his program for the uprising in Hunan had been opposed

by the Central Committe.[58] He claimed he had gone beyond Central
to advance as a slogan the idea of forming governments of the soviet
type. As a punishment for his insubordination, the story goes, Mao
was dismissed from the Politburo in December 1927. In fact, however, Mao's contribution to the rural revolutionary strategy is more
complicated, if no less important, than this simple outline suggests.

It is undeniable that as soon as Mao Tse-tung reached Hunan
from Wuhan, where the August 7 conference had convened in a
stifling attic room, he began to change the program for the insurrection. Mao's new program dispensed with the Kuomintang flag as
well as its personnel; he recommended that worker-peasant-soldier
soviets be the declared goal of the insurrection. He insisted on a
complete solution of the land problem. All three of these innovations had been considered at the August 7 conference and rejected.
Central had ruled that the KMT flag was still necessary to court the
wavering petty bourgeoisie. Soviets might be a useful propaganda
slogan, but it would be premature to establish them. Radical land
confiscation would alienate too many small landlords. The difference of views seems clear.

But in actuality these were superficial issues in the context of the
month of August. In late August Central admitted in a letter to Mao
that the Communists need no longer work for the Kuomintang. It
further granted that there was no longer any reason to fear confiscating small landlords. Central was simply reluctant to advertise its
new policies for fear of creating even more enemies. Finally, on the
question of forming soviets, it is apparent both from Mao's proposals
in August and from his behavior as insurrectionary leader that he
did not intend to set up village or local-level soviets but rather to
declare the new provincial government of Hunan a soviet once it
became firmly established in Communist hands. On all these issues
Mao's differences with Central amounted to mere cosmetic changes
on a mutually approved policy.

If Mao's divergence from Central over the slogans for the insurrection was marginal, the opposite is true of his innovations in the
action program. Almost as soon as he reached Hunan he made three
new proposals against Central's plans for a coordinated insurrection
in three main districts of Hunan. He argued there was only one district where an insurrection could succeed: the area immediately surrounding Ch'angsha. Then he contended that due to increasing

pressure from local warlords, the schedule would have to be advanced to the last week of August instead of early September as Central planned. Finally, he proposed that two regiments of troops already organized and under Communist command would bear the main burden of the offensive. On each of these points Central quickly took Mao to task for altering its August 7 plans.

Of these new practical plans, only one was truly noteworthy. Central realized that Mao would have to make some decision about which parts of Hunan were more important than others. Cadres in Hupeh province to the north were at that very moment deciding to concentrate on south Hupeh to the virtual exclusion of other districts. But Central hoped Mao would at least keep open the possibility of working in south Hunan, around Hengyang. Mao's suggested restriction of the uprisings would reduce the number of counties from twenty-four in the three regions of east, south, and west Hunan to only seven in east Hunan — those counties surrounding Ch'angsha that Mao had studied for his famous Hunan report six months earlier: Hsiangt'an, Ninghsiang, Liling, Liuyang, P'ingchiang, Anyuan, and Yuehyang.

He justified the abandonment of south Hunan by admitting candidly to Central that he lacked the forces to scatter about the province. Mao's idea of a late August starting date was already outdated when Central received it, and in any case Mao was forced by circumstances to postpone his urban insurrection. The important difference lay in the stress Mao placed on organized military units: the two regiments of his latest plan.

From the day he arrived in Hunan, Mao Tse-tung refused to let himself be put in the position of his Hupeh comrades to the north. Central had forced them to execute violent combat plans without any support from Communist military units. In his August 20 letter to the central Politburo, Mao had already proposed that the main force of the insurrection in Hunan be two units of Communist troops that he called regiments. From the start Mao intended to execute the August 7 idea by using locally organized units under local command.

Ch'ü Ch'iu-pai's Central was willing to compromise on the slogans and propaganda, but it would brook no interference with its operational commands. A stern letter to Mao on September 5 virtually accused him of insubordination in his failure to build the main force of the insurrection among the peasantry. Other letters charged him with overstressing military force for his reliance on the two regiments, and neglecting insurrectionary work in local areas for his abandonment of south Hunan. Central told him his reliance on two army regiments instead of on the peasants was a fantasy. Here, rather than in disagreements over slogans, lay the real differences between Central and Mao.

Mao Tse-tung knew well the threat behind Central's warning: in September 1927 Ch'ü Ch'iu-pai operated under pressures from Moscow far greater even than those Ch'en Tu-hsiu had endured. He had to protect himself from the charges of adventurism and putschism should the insurrection fail. He sought to pin all responsibility for failure on the local operatives. This meant, or could mean, Mao himself. Mao's replies to Ch'ü were firmly defensive. South Hunan had to be abandoned for lack of strength. The two regiments were not the main force but simply cover for the worker-peasant armies. Furthermore, Central badly misunderstood the Hunan situation. "Your policy," he charged bluntly, "is a contradictory one: You desire us not to be concerned with the military but at the same time you want a mass armed force!"[59] This contradiction Mao was determined, and indeed destined, to eliminate in practice.

But it was too late to begin anew in the autumn of 1927 to construct a real peasant army, though this is what he and his Hunanese comrades pretended to do. Instead, Mao placed his insurrectionary hopes on a motley collection of peasant militia soldiers, secret society outlaws, Nationalist renegades, and disgruntled unemployed miners. Of the four units that he ordered into battle in the second week of September, only one was legitimately composed of peasants. That unit, his third regiment, the remnants of the feeble peasant self-defense armies that had thrown themselves against Ch'angsha in May, proved the least able to follow orders and the least valiant in combat. Of the two regiments he mentioned to Central, one turned traitor at the height of combat on September 14 and the other fell victim to treachery through its own blunders. That the most effective military unit, the only one to capture and hold a county town successfully, was the miners' brigade showed how far the campaign was from Mao's expressed ideal of peasant insurrection.[60] P'eng

Kung-ta, Mao's fellow provincial who helped him run the uprising in Hunan, admitted honestly afterward that the peasantry was not yet ready for insurrection.[61]

The Communist party Central Committee authorities had already prepared their indictments before Mao's forces began to move. The written plans of the August 7 conference explicitly demanded that the peasantry be the main force in the insurrection. Central's criticism of Mao's new orders for Hunan ordered him to avoid a military adventure. As the news of the defeats trickled into Wuhan, Central moved quickly to censure Mao for his failures. They were aided by messages from a comintern adviser assigned to Hunan, Comrade Ma, who accused the Hunanese of acting cowardly under fire. Since Mao Tse-tung was already in the fire zone with his troops, Ma singled out the hapless P'eng Kung-ta for a verbal lashing. The Hunanese, Ma said, had failed to follow the tactical plans they had agreed upon, had "soiled their own diapers" when faced with a partial defeat, and had concealed their behavior from the Russians with "Chinese-style, totally sharpsterish double-dealings." P'eng was too polite to reply directly, but he was heard to mumble to a comrade that Ma was a bookish intellectual who understood nothing of Hunanese conditions.[62]

Though the Russians and the Central authorities tried to blame the defeats of the Autumn Harvest on their subordinate Chinese Communists, nothing could have produced a successful insurrection given the conditions of the day. In the rapidly shifting politics of mid-1927, non-Communist troops were not dependable. Many even within the party doubted that the Communists could succeed. How much more difficult it must have been to convince sharply pragmatic bandit or mercenary forces. The peasant militia had never received enough training or weapons to become a disciplined force. Little wonder that they tended to break and run at the first adverse turn of events. The Communists learned also that their own personnel and command structures were too weak to engineer insurrection. The umbrella of KMT cooperation allowed Communists to play a role in local affairs disproportionate to their actual numbers.[63] In part the Communists' tendency to overestimate their forces was due to a justified fear of Central's harsh criticism. But a large part of Mao's and P'eng Kung-ta's optimism, almost to the day of their final defeat on September 19, must have been due to their own rank immaturity as military officers.

The most important cause of the defeat of the insurrection ultimately was the strength of the opposition. The Kuomintang party, with the split between Wuhan and Nanking, the pause in the Northern Expedition, and the resignation of Chiang Kai-shek, was a flagging and uncertain force. Immediately ready to step into its shoes, particularly in Hupeh and Hunan, were the more modernizing elements of what must, for want of a better word, be called gentry society—represented directly by what the Communists called the new warlords. T'ang Sheng-chih and Hsu K'o-hsiang had no trouble finding out about the "Communist plot" of a peasant uprising. The Shanghai papers several times tipped readers off in advance about forthcoming Communist actions. Mao Tse-tung himself narrowly escaped execution at the hands not of Chiang Kai-shek or any modern military force but of a patrol of ignorant local anti-Communist Popular Corps troops.[64]

If the insurrection now seems to have been doomed from the start, what do we conclude about Central's motivations in urging it onward? Some have claimed along with Trotsky that the Russian and Chinese Communist leaders sacrificed the peasant movement in 1927 solely in order to undermine Russian domestic opposition to Stalin.[65] Certainly the carefully self-serving language of Ch'ü Ch'iu-pai's orders to Mao and the other insurrectionaries suggests they were playing with insurrection in no small degree. Might we not legitimately conclude that the Autumn Harvest was, as Harold Isaacs has said of the Canton urban rising that followed it, a "bloody sacrifice, imposed from above and the outside?"[66]

Such an interpretation is not wholly convincing. The new party Central Committee, despite the important roles played by foreigners such as Lominadze and Ma, was composed of Chinese who would certainly have balked had they thought their movement was being sacrificed for Russian pride. The Chinese peasant movement leaders, particularly Mao Tse-tung and P'eng Kung-ta, clearly expected mass work with peasant associations to be more effective than it was. Their rapid and pragmatic adjustment to the changing military realities of late summer suggests they were indeed serious about the insurrection. The Central Committee was as committed to rural uprising as was Mao, but it had a different strategy.

Central placed its hopes from the start in a widespread rising among the mass of peasants in the plains of Hunan and Hupeh. The simultaneous and rapid spread of armed resistance across the counties would prevent concentrations of the suppressing armies. Further, the key link in Central's plan was the capture of a number of important county towns from which offensives against the major cities could be launched. Central remained convinced to the last that it would not be difficult to put together large military forces in the course of the insurrection. It wanted its lower-level workers to spend energy not on making military alliances but on creating an effective mass base among the peasants in each county. Peasant work was one thing and military work another, and the contradiction between them was to be borne in the breast of Central itself.

Mao Tse-tung shared many of these perceptions with his Central Committee. Indeed they had become part of the peasant movement orthodoxy. If anything, Mao was more single-minded than Central on the capture of the cities. He was convinced by virtue of his emotional commitment to the revolution that Ch'angsha would be its Petersburg. After Ch'angsha fell, the creation of soviet power could not be far behind. And until the city was taken, there was basically little sense in speaking of soviets or declaring the land revolution. As he put it in one letter to Central, "The seizure of Ch'angsha and the land revolution are one and the same thing."[67]

But the situation in Hunan in 1927 differed vastly from that of the Bolshevik revolution. And since the radical peasant movement was the single remaining prop of Communist power in Hunan, Mao was compelled, and indeed his peasant movement connections made him eager, to agree that the main force had to come from the villages.

It was on the nature of that revolutionary force that Mao diverged from Central. Mao was convinced that insurrection spreading across the counties—the Jacquerie of the Communist tradition—would merely dissipate Communist energies. He therefore found it easy to abandon south Hunan and easy to cancel the insurrection after his final defeat at Wenchiashih and go into the Maquis by heading for remote and mountainous Chingkangshan. If the movement seemed lost from the cities' point of view, as he later told Edgar Snow, a simple peasant rising would not accomplish the job.

Mao's concept of the insurrectionary strategy was based on a concept of the Worker-Peasant Revolutionary Army, whereas Central admitted that organized military force would be needed at a certain stage. It limited its use to what it called bandit style operations designed to create disorder in the countryside. But Mao's Worker-Peasant Army in Hunan was a unit of a different order. It numbered in the thousands even after the bloody defeats of May, possessed over three thousand weapons, and had been intimately mixed with regular army troops and the Hanyehp'ing miners. From at least mid-August on, these units had been on maneuvers far from their homes, some even in other provinces.[68] It was not that Mao had become a pure militarist on leaving Wuhan. During a twelve-hour stay in the town of Liling, his miner's regiment proclaimed a revolutionary committee and land confiscation, thus giving the lie to Central's later charge that Mao had failed to offer any political programs beyond military liberation. It was rather that Mao's experience demanded he add the military element to Central's plans. Ch'angsha had very nearly fallen to semiorganized peasant forces only two decades earlier in an uprising that he remembered vividly from his childhood.[69] Mao found that a similar collection of forces, including informal armies with secret society and underworld connections, had emerged in 1927 and might save the revolution.

But the difficulties in September 1927 proved to be too great. Perhaps even before he set out to join his front committee, bivouacked across the border in Kiangsi in early September, he began to feel that the opposition was too strong and that he would have to call off the attack and retreat into the mountains to await the second insurrection, as several other Communist peasant leaders had already elected to do.[70]

It is true that during the disastrous skirmishes of September a number of Communists groped toward new tactics to deal with the new situation. Some voiced, before Mao Tse-tung did, the conception of a revolutionary base outside the county towns of rural China. Some preached a form of the doctrine that insurgent forces must conserve their strength and strike only when tactically superior. Some even proposed building a new strategy of guerrilla warfare in which the Communist armies would appear and disappear at will in the hit-and-run tactics that so terrified anti-Communists in the 1960s.[71] Mao's friend P'eng Kung-ta, at the height of his dispute with Comrade Ma, proposed the slogan that the "People's Movement be transformed into the uninterrupted struggle of a People's

Army." A few hundred miles south, in Haifeng county where the peasant movement had begun, some Communists had already begun to forge the tactical weapons for what was later called people's war.

But these intimations of future strategic debates for the moment fell on deaf ears. Central continued for years to insist on the same vacuous slogans of the insurrection. The nature of the revolutionary base, whether geographical or social, the types of organized force available to the revolution, and the proper sphere of political activity for the Communist party all would require reinterpretation over two decades. Mao and his small band of stragglers set their minds to this job of rethinking at the end of the Autumn Harvest.

The cycle of the peasant movement strategy lasted less than half a decade. In the five years between 1922 and 1927 a small group of urbane intellectual Marxists discovered, developed, and then squandered the political potential of the Chinese countryside. Urged on by Moscow, attracted by what appeared to be a rural power vacuum, the Communist party waded deeper and deeper into the countryside. With each step it bonded itself further into a partnership with military and Nationalist bureaucratic politicians whose interest in the countryside was marginal at best. The novelty of the countryside, the apparent ease of penetration, the convenience of roles complementary to the roles of labor or military organizers, and the populist concern with the majority population strengthened the Communists' desire to attempt a rural revolution. But only when that final option was taken did Mao and his comrades realize how near to ruin their misconceptions and fantasies had brought them and the Chinese peasantry.

The strategic discussions in the revolutionary camp during this seminal period suggest that the road to the countryside would not be easy under the best of circumstances. To be convincing, the practitioners of the peasant strategy had to produce results that would benefit not only themselves but also the larger political forces upon whom they had to rely. To be effective, they had to neutralize potential opposition by exercising restraint and discipline. To prevent early destruction, they had to avoid premature polarization and violence. And when considering armed warfare in the countryside, the weaknesses of peasant-based armies had to be known and countered.

The cause of Chinese Communist rural failure in the peasant movement period was not the absence of the concept of rural struggle. The proponents of the rural strategy could not have succeeded without first building certain essential political assets. They lacked not a concept, but credibility, unanimity, authority, and maturity.

PART TWO

Organization

Agitation is such a joy.
It is organizing that is so difficult.

Francisco Juliao

3

STAFFING THE
REVOLUTION:
THE KUOMINTANG
PEASANT
BUREAUCRACY

Just as the idea of rural work preceded the practice in the Chinese Revolution, so the template of organization antedated the casting of the Chinese peasant movement. Russian experience was the blessing and the curse of Chinese Communist tacticians of the 1920s. Two decades earlier Vladimir Lenin had urged Russian Communists to build their professional ranks and avoid relying excessively on working-class spontaneity. Lenin's success in 1917 turned what had been a tactic of the moment in 1905 into a dogma for all future Bolshevik revolutionaries. The first item on the Chinese Communist list of what to do had to be getting organized. Lenin chided his Social-Democratic predecessors for marching into battle unprepared "like peasants from the plough, snatching up a club."[1] His Chinese counterparts, however, left nothing to chance. They would march to the villages and present an astonished peasantry with their ultimate weapon—organization.

The advantages of organization quickly became evident. The Communists found themselves after 1923 acting as management consultants to a revolutionary group with little concept of human structures. Sun Yat-sen's acceptance of the idea of reorganization not only brought in the by-now standardized Leninist terminology of committees, cells, secretaries, departments—the whole idea of *cadre* in the original French military sense familiar to the Russian leader—it also opened the door to Communist party participation in the highest reaches of Sun's Kuomintang party. The disadvantages of the Leninist organizational perspective, particularly when applied to a complex agrarian society, took considerably longer to learn.

The Communist effort fell short of success. The organization that the Chinese Communists built, unlike Lenin's, belonged to someone else. The would-be revolutionaries they trained for rural work were swallowed in a tide of newly mobilized, non-Communist activists. The mass organizations that appeared so extensive on paper vanished as though they had been figments of Communist imagination. The oddities of the Chinese Revolution were responsible, it may be seen, for each of these failures.

How much credit should the Communists get for the reorganization of the Kuomintang? To many the simple evidence that Sun Yat-sen had conversations with Borodin and accepted some Communists into his entourage is enough to show that the Koumintang became bolshevized after 1924. But it was one thing to accept new terminology or to draw a different organization chart and yet another to transform the fundamental nature of a political party. The Communists were patently aware of the danger that Sun's party would accept the name and reject the reality of a Leninist party. Peasant leader Lo Ch'i-yuan had an image: the Kuomintang in early 1924 was only a lampshade of paper and paste through which the light of the president shone undiminished.

After the January 1924 congress the Kuomintang seemed to bring order and hierarchy into what had been chaos and patriarchy. The Kuomintang was to meet regularly, establish central offices, and regenerate itself from the bottom up through the cell-branch-office hierarchy. It was to spread out in ordered, geometric fashion to other provinces, where the same process of hierarchy building would begin, with the executive offices in each provincial capital providing the direction. At the central office and in each of the provinces, bureaus would be set up along clean, functional lines (the Russian word was *sektsii*—sections). The central party office would have nine such bureaus, each with a chief and a secretary and a budget of its own. This part was easy enough to achieve.

Of course bolshevization would also have meant the establishment of strict rules of admission, party life, and members' behavior; inexorable procedures for enforcing discipline; and regularization of channels for the communication of messages from central authority — a much more difficult assignment. But with sufficient motivation the restructuring and reform of the Kuomintang could have been achieved without reliance upon members of another party, which had already learned the rules. The Kuomintang acceptance of Communist infiltration thus assumed that Communists had something to contribute besides their party organizational skills. There was nothing out of the ordinary in CP members moving into offices in the new structure where their skills could be put to use.

But those who complained about Communist infiltration, which had already begun in early 1924, claimed that the Communist party selected its positions with the aim of dominating the Kuomintang party and eventually taking it over. Certainly this was one of the main charges leveled against the Communists in the peasant movement and in the regional KMT organizations. For all their usefulness to anti-Communists, such claims uniformly overestimated Communist power. The allegation that the Communist party ran the regional KMT offices after 1924 is made rather boldly in recent KMT anti-Communist histories. The evidence is not impressive. There was in fact considerable variety in Communist influence of KMT regional organization. Mao Tse-tung's proposals to the First KMT Congress in January 1924 show that some CP members hoped to push the Kuomintang into areas where it had never worked before. His departure from Canton along with that of a number of other Communists to work in regional executive offices suggests their seriousness about operating in the name of the Kuomintang. Yet even at this point, perhaps the maximum point of CP influence at the regional level, they were scarcely threatening to dominate the Kuomintang.

Far from indicating a preponderance of Communist organizers, the numbers in table 1 show that the majority of regional KMT officers were non-Communists. Anti-Communist historians claim that the Peking executive office, for example, was in the control of Li Tachao.[2] But even before the successful challenge to his position by the Western Hills faction in 1925, he and his fellow Communist, Yü Shu-te, were in a minority in Peking. It was only in the central

Table 1 Communist and non-Communist KMT regional and provincial officers, 1924

	CP	non-CP		CP	non-CP
Central (Canton)			Shanghai		
Members	1	6	Members	0	5
Alternates	2	2	Alternates	2	3
Supervisors	0	5	Supervisors	0	3
Peking			Kiangsu	1	1
Members	2	4	Fukien	0	1
Alternates	2	4	Chekiang	0	1
Supervisors	0	2	Hankow		
Shantung	0	1	Members	0	1
Chihli	1	1	Alternates	0	1
Shansi	1	1	Hunan	1	0
Inner Mongolia	0	2	Hupeh	1	0
Chahar	0	1	Anhwei	0	2
Suiyuan	0	1	Kiangsi	2	0
Jehol	1	1			
			Harbin		
			Members	0	1
			Alternates	0	1
Total	10	31	Total	7	20

Source: Li Yun-han, *Tsung jung-kung tao ch'ing-tang* (To the party purge) (Taipei, 1966), pp. 268-271. Party attributions are mine.

Yangtze valley provinces of Hunan, Hupeh, and Kiangsi that Communist organizers appear to have had a monopoly of a number of KMT offices, but their superordinates at Hankow were not CP members. The Shanghai executive office, somewhat larger since it was the reincarnation of the old home office, did have a near majority of Communist section chiefs while Mao Tse-tung was working there, but the east China provinces under it were almost completely non-Communist. We should not be surprised to find that the Communists attempted in early 1926 to have the executive office level of KMT organization abolished.[3] The same generalization holds for the supposedly sensitive functional offices below the provincial executives. Contrary to the general impression conveyed by KMT historians, the Communists were less successful at placing their men in charge of important mass organization leadership posts than they were in putting them in charge of the executive offices.

With the important exception of Liu Fen, the Communist who held both the peasants' and workers' sections of the Hankow executive office, most of the top offices in the functional posts were held by staunch KMT members (see table 2). Liu's exception is important because from 1924 to 1925 he was able to build the Communist party in Hunan simultaneously with the Kuomintang and thus establish the base for the remarkable penetration of the peasant and workers' movements into Hunan in 1926. The Communist position in these regional functional posts did not improve through time. Fierce battles in each of the offices developed in 1925-1926 and the Communist party gradually lost ground.[4]

They did not lose ground until mid-1926, however, in the central KMT apparatus. It was the presence of important Communists at the core of the party that aroused the greatest suspicion and antagonism. The obvious growth in CP presence in the central executive committee led to demands to limit the extent of acceptance of CP members in early 1926. It was especially in the functional bureaus of

Table 2 Political affiliation of section chiefs and secretaries in the KMT regional executive offices, 1924[a]

Office	Peking	Shanghai		Hankow	
Organization	*C*[b]	*L*	C[c]	*C*	2C
Propaganda	*F*	*L*	C	*R*	
Students	*C*	-		-	
Youth	-	*R*	R	*R*	C2R
Women	-	*R*	R	*R*	C2R
Workers	*R*	*R*	C	*C*[d]	C2R
Peasants	*R*	*R*	C	*C*[d]	C2R
Investigation	*S*	*R*	R	*R*	

Source: Li Yun-han, *Tsung jung-kung tao ch'ing-tang* (To the party purge) (Taipei, 1966), p. 279ff.

[a]C = Communist party, S = Socialist Youth, F = Communist Front, R = Right KMT, L = Left KMT. Italic letter = section chief, roman letter = secretary.

[b]Li Ta-chao

[c]Mao Tse-tung

[d]Liu Fen

the central party that the enemies of the Communists found their presence threatening. As table 3 shows, by 1926 right-wing influence had been all but completely removed and Communists occupied a majority of the seventeen top functional positions (chief and secretary) at the time of the Second National Congress. After Chiang Kai-shek laid down the new rules in May 1926, the CP members squeezed out of the bureaus sought to turn them over to left-wing figures favorable to the radical cause.[5]

The extensive peasant movement bureaucracy in the Kuomintang was part of this pattern of erosion at the center and sedimentation at the periphery. The peasant movement's bureaucracy and general staff, which controlled the financing, training, and coordination for the rural effort, needed a presence at the Kuomintang's center. Had the Kuomintang been a truly Leninist party, its mass movements would have been ancillary to its leader and his Central Committee. But in the Chinese case the presence of a second Leninist party within the Kuomintang generated constant tensions between the top and the bottom of the Nationalist organization.

The central bureaucratic focus of the peasant movement was the peasant bureau of the Kuomintang's central executive committee. The bureau was one of nine departments (*pu*) quartered in the same

Table 3 Political affiliation of section chiefs and secretaries in KMT central departments[a]

Department	1924		1926		1927
Secretariat	-		*C*	C	-
Organization	*C*	C	*C*	C	(C)
Propaganda	*R*	R	*L*	L	*L*
Youth	*R*	R	*L*	C	*L*
Women	*R*	R	*L*	C	*L*
Workers	*L*	C	*L*	C	*L*
Peasants	*C*	C	*C*	C	*L*
Merchants	-		*R*		*L*
Overseas	-		*L*	C	*L*

Source: Li Yun-han, *Tsung jung-kung tao ch'ing-tang* (To the party purge) (Taipei, 1966), pp. 270, 549-550.

[a]C = Communist party, R = Right KMT, L = Left KMT. Italic letter = section chief, roman letter = secretary.

converted cement factory where Sun Yat-sen had his apartments in 1924.[6] Its enabling legislation gave it broad powers to conduct rural investigations, form study groups, draft land reform programs, and organize peasant conferences.[7] But for the first half-year of its existence the bureau remained a mere name on a door behind which a handful of young revolutionaries worked alone.[8]

Only in September 1924 did the bureau begin to grow. New regulations provided for a scattering of minor officials, secretaries, translators, and high-level operatives called organizers (*tsu-chih-yuan*) empowered to create mass organization. The lower-level workers, called special assignees (*t'e-p'ai-yuan*) would do the hard work (six hours a day at least) in the countryside, reporting once a week to the bureau's secretary. The secretary, and not the bureau chief, had the power under these new rules to direct all activities, draw up all correspondence, prepare all charts and pamphlets, collect and pay all accounts, and determine the bureau's budget. All the bureau chief had to do was sign the papers.[9]

This arrangement certainly appeared convenient for the Communists. As long as they occupied the position of secretary, they could continue to dominate the peasant movement, even using it to build the Communist party in the villages. Should his enthusiasm wane, the chief would be in no position to control the Communists' activities. By early 1926 the Communists appeared well along on this path of monopolizing peasant movement work. The first two secretaries of the bureau were the Kwangtungese Communists, P'eng P'ai and Lo Ch'i-yuan. Virtually all the bureau members were overt or covert CP members. By early 1926 the most important working group within the peasant movement was not the bureau but a secret peasant committee within the Communist party's Kwangtung Regional Committee. In this sense the Communists did indeed run the peasant movement as their enemies charged.[10]

But the Communists' strong grip on the lower levels of the Kwangtung organization masked their weakness at the center. The secret peasant committee was a case in point. P'eng and Lo twice attempted to install a similar committee, called the Kuomintang peasant movement committee, legally and openly under the KMT bureau but were forced to disband it in the face of active right-wing opposition.[11] Even the post of secretary fell from their grasp after Chiang Kai-shek's coup of March 20, 1926, when Lo Ch'i-yuan was forced to resign in favor of a little-known leftist.[12] When the Kuomintang peasant movement committee reemerged in Wuhan in March 1927, it openly debated the peasant question with a promising balance of opinions represented. But parallel to this committee and sapping its powers was a new overt Communist organization called the central peasant committee, headed by Mao Tse-tung and staffed by the men who would soon lead the Communist party into the Autumn Harvest Insurrection. It was already too late to build a truly effective peasant apparatus at the top of the Kuomintang.

The difficulty was that the Communists needed more than just a passive bureaucrat as their leader if they were to capitalize on their mass work. Their minority position demanded that they have positive representation, an active broker who could speak for the peasant interest at the highest levels of the Kuomintang. The bureau chief thus played a critical role in their gamble, a role that could be successfully played only if three conditions obtained: that the chief's position as broker not be compromised by overly strident demands from his constituents, that he continue to gain the respect of his peers and superiors within the Kuomintang, and that he remain sympathetic with the Communist-peasant cause. Unfortunately these conditions, present in some degree from 1924 to 1925, had disappeared by 1927.

The rapidly changing roster of bureau chiefs illustrates the Communist dilemma. Their first choice as chief seemed ideal at the time. Lin Tsu-han was a long-time associate of Sun Yat-sen who had recently joined the Communist party. But the Communist party needed Lin's services elsewhere in central China, where new cell organizations were being built. They also hoped to dampen mounting criticism from the right.[13] So Lin resigned and was quickly supplanted by three Sun cronies, all Cantonese and all non-Communist, in quick succession. The last of these, Huang Chü-su, resigned abruptly in October 1924 amid rumors that he could not get along with his Communist secretary, P'eng P'ai. Huang was a civil servant in the Western image who later became Kwangtung's most prominent county magistrate and turned his native Chungshan county into a model of Kuomintang local government in the 1930s. He and his two predecessors clearly lacked the will to broker the Communist interest in the KMT marketplace.[14]

For ten months in 1924-1925 it seemed as though the right man had appeared. The man who eased out Huang, who was Sun's chief plenipotentiary in Canton and had rocketed to the leadership of the Kwangtung provincial government in 1924, agreed now to make the peasant movement cause his own. Liao Chung-k'ai's scholarly background, his east Kwangtung origins, which placed him spiritually closer to P'eng P'ai than to the Pearl delta Cantonese who preceded him, his Japanese education at Waseda a decade before P'eng P'ai, and his reputation as an eloquent speechmaker before working-class crowds all convinced the Communists that he would be an ideal spokesman. During his tenure as chief Liao did intervene on several occasions to protect peasant movement operatives against attacks.[15] His speeches often urged the Kwangtung peasantry to build their organizations — the appeal to strength from solidarity so often used by members of Sun Yat-sen's entourage.

Liao was gunned down on the steps of the Kuomintang central party office on August 20, 1925, the victim of alleged anti-Communist terrorists. Despite the Communist adulation of their martyred chief, there are clear indications that Liao was not in his lifetime a perfect apologist for the peasant movement cause. Liao, like Sun before him, tended to view the peasantry as an abstraction, as that element by which China differed from the more industrialized world.[16] Like Sun also he placed the peasant movement on an equal plane with the other movements that made up the national revolution. The peasantry had the right to organize themselves for self-protection in the same way that the merchants did. A key figure in Hong Kong-Canton strike negotiations in the summer of 1925, Liao divided his interest in the peasant movement with concern for Canton's labor problems and for the new Whampoa Military Academy, of which he was a founder and long-time party representative or political commissar. He took great pains not to support the notion of class struggle, especially in the countryside. His remarks, for example, to the Communist-dominated First Congress of the Kwangtung Peasant Association, a congress that roundly denounced capitalist oppression, large landlords, and traitor merchants, blandly omitted any reference to class or to economic struggle.[17] However favorable to Communist peasant activity Liao may have been, it is not hard to imagine him applying restraint on the movement's excesses had he lived longer.

After two more caretaker appointments, control of the bureau

passed to a former subordinate of Liao Chung-k'ai, a mission-edu-
cated teacher turned full-time functionary. Kan Nai-kuang in his
public performances seemed more willing than Liao to encourage
class struggle in the countryside. Pamphlets he authored urged the
Kuomintang to become a true mass party by making the peasants its
main force army. By late 1926 Kan's forward position attracted extensive praise from Ch'en Tu-hsiu and other radicals, who called
Kan the young left-wing leader with the most ideas. Nevertheless,
Kan clearly lacked Liao's prestige, experience, and authority. Moreover, Chiang Kai-shek's anti-Communist turn severely weakened the
power base of the leftist position. While Kan's populist rhetoric continued through the end of 1926, his behavior toward the peasant
movement Communists in Canton cooled noticeably from summer
1926 on.[18] In December Kan, without resigning as chief, accepted
another mission to neighboring Kwangsi, formed a moderate study
group of former leftists, and moved closer to the Cantonese militarist Li Chi-shen.[19] It is not surprising to find Kan a year later acting
as mayor of Canton in charge of executing thousands of Communists accused of rioting.

Kan Nai-kuang's desertion, coming at the same time as the secession of Wuhan during the Northern Expedition, left the peasant
movement again without representation in the Kuomintang. Although Chiang Kai-shek's entourage in Nanchang was closed to
them after January 1927, the Communists could still pick their own
man in the rump Wuhan government. Their choice was Teng Yen-
ta, again an old Sun associate, but one with Moscow training and
military command experience. Teng performed admirably, staking
out positions on the land question well to the left of all the former
bureau chiefs and appointing Communists to most of the operational offices in the peasant movement under Wuhan. But his successes came at the cost of the very support among non-Communist
politicians that the peasant movement had courted for three years.
Teng acted easily as movement spokesman, but his audience had
dwindled to an insignificant few. In July 1927 the last listener, the
warlord whose military might permitted Teng and the Communists
their brief hour in Wuhan, ceased to pay heed.[20]

The technique of placing Communists in key ministries or
bureaus was a part of the Leninist insurrectionary orthodoxy of the

1920s. Yet not in that decade, nor even later in non-Western countries, did that strategy ever produce the desired result. In the Chinese case iι is not difficult to understand why. The pathetic search for a leader or broker sympathetic to the peasant movement cause pointed up the differences between Sun Yat-sen's personalistic, antiprofessional following and the new breed of revolutionaries who had studied What Is To Be Done. The more successful the Communists were at forging an organizational weapon at the bottom, the more threatening they seemed to the skeptical old guard of Sun's party. Any non-Communist standard-bearer risked being compromised by the stridency and immaturity of his Communist subordinates. A professed Communist, on the other hand, attracted the ire of those who opposed harboring a party within the party. These conflicting pressures prevented the Communists from building an effective peasant-oriented bureaucratic force within the Kuomintang movement and forced them instead to rely upon their own underground bureaucracy and the personal favors of a few sympathetic politicians. Although the secession of Wuhan freed the Communists momentarily from such criticism and let them pretend to have staged a successful Leninist coup, it cost them access to the main body of KMT opinion, finances, and military power without which they could not survive.

4

EDUCATION FOR REVOLUTION: THE PEASANT MOVEMENT INSTITUTE

The peasant movement faced the situation that Lenin described in his conundrum: there are no people—yet there are enormous numbers of people. Before the conviction that the countless millions of Chinese peasants were a massive potential force for revolution stood the stark reality that the peasantry would never appreciate their true role unless they could be reached. The Chinese revolutionaries approached this problem through an ambitious program of professional training in the arts of rural organization.

Perhaps the deepest impression left by the wave of Soviet Union advisers to the Kuomintang in the mid-twenties was the concept of the importance of professional training for the formation of a revolutionary elite. We tend to think that the main medium of cadre training that they developed was the famous Whampoa Military Academy. Indeed, for a twenty-five-year period in Chinese history the graduates of that school did constitute the backbone of Chinese political life. China was, and Taiwan still is, ruled in no limited degree by the Whampoa spirit.

But revolutionary Canton, and later Wuhan, were very nearly nothing more than training grounds for an entire range of revolutionary activity. The KMT leadership, Communist and non-Communist alike, deeply loved the idea of training classes. The Whampoa Academy grew in part out of earlier military schools (*chiang-wu-t'ang*) that prolifcrated after 1911 in Canton. With the reorganization of the Kuomintang, the training class fever spread into the highest party echelons. About the same time as Whampoa was being founded a school calling itself the Chinese Kuomintang Institute was set up to train high-level cadres. The faculty consisted of the great majority of the KMT bureau chiefs.[1]

The Peasant Movement Institute (Nung-min yun-tung chiang-hsi-so) that was established by a June 30, 1924, order of the KMT executive committee fell into this tradition easily.[2] From its inception to its closing in Wuhan in May 1927 the Nung-so held seven classes (see table 4.) Compared with the Whampoa Academy, it was not an imposing operation. The military school over the same period produced over seven thousand military officers whose training averaged just under a year. The peasant institute alumni totaled by the most favorable count only a little over seventeen hundred and were given an average of only three months of schooling in the art of being peasant organizers.

Table 4 Classes, principals, dates of operation, and graduates of the Peasant Movement Institute

Class Principal	Date[a]	Graduates	Graduates' origin		
			Kwang-tung	Hunan	Other
1 P'eng P'ai	1924.7.3-8.3(?)	33	33	0	0
2 Lo Ch'i-yuan	1924.8.21-10.30	142	142	0	0
3 Juan Hsiao-hsien	1925.1.1-5.1	114	114	0	0
4 T'an Chih-t'ang	1925.4.1-9.1	76	63	11	2
5 Lo Ch'i-yuan	1925.9.14-12.8	113	40	44	25
6 Mao Tse-tung	1926.5.3-9.11	318	2	36	280
Wuhan Chou I-li(?)	1927.3.7-5.(?)	950	-	150	-

Source: Lo Ch'i-yuan, "Nung-min yun-tung chiang-hsi-so" (The Peasant Movement Training Institute). *Chung-kuo nung-min,* no. 2 (February 1926), pp. 1-44; Lo Ch'i-yuan, "Ti-liu-chieh nung-min yun-tung chiang-hsi-so pan-li ching-kuo" (How the sixth class of the Peasant Movement Institute was conducted). In *Ti-i-tz'u kuo-nei ko-ming chan-cheng shih-ch'i-te nung-min yun-tung,* p. 20; Chou I-li's report in "Minutes of the Expanded conference of the Central Peasant Movement Committee," courtesy C. M. Wilbur.

[a]Dates of formal beginning of study and of graduation.

In a second sense, the institute has deserved the obscurity it has been awarded in Western accounts of the Chinese revolution. Whereas a sizable number of Whampoa graduates went on to achieve considerable fame as revolutionary leaders — including some of the most important recent leaders of the Chinese Communist party such as Lin Piao and Lo Jui-ch'ing — there is not a single graduate of the institute represented at the top of the Maoist hierarchy today.[3] The small number of graduates combined with the staggering losses the peasant movement leadership suffered in the great reaction of 1927 have thus produced the impression that the institute was a rather insignificant aspect of the period.

Despite the apparent lack of long-range impact on Republican China or even on the higher-level personnel of the Communist movement, there are sufficient reasons to regard the Peasant Movement Institute as an establishment of considerable influence. The fact that its building has been turned into a museum in China indicates that the present Chinese Communist leadership believes it was the cradle of the correct peasant policy of the Communist party.[4] A list of the teachers at the various sessions is almost a roll call of the leading figures in the Communist mass movements of the mid-twenties: Chou En-lai, Wu Yü-chang, Ho Hsiang-ning, Ch'ü Ch'iu-pai, Teng Chung-hsia, Yun Tai-ying, P'eng P'ai, Lin Tsu-han, Su Chao-cheng, Hsiao Ch'u-nü, Li Li-san, Chang T'ai-lei, Kao Yü-han, Juan Hsiao-hsien, Lo Ch'i-yuan, and many more. And the very fact that the ideas Mao carried with him into Hunan directly on leaving his post as principal of the institute were generated in the course of his lectures and his discussions of rural strategy with his contemporaries there makes a treatment of the nature of the institute environment critical to an understanding of the policies he later came to espouse.

What, then, was the nature of the Nung-so? How may we characterize its student body and its faculty? What kind of training did the initiates undergo? To what posts of importance in the revolution were they assigned?

RECRUITMENT

The Communists kept a tight rein not only on the faculty but on the institute admissions policy. Although there are no facts available about CCP membership, both the CCP and the KMT accounts make the claim that it was nearly total. Chou Fo-hai gave the following description of the procedure for recruitment to the school:

> As a result of the CCP monopoly of the worker-peasant movement, those applicants who belonged only to the KMT were not allowed to participate. Let me recall the following fact: when the call to commence the first class of the institute was issued, students were brought together and given an exam. The examinations were to be graded at the home of T'an P'ing-shan. But rather than the usual method of grading, an unusual procedure was adopted: the candidate's name was read off and if he was a CP member he was accepted without reading the grade. If only a KMT member, he was failed. Thus non-Communists were unable to take part.[5]

This recruitment procedure presumably was followed throughout the six classes of the Canton institute and later in the Wuhan branch as well. The institute faculty was certainly heavily if not exclusively larded with Communist leaders; every principal was a leading Communist figure and many of the teachers were Communists as well.[6]

An examination of the geographical origins of the institute students reveals a remarkable expansion in the recruitment area over a two-year period. The native places of the original thirty-three students are not listed, but judging from those who later became known, all were from the immediate Canton region. The second class included representatives of some twelve different counties, with disproportionate emphasis on Hsiangshan, Shunte, and Kwangning; all Cantonese areas.[7] In the third session in early 1925 some thirty-three Kwangtung counties were mentioned as home counties of students, with Pearl River delta counties such as Tungkuan, Hsiangshan, Haoshan, and Hua favored. The fourth class, beginning in April of 1925, was the first to introduce non-Kwangtungese, bringing eleven Hunanese and two Kwangsinese into the institute. With the expansion of revolutionary power into the North River and Southern Route-Hainan regions, these areas began to climb above the Canton environs in representation. In the fifth class, begun in the late summer 1925, for the first time Kwangtung provincials were outnumbered by Hunanese and students from other provinces including Hupeh, Fukien, Kwangsi, and Shantung. Significantly, ten of the Hunanese were from Mao Tse-tung's native country of Hsiangt'an. Finally, in the last Canton class, begun under Mao's direction on the eve of the Northern Expedition, nineteen provinces were represented, with Mao's Hunan second only to Kwangsi.

When this geographical expansion is compared with the recruitment sources of the Whampoa Academy for the same period two significant patterns emerge.[8] (See table 5.) One is that the Peasant Movement Institute tended to recruit only from those areas into which the revolutionary movement was expanding or hoped to expand, whereas Whampoa by contrast had from the beginning a pan-Chinese student body. The second was that from mid-1925 on in both Whampoa and the peasant institute there was a remarkable surge in the recruitment of young Hunanese provincials. The important point is that the recruitment patterns for the institute seemed to reflect in a direct way the geographical hopes of its Communist leadership.

An examination of the recruitment procedures of the peasant institute reveals that from the very beginning one of the main prob-

Table 5 Provincial origins of Peasant Movement Institute and Whampoa students and active Communist peasant movement workers

Province	PMI[a]	Whampoa[b]	CP[c]
Anhwei	1	207	13
Fukien	2	144	9
Hupeh	4	504	21
Hunan	53	2189	30
Kiangsi	4	476	16
Kwangtung	380	1036	-
Kwangsi	7	218	12
Shantung	7	458	12
Unknown or other	18	2167	105
Total	476	7399	218

[a]Graduates of first five classes of the Peasant Movement Institute tabulated from lists given in *Chung-kuo nung-min*, no. 2 (Feb. 1, 1926), pp. 174-207. Excludes the sixth class in Canton and the Wuhan class.

[b]Graduates of first five classes through September 1927 tabulated from *Huang-p'u t'ung-hsueh tsung-ming ts'e* (General name register of Whampoa classmates) (Nanking, 1932).

[c]Numbers cited by Ch'en Tu-hsiu in November 1926. ("Report on the Peasant Movement for October and November," *Chiao-yü Tsa-chih*, no. 3, p. 40.)

lems was to ensure that an adequate number of real peasants were
included in the classes. That the problem was never adequately met
was considered deplorable by the movement leaders. But the result
was that the movement tended to reproduce its own kind.

The first class was unashamedly intellectual:

> The participants in this class consisted largely of conscious activists who
> had joined in the May Fourth struggles and who desired to "go to the
> people" (*ju min-chien ch'ü*). Next came a number of peasants who had
> accepted our [KMT] party program or had been in the Peasant Move-
> ment before. And finally there were some workers who had joined in the
> movement to organize labor unions.[9]

By the time the second class came along some attempt was made
to improve the distribution and quality of recruits. A general questionnaire was passed out to every applicant in which considerable
prominence was given to questions about revolutionary background
("Were you in the 1911 Revolution? The Workers' Movement? Peasant or Student Movement? Can you prove it?") family background
("How do you get along with your family? Is your family powerful?"), and ethnic identity ("What dialect do you speak? In which
county are you known the best?"). But the effect of these precautions was not immediately to increase the percentage of peasants
in the institute—the second session claimed the following recruitment breakdown: students and peasants, 30% each; those assigned
by peasant associations (professional organizers), 10%; workers,
22%; and women, 8%. It was only with the third session in early
1925 that a sharp increase in the peasant category occurred: some
92 of the 128 accepted were peasants, and of these 72 were classed as
tenant farmers (the other 20 were owner farmers). Four were
workers; 1 owned a small business, and 2 were soldiers.

In order to increase the percentage of students of worker-peasant
origin, the requirement that all applicants be middle-school graduates was dropped after the second class. The results were apparently somewhat successful. But at the opening of Mao's sixth class in
May 1926 it was again decided that a middle-school education was a
necessity and that the candidates would have to be literate men who
were able to reason.[10] Thus it was considered too great a risk to
accept ordinary uneducated farmers in Mao's classes. Though we
have no figures for the sixth and Wuhan classes' composition, we

may assume that worker-peasant proportions declined as a result of the stipulation. Forty years later, ironically enough, Mao Tse-tung, by then Communist party chairman in the Chinese People's Republic, began his Cultural Revolution on a platform that made education more available to worker-peasant elements.

An advertisement in the Hankow papers in early March 1927 suggests one reason why there was much difficulty in recruiting large numbers of potential organizers. The notice demanded high school education, teaching experience, or very high marks in primary school as the educational criteria. The age had to be between eighteen and thirty-five, and the student had to supply his own coats, shoes, and bedding since the institute would only supply a simple suit of clothes. The candidate had to be free of tuberculosis and able to walk long distances in the countryside. He had to be determined to return after graduation to his home village. Then, if he could pass the examination, he would be admitted.[11]

Rural work was clearly a hazardous and unrewarding occupation, one that required much sacrifice and involved great danger. Past applicants had entered the institute in the hope of advancing in the bureaucracy more than of returning to their villages to work. The movement would, however, be able to absorb only literate persons—a demand imposed by the heavily bureaucratic nature of peasant movement work during the period. Little wonder that the recruitment rate lagged behind Communist hopes.

The students at the institute, and by extension the leading figures in the peasant movement, constituted a kind of elite drawn from the same sources as the labor movement and to some extent the new military. In fact the lines between these groups were extremely fluid—as Mao's easy transition might indicate. But usually those who joined the peasant movement elite had had some connection with rural problems in China: either they had been born in the countryside or were assigned there by the Kuomintang or the Communist party.

Some idea of the type of persons who became important in the movement after graduation can be gleaned from the obituaries of graduates printed occasionally in the main journals.[12] The most striking thing about these accounts is that practically none of the martyrs—men whose professional commitment to the movement led to death in service—was a peasant, either in family background or in actual work. There was a strong bias in favor of those who had received some education; even those boys from rural backgrounds had as a rule attended the private Confucian school (*ssu-shu*) — and particularly those who went to school in Canton around the time of the May Fourth movement. A number of these men appear to have had some south seas (mostly Singapore) experience, although this fact is often concealed in the official listings because the native place of a Chinese person always refers to a location on the mainland. Those who came from peasant backgrounds generally had made the break with agricultural society quite early, whether by going to school or by moving to the city. There were a number of school-teachers who became prominent.

A composite picture of the typical peasant movement leader gives us a very unpeasantlike character: not all the cadres of the movement resembled their Japanese-educated leader P'eng P'ai, but it certainly helped to have had an urban intellectual upbringing, particularly if that upbringing brought one into the circles of May Fourth or the labor movement in Canton. Presumably Mao's Hunanese trainees at the institute would have been even more likely to have come from intellectual and middle-class backgrounds, since the difficulties and costs of transportation alone from Hunan to Canton would have been prohibitive for ordinary rural boys.

TRAINING

The training received at the Peasant Movement Institute reflected the hopes of its creators and teachers and also provided a mold for the shaping of younger movement leaders. Certain aspects of the curriculum were present from the very beginning and others were introduced only after a time and because of shifting commitments on the leadership's part.

One of the most consistent stresses in the institute program was its military training program. In the very first class ten of the thirty days of sessions were spent in military drill on the premises of the Whampoa school. The second class would have had at least a half-month of drill had it not been thrown almost immediately into combat at the time of the Merchants' Corps incident. It was this group of students that almost exclusively formed the Peasant Corps Army that Sun Yat-sen so noisily led to Shaokuan on his Northern Expedi-

tion and then back to fight the merchants' "paper tigers." Little
wonder that Lo Ch'i-yuan could explain that "an examination of
the first two classes reveals that those students who were most eager
about the military aspect of their training have been able to put the
most effort into the peasant movement."[13] During the third and
fourth classes the students were prepared more for becoming the
organizers and commanders of their own peasant self-defense
armies in the various counties. Military training was thus made a
daily affair; during the fourth class, three hours every morning were
devoted to drill. By the time of Mao's sixth class military training
had been fully integrated into the institute program. The class of
over three hundred was divided into two squads and given cadres to
lead them in a 10-week, 182-hour program of formal military training.[14] This arrangement presumably was continued when the school
moved to Wuhan. There is little reason to doubt that the young
peasant movement students constituted one of the most effective
battle units in the city.

A second constant aspect of the institute's curriculum was the
emphasis on what was called practical training. Every class was at
some point thrown as a group into either some extracurricular political activity or an inspection tour of some realm of peasant movement success. P'eng P'ai, principal of the first class, insisted that the
students spend as little time in the classroom and as much in practical work as possible. Every Sunday he led them into the villages on
the outskirts of Canton and directed them in a program of investigation, propaganda, and the organization of peasant associations
there. This group of students created the first associations in the
Canton suburban area. Even the harassed second class in the midst
of its hurried trip to Shaokuan was divided up into squads and sent
out into the neighboring villages. For five days these groups, led by
local students, went into the villages to make their own investigations. For its practical experience, the fourth class was allowed to
attend en masse the first Kwangtung Peasant Congress in 1925.

The fifth and sixth classes, enjoying the relative calm of the Canton political situation, were permitted more systematic forms of
practical exercises. In the former the student body was sent first to
attend a founding meeting of a district association in the suburbs of
Canton, to visit an arsenal, and then to join in the founding meeting
of the Ch'üchiang County Peasant Association in the north. The

sixth session, apparently led by Principal Mao, went as a body to inspect the peasant mass organizations in Haifeng, far to the east. A contemporary account of their visit provides us with some local color:

> The steamer departed from Canton, tooting its whistle, at 4 P.M. on August tenth. It arrived at the same time on the twelfth at Swatow, where it was met at the dock by a group of all ages and sexes representing a KMT district party office, the peasant associations, the labor unions, the merchant association, the peasant self-defense army, the Corps of Young Laborers, and the (Swatow) city authorities. As they formed into ranks they were greeted by beating drums and popping firecrackers. When they marched, shouting slogans, the sounds resounded from the surrounding hills. Their courageous, fighting air resembled the front lines of the revolution and demonstrated their unshakeable solidarity.[15]

Whether such a festive welcome had any real value in terms of practical training may well be doubted. But there is no question that it had an impact on the students. It also deeply affected their principal's contribution to the rural strategy.

In the classroom, the institute demonstrated a certain change over a period of time in the intellectual content of the curriculum. When the concept of the school was first being formulated in late June 1924, the projected courses were rudimentary. There were only ten subjects to be offered, running from the theory of the peasant movement through the agricultural conditions of Kwangtung and methods of improving them to simply peasant self-defense armies.[16] The details of the curriculum were not published until 1925. By that time the course offerings had expanded to twenty-six and included such arcane subjects as statistics, the history of Chinese secret societies, and singing.[17] There were basically four major divisions of the curriculum: KMT party principles, basic knowledge about the national revolution, peasant movement theory and practical tactics, and propaganda training.

After the central peasant school shut down, the curriculum and practical training of the peasant movement continued on a smaller scale. In place of the central school came a number of smaller, ad hoc training classes (*hsun-lien pan*). The first of these was largely under Mao's direction. Established at the insistence of the Communist Central Committee and the Kwangtung Peasant Association

in July 1926, this school was rather strictly watched by the Kwangtung Communist apparatus and admitted only students from
Kwangtung—thirty from each of the ten counties surrounding
Canton. The teachers were under instructions to induct every student into the Communist party or failing that to recruit at least a
third of them. "In this way," the resolution setting up the school
said, "at the end of six months we will have cultivated 1800 people
. . . and absorbed 800 [600?] new party comrades to scatter to the
counties by the end of the year."[18] The lecture schedule at this peasant movement training class was grueling and purely Communist.
Three of the five regular lecturers were the Russian agrarian experts
assigned to Borodin's entourage: Volin, Tarkhanov, and Iolk, who
lectured on the theory of the land question, agrarian statistics, and
investigative sampling techniques. Lo Ch'i-yuan, the director of the
Kwangtung Provincial Peasant Association, lectured on the Chinese
land question and the Communist party, and Mao Tse-tung, now
boning up on his Marxism-Leninism, did the nineteen-hour course
on the Comintern and the land question.[19] This class was nominally
run under the Kwangtung Provincial Peasant Association, but the
announcements of it in the official Kuomintang newspaper censor
out the names of the instructors—a clear indication that the Russian
and perhaps the Chinese Communist presence was an embarrass-
ment to the provincial KMT authorities.[20]

Despite the growing suspicion, Communists continued to be
active in the new training programs until late in the fall at least. At
the end of October a group of thirty Whampoa graduates ran a two-
week special institute to train peasant army officers. Mao Tse-tung,
Lo Ch'i-yuan, and Juan Hsiao-hsien were among the teachers. This
was Mao's last job in Canton before he left for Shanghai to join the
Central Committee as the CP peasant committee chief.[21]

After Mao's departure and with the evacuation of many Communists northward to join the Wuhan administration, the training
of peasant cadres fell to lesser hands. By March 1927, the last training program documented, the KMT military's suspicions of the
Communist training programs had been aroused. The last class
admitted in March had rather strict qualifications for membership:
high school or upper primary education, age eighteen or over (a
dozen members of the first five institute classes had been under
eighteen), proficiency in the Canton dialect, and above all KMT

membership. Graduates of this program doubtless participated in the dismantling of the Communist peasant unions after April.

The curriculum of Mao's sixth class, although adhering to this general outline, shows that a subtle evolution was taking place in course content. Whereas the original charter curriculum had such harmless items as simple theory of sociology and everyday legal knowledge, the sixth session was pared of offerings that did not have a blatantly Marxist orientation. There were also new courses to be taught, including social problems and socialism, the Soviet Union, and the Chinese peasant question (the last taught by Mao).[22] Where the teaching materials for the earlier classes had most probably been the publications of the KMT central peasant bureau, the sixth session began a program of systematically compiling its own textbooks. These materials began to provide a body of often translated theoretical and practical knowledge that could be used, developed, and preserved independent of rival information.[23] The increasing self-sufficiency of the peasant movement curriculum can be seen from a type of study technique Mao initiated at his sixth session. Before assigning any book to read, the teacher would first make an outline of the important questions that the student was to answer. The student would be expected to supply written answers within a fixed period of time. The best of these would be selected by the teacher, corrected, and then posted on the wall for all to read. Later all answers would be returned to the students and each would be required to retrace his errors and correct them according to the approved essay.[24] This process of closely directed indoctrination under Mao replaced the more libertarian methods of his predecessors.

ULTIMATE ASSIGNMENT

The assignments that the institute gave to its graduates indicated the fatal flaw in the program: the movement could produce enough men to, in the classical phrase, "mount steeds and chase thieves," but not enough to "dismount and post the victory proclamations."[25] The problem was that the institute produced barely enough personnel to staff itself and the central organs of the Kuomintang, much less to bring under control the vast reaches of Chinese rural society. Of the first class of thirty-two, three-quarters were assigned directly as special delegates of the central peasant bureau. One hundred and forty-two members of the second, after its brief use as a military unit, were sent directly to their home villages around Canton to become organizers. In the third class, where military training had been particularly stressed, the best fifteen students in the military training program were kept on to teach the next class, and an additional twenty remained in Canton as on-the-spot study personnel—guides for future classes. By the time of the fourth class it was reckoned that over one-third of the graduates had been kept in the central KMT apparatus.

It is likely that as the size of the classes grew the flow of trained personnel out into the villages increased. The majority of the Hunanese students at the fifth session left school before classes were over to assume posts along the railway to Ch'angsha. Presumably the three hundred-odd members of the sixth class followed in their footsteps. The assignment of the last and largest class in Wuhan again suffered somewhat from the demands placed on it at the time of the Hsia Tou-yin mutiny, but the class probably contributed a sizable portion of the four hundred men that the Hupeh Communists assigned to the villages in the preparations for the Autumn Harvest Insurrections.

We may assume that of the total seventeen hundred graduates of the various classes only somewhat fewer than one thousand actually involved themselves in the turmoil of village work. The rest either became tied up in one way or another with the elaborate central and provincial apparatus of the movement or simply dropped from sight like half the assignees in Hupeh. Even in Kwangtung, perhaps the best developed in terms of trained, experienced peasant movement leadership of all the provinces, by 1926 there was only one trained peasant organizer for every thousand peasants already in the peasant associations.[26] In the area controlled by Wuhan the proportion was far lower.

This fact appears to have been one of the primary concerns of Principal Mao during his move from Canton to Wuhan. As Mao passed through Kiangsi on his way to Shanghai to take up his post as secretary of the new Communist peasant movement committee, he paused to discuss the peasant movement problem with a local KMT member named Wang Li-hsi, who later became his arch enemy in the battle to control Kiangsi in the 1930s. Wang later recounted how concerned Mao was with the fact that in all of Kiangsi there were only ten graduates of the Peasant Movement Institute.[27] When Wang informed him that he planned to organize a peasant training school, Mao replied, "I too have been thinking precisely the same thing. My own thought is that Hunan, Hupeh and Kiangsi should operate one together and locate it in Wuch'ang. The reason is that we plan to concentrate our forces there in the future and that within such an environment the student body will purify itself through natural processes."[28] Mao's remark reveals a final problem that delivered the *coup de grace* to the new revolutionary elite: loyalty to the Communist party. The purification that he alluded to came to a head in April 1927 when an extensive purge of Kiangsi students at the institute was carried out after the Kiangsi peasant movement, under Wang Li-hsi, went over to the anti-Communist side.[29] Thus by the time of the Wuhan institute the problem of loyalties had begun to eat into the reserve of potential peasant leaders.

THE PEASANT MOVEMENT INSTITUTE started with a small band of committed intellectuals, all from Kwangtung. It grew within its three-year life span to almost thirty times its original size, with a student body from all over China. Perhaps more than any other single institution it symbolized the youthful ambitions of the movement.

Patterned on the Whampoa Academy, on which it occasionally drew for space, faculty, and even weapons, the institute developed its own exclusive spirit of devotion to the cause of expanding the peasant mass organizations. Its graduates became, in effect, the bearers of the "sedan chair" of the movement.

In the beginning the countryside was an unknown factor in Communist calculations. The institute was a means of breaking through the ignorance barrier. Through an unending process of collecting experiences and practical work, and compiling reports and documents it became the intelligence center for the entire peasant apparatus. Here we discover one of the origins of the Maoist faith in research and study. The classroom styles, the group discussions, the self-government exercises, and the constant stress on military discipline and training were likewise hints of educational trends to come.

The institute's rapid growth reflected the hopes the Communist movement leaders placed in the potential of a trained agitational

elite. The increasingly dogmatic content of the lectures and materials was designed to ensure that the elite shared few illusions about
which party was the true savior of the peasantry. But at every turn
the institute suffered from the insatiable demand for revolutionary
leadership cadres. The constant interruption of class work by
emergency mobilization in times of crises — the last such call leading
to the dissolution of the Wuhan school — took its toll in reduced
effectiveness. The never-too-large output of trainees found themselves swallowed up in the problems of leading immense and unruly
mass organizations and were forced to yield ultimately to the power
of the professional military.

5

ORGANIZING
THE MASSES:
THE PEASANT
ASSOCIATIONS

One of the most persistent generalizations of our time holds that peasants are not easily organized. Karl Marx's observation that the peasantry of France was, like so many potatoes in a sack, undifferentiated and shapeless grew out of his bitter experience with agrarian parties of a century ago; but it has become a virtually indispensable part of our modern intellectual baggage. Many observers of peasant behavior have cited it without noting Marx's own belief that even the French *paysan* might, under certain circumstances, be made susceptible to socialist organization.[1] Neither did the sweeping successes of European peasant parties in the half-century after his "Eighteenth Brumaire" was written affect this judgment. American foreign-aid officers only recently returned from the paddies of a tightly Communist-run Vietnamese province to complain that the villagers seemed unable to work together.

To some this difficulty of organization seems to stem from the peasant mind, which in its powerful conservatism, its monomania toward the land, its familism, and so on is essentially incapable of a higher, nonpersonalistic political orientation.[2] To some it results from the essential isolation of village life that prevents the easy exchange of leadership, experience, and ideas that make urban movements spread.[3] And to some the difficulty stems from the powerful stranglehold that the agrarian upper class has upon its minions.[4] Still others, such as E.J. Hobsbawm in his work on social bandits, have suggested that the problem may be simply the lack of an over-arching modern organization and political awareness. But whatever the underlying reasoning, many seem to agree that the task of any-one who wished to introduce the rural underdeveloped into a national polity is not easy.

The early Chinese Communists faced these difficulties with neither a theory of organization nor any experience in rural work. But those who knew something of Chinese village life perceived that Chinese villages, far from being disorganized, enjoyed a powerful degree of internal solidarity. This solidarity revealed itself in south China particularly in the form of the agnatic lineage, strengthened by the age-old normative system of filial piety. Lineages, or clans, as they are sometimes called,[5] employed clearly defined membership qualifications, hierarchical structure, and a careful balance between inducements to participate and requirements to contribute — all the signs of higher-level organization.[6] In north China village solidarities often extended beyond the family, admittedly weaker than in the south, to include all residents. The crop-watching societies that Ch'en Tu-hsiu briefly admired in 1926 performed villagewide de-fense, constuction, and sometimes even production functions.[7] Early Communists like Ch'en were tempted to borrow heavily on the latent organization of the Chinese countryside to build their new rural political force.

It was, however, this very strength of latent organization that doomed Communist efforts to co-opt and exploit clan structures and secret societies. A classic example of their failure was the famed Red Spears Society of Honan province. When in 1925 Russian advisers to Marshal Feng Yu-hsiang discovered that this powerful armed society held the balance of power in the struggles between Feng and the Manchurian warlords, they exalted it into an example of an ideal peasant movement.[8] Ch'en Tu-hsiu and Li Ta-chao picked up the litany and the comintern proclaimed in article after article the importance of working with the Red Spears. But opera-tives in the field soon found that reality did not correspond to theory. Red Spear ideology, if that is a proper word for deep-rooted superstitions and beliefs, did not go beyond the traditional goal of restoring the emperor to the throne.[9] The Red Spears were a fiercely independent, loosely defined band who could be won over not by persuasion but only by massive force or extensive bribery, weapons that Communists lacked.[10] Not only were such societies as the Red Spears, the Great Sword, or the Triads unreliable allies, they quickly became the bitterest enemies of the Communist insurgents in 1927.

The Communists could not wait for the outcome of their attempt to exploit secret societies. Many of them distrusted implicitly the habits and patterns inherited from the older society. Many felt that China needed not just reform of the old but importation of new forms of organization. Leninism offered them the idea and Eastern European peasant movements the practice of taking labor union organization into the countryside. Many of the peasant movement's successes and failures resulted from the imported principles of organization.

Curiously, the earliest versions of the peasant association imported into south China relied heavily on the Eastern European peasant movement experience. In countries such as Bulgaria and Poland in the early twenties Communists and non-Communists alike treated the peasantry as they did the proletariat: a working-class population divided into its trades and classes. Thus agricultural laborers could be organized separately from, for example, parcellized peasants. The earliest Chinese regulations on peasant organization provided for four different groups, one for each of the three major classes of farmers (owner, tenant, hired) and one so-called peasant self-defense organization. On top of these would preside a peasant joint association to provide an umbrella for the more specialized type of organization. It was not long, however, before these distinctions were dropped. Chinese farmers, even in property-conscious Kwangtung, did not distinguish clearly among themselves on the basis of land ownership, since other cleavages such as village loyalties, lineage distinctions, and ethnic or linguistic barriers proved to be far more important. By 1926 the nominal form of rural organization was simply called the peasant association (*nung-min hsieh-hui*) and included basically every organizable village resident.[11]

The fundamental principle of peasant association organization as spelled out in the peasant association charter was hierarchy. The associations would accept as a member any farmer, whether he owned his own land wholly or in part, rented someone else's, or hired himself out as a laborer or craftsman, so long as he earned his living by physical labor. Members had to be adults over sixteen, free of gambling and opium habits. Excluded were owners of large tracts of land (sixteen acres or more), professional men or men of religion (such as Taoist priests or missionaries), and persons in the hire of imperialists — that is, foreign residents. Whenever fifty or more such qualified farmers could be assembled, they could petition to form a provisional county association. This self-appointed core group could, after gaining the permission of higher authority, proceed to sponsor separate village associations underneath. Thenceforth growth would be by threes: when three village associations existed, a district association could be set up; and with three district associations in existence the formal county association structure would follow. County associations then begat provincial associations, and as the grand finale the All-China Peasant Association would come into being when three or more provinces had built up their respective pyramids.[12]

By their chartered structure the peasant associations thus resembled the labor unions, women's associations, China Youth League, and indeed the Communist party. But there were significant differences.

First, the peasant association rules gave a special place to the level of the county in the hierarchy. Provisional associations were provided for at the county level because the movement found counties to be the most effective entry point into rural work — there were only a hundred of them in Kwangtung and fewer than ninety in Hunan. Rural Chinese identified themselves most often by county origin, not by town or city. Associations were not to grow spontaneously but rather in a planned fashion so that local authority had to be established first, conveniently at the level of county seat, before the villages could sprout their organizations. At the same time, provinces really needed more than three counties to represent a substantial association growth — so the number of counties required to make this transition was set at five.

The second way the peasant organization differed from that of other mass groups of the period was in its relationship to local authority. Communists desired a controlled growth of their rural associations because they justly feared the watering down of their influence might permit their enemies to control the mass organizations. Hence their stress on the careful scrutiny of credentials, a formal application procedure prior to granting permission to form, and regular checks on the quality of association leadership. Hence also the careful attention to bottom-to-top buildup of the pyramid structure. Because peasant organization, unlike industrial worker or student organization, spread across the landscape into territories at first only questionably under Nationalist control, the illusion grew that associations might gain a certain autonomy as against the local KMT government.

But the reality proved to be quite different. Ironically, the very insistence on controlled growth made autonomy, even in favorable circumstances, difficult to develop. Although peasant associations in the early years of 1924-1925 obtained a wide range of powers from tax collection to the right of recall of corrupt officials, the enabling legislation always stressed they were not to be given direct administrative power in the villages and were to obey higher government authorities without question.[13] In these years the naïve belief in the common interest between the Kuomintang and the Communist party made it natural to grant KMT party district and subdistrict offices, which in many cases had been created by Communists in the first place, full responsibility over the process of association formation. But later, as the local KMT branches became less reliable allies of the local Communists, the rules were changed to give more power to the central peasant bureau or its equivalent in the KMT provincial party bureaucracy. The higher rationale of the two-party alliance made it impossible to give controlling authority to the provincial or national association, and thus the slowly evolving Nationalist government became the final arbiter of local disputes between the movement and other local powers. In 1925 the Communists, hoping to discourage attacks on the peasant mass organizations by local conservatives, invented the slogan "the KMT is the father, and the peasant association is the son." By 1927 it was too late to disclaim the paternity.

Congresses (*ta-hui*) played a major role in the peasant movement, as they did in the later life of the Chinese Communist party. Holding a congress served notice that a mass organization was ready to perform its designated work. Congresses were signs of completion, not of indecision. A provincial association congress could be held only when the base was ready—when at least five counties had already convened their own subordinate meetings. Between 1925 and 1927 only five provincial congresses took place, two in Kwangtung and one each in Hunan, Hupeh, and Kiangsi.[14] In these provinces the congresses signified that the movement had come of age.

Congresses also served to present to the outside world the image of a tightly knit, unanimous, and unshakable mass base. Painstaking preparation readied the way. The size of each county's delegation depended on the number of association members in the county. In Kwangtung there were from two hundred to a thousand members per delegate.[15] The movement was careful not to permit unauthorized elements with poor credentials to join in and possibly disrupt legitimate meetings.[16] Unruly behavior, like inaccurate representation or poor preparation, was a sign of lack of control that could not be tolerated.

Higher authorities also often made use of congresses, both of the peasant movement and of other mass organizations. Peasant congresses usually featured a number of speeches by nonpeasant leaders stressing the importance of rural organization for the revolution. Chiang Kai-shek's speeches, for example, at the second Kwangtung peasant Congress of 1926 and the Kiangsi Peasant Congress of early 1927 ranked among the more spirited exhortations of the mass movement during his Red period.[17] Mao Tse-tung used the platform of the All-Hunan Peasant Congress to launch his radical initiative of December 1926.[18] The resolutions passed by the congress in response to speeches often conveniently rephrased the speaker's remarks in the more rigid language of the Marxism of the moment. Resolutions, unlike long-winded speeches, were meant to be used in later propaganda circulars and therefore had to be precisely worded to conform to policy.

The founding congress of the Kwangtung Provincial Peasant Association may be taken as a typical peasant movement congress despite its early date. In fact, its sponsors intended it to meet as early as September 1924,[19] but either the confusion surrounding the Merchants' Corps squabble or the slow start in organizing associations around Canton caused the congress to be delayed until May 1925.[20] Opening the congress on May Day made it easy to underline the slogan of great unity between the workers and peasants that

Communist leaders made into the theme of the congress. This theme was enhanced by bringing the peasant delegates to Canton at the same time as the convening of the Second All-China Congress of Labor. Peasant organizations were made to feel they were the younger siblings of the growing labor movement.[21]

The proceedings of the congress remained in firm hands. On the morning of May 1 provincial leader Lo Ch'i-yuan presided over a preparatory meeting that selected the presidium, approved the credentials of each delegate, and laid down the rules for the congress. The presidium, like the observer delegation sent from the central peasant bureau, consisted mostly of Communists. The chairman for each day's session emerged in rotation from this presidium, according to standard Leninist practice. The rules limited discussion to fifteen minutes per person, with five votes required to bring a motion for discussion and with the final form of a resolution to be decided by the chairman pro tem. There was little likelihood that the discussion would get out of hand.[22]

Subcommittees did much of the drafting work for the congress, such as writing certain proposed modifications of the peasant association charter. The full congress spent much of its deliberative time passing these resolutions and ratifying protests and letters to other parts of the government. An incident in Tungkuan county, thirty miles to the east, caused an uproar at the congress because the leader of the movement in that county happened to be on the presidium. But conditions in other counties were also brought up in some detail since every delegate was required to give a brief report on his home county.[23] Provincial association leader Lo Ch'i-yuan stressed the importance of local affairs in a lengthy speech on improving the quality of reporting from the counties.[24] The protests were addressed mostly to the Kuomintang provincial authorities who, it was hoped, would intervene to protect association members from their enemies. But one telegram went out addressed to the American peasantry requesting that they stop the U.S. government from granting further loans to anti-KMT warlords in southern Kwangtung.

The peasant congress was, however, less a deliberative than a celebrative organ. Its speakers ranged from those at the top of the revolutionary hierarchy—Liao Chung-k'ai, for example—to the lower reaches of the peasant activists. They included Communists from the workers' movement (Li Li-san, later general secretary of the Chinese Communist party, 1928-1931), a representative from Krestintern, the Red Peasant International, and a Russian adviser to the Kuomintang. The huge rally held on May Day in the auditorium of Kwangtung University (now Chung-shan University) must have been most impressive. The rally opened with the Internationale; then followed addresses by several Russians as well as Governor Liao Chung-k'ai, the songs of a girl's chorus, folk dancing and music, and a silent movie of a comintern congress before the audience adjourned to a massive reception. By the end of a week of similar festivities the peasant delegates returned to their home counties impressed indeed with the warmth of Canton's revolutionary fires.[25]

In between the rare congresses of the provincial associations a permanent office maintained contact with local operations out in the counties. The first such office grew up naturally in Kwangtung, the cradle of the peasant movement. It began shortly after the association's founding congress on May Day 1925 in the form of an operations office with five thinly staffed bureaus. During the crises of late 1925 this staff spent most of its time outside the provincial capital, leaving behind only a bookkeeper and stenographer. This first provincial bureaucracy had no fixed income, no claim on taxes, and relied for its funds mostly on personal loans from the more affluent officials — some of whom pawned their clothing and went without food for days to contribute to the new organization. The bureaucracy existed from June to October 1925 on contributions of one hundred yuan. But the growth of the movement in 1926 rapidly changed the financial and personnel picture.

By early 1926 the Kwangtung association became a large bureaucracy in itself (see table 6), with an income of over fifteen hundred yuan a month promised by the Kuomintang central executive committee. The growth in responsibility forced the Canton organization to expand by adding seven regional offices, in which the best graduates of the Peasant Movement Institute quickly found jobs.[26] These offices carried the burden of the difficult work of 1926. In addition, the provincial apparatus began a series of expanded conferences that assembled all the county-level operatives from across the province in Canton. In February and August 1926 and again in January 1927 expanded conferences of the provincial association gathered to establish new policies to deal with bitter attacks on the movement.

Table 6 Structure of Kwangtung Provincial Peasant Association, 1926

Peasant Congress
Executive committee (12 regular, 5 alternate)
Standing committee (5 members)
Secretary-General
Provincial office (including Central Route)
Staff committee

West River office	Hainan office	Southern Route office	North River office	Huichow office	Ch'aomei office
Peasant Self-Defense Army Department	Education Department	Organization Department	Coop Movement Department	Statistics Department	

Source: T. C. Chang [Chang Tzu-ch'iang], The Farmers' Movement in Kwangtung (Shanghai, 1928).

Each conference was dominated by the KMT Communist faction.

During the critical summer of 1926 the provincial association's executive committee, headed by its chairman Lo Ch'i-yuan, waged a steady battle for public attention. Hardly an issue of the Canton Kuomintang newspaper lacks a pronouncement, warning, telegram, or resolution from this body. The executive committee signed letters to Chiang Kai-shek demanding the dismissal of a military officer who permitted local forces to attack the associations.[27] It demanded the dismissal of a military officer who permitted his subordinates to fire on peasants.[28] It recommended rural educational reforms and the elimination of banditry.[29] And when the Kwangning county peasant movement came under severe attack in midsummer, the executive committee interceded for it with the Canton military authorities.[30] On this last occasion the association organized a protest march of twenty-three delegates from eighteen counties and more than a thousand sufferers from Kwangning that was led by Lo Ch'i-yuan to the front steps of the military headquarters. The provincial *apparat* was, as one contemporary account suggested, the "soul and spirit of the movement."[31]

Other provincial associations established later tended to follow the Kwangtung model in relying on a small core of professional communist bureaucrats. These bureaucrats had a dual responsibility: they acted in the capital as the representatives of peasant interests and they transmitted directives from the Kuomintang provincial governments downward to their own subordinates. These two roles often came in conflict, as in Hunan in early 1927 when the provincial peasant movement bureaucracy, notorious in Wuhan for its radicalism, harshly restrained the Maoist zeal of several local county associations. But even in the cases where the provincial KMT peasant bureau drifted out of Communist hands, the provincial association remained in CP hands until the very end.

The final glory of this incipient Communist peasant bureaucracy was to have been the All-China Peasant Association. As early as 1926[32] the Communists had planned to set up this organ on May Day in Canton, but Chiang's March 20 coup cut them short. Not until late spring 1927 did they revive their hopes and begin to issue pronouncements in the name of the All-China Peasant Association. However, because the congress plans first for May Day, then for July 1, and then for October 1 never materialized, the association remained a provisional body without a real bureaucracy. The tentative executive committee of this umbrella organization included all the major peasant movement leaders from Mao in Hunan to P'eng P'ai in Kwangtung, as well as enough Kuomintang members to make it fit in with the united front concept of the Wuhan period. Ironically, virtually the only act of this committee was to issue the fateful directives of May 1927 urging the movement not to struggle against the reaction engulfing it.[33]

For the peasant movement to have a claim of privileged access to the millions of Chinese peasants it needed proof that in some real sense it represented the peasantry. That proof was thought to be provided by the membership of the peasant associations. Carefully built up, block by block and layer by layer according to the charter, the associations' mounting membership gave the leaders a certain confidence. The peasant association structure had many of the aspects of a chain letter: the more people who could be brought in at the bottom of the pyramid, the greater the profit at the top.

Much of the peasant movement mystique was based on the metaphor of momentum. Such words as locomotives, sedan chairs, waves, and surges were the stock in trade of the peasant movement organizer. For them to continue to have significance the peasant movement would have to demonstrate growth. Thus it can be expected that the statistics provided by the peasant movement would have a certain built-in bias. Consider, for example, the following passage from a sober report by Lo Ch'i-yuan:

> Sixty-six of the ninety counties in Kwangtung already have peasant association organization — more than two-thirds. Their total membership now amounts to 626,457 persons. Included in this figure are some counties which reckon their membership by the household, not the individual. Moreover, the majority of members are male, and if a male member of the family belongs, the women will naturally be sympathetic. Then if we exclude those portions of the population under 16 and over 60 — totaling 20 percent — as well as the 50 percent which is female we have a remainder of 30 percent who are capable of becoming members of the 30 million population of Kwangtung. The 620,000 members of our association *thus constitute almost 60 percent* of the eligible population — already a majority.[34]

It might seem incredible that the leader of the Kwangtung peasant movement should make such an arithmetical blunder. But the careless calculations of this passage were in fact rather typical of an attitude that demanded numerical results. Mao Tse-tung had his own mathematical formula: he estimated that a secure victory for the national revolution would be possible if only 10 percent of the three hundred million peasants in China—especially those in the politically more important provinces—could be organized into peasant associations. It was but a short step to the assumption that once more than 10 percent of the peasantry were organized, victory was assured.[35]

As the peasant associations grew across southern China there was a natural tendency to inflate the figures. Only Kwangtung appears actually to have made efforts to assure the accuracy of its numbers, and they were much lower than the spectacular statistics claimed for other provinces. A glance at table 7 reveals the startling case of Honan, a province that never received much peasant movement attention. Despite this negligence, the province claimed an association membership that ranked second in all of China in the sum-

Table 7 Peasant association membership claimed by organizers from 1924 to 1927 in four provinces and all of China

Date	Kwangtung	Hunan	Hupeh	Honan	All China
1924.10	60,000	-	-	-	-
1925.5	210,000	-	-	-	-
1925.10	450,000	-	-	-	-
1926.1	320,000	-	-	-	-
1926.4	626,000	38,150	-	-	-
1926.5	-	60,000	-	-	-
1926.6	647,766	-	-	270,000	-
1926.7	665,441	-	72,000	-	-
1926.8	689,214	-	-	-	-
1926.10	-	138,150	-	-	1,096,841
1926.11	-	1,071,137	-	-	-
1926.12	-	-	287,000	-	-
1927.3	-	-	797,000	-	-
1927.4	-	-	1,000,000	-	-
1927.5	700,000	4,517,140	2,502,000	-	9,153,093
1927.6	-	-	2,842,239	245,500	-

Source: Roy Hofheinz, "Peasant Movement and Rural Revolution: Chinese Communists in the Countryside, (1923-1927)." (Ph.D. dissertation, Harvard University, 1966), p. 82.

mer of 1926, and the movement happily repeated the figures. Statistics from other provinces as well all show more or less the same padding. The figures for April and October 1926 for Hunan differ by a suspiciously round one hundred thousand members.

But again, it was not accuracy that counted, but the general impression. As the chart shows graphically, the movement claimed a more rapid rate of growth than any of its rivals for Kuomintang attention. It was important for Teng Yen-ta at the meeting of the peasant movement committee to be able to claim that after the break with Chiang Kai-shek "the peasantry has obtained progress by leaps and bounds. The peasantry[36] in Hunan have increased from three to five million . . . Although their strength may be dissimilar, still they can without a doubt all become a revolutionary force."[37] It was only weeks later that Teng and his peasant movement associates discovered that figures alone do not constitute a revolutionary force.

The essence of the peasant movement organization problem could be seen in the history of the Peasant Army. The earliest attitude of Communist rural organizers was similar to that of Sun Yat-sen. They maintained that local peasant forces should be combined with merchants and other classes into a generalized people's militia, the Popular Corps or Min-t'uan. T'an P'ing-shan and Feng Chü-p'o wrote a pamphlet for Sun's propaganda committee in late 1923 praising the local *t'uan* in Kwangtung for its efforts in helping to drive out anti-Sun warlords Shen Hung-ying in the West River area and Ch'en Chiung-ming in the East River area. T'an and Feng, in language they were to regret a year later, recommended expanding the powers of the Min-t'uan by setting up a general office for them in Canton, giving them training, and providing them with weapons. The Communists even suggested that the *t'uan,* traditionally a rural self-defense organization, move into the cities and thus provided the foundations for the Merchants' Corps chaos of later 1924.[38] The earliest versions of the Peasant Self-Defense Army, called the Nung-t'uan or Peasant Corps, joined with the Whampoa cadets in the defeat of the merchant force.

But peasant army organization remained at the bottom of a long list of military priorities for the Canton and Wuhan governments. The central peasant bureau petitioned to have some students at the peasant institute admitted to the Whampoa Academy as auditors.[39] In late 1924 a Peasant Self-Defense Army charter was drawn up

Forces of the National Revolution

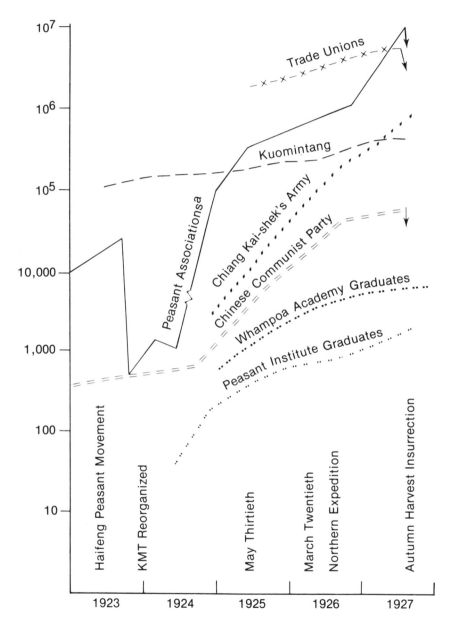

aBased on statistics given in Hofheinz, "Peasant Movement and Rural Revolution," pp. 82-83.

along the lines of the association charter.[40] Movement workers in Kwangning county did begin to build such an army, but very quickly found the problems of weapons and training overwhelming. At the height of the Kwangning incident in late 1924 the Peasant Army was thrown against a much larger Min-t'uan force with much better weapons and was virtually destroyed.

Only in Haifeng, where the Whampoa graduate and Communist party member Li Lao-kung launched a concerted program of army building with the support of the Communist-controlled county government, did the Peasant Army develop into a usable force. And even there Li's unit by mid-1926 numbered only eight hundred to a thousand poorly armed and supplied men.[41] In the spring of 1926 Lo Ch'i-yuan set up a Peasant Army training class in Kukong (Shaokuan) in the North River region that ran eight months and graduated several dozen peasant officers.[42] Lo was forced to steal money from local temples to finance the purchase of arms. In the spring of 1927 this Peasant Army was the only one outside Haifeng that attempted to resist Li Chi-shen's coup; but even this army had to rely upon the support of a former KMT regiment under Ch'en Yu-liang, who sided with the Communist party. In late 1926, when the Kwangtung Regional Committee attempted to push forward Peasant Army construction,[43] it was soon discovered that the Communist party had kept no record of military activities under the associations. A quickly researched report soon revealed that all Kwangtung could count only eleven thousand Peasant Army troops scattered about the province.[44] A number of these were in the control of non-Communist Popular Corps commanders.

One of the major charges against Ch'en Tu-hsiu's leadership was that he had failed to arm the peasants. It is doubtless true that Russian advisers refused to siphon off weapons to the Peasant Army leaders. Particularly after March 20, 1926, any such requisition would not have been popular with Chiang Kai-shek or any other military officer. The peasant armies were meant for local self-defense and would make no contribution to the greater military plans of the new Nationalist elite. The Wuhan land committee did recommend in early May 1927 that 5 to 10 percent of the Wuhan arsenal output go to the peasants, but Wang Ching-wei would not consent to delivery. His suspicions could not help but be aroused by Stalin's secret instructions, foolishly shown to him by Roy in early June, to arm fifty thousand peasants for a great insurrection. The attempt by Hunanese self-defense groups to disarm police to gain a few guns precipitated the bloody reaction.

The issue of the Peasant Army thus was not weapons but subordination. Only where the Communists could control entire territories, as in Haifeng, would rural militia be given protection from other armed groups. So long as the peasant movement remained a tiny portion of the greater tide sweeping China, it could not claim the resources it needed to become armed masters in the countryside. An armed peasant militia fighting in the name of the revolution would require a revolutionary army and elite that truly needed it.

WERE THE PEASANTS of south China in the 1920s organizable or not? Clearly the Kuomintang's bureaucracy was not the powerful Bolshevik tool Communists needed to build bridges to the countryside. Their hastily developed training facilities could not supply enough cadres to meet the needs of expansion. But even given these preconditions, there is still some question whether the peasant associations could have become true mass bureaucracies capable of struggling for the interests of the farm population. No matter how successful a party is at developing a rural strategy and an ideology of peasant revolution, the critical element in success will always be organization.

There are three prerequisites to building a political organization in a peasant society. First is the ability to link goals with capacities. The tendency of radicals in general to move beyond reality into fantasy is accentuated in a rural environment. Whether this phenomenon is due to what Beqiraj calls the "extremism of peasantry"[45] — the tendency of villagers in a traditional culture to react suddenly and irrationally when overwhelmed by threats or burdens — or simply due to the difficulty of learning what is in the minds of the village rank and file, it is a destructive tendency. When combined with a poorly thought-out intellectual romanticism at the top it can be disastrous, as it was in Hunan. If peasant movements are to survive independently, they must be able to provide sufficient payoffs short of the millenium to compensate for the contributions in time, money, and security they demand of members.

Second, to be an effective organization a peasant association needs good communications. Communists discovered only too late that their machinery for reporting conditions at lower levels was inadequate. Congresses, with their reports from the regions, were too sporadic and too enthusiastic to convey a true sense of the local scene or to debate real strategy on the basis of real information. Perhaps it was the peasant movement failure that, overcompensated, produced the massive outpouring of local reports from Communist operatives in the Kiangsi and Yenan periods. Without reports, rumors informed policy. Without information, feedback for introducing corrective measures was missing. And without the machinery for imposing discipline, later developed within the Communist party through elaborate self-criticism and personnel controls, a correct policy, if devised, could not be enforced.

Finally, a peasant-based organization needs a committed nucleus of office-bound professionals at the lowest levels. Peasant leaders cannot be functionaries or circuit-riding agitators. Village-based organizations in particular must have permanent resident personnel with a career commitment to the goals and the structure of the movement. Hinton's *Fanshen,* describing a Communist organized village in the late 1940s, is candid on this point. By 1947 3 percent of the thousand villagers in his Longbow Village were Communist party members — a higher ratio than obtained even in Haifeng during the height of the peasant movement period, though it may have been reached in some of the more ardent movement villages there. These core cadres worked in secret with powerful outside support from the Communist Eighth Route Army in the hills and monopolized positions of authority in the village mass organization structure. "There was no question," Hinton says, "but that the Party members were the backbone of this whole structure, but since the average peasant did not know this, it was the whole structure that took the credit or the blame and not just its guiding core."[46] Though the central Communist leadership in the 1920s saw clearly the need for such party construction in the villages, they lacked the experience, the elaborate skeletal framework, and the capacity for support that enabled their successors to penetrate the villages with more than just an idea.

6

THE SOCIAL
BACKGROUND:
EXPLANATIONS
OF SUCCESS
AND FAILURE

Theories of revolution abound, indeed they are more numerous and persistent than are theories about how humans produce war, democracy, or the good life. But virtually every theory of revolution, at least since the eighteenth century when the French word came into widespread use in its current sense, involves some proposition about the environment, the background, and the conditions that are likely to produce revolutions. The nineteenth-century positivist philosophers created a still potent tradition of seeking the causes of political events in the social and economic forces that were seen as somehow underlying them. It is this intellectual tendency that most social science explanations of revolution share with Karl Marx.

Empirical work on the environment of revolution has focused largely on the European phenomenon. Rudolf Heberle's classic work on the origins of Nazism argues that radical rural movements such as Hitler's Nazi party flourished particularly in small-holding peasant populations remote from the centers of industrial growth. Eric Hobsbawm noted that the phenomenon of banditry in Mediterranean Europe shades over into revolutionary anarchism and communism under the subtle changes brought by modernization. Eastern European historians, for example R. V. Burks and Eugen

Weber, stress the importance of such noneconomic factors as ethnicity or recent political history in the background of the rising Communist or Fascist parties.[1]

There is a growing new body of information about Asian political sytems that echoes this great variety of interpretation. Donald Zagoria's work indicates that in India the Communist party dominates more easily in districts where rice is the major food crop. In the Philippines, however, where rice is also grown, support for the Hukbalahap insurrections of the 1950s came largely from ethnic minority areas. Analysts of the Vietnam insurgency in the 1960s stressed the inequality of land holding as a major factor in the ability of the South Vietnamese government to suppress their rivals — though they are challenged by those who make the opposite claim.[2]

China, too, has been the subject of this sort of environmental analysis, though often by theoreticians with strong biases or a short memory for political history. One school has insisted that the Chinese agricultural economy systematically declined under the assault of industrial products in the present century, despite evidence of gradual, if nonmonotonic, improvement. For those who claim that in China land-holding patterns discriminated against a large tenant class that grew during the last century, there are others who answer that tenancy has never been as severe in China as elsewhere and that there is little evidence it grew substantially in modern times. Finally, many accounts of Chinese political disorders from the Opium Wars to the anti-Japanese struggle during World War II stress the common theme of xenophobia — antiforeignism or nationalism — underlying the virulent Chinese response to the West.[3]

There is thus no dearth of attractive hypotheses about the origins of Chinese peasant communism. Some have already been put to crude tests elsewhere by examining the entire sweep of the Communist movement up to the point of victory in 1949.[4] Devising more accurate tests by limiting the focus to the peasant movement is a tempting tactic, for here we have the concrete, quantified measure of peasant association membership as an apparently reliable measure of success for the radical movement. These figures are found in scattered sources for the three provinces of Kwangtung, Hunan, and Hupeh. As we might expect (see table 8), the three provinces differed considerably in their movement results, not least because the figures were issued at different times for each province. Hupeh ap-

Table 8 Peasant association membership statistics for three provinces, 1926-1927

Province	Counties	Counties with associations	Average county membership (thousands)	Average membership per 1000 population
Kwangtung	107	68	118	38
Hunan	88	52	260	48
Hupeh	74	44	709	144
Total	269	164	322	73

Source: Data bank on Republican China county development, East Asian Research Center, Harvard University.

pears the most successful province only because the data are from the weeks just before the Autumn Harvest Insurrection in 1927, whereas the Kwangtung data come from mid-1926. For Hunan, the figures are those released by Mao Tse-tung as an addendum to his famous report on the peasant movement.

The membership figures show that the movement was less widespread than might be supposed, even among these successful provinces, more than one-third reported no associations whatever. Kwangtung had a slightly better geographic distribution of associations than the other two provinces. Of those counties having associations, the average membership was less than 8 percent of the total population, even when vastly more successful counties such as Haifeng (55 percent) are included. Nevertheless, membership was sufficiently widespread to permit an attempt at an explanation of the variance in success.

First, for our dependent variable we must convert the raw membership figures into a usable measure of success by dividing the raw figures by our best estimate of the total population of the county. Then, to correct for the different dates of release of the figures, we relate each county's per capita membership to the mean for its province by calculating its T-score. This success measure sets each province on an equal footing and allows us to examine the distribution of movement success around the provinces.

Second, we must derive measures of potential independent variables that represent potential explanatory factors. The nine variables in table 9 were each chosen to represent a particular theory or

Table 9 Correlations of some explanatory variables with peasant association success.[a]

	All three provinces r counties		Hupeh r counties		Hunan r counties		Kwangtung r counties	
Proximity to provincial capital	.18	(160)	.35	(43)	.43	(51)	.00	(66)
Years of Protestant missionary effort	.13	(143)	.21	(40)	.33	(45)	-.01	(58)
Population growth, 1920-1947	.09	(146)	.16	(42)	.19	(51)	-.02	(53)
Rice acreage, percent of arable land	.10	(158)	.25	(42)	.15	(51)	.02	(65)
Years of railway access	.04	(43)	.15	(12)	-.24	(13)	.05	(16)
Agricultural population, percent of total	-.03	(157)	.10	(51)	-.10	(51)	.06	(65)
Land owners, percent of all farmers	-.07	(123)	-.01	(24)	-.15	(52)	-.01	(47)
Rank of largest urban place (1 = 20-50.000 5 = over 1 million)	.07	(43)	-.74	(7)	.20	(13)	.18	(23)
Students, percent of population	.02	(161)	-.11	(43)	.23	(52)	-.02	(66)

Source: Data bank on Republican China county development, East Asian Research Center, Harvard University.
[a] Peasant association membership per capita t-scores computed separately for each province.

hypothesis about how peasant radicalism might gain support. Responses to urbanization and to Western impact might be gauged by the measures of proximity to the provincial capital, of rank of the largest urban place within the county, of the length of time in which a railroad has passed through the county, and of the number of years Western missionaries have been at work in the county. Additionally, the youth and education factor may be tested by the proportion schoolchildren are to the total population. Finally, several economic propositions may be tested by referring to the extent of rice cultivation, the percentage of the population engaged in agriculture, the amount of population growth during the decades of turmoil during the Republican period, and the extent of land ownership as opposed to tenancy.[5] Notably high correlations between any of these variables and the dependent variable of peasant movement success would suggest the validity of one or more of the theoretical hypotheses.

Unfortunately, these data refuse to yield such a simple clue to the politics of the early Communist efforts. The majority of measures are strikingly insignificant. The strongest relationships for the entire three-province sample are the date of railway penetration and the proximity to the provincial capital, suggesting that the peasant movement did better on the whole in counties that communicated more readily with administrative centers. This conclusion must be qualified, however, by noting that in Kwangtung these measures of centrality are quite unimportant and that in Hunan the movement developed in counties with younger, rather than older, railway trunk lines. And in any case, the correlations for the three-province sample all fall below the 5 percent confidence level, so the chances are better than one in twenty that the positive relationships shown occurred by chance.

A closer look at the provinces, however, suggests something of the intriguing variety that lay behind the efforts of the peasant organizers. In Hupeh, for example, a province in which rice agriculture mixes in its northern portion with wheat cultivation, the rice ratio seems more important than elsewhere in explaining movement success. Among urbanized counties in Hupeh, the movement did better near the small towns than it did near the metropolis of Wuhan. In Hunan, the dominance of Ch'angsha, the provincial capital, over the peasant movement's fortunes is shown by the significantly high correlation of the proximity measure with association success as well as by the positive relationship with city size among counties with cities. The notable insignificance of the correlations for Kwangtung suggests the complexity and variety of the underlying social and economic background in that province. Clearly if we are to make sense of this variability in the impact of Communist efforts we must go beyond the aggregate statistical data.

The variety of the provincial responses to the stimulus of peasant movement agitation may be turned to our advantage, however. We suspect, for example, that the political conditions that prepared the way for the Communists from 1923 to 1928 may have been as important as the social or economic conditions. Such an interpretation receives support from table 10, which shows the correlation between our measures of peasant association success and a number of the important political forces that developed in the Republican period. Although the total sample of all peasant movement counties shows little correlation with the non-Communist political movements that preceded and followed the period, Kwangtung province differs sharply from Hunan and Hupeh. In Kwangtung the peasant movement appears to have succeeded in counties where Sun Yat-sen's T'ung Meng Hui lacked any basis several decades earlier and where the later Kuomintang elite did not take root; in Hunan and Hupeh the relationship is the opposite. This intriguing puzzle is worth exploring further.

IN THE EARLY twentieth century Kwangtung shared with other provinces the rapid shifts caused by the fall of the Ch'ing dynasty in 1911. Political instability and accelerated militarization dominated the history of the province after the new Republic of China collapsed into civil warfare in 1916. A succession of governors, largely from warlike Kwangsi and Kweichow to the west—with names like Lung Chi-kuang, Lu Jung-t'ing, Yang Hsi-min, and Shen Hung-ying—dominated the politics of the capital city of Canton and fought with one another for control over the provincial hinterland. Kwangtung produced her own fair share of militarists, including the first Kuomintang governor of the province, Ch'en Chiung-ming of Haifeng county, Wei Pang-p'ing, and Hsu Ch'ung-chih. The father of the Chinese Republic, Sun Yat-sen, was forced to rely on such militarists several times in his attempts to build a political base in his home province after 1918.

The relationship between provincial rulers and their regions was

Table 10 Peasant association success correlations with political measures

	All three provinces r counties		Hupeh r counties		Hunan r counties		Kwangtung r counties	
T'ung Meng Hui members, 1904-1906	.07	(72)	.13	(25)	.20	(26)	-.39	(21)
Kuomintang elite, central executive committee members, 1947	.09	(52)	.51	(13)	.51	(16)	-.23	(23)
Kuomintang members, 1929-1931	.10	(81)	.01	(30)	.14	(51)	-	
Whampoa Academy students, 1924-1927	.10	(143)	.23	(39)	.14	(49)	.02	(55)

Source: Data bank on Republican China county development, East Asian Research Center, Harvard University.

tenuous at best, dependent as it was on the clientele of petty local militarists who were in charge of the subregions of the province. The garrison armies (*chu-fang chün*) at the county level and above obtained foraging rights in these subregions, supposedly in return for bringing order to them. This garrison system provided a symbiosis in which politically minded warlords, including later those of the governments of Sun Yat-sen and Chiang Kai-shek, purchased financial and recruitment support for their greater ambitions by leaving the lesser fruits of local rule to poorly armed, venal local armies.

Below the garrison commanders at the base of the social order in the unruly twenties lay the remnants of the nineteenth-century village self-defense system. The elaborate local gentry-led paramilitary organizations described by Frederic Wakeman and others that stretched across south China during the great rebellions of the 1800s had fallen into disarray first because of the dynasty's success at suppressing the Taip'ing and other rebels and then because of the increasing inability of local notables to attract support from central authorities. The county chief, called *hsien-chang* after 1911 instead of *chih-shih* (magistrate), commanded only the most rudimentary administrative apparatus, consisting sometimes only of a court of law and a few dozen roving police (*yu-chi-tui*).[6] The remarkable rise of disorder after 1911, however, brought a rapid revival of the old organizational forms. One peasant movement author described the process in the following way:

> After 1911 banditry spread day by day. The people began to feel that the old watchmen-police (*keng-fu hsun-ting*) were not strong enough to preserve public order in the villages. *Pao-wei-t'uan*, composed of an ever ready force of unemployed vagabonds (*yu-min*) from the villages grew rapidly as a result. The chief of the *t'uan* was drawn from the most influential of the local bosses and base gentry (*t'u-hao lieh-shen*). Weapons were purchased mostly of the modern type, financed by tax levies. In this way, bit by bit, an extremely powerful armed force arose in the villages, commanded by a chief who also led the village administration . . . and who in fact became nothing more than another petty despot.[7]

Amid this spreading local tyranny the residual power of the traditional gentry may still be discerned. The peasant movement radicals favored an expression that grouped all such notables together into one class of evildoers. The terms *t'u-hao* (lit. "local or land-holding bigwig") and *lieh-shen* (vicious or evil gentry) were usually thrown together in a phrase with almost amuletic qualities. During Ch'ing times, local notables who chose to take the side of rebellious groups were called *t'u-hao-lieh-shen.* In Republican China the term was reserved for those who, unlike the new liberated men and women after the May Fourth movement of 1919, wore long gowns and spoke and wrote in a strange and laughable way. Despite the Communists' penchant for caricature, the villages of Kwangtung were still largely ruled by men with some claim to cultural superiority or local economic power or both.[8]

Nevertheless, there were strong signs throughout the province that the informal private government of the subcounty countryside was breaking down. Particularly in the outlying areas surrounding the Pearl River floodplain, serious disorders had broken out even before 1911. In Haifeng in 1895 and in Kwangning in 1898, to pick two important peasant movement strongholds, there had been extended riots in which peasants fought for an exemption from rent payments. The constant marching and countermarching of warlord troops after the turn of the century was accompanied by extensive recruitment and, more important for local order, helter-skelter demobilization of defeated troops. These disorders contributed directly to the problem of banditry.

One Japanese ex-policemen with some first-hand experience in the area observed:

> Kwangtung Province, the very birthplace of the National Revolution, could not be outdone by any other in the way of banditry. Bandits increased in number there especially sharply after the beginning of the revolution. From the start of the Chinese Republic the province was higgledy-piggledy thrown into a state of incessant warfare. In addition, after the creation of the Canton Government [of Sun Yat-sen] the armies of Yunnan, Kweichow, and Kwangsi all concentrated within its boundaries and began a struggle for power, in which it was the plight of the troops of the losing side to take up banditry. The entire province thus filled to the brim with such *t'u-fei.*[9]

Just as elsewhere in China, there were bandits of all sizes and stripes in Kwangtung. Some plied the trade of protecting riverboat travelers for small sums. Some preferred the more lucrative business of train robbery, resulting in an average of eight major train holdups a year during Sun Yat-sen's last reign. Some simply settled in an area and lived off the opium or crop protection rackets. As the Japanese described them,

> the more famous bandit groups were organized like armies, possessed modern weapons, underwent training, and were a match for any regular soldiery. And since the authority of the armies seldom extended all the way to the boundaries of an area, the people in the outer reaches were forced to obey the orders of the bandit chieftain in order to protect their lives and property. Furthermore, since these groups exercised effective authority in the vicinity of their dens (*ch'ao-hsueh*) they often attracted to their ranks the local *t'u-hao-lieh-shen* . . . and thus gradually expanded their domain.[10]

And since, under certain circumstances, soldiers could be worse than bandits, entire villages often went over to the underworld. By the beginning of the peasant movement period, Kwangtung was in danger of becoming almost literally a bandit world.[11]

A final element of the social landscape in Kwangtung during the peasant movement period was the secret society. Part underworld brotherhood, part religious sect, part self-defense militia, these organizations survived relatively intact well into the twentieth century and became a focal point for political support of the 1911 revolution.[12] Many of the more ancient societies dated back to the end of the Ming dynasty in the seventeenth century or even to the heterodox sects of the Maitreyan sect of eschatological Buddhists earlier. In the twenties three major societies were active in Kwangtung.

The oldest was the Triad Society (San-ho-hui or San-tien-hui), which had flourished throughout the province in the nineteenth century and which still has deep roots among overseas Chinese communities outside the motherland.[13] The Triad's strength of tradition, the difficulty of penetrating their secrecy, and their involvement in illicit trades such as gambling and prostitution made them a difficult target for Communist penetration. Triads were also extremely active in the protection rackets that flourished in the lawless *sha-t'ien* polder districts of the delta. Similarly the Small Knives Society (Hsiao-tao-hui), which had launched a major riot among Cantonese sojourners in Shanghai in 1854, continued to operate in the Canton region in the 1920s, though their tendency to divide into and follow separate clan interests kept them out of political involvements.

The most likely prospect for Communist agitation among the

societies was the Great Knives Society (Ta-tao-hui) of the West River region — a religious-military organization with strong gentry participation. Here again, the very traditionalism of the Divine Strike (Shen-ta), as the Great Knives were also called, made them amenable to appeals to high patriotism, anticommercialism, and the need for local autonomy and self-defense. For a brief while in 1925 and 1926 this element of the social landscape gave peasant movement leaders some hope.

The picture we have of rural economics in Kwangtung is even less clear than that of the political and social scene. On the one hand Kwangtung remained one of China's most advanced provinces in its rate of commercial and industrial growth even during the turmoil of the twenties. But on the other, the continued growth of native and foreign industry was restricted largely to the major cities of Canton, Swatow, Chaochow, and Hong Kong and was not matched by uniformly rising prosperity in the countryside. The rich delta floodplain around Canton saw the growth of profitable large plantation enterprises such as the Ch'ingfen Agricultural Company of Chungshan county, and areas close enough to the cities felt the attraction of urban jobs and enjoyed the benefits of inexpensive industrial goods.[14] But the other more distant counties such as Haifeng on the east coast or Kwangning in the western mountains did not benefit much from the rising economies. They experienced instead the disruptive effects of emigration of able-bodied males, the increased employment of local female agricultural labor, and the pinch caused by rising expectations and demands for a better life.

Later Marxist interpretations of the peasant movement insisted that the main source of support for the early radicals was the dissatisfaction produced by the modernization of agriculture. In these interpretations it was assumed that the growth of market economics, especially in the produce market necessary to feed growing cities, would push up the price of land, encouraging the sale of small holdings to more and more concentrated agribusiness companies and increasing economic pressures on small holders. Rising tenancy, it was assumed, would signal hard times for those who remained home on the farms; rising indebtedness required by the larger investments of modern agriculture would produce great hardship and bankruptcy in years of poor crops or of declining market prices. The market economy in this view helped produce the successes of the peasant movement.

The facts seem to demonstrate the opposite relationship between market improvement and the incidence of rural unrest in Kwangtung. It was precisely in those areas where tenancy was the highest — the delta counties to the south of Canton — that the peasant movement had its greatest difficulty. Peasant movement accounts of Kwangtung economic conditions, while normally complaining about the declining profitability of agriculture, only seldom mention the percentage of tenancy in their discussions of village problems. Far more important than the extent of market penetration or of tenancy was the quality of the man-land relationship.

In the area around Canton the peasant had become a highly sophisticated farmer of the rich reclaimed polderland of the delta. Either he hired himself out at high wages to one of the large companies growing cane or bananas or he applied his skills to matching the market demand for rice and other foodgrains. Because of the high probability of flooding, polder rents were low compared to land in other parts of the province; a clever bidder could turn considerable profit by farming the polder so long as he could get his crop to market. In many cases the actual ownership of the land had become obscure, so that rents often went unpaid, particularly since the unsettled conditions of the countryside made landlords reluctant to make their rent-collecting rounds. High tenancy in this part, as in many other parts of China went hand in hand with increasing well-being for prosperous paddy farmers.

By contrast, the relationship between farmer and landowner in more remote sections of the province such as the West River watershed and the east coast above Hong Kong remained more traditional and provided more opportunities for political agitation. Characteristic of both these areas where the peasant movement developed rapidly and strongly were the customary obligations between lord and tenant, which resembled the bonds between master and servant in medieval Europe. In addition to the ordinary payment of rent, tenants were expected to provide special year-end gifts — poultry, pork, or grain — to their lord in return for the use of their land. This system, generically known as the system of contractual cultivation (*pao-nung-chih*), bound the lord and tenant closely together in a bond that lasted through bad harvests and natural disasters, at least in traditional times. In return for the willingness to reduce burdensome rents in bad years, the landlord regularly exacted small fees, services, and gifts from his tenants. In certain districts in the West River the practice of recording the names of tenants as field slaves in the familial funeral registers still existed. The subtle effect of modernization on these old patterns is difficult to assess, but it seems likely that landowners, learning of the growth of impersonal trading patterns near the cities, were the first to insist that the old obligations were no longer binding in years of poor crops. This probably helps explain the spate of rent reduction protests in these regions in the decades prior to the peasant movement.

Kwangtung was a province divided by many loyalties and many rivalries. But the most powerful forces in each village were undoubtedly the ties of agnatic kinship—the ancient groupings of clan and ethnic group. Kwangtung contained entire villages of tens of thousands of inhabitants with only one surname.[15] Large sections of the countryside were divided checkerboard fashion into villages speaking Cantonese or a Chaochow dialect or the outsider tongue of Hakka.[16] Wars between clans, villages, and dialect groups were endemic in a countryside to this day strewn with makeshift and permanent fortresses against known and unknown enemies. In this maelstrom of disorder, banditry, and civil strife the Communists could find many cleavages to exploit as well as many sources of support. They also found many natural enemies.

Rural communist leaders were painfully aware of the complexities of the village scene in Kwangtung. A questionnaire circulated by the Kwangtung Peasant Association in 1926 illustrated their sophistication. Rural party workers were asked to locate the pressure points of economic discomfort in their home counties: How many landowners owned how much land? Was there a contractual farming system in effect? Did multiple-level land ownership offer a chance to rally disaffected tillers? The questionnaire, drawn up by association leader Lo Ch'i-yuan, stressed political conditions as much as economic: What was the ideology (*ssu-hsiang*) of the county chief? Who collected supernumerary taxes? Who commanded the garrison army and was it local or outsider in origin? Were the secret societies and the Min-t'uan (Popular Corps) active and with what kind of leadership? Answers to these questions and sixty-odd others presumably supplied through the private channels of the party and the Kuomintang peasant organization gave the provincial leadership indications of where to concentrate their efforts.[17]

The movement's flexibility in Kwangtung therefore comes as no surprise. Not only was the provincial leadership prepared for a variety of opportunities depending on the conditions in each county, but the policies of operatives, despite attempts at central direction, inevitably had to adapt to changing local situations. An example of Communist flexibility was the cherished tactic of rent reduction. The party waited until late 1926 to lay down demands for a fixed reduction. The movement operatives had insisted up to that point that the delta counties around Canton would not support a rent reduction movement—although the practice of auctioning land rights might have offered a chance to organize collusion among the bidders.[18] In the West River watershed, where rents were artificially high given the low productivity of mountainous land, such a drive might have made more sense. Even after the politics of the alliance with the Kuomintang drove the Communist party to adopt a rent reduction platform, local workers often failed to comply.

The flexibility of local workers was encouraged by an important ideological distinction that the Peasant Movement Institute instilled in its students: that between political and economic struggle. Economic struggles, such as rent reduction and land confiscation, were long-term goals that might prove elusive if striven for prematurely. The movement insisted that a firm organizational foundation be built through political struggle before moving to economic targets. In practice, however, the schedule was sometimes advanced—after considerable intraparty discussion—in the heat of battle. For example, the transition to economic struggle was ordered by local workers in Haifeng county in 1923, in Kwangning county in 1924, and again in Haifeng in 1925. These cases probably prompted some Communist leaders later in 1926 to claim that the Kwangtung peasant had demanded a solution to the land question. But many localities never reached the point where rent reduction could be demanded.[19]

The tactics used toward secret societies are another example of peasant movement flexibility. Movement workers were warned that societies were risky allies, though some might be susceptible to

radical suggestion. In Hua county, where the movement established
a tiny base in 1923, its prime ally was a society related to the Great
Knives.[20] Movement leaders P'eng P'ai and Lo Kuo-chieh attempted
to secure at least the neutrality of the Divine Strike Society in
Kwangning county in 1924, but their effort failed. In the delta
county of Chungshan the Triad-related societies were hostile from
the beginning and the associations there took a correspondingly
wary attitude.[21]

Even more difficult to use effectively were the village ethnic and
clan cleavages. In many cases the underlying motivation of the peasants who joined the associations derived from historical rivalries and
feuds. In Haifeng and Kwangning many farmers felt hostile to
large, powerful landowning clans. In Kwangning county the geographical concentration of association support in one small corner
of the county suggests a role played by village rivalries. In Kaoyao
county, down river from Kwangning, and in Hua county, just north
of Canton, the Hakka-Punti rivalry between Cantonese and outsiders flared up more than once to the advantage of movement
organizers. The most striking use of clan hostility occurred in
P'uning county in the East River valley, where a single clan of the
surname Fang composed half the population of the county capital
of two hundred thousand persons. The movement made conscious
use of resentment against the Fangs—as well as of country people
against the city—to gain the allegiance of large sections of the villages. Just as often, however, the anti-Communist opposition could
use the same forces against the outside agitators from Canton, as in
Hua county in 1926, where the Min-t'uan grew to a powerful force
based on hostility to intruders.[22]

The notion of political struggle and the apparent flexibility
offered to local workers suggests a degree of prudence about local
political conditions that Communist leaders did not always display.
In fact we may distinguish several phases in the techniques used by
the peasant movement to penetrate new counties with their associations. In the earliest phase activists such as P'eng P'ai in Haifeng
county adopted approaches resembling Christian social action. To
achieve their goals, they operated independently of existing organized forces, relied strongly on preachment and on generalized public welfare programs, and made alliances with important gentry
groups. P'eng P'ai's first association in Haifeng, for example, set up

a farmers' pharmacy and a funeral aid society—paternalistic social aids very different from the tightly knit revolutionary cells of later years. At the beginning of the cooperation with the Kuomintang the movement made use of its new-found patrons by simultaneously stirring up trouble at the local level and demanding help from Canton. Kwangning county in 1924 became the paradigm for this type of operation, which always ran the risk that someday Canton might not rescue an association besieged by its natural enemies. Finally, in the last phase of the movement's expansion across Kwangtung, particularly during the Eastern and Southern Expeditions of 1925 and 1926, the movement entered new areas on the shoulders of the Kuomintang armies.

This protective shield emboldened movement organizers to deal sharply with potential enemies. Thus in the recapture of Haifeng in 1925 the movement under P'eng P'ai undertook more radical rent reforms and harassment of local gentry leaders than had been possible earlier. This last form of blitzkrieg on potential opponents depended, of course, on the willingness of the expedition's military commanders to avert their eyes while the movement waged a minor civil war. Although this technique brought quicker results than moderate reformism, it also risked provoking the reaction of apolitical militarists.

How EFFECTIVE was the peasant movement in dealing with the promise and the complexity of the Kwangtung rural scene? The answer is as multifaceted as the question. In certain parts of Kwangtung, particularly in the West River section and on the eastern seacoast, the movement successfully incorporated about half the rural population into its associations, raised sizable local forces, and for a brief period controlled local government. In other parts, most notably in the populous districts around the provincial capital, the movement never captured more than 5 percent of the peasantry and remained under constant threat from internal and external opponents.

One clue to this variability may be seen in the quantitative measures; in Kwangtung province peasant association membership figures correlate negatively with measures of previous non-Communist political activity. The peasant associations grew rapidly in counties such as the two regions east and west of the capital where there had

previously been little work done by Sun Yat-sen's revolutionary followers. Sun's coconspirators from the 1890s up to his death in 1925
tended to come from the delta region near his home county of
Chungshan, and the Kuomintang party of the mid-1920s resembled
Sun's entourage strongly in its geographical origins. As late as mid-
1925 fewer than half the counties of Kwangtung had any significant
Kuomintang membership, and these did not include the areas of
maximum peasant movement penetration.

Thus the movement appears to have grown up in an environmental niche as yet unpopulated by revolutionary politicians. In this
it resembled to a degree its major rival for political control of the
Kuomintang, the Whampoa military elite, which came heavily from
nondelta counties as well. The difference between the two is that
Whampoa drew students from remote corners of the province such
as Hainan Island and from the ethnically distinct counties of the
largely Hakka upper East River watershed. The enrollment records
(see table 11) show that outside the Pearl delta, counties that contributed students to one academy were unlikely to contribute them
to the other. This rivalry in Kwangtung contrasts sharply with the
pattern in neighboring Hunan province to the north.

However necessary these broader political preconditions were to
early peasant movement penetration into the counties of Kwangtung, they were not alone sufficient to determine the outcome.
Equally important was the nature and strength of the local opposition. In Pearl delta counties such as Hua and Chungshan the deep
natural cleavages in Kwangtung society, the strength of the bonds
between local gentry politicians and the new Kuomintang elite of
the provincial capital, and the advanced degree of paramilitary
organization into militia self-defense forces controlled in part by the
underworld made consolidation of power by the radicals difficult
even at the height of their influence. In more peripheral counties
such as Kwangning and Haifeng, in the penumbra of the shadow
cast by the modernization of Canton, native opponents had greater
difficulty denying the claims of young Communists that they represented the wave of the future. And in the truly remote reaches of the
province, such as Hainan Island, the Leichow peninsula, and the
deep Hakka country around Mei county in the northeast, a strong
sense of traditional values produced a surge of interest in military

Table 11 Regional origins of Kwangtung students at the Whampoa Academy and Peasant Movement Institute

	Chaochow, Leichow, Hainan Island	Hakka and West Delta	Delta, East and West River	Total
Counties	21	29	30	80[a]
PMI students	57	51	219	327
Whampoa Academy students	392	221	221	834
PMI and Whampoa students	449	272	440	1161
Percentage of students to PMI	12	16	42	20

Source: Tabulated from name lists found in *Chung-kuo nung-min,* no. 2 (Feb. 1, 1926), pp. 174-207, and *Huang-p'u t'ung-hsueh tsung ming-ts'e* (General name register of Whampoa classmates; Nanking, 1932).

[a]About four-fifths of the counties in Kwangtung sent students to one or both of these training institutions.

work through the Whampoa route but rejected out of hand the disturbing demands of would-be agrarian revolutionaries.

Hunan and Kwangtung. Readers of Mao Tse-tung's Report of an Investigation into the Peasant Movement in Hunan are left with an impression of sharp discontinuity from the earlier Kwangtung experience. If Mao is correct about the upsurge of the peasantry in Hunan, then that province must differ considerably from Kwangtung. Otherwise we might be tempted to conclude that the alleged upsurge was simply a figment of the young romantic's imagination. The answer lies somewhere between these two extremes.

One dimension of difference may be found in the historical background of the national revolution in Hunan. Although both provinces had been virulent centers of anti-Manchu feeling before the 1911 revolution, by the early 1920s the Kuomintang had lost most of its base in the province because Hunan was controlled after

1916 by a succession of repressive warlords. Only after April 1923 did the Kuomintang begin to revive in the Ch'angsha area, largely through the efforts not of old partisans of Sun Yat-sen but of Communists named Hsia Hsi and Liu Shao-ch'i. These youngsters naturally focused on their home counties near the provincial capital where small Communist cells already existed. In P'inghsiang, for example, the 170 members of the Kuomintang cell were mostly workers from the railway and miners from Anyuan—two centers of Communist agitation. There was no established base of labor unions under Kuomintang hegemony as in Canton, so the new Kuomintang lacked a mass base. The Communists therefore built the Kuomintang in Hunan by means of underground work among the traditionally disaffected student population in the main city, that same population from which Mao Tse-tung, Hsia Hsi, and others emerged as leaders in the late teens.

Though we have few details about Kuomintang organization from 1924 to 1927 in Hunan, the experience of neighboring Hupeh suggests that the Kuomintang spread into the countryside through the efforts of students and disaffected schoolteachers. Whereas Kuomintang membership in Kwangtung in 1925 was overwhelmingly bourgeois—merchants, laborers, army officers—in Hupeh nearly 80 percent came from the intellectual classes.[23] In any case, by the time of Chiang Kai-shek's Northern Expedition in 1926 Communists dominated the Kuomintang organization in much of the countryside in Hunan and offered support, not resistance, to the rapid growth of the peasant movement.

This background helps explain the impact of the so-called May Thirtieth movement on the Hunan countryside. Hunan responded far more quickly than Kwangtung to the news that British police had fired on student Nationalist demonstrators in Shanghai in late May 1925. By June 3, under Communist leadership, a revenge association held mass meetings of tens of thousands in the provincial capital to protest the massacre. When on June 7 the warlord governor Chao Heng-t'i ordered the suppression of this protest, the leadership decided to take their appeal to the countryside, beyond the city walls of Ch'angsha. They telegraphed every county in Hunan requesting the expansion of the protest movement into the villages through students returning home on summer vacations and through local teachers.

Though later Communist historians have claimed a widespread response from the Hunanese peasantry to these patriotic appeals, it is clear that the revenge associations built at the time did not penetrate deeply into the countryside. They were organizations of local intellectuals and took root in only seven counties—those where Communist influence in 1925 among students or workers was greatest.[24] One of the few Communists actually resident in a village at the time the appeals went out was Mao Tse-tung, who had returned to his home from Canton to recuperate from an illness.

The official post-1949 accounts of Mao's role in 1925 avoid claiming that Mao engaged in organizing the peasantry. Mao allegedly formed friendly relations with a number of peasant activists and caused them to set up peasant associations in his home town of Yint'ienssu in the summer of 1925, but no one claims he personally saw to the growth of peasant organizations on the model of P'eng P'ai. His role appears to have been limited to forming a small revenge association that lasted a few days before Chao Heng-t'i's order for his arrest as an agitator drove him and twenty-nine other Hunanese to flee back to Canton.[25] It is noteworthy that Mao's first peasant movement efforts dated from a decision by essentially urban Communists to carry antiimperialist slogans to the villages and that this decision appeared to have little impact on villagers.[26]

In fact, the origins and the earliest successes of Communist peasant organizers in Hunan were independent of Mao Tse-tung. As early as 1923, shortly after P'eng P'ai began his work in Haifeng, Kwangtung, two miners from the Shuik'oushan lead mines near Hengyang in south Hunan took on a party assignment to organize peasants in nearby Paikuo county. Disguising themselves as fortune tellers, the two Communists attracted dozens, then hundreds, of farmers into a Yuehpei peasant-workers' association—a title illustrating their labor movement origins. By the time of its liquidation by an aroused warlord in autumn 1923, the Yuehpei association they created had amassed over ten thousand members and had organized protest marches of nearly a thousand farmers.

A second, little known effort to organize Hunanese peasants came in late 1925 in Mao Tse-tung's home county of Hsiangt'an long after his departure for Canton. Labor union support was again the key to the Chuchow Peasant Association, which by November 1925 had collected a membership list of over five thousand names. Chuchow

was the large railroad town just south of Ch'angsha, and the
founder of the association, Wang Hsien-tsung, was a weaver by
trade. Wang was arrested by the local militia, declared a bandit,
and forced to confess his Communist party membership before his
public execution in the marketplace of his home village.[27]

Hunan differed from Kwangtung in having a period of underground growth of peasant organization prior to the imposition of
Kuomintang control during the Northern Expedition of 1926. The
forty-three Hunanese who left the Peasant Movement Institute in
December 1925, including the brothers of Mao Tse-tung and I Li-
jung, returned to their home counties as special delegates to get the
movement started. By April 1926, on the eve of the Northern Expedition, twenty-eight of the eighty-odd counties of Hunan had some
organization, with a total association membership of nearly forty
thousand. Not accidentally, most of these associations grew up in
counties along the railway—the lifeline of political ideas and the
easiest path for returning exiles.[28] This early preparation meant
that once the province was liberated, as it was during the expedition, there would be rapid development on an existing organizational base.

Some of the claims made for peasant participation in the Northern Expedition in Hunan remind us of the Kwangtung expeditions:
farmers offered coolie services to the troops as well as intelligence
data on enemy movements.[29] But there is a striking new element in
Hunan. Chiang Kai-shek's advancing forces were greeted and
helped by already organized armed bands of peasants in some parts
of the province. In the most famous case, the battle for Hsiufenshui
outside Ch'angsha on July 11, 1926, the Northern Expedition Army
passed untouched through enemy lines in the wake of a suicidal
charge by a local unit. This unit, called the Common People's
National Salvation Corps, was composed of workers, students, and a
peasants' armed force of over three hundred men.[30] It was no accident that the regular army unit receiving this boost was the only unit
with a Communist commander—Yeh T'ing's independent division.
In the three counties to the east of Ch'angsha—the same counties
that a year later became the scene of the abortive Autumn Harvest
Insurrection led by Mao Tse-tung—Communists put together a
force of members of a local secret society, the Elder Brothers' Soci-

ety (Ko-lao-hui), and unemployed miners that would later become the first unit of the Red Army.

After the conquest of the province, the new Kuomintang government, staffed in part by Communists, moved rapidly to support the peasant associations in ways unheard of in Kwangtung.[31] Resolutions of the new provincial party called for a guaranteed income to tenant farmers, a 2 percent limit on the interest rate, and funding for the peasant movement at all levels. The construction department of the Hunan Kuomintang, unlike its road-and-sewer-minded Kwangtung counterpart, ordered the abolition of the old-fashioned agricultural associations and demanded that newly appointed county chiefs consult at any time with the delegates from the peasant bureau. Under this official pressure, by the end of September associations were growing at a rate far faster than they had to the south, and by the end of the year at a rate of twenty thousand new members per day.

The Report on the Peasant Movement in Hunan broke the news of this rapid growth upon a disbelieving Communist party audience in early 1927. Mao described a movement that was not only growing by leaps and bounds but that had also seized power in the villages by using far more violent tactics than anywhere else.[32] But a closer look at Mao's document reveals that Hunan may not have been so different from Kwangtung as Mao wished his readers to believe.

One striking characterisitc of Mao's report was its narrow geographic frame of reference. His trip to Hunan from early January to early February took him to only six counties: Hsiangt'an, Iyang, Hsianghsiang, Ch'angsha, Hengshan, and Liling. That this was hardly a scientific sample of the entire set of nearly eighty counties in Hunan is obvious from a map. Except for the eighty-mile side trip up the Hsiang River to Hengshan, he remained within a twenty five-mile radius of his home county of Hsiangt'an. Moreover, the counties he chose for his survey happened to be the most thoroughly organized and heavily populated of all the counties in the province—their total association membership amounting to about three-eighths of the Hunanese total. Most of the examples of peasant movement success of various kinds were adduced from these six counties. Hunan, like Kwangtung, was divided into areas of striking success as well as striking failure. Mao's report also revealed essentially the same characters that played in the drama of struggle in Kwangtung. Mao speaks of clans and magistrates, *t'u-hao-lieh-shen* and *min-t'uan,* secret societies and bandits in such a way that we feel we are on familiar territory. The cast was the same; only the script differed.

To be sure, Mao asserted that the secret societies in Hunan were behaving uniquely by joining the peasant associations so there was no further need for the secret lodge form of organization. But the great homes of the societies, as of the bandits, were in the south and west of the province, areas of weak or nonexistent peasant movement support, far from metropolitan Ch'angsha where Mao's examples came from. The strongest society in the Hsiang valley was the Elder Brothers' Society (Ko-lao-hui). Members of this society, often jobless handicrafters rather than peasants, certainly joined in destabilizing actions periodically after the mid-nineteenth century.[33] But their main lair in the Ch'angsha area, the southwestern corner of Liling county, received mention in Mao's report as an area where peasant association authority was being surreptitiously competed with.[34] Only four months later Mao Tse-tung would complain that the reason peasant associations would not accept Communist discipline in Hunan was that they were controlled by the Ko-lao-hui.[35] We must conclude that Mao overestimated the movement's success in co-opting the societies to its purpose.

Mao further claims that, in contrast with the Cantonese Min-t'uan, the Hunanese gentry-led local self-defense units had "largely capitulated to the peasant associations and taken the side of the peasants."[36] Yet he admits at the same time that such landlord-supported organizations were naturally weaker in central Hunan than in the more remote regions of the province.[37] Unlike the situation in central Kwangtung near Canton, near Ch'angsha it might have been possible for a small group of unarmed peasants backed by the acquiescence of the authorities to surround and disarm the poorly equipped Hunanese Defense Corps (T'uan-fang). Furthermore, the concerted policy in Hunan demanded by General T'ang Sheng-chih was to transform the t'uan into a local police force, which he renamed the Door-to-door Corps (Ai-hu-t'uan). The Communist party obeyed by avoiding setting up rival peasant self-defense armies in Hunan. The Communist press during the days Mao was in Hunan (mid-December 1926 to mid-February 1927) published many examples of Hunanese T'uan-fang refusing to cooperate with the peasant movement and in fact resisting as aggressively as their Kwangtung counterparts.[38] Even at the time of his writing, Mao's assessment that the garrisons and the Hunanese Defense Corps had been neutralized was premature, if not misinformed.

Finally, Mao's assertion that the Hunanese gentry were in full flight before the onslaught of the Kuomintang needs a second look. Mao's biographer Li Jui admits that landlords in practically every locality had some reactionary organization under one name or another. In Hengyang one of the higher ranking generals in the Northern Expedition Army helped set up the White party to oppose the Communists. In Iyang to the north a property protection association similar to those in Kwantung sprang up. Even Mao's own Hsiangt'an county harbored a property protection party active during the days he was collecting his information. There were strong signs that the same forces that produced the collapse of the rural revolution in Kwangtung were present in embryonic form in its northern neighbor.

HUNAN is an anomaly in the pattern of peasant movement success. In Kwangtung the most modernized portions of the province proved the most difficult to penetrate. Elsewhere, the large cities of Hankow, Kiukiang, Nanch'ang, and of course Shanghai showed no signs of supporting an aroused and politicized peasantry, as did Hunan in the twenties. Hunan's uniqueness helps to explain the dominance of Hunanese such as Mao Tse-tung, Liu Shao-ch'i, P'eng Te-huai, and Ho Lung in the later history of the Chinese Communist party. But the uniqueness itself demands explanation.

Rural conditions around the provincial capital differed slightly from those in Kwangtung, for example. The Hsiang River valley was one of the rice bowls of the Chinese agricultural economy, each year supplying a sizable surplus of foodgrains to other provinces. This agricultural wealth made for a tradition of high rent payments to landowners, who tended to be heads of large extended families rather than agricultural entrepreneurs as in the Pearl delta. The peasant in the Hsiang valley lacked the security of tenure guaranteed by social custom, as well as by local disorder in recent times, near Canton. Hunan had no counterpart to the underworld gangsterism that characterized the Pearl delta; hence the profitable trade in rice remained in the hands of traditional gentry merchants. The lack of extensive paramilitary development that in Kwangtung produced the Merchants' Corps and the Popular Corps, with their virulent opposition to Communist penetration, also benefited the Communist party.

These background social or economic elements to the Communist success in Hunan seem, however, less important than the political tactics the peasant movement employed in that province. Not only did the peasant movement gain support from a Kuomintang government that was largely created and staffed by Communists, the peasant associations employed tactics that maximized the influence, at least in the short run, of the more radical wing of the Northern Expedition forces. They moved directly to an attack on their enemies, whom they were empowered to try and to execute if necessary without consulting higher authority. They established village citizens' congresses that were easier to control than were the independent county chiefs who were appointed in Kwangtung. They avoided rent reduction drives that might have alienated the land-owning class and worked instead to ensure the availability of food-grain for all villagers. Using the slogan of "all food for the people," they seized grain storage warehouses and prohibited the export of rice to other counties and provinces, thus appealing, as had the earliest Communist rural agitators in Hunan in 1923, to the less well-to-do farmers who resented continued exports in the face of local malnutrition. For a few weeks in late 1926 Hunan was indeed a peasant association empire. But the quick success of these tactics in Hunan bore the seeds of the quick failures of 1927.

WHAT LESSONS should be drawn about the secret of Chinese Communist success at rural revolution? The search for parallels and contrasts with the later efforts of Mao Tse-tung's armies, first in the central provinces of Kiangsi and Hupeh and later in the north China plain during the anti-Japanese war, is intriguing. Was the peasant movement merely a false start with few implications for the future or did it reveal patterns of support in the Chinese countryside that could be drawn upon later?

It is easy to demonstrate the profound differences in the social background of the areas of later Communist success. Table 12, which gives the average value for several major background vari-

Table 12 Characteristics of Communist base counties in three periods, 1924-1945: average value on five variables potentially affecting success

	All-China average	Peasant move-ment (1920s)	Soviets (1930s)	Anti-Japanese war (1940s)
Number of counties in base area		128	100	224
Date of first Protestant missionary activity	1900	1897	1901	1900
Percent rural	78.0	71.9	72.4	83.9
Foodgrains per rural household (kg/yr)	199.0	253.1	219.1	159.2
Population density (person/km^2)	169.5	147.3	91.3	217.7
Whampoa students (per million population)	34.7	49.7	27.0	22.8

Source: Data bank on Republican China county development, East Asian Research Center, Harvard University.

ables of Communist-occupied counties in each of the major periods, displays some striking contrasts. As the Communists moved farther from their original peasant movement bases in Kwangtung and Hunan, they moved into territory that was less urban, less Western-ized, less well-fed, and, of course, less touched by the forces of the national revolution of the twenties. One might conclude from this that the Communist party, suffering defeat in one of the most modernized portions of the country, was driven against its will into the more remote regions of the country. In those regions Com-munists managed to hold out against their Nationalist opponents, either because the poverty and backwardness of their new habitat welcomed their progressive ideas or, more likely, because the very isolation of these bases made them better fortresses against extermi-nation from without.

This simple conclusion, however, hides what may be the most important fact about the later Communist efforts: that they were built on the experiences and lessons of an earlier failure. The strik-ing performance of Mao Tse-tung's forces after 1927 can only be explained as part of a cumulative experience of rural work that began in the peasant movement period. The future movement would face, despite the differences in socioeconomic conditions, political circumstances not so remote from those faced before 1928 in south China. There would be local gentry, garrison armies, Kuomintang rivals, secret societies, and above all, the profoundly suspicious, hard-working country people to win over or to overcome. Tactics would have to be flexible, radical tendencies controlled, local opportunities taken in much the same way as in the days before Mao Tse-tung entered the Chingkang Mountains. That the Chinese Communists learned the secret of rural political work before 1928 would be too pat a conclusion. But we must not ignore the importance of practice and experimentation in the evolution of their political maturity.

PART THREE

—◆—

Practice

For peasants, prudence is essential.

Sun Yat-sen, August 1924

7

ORIGINS OF A REVOLUTION: P'ENG P'AI IN HAIFENG, 1922-1924

On a clear day the rocky coastline of eastern Kwangtung province can be seen from a jet approaching Hong Kong to the west. Crowded against the South China Sea, its sheets of paddy fields sparse and perforated as though crushed in the granite molars of the Kwangtung coastal range, the eastern shores of the province resemble the Aegean coast more than the teeming plains of most of rural China. It seems hardly the obvious place for the first explosion of the peasant revolutions of the twentieth century.

Haifeng and Lufeng, the two counties where the Chinese Communist peasant involvement began, scarcely qualify as peasant counties. Much of their population depends on fishing and salt manufacture, occupations that in Kwangtung produce independence, mobility, and resistance to collective effort. Bypassed by the lively steamboat trade between Hong Kong and Swatow, these two counties remained isolated from the spread of commerce or foreign influence alleged to generate modern peasant unrest.

Hindsight, however, suggests several peculiarities of the Hai-Lufeng region that help explain its prominence in the 1920s. A proportion of the local population is ethnically Hakka, a minority subculture of the Han Chinese famous for its ambition. Secret societies

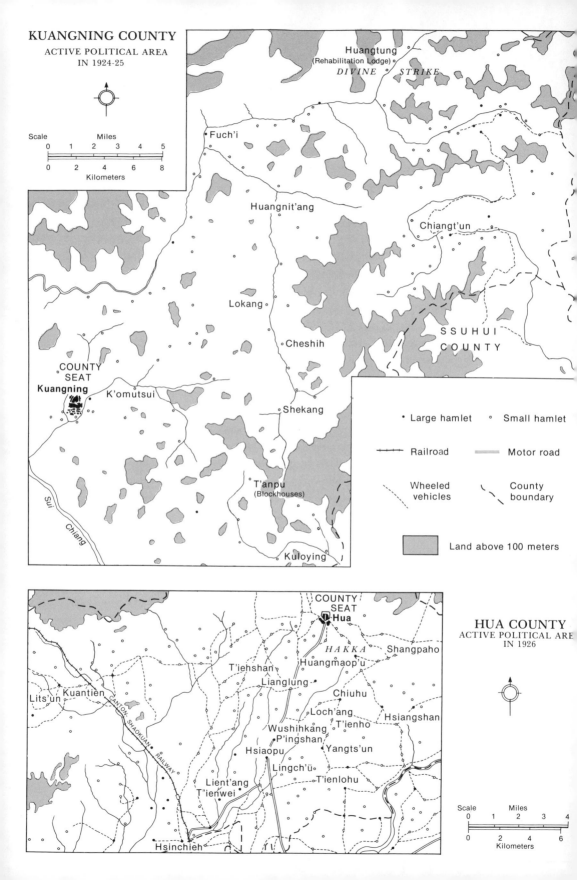

KUANGNING COUNTY
ACTIVE POLITICAL AREA
IN 1924-25

Scale

Miles					
0	1	2	3	4	5

Kilometers				
0	2	4	6	8

Huangtung
(Rehabilitation Lodge)
DIVINE STRIKE

Fuch'i

Huangnit'ang

Chiangt'un

Lokang

Cheshih

SSUHUI
COUNTY

COUNTY
SEAT
Kuangning

K'omutsui

Shekang

Sui Chiang

T'anpu
(Blockhouses)

Kuloying

• Large hamlet   ○ Small hamlet

+++++ Railroad   ══════ Motor road

········ Wheeled
vehicles

╲ County
boundary

Land above 100 meters

HUA COUNTY
ACTIVE POLITICAL ARE
IN 1926

COUNTY
SEAT
Hua

HAKKA

Shangpaho

T'iehshan

Huangmaop'u

Lianglung

Chiuhu

Lits'un

Kuantien

Loch'ang

Hsiangshan

CANTON-SHAOKUAN RAILWAY

T'ienho

Wushihkang

P'ingshan

Yangts'un

Hsiaopu

Lingch'ü

Lient'ang

T'ienwei

T'ienlohu

Hsinchieh

Scale

Miles			
0	1	2	3	4

Kilometers		
0	2	4	6

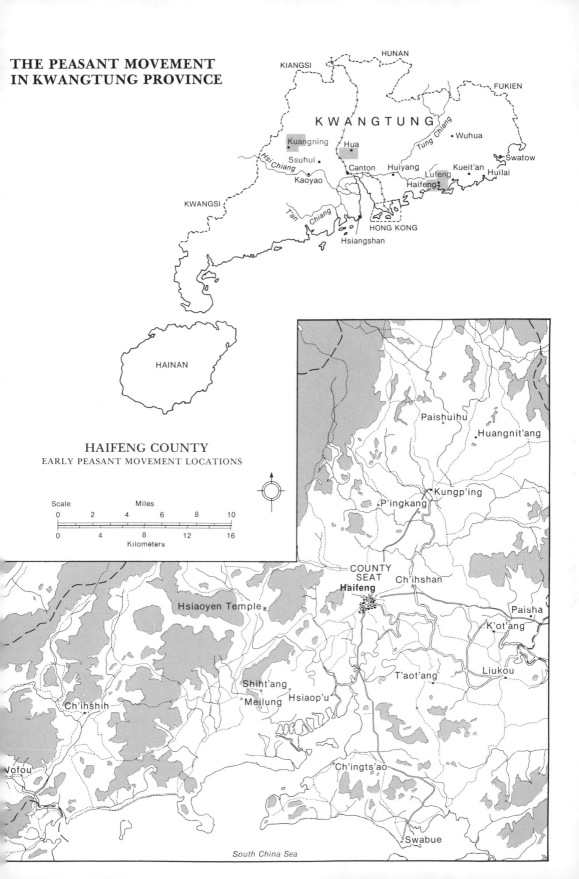

THE PEASANT MOVEMENT
IN KWANGTUNG PROVINCE

HUNAN

KIANGSI

K W A N G T U N G

FUKIEN

Kuangning

Hua

Wuhua

Tung Chiang

Ssuhui

Swatow

Hsi Chiang

Canton

Huiyang

Kueit'an

Huilai

Kaoyao

Lufeng

Haifeng

KWANGSI

T'an Chiang

HONG KONG

Hsiangshan

HAINAN

HAIFENG COUNTY
EARLY PEASANT MOVEMENT LOCATIONS

Scale

Miles

0   2   4   6   8   10

0   4   8   12   16

Kilometers

Paishuihu

Huangnit'ang

Kungp'ing

P'ingkang

COUNTY
SEAT
Haifeng

Ch'ihshan

Paisha

K'ot'ang

Hsiaoyen Temple

Liukou

T'aot'ang

Shiht'ang

Ch'ihshih

Meilung

Hsiaop'u

Vofou

Ch'ingts'ao

Swabue

South China Sea

such as the Triads flourished there in the late nineteenth century, both on a strong sense of regional loyalty and on underground links with the salt smuggling trade. Social violence, perhaps bloodier than elsewhere in Kwangtung, swept through the region and provoked retaliation from an activist local gentry determined to restore order. The Haifeng general, Ch'en Chiung-ming, drawing on these forces, rose to control all Kwangtung after the 1911 revolution. And during the teens Ch'en capitalized on traditional ambitiousness to push backward Haifeng to the front of the movement for educational reform in China.

Any one of these elements—a disadvantaged minority, a history of violence and cabalism, strong regionalistic loyalties, or rapid educational progress—might be declared the decisive factor in preparing the ground for a peasant movement. But the menton of Ch'en Chiung-ming's name presents an even more probable reason why Hai-Lufeng was the birthplace of the peasant movement: the general's encouragement of the progressive youth in his home town. Ch'en's political career sprang from his close association before 1911 with the Cantonese anarchists Liu Ssu-fu and Wang Ching-wei. Though in later years Ch'en in many ways compromised the ideals of his revolutionary youth, he maintained an interest in those issues that the intellectuals of his generation regarded as advanced, particularly universal education and democracy. Hence he financed a number of young activists during the late teens, though he scarcely shared their increasingly radical outlooks.[1] He could hardly have suspected that a sensitive, thin graduate whom he helped to go to Japan in the summer of 1917 would in ten years destroy the last vestiges of his declining authority. But without this young man, P'eng P'ai, Haifeng would not have produced China's first Communist peasant movement. And without Ch'en Chiung-ming's help P'eng would have remained just another disgruntled Chinese student.

P'ENG HAN-YÜ was the scion of a clan that owned several hundred acres of rich paddy in the suburbs of the walled town forming the county seat.[2] More than fifteen hundred persons worked the P'eng estate as tenants or lived with those who did: fifty persons for each of the P'eng family's thirty members. Born in 1896—three years after Mao Tse-tung, who later succeeded to his mantle as leader of the

Communist peasant movement—P'eng grew up to despise his family's wealth and privileges and to reject the powerful traditionalism that helped protect them. At age sixteen, in 1912, he was forced to marry a well-selected girl of gentle birth who had been hobbled from childhood by ceremonial foot binding. P'eng accepted the marriage, but freed the girl's feet and broke tradition by strolling hand in hand with her in public.

In early 1916, at nineteen, P'eng began his political career by joining a student group known as the Society for the Progress of the Masses (Ch'ün chin hui). The most controversial local issue in 1916 in Haifeng was the construction of a statue honoring a powerful military figure in the county, the incumbent garrison commander. The statue was to be located on the very spot where the Mongol armies in 1278 A.D. had killed a Chinese loyalist martyr. Young P'eng's contribution to the fight against the statue was impulsive: he broke into the sculptor's atelier one night and whacked off the commander's nearly finished nose with a chisel.[3] Though P'eng may have had many other reasons to dislike the local warlord, nationalism rather than social justice drove him to his first political act. In this regard he was not unlike many youngsters of the May Fourth movement generation.

Ch'en Chiung-ming apparently failed to connect P'eng's name with the vandalism, for in the summer of 1917 he financed P'eng's trip to Japan to join hundreds of other young Chinese learning modern legal and technological skills. It was at Waseda University in Tokyo, where P'eng began studying political science and economics in the fall of 1918, that he first heard Marxist ideas, though as an independent traveler in Tokyo from 1917 to 1919 he had joined in a number of Chinese nationalist meetings.[4] As an undergraduate at Waseda, P'eng moved in a closely knit circle of agrarian reformist intellectuals that called itself the League of Reconstruction Societies (Kensetsusha dōmei). The league included many young Japanese who threw themselves headlong into the agitation for reform that followed a series of rice struggles in rural Japan after World War I. P'eng was an outsider on the periphery of the young Japanese agrarian socialist movement, but the brief contact nonetheless was valuable. It undoubtedly helped him to resist, on his return to China in 1921, the preoccupation with industrial problems that distracted many young Chinese socialists from the countryside. Mao Tse-tung

and Chang Kuo-t'ao, to pick two other examples from his generation, lacking the exposure to rural-oriented Marxism, took years
longer than P'eng to realize the potential value of village politics for
a radical political movement.

Nonetheless for nearly a year after his return home to Haifeng in
the summer of 1921 P'eng had little to do with the countryside. In
part this was due to the conditions of his return. While P'eng was in
Tokyo, Ch'en Chiung-ming had reestablished his control over Canton and in a bid for wider support had attempted a rapprochement
with the fledgling Chinese Communist party. He invited Ch'en Tu-
hsiu to Canton to be his chief of education and moved the leftist
magazine *New Youth* (*Hsin ch'ing-nien*) to Canton as well. P'eng
P'ai returned to Kwangtung via Shanghai and passed through Canton, presumably sometime in July of 1921. There he met both
Ch'ens, who urged him to return home to Haifeng. He joined the
Communist party under Ch'en Tu-hsiu and accepted from Ch'en
Chiung-ming the post of chief of the education bureau for Haifeng
county.

P'eng later confessed that his educational work was as much a
matter of conscience as convenience. He saw how much the educational system of the county needed reforms and hoped that school reform would in turn help attack the other evils of society. He still
hoped that social revolution could be brought about through education. Though Ch'en Chiung-ming's educational construction program for Haifeng had built new schools, the taxation that financed
them still fell heavily on the rural population, who were unable to
take full advantage of them. Lessons were still conducted in the
elaborate and difficult literary language, and even the vernacular
writings of the May Fourth Movement were incomprehensible to
peasant children who spoke only the local dialect. The style of the
new schools was imported directly from the traditional tutorial, with
its rote memorization of nonsense phrases and its corporal punishment. The content of the new education angered P'eng most of all.
It strongly discouraged independence or self-reliance in political
matters; students were unwilling to accept any responsibility for the
state of the world or for their own salvation. Poverty and misery
were simply the will of heaven or the result of religious transgressions.
This view of politics as part of the religious sphere was strengthened
by extracurricular activities such as operas, lion dances, and even

gymnastics, which stressed compliance or satisfaction with one's status.[5]

The problems were not unique to Haifeng, nor to China. So too the dilemma of P'eng as a school reformer was similar to that of other educational critics elsewhere. Is education a mere product of the attitudes and the distribution of power in the greater society? Or does a social and political system draw its form and content from the way its children are raised? Where should a man of limited power and resources begin his work of intruding in the cycle of enforcement and reinforcement of old habits that produce a society seemingly bent on self-destruction?

Like many impatient radicals before and after, P'eng soon became disillusioned with educational reform. Traditional schools, for all their banality, still performed useful functions as systems of mutual reward. P'eng complained that his reformers met as much hostility from the students as from the teachers. He could not yet demonstrate to them the value of modern education in mathematics, history, or even physical education, since Haifeng supported no modern enterprises where such knowledge would be of use. Instead, the school children, "with their pale faces and their large eyes would think back on what 'Confucius said . . .' and on how the osprey honked and conclude that the old education was much less bother and effort."[6] These remarks in his memoir suggest the frustrations with educational change that pressed P'eng P'ai toward more spectacular activities.

P'eng entered Haifeng politics with a piece of theater. Inspired by the student snake-dance demonstrations he had seen in Tokyo, he organized a May Day parade in 1922 that awakened a sleepy Haifeng. Boys and girls from the county's handful of urban schools—all sons and daughters of the wealthy—mostly students from the First Higher Elementary School scarcely in their teens, marched down the street bearing a single red banner on which the two characters *ch'ih hua* (lit. "red-ize!") were boldly emblazoned. Not a single identifiable worker or peasant joined. P'eng later admitted that the entire scene was ridiculously infantile. But it did bring him local notoriety. Influential local figures soon complained to Ch'en Chiungming that P'eng and his young supporters were trying to communize property and women in Haifeng, and Ch'en agreed to fire his young education czar.

P'eng soon regrouped his intellectual followers around a new weekly publication, the *Sincere Heart* (*Ch'ih-hsin chou-k'an*), whose purpose was to bait the existing publishing authorities. The weekly ran a few issues full of diatribes against Ch'eng Chiung-ming's newspaper, the *Lu-an Daily,* and then came to a sudden halt. Though it claimed to be the voice of the worker-peasant masses of Haifeng, in fact P'eng later admitted that there weren't any workers or peasants behind them and neither the workers nor the peasants had any idea of what they were doing.

The true reason for the shutdown was a family squabble among the P'engs. One day on returning home from an editorial session P'eng was blocked at the doorway by his sister. His mother was hysterical and had been threatening to kill her son on sight. P'eng had carelessly left behind a signed *Sincere Heart* editorial in which he called on the peasants to take power into their own hands. P'eng's seventh younger brother had discovered it and read it aloud for all to hear. P'eng suffered his mother's wrath. "If ancestors fail to collect merit," she parroted the classic, "a son will bring the family to ruin. How can you continue to behave this way? Think of the bitter effort your forefathers put into our family's fortune. You will ruin us all!" she sobbed.[7] Madame P'eng, who after the Communist victory in 1949 was made into a revolutionary heroine only to suffer humiliation during the Cultural Revolution of 1967, was deeply concerned about the effect of her son's agitations on the large family estate. The P'eng family would be among the first of the clans wiped out by any reform of agrarian relations. P'eng did his best to explain his actions to his elders but later reflected that he would have gotten more understanding from ignorant peasants. This abstract faith in the peasantry rather than any concrete experience with Haifeng villagers turned him to the new job of rural agitation.

P'eng made his first attempt at what he called a real movement (*shih-chi yun-tung*) against the advice of his closest friends. His fellow Communists argued that the villagers were an inchoate mass, ignorant and difficult to convince. He would only be wasting his time trying to make them pull together. So even though his eldest brother threatened fratricide and the rest of his family refused to speak to him, P'eng P'ai, one day in May 1922, took his first fateful steps into the nearby countryside, hoping to find ears receptive to his revolutionary message.

P'eng walked a few hundred yards to a village near his home called Red Hills. He was wearing a Western suit and a white hat in the student style. He spoke hesitatingly, using the simplest language, to the few villagers he found at home. He pretended to be out for a stroll, interested in just making friends. He insisted he had not come to collect the theater tax or anything else, but he met nothing but stares and the hostile barking of village dogs. He gave up on Red Hills, unsuccessfully tried a second village, and was about to enter a third when the sinking sun and his own ebbing enthusiasm turned him back home. His family treated him like a traitor to his class that evening. He had a bowl of soupy rice in his own room, scrawled a large ZERO in his diary entry for that day, and lay awake in bed the entire night mulling over his failure.

The next day P'eng altered his approach. He used honorific language like "elder brother and sister," was humble, allowed farmers carrying their nightsoil pots to pass on the narrow paths, and let them know that at least one city boy considered them important. Again in Red Hills he tried to strike up serious conversation, to convince villagers that he was not collecting debts against them but interested in relieving their debts. "Your landlord owes you a fortune," he reasoned with one fortyish farmer he encountered in Red Hills, since "you have tilled his little plot of land for him for centuries." But the answer quickly came back: "we get the hell beat out of us when we're a peck short on our rent. Now how do you expect us to grab back what you say is ours?"[8] At the end of the day P'eng's diary contained another ZERO, but he had gained some valuable advice: avoid using empty concepts and intellectual expressions; don't dress in a sharkskin suit; minimize the class distinctions that divide the would-be agitator from his audience.

The third day rather than walk in on villages unannounced, P'eng stationed himself at a strategic crossroad where the paths to two local markets intersected. There was an attractive small temple at the crossing and marketers often paused to rest from the late springtime sun. After waiting a decent interval, P'eng approached one such group of people and struck up a conversation. Speaking quickly but directly and in something like the local patois, P'eng cited some instances of landlord-imposed injustice and suggested that only by some form of mutual solidarity could farmers rectify such wrongs. Only a small number spoke with him at first, but the crowds grew larger and larger and soon he was giving a lecture. The peasants listened half-incredulously, but there was an audience of forty or fifty. Of these nearly a dozen reacted positively to what he was saying.

P'eng continued his crossroads lectures well into the summer. The dozen-odd men who showed early interest became his regular listeners. He began to develop a reputation. Storekeepers stared at him when he visited the city. Relatives from far afield visited his home to ask about his health. Eventually one of his family servants whispered to him that he would do better to stay at home a while because people were saying he had had a nervous breakdown and should take a long rest. P'eng burst out laughing at this remark and took shelter in the notion that his enemies were spreading noxious rumors about him. His behavior doubtless seemed strange, however, even to those who were not aware of what he was about.

One day P'eng was in the middle of his by now well formulated lecture—the part about how one day the landlords would sit back and await their own execution at the hands of an aroused peasantry. Suddenly a fortyish farmer stood up from the squatting crowd and began to shout. "Stop shooting off your mouth with this nonsense about rent reduction. If you P'engs can just get your own company, the Ming Ho, to stop demanding back rents from me, I might begin to believe you are real!" P'eng was just about to respond to the heckling when a young peasant next to him rose to the dispute. "You are wrong about that, my friend. You may be tilling Ming Ho's land and would benefit from their reducing rents. But I am not. What am I to do? Our problem is not to solve our grievances with individuals but to find our own solidarity. It's like playing chess—he who moves methodically will win." P'eng had found his first vocal supporter and thought to himself, "finally, a comrade!"[9] The comrade was Chang Ma-an, soon to become a powerful peasant movement organizer in his own right.

P'eng quickly arranged a meeting with Chang and some of his young farmer friends. Chang introduced several, including Li Lao-ssu and Lin P'ei, all under thirty. It was Lin P'ei who suggested that the essence of P'eng's problem was that he lacked the proper introduction to village life. To get into a village properly he would have to be introduced by someone from the village and he would have to go at one of the idle periods of the diurnal cycle, say just after supper. Finally, he must not be disrespectful to the village gods. Another of the group suggested — P'eng admits the idea was not his own — that some form of corporate association something like the old agricultural association (*nung-hui*) that had been run by village gentry as a vehicle for financing development might be a real help. After this meeting P'eng wrote in his diary that success could not be far behind.

With introductions provided by his half-dozen new comrades, P'eng marched back into the villages where he had been cold shouldered. He found respectful audiences of fifty or sixty, children standing closest, then males, and then the women. He lectured in question and answer format so as not to seem to lecture. Soon he introduced new techniques that could not fail to attract attention: puppet shows, an imported phonograph and the tour de force, his own sleight-of-hand and magic show. His audiences began to number in the hundreds.

Throughout the summer and fall of 1922 P'eng worked to fill his schedule with such meetings. Accepting Lin P'ei's idea, he began to enroll members in what he called the Red Hills Agricultural Association. Unforeseen obstacles soon appeared. First, his newfound comrades came under strong pressure from their families to go back into the fields and work. Lin P'ei's mother warned him that though P'eng P'ai had no need to fear starvation, the Lin family was not so fortunate. P'eng claims that he bought some time against this threat by a Tom Sawyeresque ruse. He borrowed three dollars from a friend and loaned it to Lin, who took it home and showed it off proudly. After he had convinced his wife and parents that he was earning hard cash for his work with P'eng, he passed his tiny nest egg on to Chang Ma-an, who repeated the trick. Eventually the three dollars, its demonstrative purpose served, went back to its original owner. Later agitators would not have such easy access to wealthy men such as P'eng P'ai, who could finance such clever schemes.

A second obstacle was the reluctance of villagers to join anything. Convincing people who seemed to approve of association goals that they should become members P'eng called the most difficult job of all. "After everyone else has joined, then I will come in," was the standard reply. P'eng pleaded, argued, and cajoled his reluctant peasants. "Joining is like crossing a river from a dismal swamp to a blissful paradise on the other side. Everyone is so afraid of being drowned that no one ever makes it across," he chided, urging farmers to "hold hands and pull one another over."[10] He soon discovered that his chances of enrolling a member were far greater if he did not record the fact anywhere in writing. Several interested customers had run off in dismay when he pulled his membership book out of his pocket to write their names. But still it took more than a month of enrollment effort to induce thirty people to join the tiny association.

A DOMESTIC TRAGEDY gave the Red Hills Agricultural Association its first real challenge and an opportunity to grow. A six-year-old child bride in the family of a peasant association member tripped on her way to the privy and drowned. Her clan, thirty or forty persons in a neighboring village, stormed into Red Hills to take vengeance on the head of the hapless family. P'eng hastily called together his thirty association members, who decided to go en masse to the tragic scene to discuss the case with the child's clan. Reaching the village, P'eng crossexamined the angry outsiders one by one, making obvious notations in his pocket notebook. He knew that having their names would act as a sobering influence, particularly when he added veiled threats of retribution if his association members were mistreated.

Red Hills was one of a dozen *yueh,* or market districts, in Haifeng. An official from the district government soon came to arbitrate the dispute in the name of the county authorities. When the arbitrator announced upon arriving that he was taking the association member back to Haifeng for trial and punishment, P'eng's men charged at him in anger and drove him off. The dead girl's relatives, seeing that the association youth meant business, quickly backed off from their threat of violence. Now they demanded only to be able to see the body in its pine coffin. "If you are not afraid of going to jail, open it!" P'eng sallied. The child bride's womenfolk tugged at their men's shirttails and the crowd dispersed.

P'eng was quick to turn his successful bluff to good effect. "Powerless men will be tricked," his propaganda leaflets said. "If you want power you should join our association quickly." Recruitment increased perceptibly and P'eng felt he was able to take issue with the landlords. His first battleground was the increasingly prevalent practice of tenant replacement, in which landlords were removing lifelong tenants for trivial reasons in order to increase the rent. P'eng's association agreed on rules that members could not, without the permission of other members and the approval of the association, occupy land freed in this way. Any member whose land was taken from him would qualify for welfare payments from the association. The system worked well within the small membership of the associations, but leverage with nonmembers was still small. The association became involved in another type of protection insurance. Farmers who transported their produce to Haifeng city by boat often were forced by wharfmasters to pay exhorbitant fees, the penalty for nonpayment being seizure of the cargo. P'eng's men began to watch the movements of these and other local bullies (*t'u-hao*). When suspicious characters passed near Red Hills, the association would demand a large fare for their passage. This income was used to pay the exorbitant fees in the city, and the threat of retaliation against cargoes allowed P'eng to negotiate a reduction in the wharf fees themselves.

P'eng's strong-arm tactics made him the most important man in the entire market district. Villagers turned to him and the association for the arbitration of disputes and for handling criminal cases. Considering the feebleness of state authority in his villages, it was probably not a great exaggeration for him to claim that already by late summer 1922 all power was transferred from gentry and local landed bullies to the peasant association. By November 1922 there were over five hundred members in the Red Hills association, the majority of them from the twenty-eight villages of the market district. At a September congress the principals of the middle school and of the upper elementary school graced the new association with elegant speeches.

By the time of this congress the recruitment rate had jumped to ten per day and by November it had reached twenty. Income grew from entry fees and yearly dues. A simple membership card giving the name of the member, the date of initiation, the district number, and the village name of the association was issued. Printed boldly on the face was the motto: "No Work, No Eat. Think and Work Together." By October more than ten district names were found on the cards, so each of the ten districts was given its own association. These first districts to be organized fanned out radially from the first association at Red Hills. All were within a twenty-mile radius.

The expanding associations began also to perform a wider range of tasks. P'eng hoped to transform them from shadow governments or strong-arm protection societies into full-fledged community organizations, but his first step in this direction was not very successful. He formed a burial association with a hundred and fifty families as volunteer members. Funeral charges, in fact potentially ruinous expenses for small families, would be drawn from a common fund produced by a levy of two cents per family. Only twenty-four hours after the plan was announced an elderly participant died, and the families happily contributed their two cents, adding their own small gift sacrifices. On the fifth day another member's father passed on, and many members balked at repeating the performance. P'eng stepped in, paid for the funeral out of association funds, and mulled over how he could pay the money back. Several more deaths in the following few days put an end to his speculation. Members were simply unwilling to support the risk any longer, and P'eng's first cooperative welfare project collapsed. Although it made good sense, the idea of a burial insurance association never again caught hold in the history of the peasant movement.

The second project fared better. It was a farmers' pharmacy financed by the association and located in the main marketplace of Haifeng. The druggist was a Western-trained doctor who was interested in the peasant movement. All the association member needed to do to obtain drugs at half price was to present his membership card. The doctor's wife offered her services as midwife free to members. The pharmacy and clinic were so successful that membership cards were freely passed around and new regulations controlling them had to be issued. The doctor and his wife remain nameless in P'eng P'ai's 1926 account. It is possible that they, like a number of other doctors with foreign training, became disaffected by the movement's antiforeign turn in 1925. By the soviet period of 1927 it was just such Western-trained doctors who caught the brunt of Communist hositility. But in 1922 the farmers' pharmacy still projected an attractive future for the Haifeng peasant associations as the vehicle for social welfare reform.

By the end of 1922 all ten districts of Haifeng had peasant associations and P'eng was ready to move into county politics. On January 1, 1923, he staged a countywide congress attended by more than sixty delegates from the various villages. These delegates represented over one-hundred thousand individuals whose twenty-thousand-odd families had been enrolled across the county. The first Haifeng peasant congress in a sense set the tone and the format for hundreds of later meetings of this sort, both in Haifeng and elsewhere. Naturally P'eng P'ai was voted chairman of the association, and his slate of officers included familiar friends from the Red Hills Agricultural Association and the *Sincere Heart* staff. Reports, resolutions, and long-winded lectures on rural economics filled the days and effusive banquets, fit for the New Year season, occupied the delegates at night. Over the meeting hall flew the symbol of the Haifeng peasant movement, a checkerboard flag with red and black panels, symbolizing the unity of feudal lineages and the ancient spirit of struggle of the county.[11] Unity would be the theme of most peasant movement congresses thenceforth, a theme that would limit open public discussion of policy matters.

The only policy question raised at this first Haifeng congress was a financial one. Speakers at the congress pointed out that the association would double its income if it could seize control of the markets for agricultural products in Haifeng city. The yam market alone turned up cash of $500 a year, which presently went to the owners of the market stalls. Control of the markets would bring great political benefits as well, since it would demonstrate the associations' real economic power. Though there was no public resolution on this question, P'eng P'ai took the discussion as a mandate to move into marketing. Within a matter of weeks after the close of the congress he had gained control of the yam market in the county town and was using its income to finance the farmers' pharmacy.

The new business of the association in early 1923 was determined by bureaucratic considerations as much as anything else. The first peasant congress had endowed the general peasant association with nine departments, each with its own chief elected by the congress. The propaganda department was perhaps the most active of the lot. P'eng's association was beginning to pick up support from the urban middle and upper elementary school students. The department organized these new converts into lecture teams, gave scheduled performances in the town, moved on a regular circuit through the districts, and made themselves available for special occasions such as operas or festivals. By the spring of 1923 the invitations exceeded the department's capacity to provide speakers.

P'eng P'ai moved quickly back into his early field of interest—

rural education. His new program, which he called peasant education, in many respects resembled the rural educational experiments
being carried on elsewhere in China by other foreign-trained students. It offered subjects that would be immediately useful to the
ordinary farmer: bookkeeping, reading and writing of the names of
foodstuffs and implements, and basic arithmetic. To pay for it all
P'eng encouraged villages to set aside a portion of tillable acreage as
school land for the association to lease from the owner. The association provided the seeds, fertilizer, and some of the tools. Students
took time off from their class work to till the school's plot. At harvest
time, the teacher met his class at the plot, divided it into four, and
gave each group a section to harvest. Each competed with the others
to do the best job. The owner got his rent and the surplus paid the
teacher. Despite the obvious loopholes for corruption, these self-sus-
taining schools grew in number and within a month more than a
dozen came into existence — all supervised by the association's education department — with hundreds of eager pupils.

The difference between these peasant schools and the experiments being conceived during this period by men such as Liang Sou-
ming in Shantung or James Yen in Hopei lay in the intensive indoctrination that accompanied each lesson. Farm children were taught
to count, they were told, so that the landlord could not cheat them,
to read so that the storekeeper could not trick them, to till their own
crop so that they could be masters over their own land by and by.
They attended their own schools because nothing run by the government could satisfy their true needs.

The activities of the arbitration department illustrated how deeply
the general peasant association injected itself into rural life. Essentially the arbitration department combined several traditional roles
in one: that of the village gentry as representatives of villages in their
contacts with government, that of lineage elders as go-betweens in
family squabbles, and that of the yamen runners and court bailiffs
in investigating and prosecuting crimes. Nearly a third of the cases
it handled in the first few months concerned marital difficulties, divorce, and disputes between collateral lineages. More than half
dealt with money: the settlement of debts, relations between landlords and tenants, and other disputes over property. P'eng P'ai saw
each of these matters as opportunities for spreading his message. In

each case he acted as peacemaker and used each incident to attack the existing system of private property.

Though P'eng's association bore the name that traditionally had adorned the grangelike agricultural associations of the past, it did not perform the same functions. The old associations were more like chambers of agricultural commerce than mass organizations; their goals were more promoting agricultural prosperity for property owners than spreading education or redistributing political influence.[12]

Ch'en Chiung-ming had established a mulberry bureau in the city with the aim of bringing some of the profits of the silk industry up from the Canton delta where it flourished. But P'eng's agricultural bureau studiously avoided this developmental project, fearing that the profits would inevitably accrue to the owners of the larger estates. Instead they substituted a pine afforestation program to turn the hillsides green in three years. The obvious advantage of the program was that, under Haifeng custom, the pioneer who introduced cultivation to a new tract of wild land obtained the ownership of it. The pine seedling plan thus obtained for the association, and at least theoretically for the villagers who belonged to it, title to new territory, however infertile and inaccessible. A natual by-product of this afforestation effort was the sense of solidarity gained from village wide efforts to clear and seed whole hillsides.

All these activities prospered in an atmosphere peculiarly devoid of hostility. In part the peaceful growth of P'eng's movement in early 1923 was due to the mystification of the local powerholders. The magistrate of Haifeng county, Wang Wei-ch'ing, though himself rather suspicious of P'eng's motives, was held in check by Ch'en Chiung-ming, who was unwilling while still in forced exile to bear the stigma of suppression of a new mass movement. But in part the boom of early 1923 was a function of P'eng's own cautious policies. The decision to postpone implementing the rent reduction slogan for five years was well publicized in statements that the association had no intention of reducing anyone's rent at present. P'eng craftily adopted different slogans for distribution to the general public from those that he used to drum up interest among his members. Where outsiders knew the association supported improved agriculture or increased knowledge for the peasants or forms of philanthropic work, association membership was being expanded by appeals to eventual reduction of the rent, elimination of the more glaring abuses landlords imposed on tenants, and the control of graft and corruption in the police. That these appeals were taking effect was shown by the association's spectacular Chinese New Year's festival meeting on February 16, at which more than two thousand new members joined.

THE GROWTH of P'eng P'ai's influence in Haifeng did not long go unnoticed. Close associates of Ch'en Chiung-ming had already sensed that P'eng's association threatened their interests. P'eng's new enemies included many important men in Ch'en Chiung-ming's entourage. One of them was Ch'en Yueh-po, a distant relative of the general and the elder brother of two high officials in Ch'en's short-lived Kwangtung provincial government. Another was Chung Ching-t'ang, the general's former chief of staff, only recently returned to Haifeng after a series of disastrous defeats in northern campaigns at the head of a ragtag lot of Haifengese professional soldiers. These two enjoyed the confidence of many others, including the officers in charge of Ch'en Chiung-ming's personal office in Haifeng and the commanders of the informal county militia, the 'Protection Corps.' Both men, the former a practicing Buddhist who hoped to turn his followers away from P'eng by religious suasion, the latter suffering from battle fatigue, hesitated until February 1923 to confront the associations openly. Behind their hesitation lay also uncertainty about the old general's attitude toward P'eng P'ai. It took six months to organize an opposition to P'eng P'ai and a year to produce the first major victory.

The incident that first polarized Haifeng into two armed camps was a fine stereotype for future peasant movement workers. It included all the elements of the radical critique of Haifeng government. There was absentee landlordism, extortionate rent, violence by hired thugs, graft by the police, and the corrupt purchase of a judge. The villain, Chu Mo, soon became a classic example of what the peasant movement would later call an "evil gentry and local bully." He lived in sumptuous quarters within the city walls and drew his income off the rent from dozens of plots of paddy land in his ancestral village three miles northwest of town. The heroes were tenants whose ancestors had begun to work poor land decades ago on a promise of permanent tenancy. Though they had never obtained written agreement on the level of rent charges, they paid a small rent on these inferior plots for decades. Suddenly in 1923 Chu Mo demanded a modest increase in the land rent rate. One of his many tenants refused to pay.

Landlords had a great variety of weapons to wield in case of disagreement with their tenants in Haifeng. Chu Mo tried most of them. He sent professional rent collectors who verbally threatened and physically attacked the tenant. But the tenant now could call on P'eng P'ai and seek peasant association support. P'eng convinced another five of Chu's tenant families to leave his land and refuse the rent. Chu Mo then turned to the courts, filing a suit that argued that the six were robbing him of his rightful income from the land. But now the association had some influence at court, since the district magistrate was a former schoolmate of P'eng's and had received some favors from the association. After a brief hearing the judge dismissed the case. Chu Mo had only one recourse: to seek help from other landlords and from county government officials. He turned to P'eng's new enemies.

Within a few days of the courtroom defeat, Chu Mo was addressing a meeting of more than five hundred men who owned land near the county town. P'eng P'ai later wrote of this gathering that every man wore the traditional scholarly long gown and riding jacket, gold rimmed spectacles, and gold watch with gold chain. We may doubt that every one also had round faces and fat paunches as P'eng claimed, but it was hardly a gathering of the local poor.

"We landowners have bought our land with good money," shouted Ch'en Yueh-po. We have paid our taxes to the government, and now these criminals from the peasant association, who are demanding our land and wives, have begun to buy the courts and use them to mistreat landowners. If this local vandal P'eng P'ai is not quickly put in his place our industry will suffer great losses, and so, Ch'en said pointedly, will the county government. The government may not receive full payment of the grain tax in the short run, and in the long run may have to contend with anarchy and rebellion.[13] Ch'en finished, and the platform was taken by Wang Tso-hsin, a large landowner who would become the next magistrate of the county. Wang proposed that the owners form their own association like the peasants. Ch'en Yueh-po's seconding speech proposed the name "landlord association," but to implicate the government somewhat more, this appellation was soon changed to Grain Industry Protection Society (Liang-yeh wei-ch'ih hui). Ch'en Yueh-po was quickly elected chairman and Wang Tso-hsin vice-chairman of this new organization.

The new society moved quickly to appeal the Chu Mo case. They sent a delegation to demand that the judge reopen a tribunal. They let it be known that they expected to have a fund of over a hundred thousand dollars collected in a few weeks. They arranged with the county magistrate's police to admit to the courtrooms only spectators they approved. The judge, impressed by this new display of wealth and power, reversed himself at the tribunal and put the six tenants in fetters and behind bars.

P'eng was prepared for the setback. That evening he convened a meeting of association delegates and sent out a mobilization order. The next morning six thousand farmers converged on a temple hall within the city walls. P'eng gave them a rousing speech declaring his peasant friends in the jail guiltless. He offered to lay down his life if necessary to free them. Other speakers allayed growing fears of the landlords' wealth. Their money came, after all, from the grain that peasants produced. A rent strike would sharply curtail the opposition's power. If the conflict should come to open warfare, another speaker declared half-convincingly, the peasants could simply tear down all the field boundaries and let the lords fight among themselves about their parcels. Adjourning the meeting, P'eng led the spirited crowd to the county yamen, where he met the vacillating judge. He demanded immediate release of the farmers, a marching band and firecrackers to welcome them home, and apologies from the public prosecutor.

The judge was in a state of confusion. The poorly armed magistrate's police were no protection against a mob of thousands at his door. He tried briefly to appeal to P'eng's personal feelings, then ordered the captives released to avoid a raid on the prison. Mass action had worked. P'eng's skeptical followers were delirious and amid shouts and the staccato of fireworks returned to the general peasant association for a large victory meeting. P'eng P'ai squeezed every advantage from the success. He asked the crowd to identify who was responsible for the victory. Some shouted his name; others named the general peasant association; still others volunteered that it was the work of all toiling comrades. But P'eng insisted that he and his cadre comrades had little to do with the victory. Though P'eng admitted that he might have a little influence, it was the six or seven thousand people of the association who had turned the deed. "Even if he had the abilities of heaven itself, one P'eng P'ai could not abandon his peasant friends." From this day on P'eng would consistently employ this combination of authoritarian discipline over his followers and self-debasing flattery of mass potency. It was part of the secret of his success, as twenty years later it was of Mao Tsetung's.

The indirect effects of this successful confrontation were more important than the direct ones. First, the clamor of the event spread rapidly to the surrounding counties and made outward expansion far easier. Within two months P'eng's association reached Ch'aochou, P'uning, and Huilai in the three available landward directions and P'eng seized the chance to declare himself head of the Kwangtung Provincial Peasant Association. Membership increased now at the rate of three or four hundred a day. Second, the quality of P'eng's leadership cadre was greatly improved by recruits gained after the Yü K'ang case. Li Lao-kung, later the military genius of the Haifeng soviet but now a recent graduate of P'eng's alma mater, the Tansang Elementary School, joined after introducing himself in a passionate letter to his new hero. Other young intellectuals accompanied him into the ranks after the successful show of force. Third, the landlords' grain protection association was thoroughly intimidated by P'eng's *coup de main*. Ch'en Yueh-po quickly took the exit that his relatives and associates would often take in the coming half-decade: escape to Hong Kong.

By EARLY SUMMER 1923 the Kwangtung Provincial Peasant Association covered six counties and included over one hundred thirty thousand members. Already a sizable bureaucracy was required to run it. Each of the counties had its own county peasant association, though only Haifeng and Lufeng had subordinate district-level organizations. The provincial office, set up in the same headquarters as the Haifeng county association, was composed of ten bureaus, including ones for publications, investigation and research, and liaison. P'eng P'ai headed this last one, along with three other bureaus and a number of other positions in the Haifeng county association.

The investigation and research department tried to find out something about the nature of the growing membership in early summer and produced a set of figures that suggest the extent of its ignorance. The Haifeng county association knew precisely how many students, teachers, and petty merchants had joined. There were exactly three members of Ch'en Chiung-ming's private bodyguard staff, one professional fortune teller, ten gentry who worked at tutoring the young, and fifty Christians. A number of the largely protestant Christian members had turned on the church, and the investigation turned up one, Wan Ch'ing-chu, who had been a Presbyterian elder before renouncing religion to join the association. But the investigators could find out practically nothing about the peasant members of the peasant association. Rural membership was taken out not by individuals, but by households, as was the case in tax records and census returns. But even here there were no precise figures available. The investigation merely reported what it thought to be the percentage makeup (*ch'eng-fen*) of the peasant membership in the traditional categories of land ownership: owners, part-owners, tenants, and landless laborers. That these percentages were in even tens suggests that they were wild guesses rather than the result of any significant study. For the next half-decade the peasant movement would suffer from a similar disparity of knowledge: it was far easier to examine social questions in the towns than in the countryside.

But whatever its composition, the Haifeng Peasant Association was in the middle of county politics by mid-1923. One issue was bandit support. The associations in counties surrounding Haifeng—especially Huiyang to the west and Tzuchin to the north—had attracted the favorable attention of some rural notables who were regarded as local bandits, a term that meant that the gentry in power regarded them as threatening legitimate authority. The Huiyang association was located in a mountain market town called Kaot'an, traditionally the site of agitation against the officialdom of both county seats. Bandits in these counties recognized kindred souls in the peasant association organizers and took care not to rustle cattle from association villages. By 1923 Haifeng's peasant association influence ran along the corporate lines of villages or lineages rather than occupations or social statuses, and out-of-power groups were quick to sense this segmentation. By March 1923 the Haifeng association attracted criticism from officials in the entire East River area for their symbiosis with the outlaws.

An even more important issue was the job of magistrate for Hai-feng county. The incumbent, Lü T'ieh-ch'a, was an elderly scholar who could scarcely control his dislike for the new radicals. When Lü resigned in the spring of 1923, local notables pressed for the appointment of Ch'iu Ching-yuan, a more vigorous man of Lü's persuasion who had earned the particular enmity of the small but influential group of teachers and students of modern education. The two worlds—peasant and educational—met to discuss Ch'iu's appointment and decided that, though their joint opposition would likely prevent him from taking office, they would be unable to get their own man appointed. During these discussions P'eng's old adversary, the editor of the *Lu-an Daily*, published rumors that P'eng was an active candidate. To squelch this gossip, P'eng offered the name of Ma Huan-hsin, the chief of the peasant association's education department and scion of the large gentry family of the military leader Ma Yü-hang. But before this balloon could rise, Ch'en Chiung-ming let it be known that his appointment was Wang Tso-hsin—the man who had led the Grain Industry Protection Society. P'eng called a large citizens' meeting, which was attended by six or seven hundred persons, to protest the appointment and used it to pass the blame onto an uncooperative educational world. Wang's appointment was a fateful indication that Ch'en Chiung-ming's romance with peasant radicalism might not last. P'eng turned from county politics to domestic association work.

JUST AS THE child bride's death produced P'eng's first organizational breakthrough in Red Hills, the disastrous typhoon of August 1923 allowed him to strengthen and expand his regionwide associations. The cyclonic winds killed nearly a thousand and brought a week of floods to the low-lying polderlands where half the village population lived. P'eng P'ai moved quickly to surmount the crisis. The peasant association organized rescue teams to pick up moored and stranded families and repair squads to rebuild the dikes and channel away the flood waters. When the flood began to recede, association headquarters was inundated by a human sea of suffering villagers. Five or six hundred a day came in reporting new horrors or begging for money. The association eagerly embraced its new role.

Now the question of tactics arose. How should the association behave toward the applicants, and particularly toward their obvious desires for relief from rent obligations? In past years custom in the county took care of tenants in bad times. Landlords traditionally expected a request for relief and traditionally responded that if they could witness the extent of the damage, they would be willing to take merely a share of the actual crop. But the presence of the peasant association had altered this ancient understanding. Even though the peasant organizers refrained from pressing for rent reduction, the landowners refused in many cases to consent to crop splitting. The injection of an element of advocacy in what had been a purely informal and personal relationship paralyzed the normal processes of compromise.

At first the peasant association hesitated, then approved of seeking the traditional redress. But a dispute was shaping up among the few dozen men who were spearheading the movement. Just after the typhoon there were two alternate views: the association should do no more than intervene in extreme cases of landlord harshness, be the rear shield of farmers who chose freely to refuse to pay their full rent. The association was still too feeble to try to implement the rent reduction slogan. That move would not come for five years. To do so in 1923 would be highly adventuristic and might risk losing more than it gained. A second view argued that the typhoon had greatly altered the balance of power and justice in the county. Its advocates noted that in Haifeng there were few armed defenses against mass action. The landowners were not armed and there was at the moment no army garrisoning the county seat. The few district policemen feared the peasant association's power in normal times, they argued. The magistrate had only thirty or forty men in his private police force and was not likely to put his reputation on the line by acting harshly in a disaster year. He might try to take association leaders to court, but his eight bailiffs had already felt the muscle of peasant organization. In short, this group argued, the time had come to declare rent reduction in the entire county.

A resolution was impossible on the question, since a number of the important executive committee members had been caught by the floods across the border in Lufeng and were unable to return quickly. For several days the leadership waited. Meanwhile reports of the extent of damage continued to flow in, as did details of landlord lack of cooperation. There were also some heartening cases of defection from the landlord side. But absentee landlords were unwilling to throw in the sponge and even less inclined to travel outside their walled towns in this time of unrest. The teahouses were full of heated discussions about what was going to happen next.

P'eng had to act. As soon as the committeemen from Lufeng arrived, he called a secret meeting of association cadres to make a decision on the rent question. The outside agitators who had been working to expand the associations in Lufeng were more radical than either of the two groups that had spoken their pieces. They questioned how the peasants could consider continuing to pay any rent at all when nearly 90 percent of the crop had been destroyed. They pointed out that the slogans already allowed for rent reduction in bad years, but they were not willing to meet even that minimum standard. Adventurism (*wei-hsin-hsing*) is a label they used, but not to act would be to lack common revolutionism (*ko-ming-hsing*) by any standard. What was needed was not rent reduction, but rent *abolition*. The third radical wing argued that there was no alternative but to struggle with the enemy to preserve the association's values.

The conservative wing of the association, which had favored the slogan "individual right to reduce rent payments," became silent. The second group, now classed as moderates, argued against taking too radical a stand and suggested a compromise platform of setting a maximum rent. This year, they suggested, in no case should a farmer pay more than 30 percent of his usual rent. The third group accepted the compromise with the proviso that individual farmers retain the option of refusing to pay any rent at all. The slogan of "30 percent at most" became association policy. It was ratified at an emotional conference of association cadres on August 5. The gallery at the conference interrupted P'eng P'ai's careful report of the executive debate to clamor for immediate abolition. The 30 percent compromise passed by a majority only on the strength of P'eng's prestige and his promise to personally guide the interpretation of the demand.

Now the slogan had to be taken to the countryside. P'eng prepared the way by drafting a rousing manifesto on rent reduction intended for wide circulation within Haifeng. Likewise he drew up dozens of telegrams to go to various all-China groups and associations outside Haifeng in a claim for national publicity. Ch'en Chiung-ming, P'eng's former supporter, got a message to disregard nasty rumors about the association's work. The police chief in each of the county districts received detailed instructions about the rights of farmers in disputes with their landlords. Members of the executive committee were reminded to prepare for the coming association congress. Having won his private battle to push the association leftward, P'eng now tried to spread his movement's reknown abroad.

Confrontation and Defeat. The association developed a new-found self-confidence and solidarity in the face of the typhoon disaster. P'eng P'ai boasted that he had succeeded in dividing the county into two classes: the peasant and the landlord. But this very success at dividing rural society bore the seeds of future failure when the division between the two sides became unbalanced. One important swing group was the educated youth, the group on which he had relied when he first began his work a year earlier. There were two effects of P'eng's program that alienated the student population. They felt the first through their families, for high school education was a luxury that only the wealthy could afford. Many children of such families inherited strong antipeasant biases that made it easy to recruit them against P'eng P'ai's agitation. Others, particularly the gifted children of less well-to-do families, soon found that the reduction in family earnings from rent cut off their tuition funds and some schools went out of business for the same reason.

This disaffection reached into the heart of P'eng's association. Ma Huan-hsin, the chairman of his education department, was a young man from a small landlord branch of the powerful Ma clan—the elder of which was the general Ma Yü-hang. Young Ma had been P'eng's nominee for magistrate only a few months earlier. P'eng first noticed Huan-hsin's uncertainty during the debate over the rent reduction slogan. Ma had first sided with the moderates and then inexplicably switched to the radical side. Shortly afterward he disappeared from movement activities and soon requested a leave of absence. When he was chastized for his negligence, Ma turned on the association and published a scathing criticism of what he called the extremist 30 percent rule. Here was a clear example of what an astute observer of rural politics has called the utopian romanticism of the young peasant scholar.[14] Fortunately for P'eng, not all the youth were so committed to the process of education.

Deepening the cleavages in the county had another effect: to strengthen the resolve of landowners to fight for their rights. Propaganda is seldom the sole monopoly of the Left. The *Lu-an Daily* continued to publish anti-Communist editorials and gentry groups published handbills with their own slogans. In addition to the already traditional claim that the associations were instituting communism and colluding with the local bandits, there was the new mention of the mistreatment of the "cooking pot families." *Kuo-t'ou* or cooking pot was the local slang for persons who lived entirely off rental incomes — the small rentier class. P'eng P'ai described such persons with hostility as "families who refused to go out and find a job, who rode on the coattails of rich landowners, who were able to wear the long gowns of the gentry and live entirely off rents."[15] But gentry documents make such families sound more like persons incapable of work — elderly, infirm, or feeble-minded. The cooking pot appears to have been a form of clan-maintained welfare system that was severely hit by the typhoon and the resulting decline in rent income. P'eng P'ai's response to the appeal for mercy was simple: there were many more tenants in the county than there were cooking pot families. "Do you mean to say that the *kuo-t'ou* are afraid to die of starvation but the peasants are not?"

The 30 percent slogan was not an unqualified success everywhere. There were some instances where the association could intervene in disputes over the maximum. It could send a handful of pickets (*hsiu-ch'a-tui*) — a name taken from the parlance of urban labor unrest but in Haifeng resembling more the unarmed bailiffs of the gentry than protesting workers — to stand by a family that refused to pay more than the agreed amount. In one case at least the pickets were used to punish a peasant who willingly paid half his crop in rent. But one incident revealed that the association had not entirely taken over the functions of rural arbitration.

In early August a man who had contracted with the county education department to collect its rents found himself in trouble in a hamlet a few miles west of the county seat. As was the practice with such rent farmers, he had insisted on payment of the rent in full, plus his own fee. He was refused in one village and soundly beaten up in a second. There were two points in his favor, however. He was collecting not for a private landlord but in the name of the county government; and he was in fact a nephew of the chief of the Protection Corps in Haifeng city. Dismissing the niceties of legal procedure, which would have required him to lodge a complaint with the branch court, this man took his case directly to the county magistrate.

Magistrate Wang Tso-hsin had been looking for a useful incident to make a show of authority. He assigned twenty of his personal guerrillas (*yu-chi-tui*)[16] to the offending village, where they fired warning shots in the air and chased the inhabitants into the still-flooded paddy. The magistrate's men demanded that the village pay forty or fifty yuan in damages (much of which was doubtless destined for their own pockets, in the traditional fashion) and being rebuffed, arrested three elders. Wang Tso-hsin summarily placed them behind bars.

The association moved quickly. Delegates visited Wang's office to protest that this was a civil case, but the magistrate responded that the collector had been on official business. P'eng P'ai reminded the magistrate that the man was in fact a businessman working on a contract, but his argument was to no avail. The executive committeemen met to discuss the case and decided that there was nothing the association could do. The pickets were no match for even the small armed force of the magistrate, much less for the armies stationed in neighboring counties. The peasant organization would have to be satisfied with collecting relief funds and paying a bribe to the jailer to ensure good treatment of the prisoners. It would not be the last time that a peasant organization would have to back down before the force of the magistrate.

P'eng knew well that his association's powerful reputation depended on his ability to assemble a large mass gathering in the county seat. He had done so earlier in the year in the name of the wronged tenants. A crowd of five or six thousand well-disciplined rural people milling about the streets of a town of only eight thousand was an awesome sight. He doubtless hoped that just such a demonstration of crowd power could be used to enforce the 30 percent slogan. He laid plans for a large-scale peasant congress to convene in the town a few days after the arrest of the village elders.[17]

Wang Tso-hsin was a crafty old scholar, probably in his seventies at the time, who had read his history of Chinese statecraft well. He was the tutor of prominent politicians, including Ch'en Chiung-ming. He had learned the classical lessons about how to preserve authority in the county seat—the first principle of crowd control being not to permit crowds to form. At dawn on the morning of August 15, the announced date of P'eng P'ai's peasant congress, posters went up through the town. They declared that this was the day on which the bandit chief, P'eng P'ai, planned to instigate a revolt. The people from the surrounding villages should not allow themselves to be tricked into courting their own disaster. To remove the temptation he stationed policemen at the four gates to the walled town with orders to prevent anyone from entering. The police were, however, typically unarmed and were easily pushed aside by villagers determined to watch the excitement. Wang, having overestimated the power of proclamation—perhaps itself a classic Chinese error—was reduced to ordering trenches dug around his own offices and preparing for certain combat.

Combat never came. Four or five thousand farmers had collected in the streets by ten in the morning, all the stores were boarded up, and Wang Tso-hsin was furiously drafting telegrams declaring the emergency. He had earlier requested the small garrison in the coastal town of Swabue under Chung Ching-t'ang to come to his aid, but Chung had replied that he was too busy. "The affairs of heaven are on my shoulders, not yours!" Wang fired back and signed the message with the name of a number of the major gentry figures in the county. Chung sent a hundred armed men.

P'eng P'ai was forewarned of Chung's arrival and decided to ignore him and proceed with the meeting. By noon the congress had begun. A series of rousing speeches stirred the crowd to ever greater heights of enthusiasm, and by the final slogan-shouting time the noise was, according to P'eng's report, like thunder. The magistrate clearly assumed that the mob would head for his office, for he escaped as the noise grew louder. So too did his guerrillas and police. In fact P'eng P'ai later learned that Chung Ching-t'ang's troops, hearing rumors that peasants had seized the county seat, had refused to go a step farther and remained several kilometers away. But the congress merely adjourned and the association leaders assembled at their headquarters near the Lungching Bridge outside the eastern gate of the city. P'eng assumed, wrongly as it turned out, that by avoiding contact with Chung's soldiers he would not attract their ire.

That evening a highly secret meeting of forty or fifty top Haifeng gentry met to discuss how to handle the threat posed by the association. Unknown to P'eng P'ai, the dominant view at this meeting was that the authorities should stage a preemptive strike—the Chinese phrase was more mellifluous: "one effort-eternal leisure." At dawn on August 16[18] Wang and his brother, who was commander of the guerrillas, launched a raid with three hundred men on the association headquarters at Lungching Bridge. They covered the front and the side doors and began shooting at the rear. Until the first shot was fired, the association officials were asleep. Ch'en Meng started to escape through the front door, but was blocked by a burly policeman. He sliced the raider across the belly with a sharpened bicycle chain he kept ready and leaped out a window. A handful of others, including P'eng P'ai, escaped through the roof. Twenty-five were taken captive after being beaten with sticks and the blunt end of spears. The doors of the association building were locked and all its documents taken. Not until February 1925, when the Kuomintang armies swept through the region in their campaign against Ch'en Chiung-ming, would the Haifeng Peasant Association come back to public life.

THE AUGUST 16 coup spectacularly defeated P'eng P'ai's strategy of mobilization and the escalation of demands. He toyed briefly with the idea of an angry retaliation and spoke of raising a giant army of peasants to unleash widespread slaughter. But his more reasonable brother persuaded him first to try a subtler tactic, to try to win back the protection of his former supporter Ch'en Chiung-ming. The old warlord, defeated in March 1923 by the allied forces of Sun Yat-sen and several Kwangsi warlords, seemed still willing to flirt with the young radicals. He had even offered financial aid to the struggling association.

By late 1923 Ch'en was walking a tightrope between his gentry supporters in Haifeng and the new Kuomintang government in Canton. The old general knew that Sun Yat-sen's power base in Kwangtung, regardless of the promises of the adviser, Borodin, would have to rest on local military and financial forces. Ch'en prided himself in his progressive thinking, which he rightly thought was more firmly based on socialist theory than Sun's. He knew that a resurgent Kwangtung would need the services of young radicals such as P'eng P'ai, as well as of old scholars such as magistrate Wang Tso-hsin. He felt that a benevolent military government could lead Kwangtung, and eventually China, toward his favored guild social-ist society through what he termed a cultural revolution. Unfortu-nately for him, and perhaps for the peasantry of Kwangtung, his fortunes as a military figure were already eclipsed by the rising power of Sun's new government.

The old general had retired to his summer mansion in the ancient town of Laolung in the upper reaches of the East River. P'eng made the trip to Laolung on foot begging for his lodgings, avoiding mili-tary units, occasionally exploiting his own gentry background. His peasant movement cause received greater support from the Hakka minority than from his lowland ethnic group, so he could travel more easily in Hakka areas like the East River valley. He found his wel-come at Ch'en Chiung-ming's home less warm than before, but still correct.

Ch'en had been disturbed by letters from the magistrate of Hai-feng about P'eng's behavior during the typhoon crises. He was obvi-ously shaken by the gentry's reports of riot and rebellion, with their references to red flags, knife fights, and sharpened chains. P'eng P'ai defended himself by blaming magistrate Wang for failing to ac-cept the traditional obligations of relief in time of disaster. P'eng de-manded the release of the prisoners, official approval of rent reduc-tion, restoration of the association to its rightful legal position, and punishment of the county magistrate. Ch'en agreed to the first three, but refused to indict Haifeng officialdom. He signed a telegram to the magistrate requesting leniency for the association and recom-mending fair arbitration of the disputes at the hands of the former county magistrate. This essentially moderate telegram P'eng P'ai later tried to use as continued proof of Ch'en's support for his move-ment.

Despite Ch'en Chiung-ming's telegram, Haifeng remained unsafe territory for P'eng P'ai. He returned by inconspicuous sampan, dis-guised in peasant garb. Since he had left, his brother reported, the movement had deteriorated drastically. A number of unsuspecting peasants had been mistreated for refusing to pay their rents. The 30 percent rule could not be enforced. Just after the raid on the cadre dormitory, the magistrate's police had closed the farmers' pharmacy. Even the food sent to the jailed farmers had been confiscated. Calming words from the old general would not be enough to restore the peasant associations' midsummer powers.

The peasant leaders met furtively to discuss the next move. As always the possibility of insurrection was in the air, but now it seemed more remote than ever. P'eng P'ai realized there would be little sense in trying to threaten the powers by resorting to violence. The first task, the group resolved, was to raise funds to replace those wasted and stolen, just in order to keep their comrades in prison alive and to prepare for the eventual restoration of the organizations. There was some point, it was resolved, in pursuing further contacts with those gentry and intellectuals who had voiced private and public support for P'eng; there was always the chance that they might have some future influence. P'eng P'ai elected to move out of Haifeng for a while to operate in Swatow and Hong Kong, where there might be excellent opportunities to raise money and gain outside support. He would gladly have gone to Canton, but he feared he would be immediately arrested by the Kuomintang as an enemy agent. His East River origins and connections with Ch'en Chiung-ming, Sun Yat-sen's latest bitter enemy, put him in the opposite camp from the very men whose support he would have to seek three months later.

The first stop was the British colony of Hong Kong. Lin Shu-sheng lived there and might have some useful contacts. P'eng and Li Lao-kung moved into the Hong Kong headquarters of Ch'en Chiung-ming's private intelligentsia, where the editors and reporters of the *Lu-an Daily* stayed during their visits. While Ch'en Po-hua wrote editorials on the first floor attacking the peasant association, P'eng P'ai wrote letters and articles answering him on the second. P'eng fared much better with East River exile intellectuals than he did with exile peasants. He found it impossible to raise funds in Hong Kong. His complaints about the apathy of the crown colony Chinese were later echoed by many political activists. His only breakthrough came with the introduction of a former Haifeng poor farmer who had become a well-to-do small merchant in the colony. This man took P'eng and Li Lao-kung to a meeting of the Hong Kong rick-shamen, a trade dominated by Haifengese in the 1920s. With Wang's introduction P'eng raised nearly eighty dollars in small change from the several hundred members.

P'eng remained frustrated in Hong Kong about a month, until

perhaps early November 1923, before deciding to pay Ch'en Chiung-ming another visit. This time P'eng moved right to the point. How did the general explain that his many telegrams to Haifeng were being ignored and the men were still in jail? Ch'en blamed it all on the gentry, who he asserted were now saying he was being influenced by P'eng P'ai. Ch'en claimed that he was afraid of his former teacher Wang and of his uncle Ch'en K'ai-t'ing. With perhaps more humor than was appreciated, he punned with the Chinese words for new society and gentry society (*hsin she-hui, shen she-hui*—in East River dialect they are even closer in pronunciation), saying that there seemed to be little distinction between the two. His remarks were too direct and disarming. P'eng understood only when Ch'en began a long plea to P'eng to join his entourage, which was just preparing to move to Swatow to be closer to Haifeng. Ch'en's military disagreement with Hsu Ch'ung-chih had resolved itself with a stalemate.

P'eng had never wished his relationship with Ch'en to be too close. But now he found it more prudent to go along with the old man. Partly it was his sense that the general was losing his grip on reality. At one point, after P'eng gave him a rousing speech about the need for the liberation of workers and peasants, Ch'en dashed off a rash (and quite empty) order to prepare for an immediate offensive against Canton. The young agitator, realizing that his own rhetoric could push Ch'en into flights of fantasy about climbing once again the slope of power that peaked at the provincial capital, knew how close to real collapse the man was. P'eng also knew he needed to squeeze Ch'en for all the Haifeng influence he was worth. He needed more time to work his propaganda.

In Swatow P'eng continued to discuss Haifeng with Ch'en at every chance. The responses became more concrete but less serious. The way to free the prisoners, Ch'en suggested surely in jest, was to write one thing to his Uncle Ch'en and another to his teacher, Wang. This would so scatter their forces that P'eng's men would have easy going. Each time P'eng got Ch'en to think about the question, the old charges kept coming back to him: did P'eng really purchase weapons for the association? Did he really borrow an automatic from so-and-so? Conversations always ended on the same mildly accusatory note. P'eng saw the handwriting but could not decide to abandon the work.

His memoir informs us that he very nearly refused Ch'en's next whim, that P'eng accompany him back to Huichow. Nevertheless, he had accepted twenty dollars traveling money and a majority of his closest friends urged him to go along so people would think he was a big official. P'eng packed his bags and made his way along the well-guarded streets of Swatow prepared for Ch'en's departure. As he entered the anteroom of the headquarters he had a change of heart. "I saw them all," he recalled later, "the gentry, the landlords, the capitalists, the officials, the compradores, the whole lot of them. A bunch of round-faced, fat-bellied monsters crawling around Ch'en like flies. I boiled with anger, and hated the fact that I was unable with one sweep of a machine gun to mow them all down."[19] Li Lao-kung arrived to go along but was hesitant also, fearing that fund raising would suffer with their absence. P'eng, his indecision resolved, reached for a telegram blank and wrote Ch'en a message excusing himself because of his mother's illness. Even the stern old matriarch who had drummed him ceremoniously from the family had her uses in times such as these. P'eng admitted that his spirits lightened immeasurably as he left Ch'en.

The Ch'aochou Bay region was far enough away ethnically, geographically, and at the time politically, to have avoided all influence from the peasant movement to the west. P'eng saw his month and a half in Swatow as an opportunity to move out from his original base into a potentially fruitful shield for organization — the outward expansion that became such a crying need for peasant movement development later was already felt. P'eng traveled during this time back and forth across the ten counties in the eastern tip of Kwangtung and established association offices in each of them. In Swatow itself his umbrella was a Hui-Ch'ao-Mei Peasant Association Preparatory Office (for Huilai, Ch'aoan, and Mei, the counties typical of the three distinguishable regions of the bay area). P'eng had no trouble renting space and declaring his offices open. In part this was due to what he termed a typical Ch'aochou reverence for officialdom. As ever, P'eng passed himself off as a member of Ch'en Chiung-ming's civil staff. On his own admission his Swatow-based associations did nothing whatever — his apt classical phrase was the name without the reality (*yu-ming wu-shih*). The wealthy and powerful in each county were unable to see into Ch'en Chiung-ming's mind and so thought him to be supporting P'eng, so they donated large sums of money. P'eng gladly used their support in turn to impress Ch'en with his progress. The claim of having organized ten counties and brought several hundred thousand peasants into his camp naturally did not go unnoticed in Ch'en's headquarters, and the old general sent a steady stream of telegrams to P'eng care of his papier-mâché Hui-Ch'ao-Mei association.

Practically each one of these messages requested, pleaded, or cajoled P'eng to come to Huichow to stay with Ch'en's staff. P'eng guessed that Ch'en's motives had now changed. Instead of wanting P'eng for his own intellectual stimulation, Ch'en seemed now to need to keep the peasant organization under closer surveillance. To refuse him at this juncture might invoke his wrath and make it even more difficult to make progress back in Haifeng. So P'eng abandoned Swatow and headed once more on a pilgrimage.

This time he was able to pass openly through Haifeng. In fact many of his gentry enemies seemed obviously deferential to him. Word that P'eng was still in Ch'en's good graces had arrived, and even Wang Tso-hsin was heard to mention that he was a distant collateral relative of the P'eng clan. The news of P'eng's apparent successes in Swatow had spread to the outlying villages, and there was a steady stream of visitors asking when the Haifeng associations would come back to life again. In one district, the Meilung district nearest Huiyang on the west, an association had sprung into being on its own. A young intellectual named Yeh Tzu-hsin had organized a concerted strike against the large estate owners of the town, obtained a reimbursement of some of the key money on the land, and brought some three hundred persons into an underground peasant association. Yeh Tzu-hsin would later rise to high office in the Haifeng soviet government and the district of Meilung would become the showpiece of China's first rural soviet. But in December 1923 the activity in this corner of Haifeng was subdued and clandestine. Still P'eng's return made Yeh and many others anxious to begin the task of restoration.

A small congress of forty district delegates in mid-December heard P'eng conjecture that the situation had changed in their favor, that the prisoners would be released in a few days. This new situation, he said, was not due to his own skill. Although P'eng attempted to persuade the delegates that it was the strength of the peasants that had brought about the change, the example he cited would hardly have convinced a critical listener. He claimed that the Hui-Ch'ao-Mei association, though not perfect, had convinced all the oppressors from Wang to Ch'en that the more they disband the associations, the more they grew. It was this threat of peasant unity rather than internal gentry politics that would bring Ch'en Chiung-ming to a supine bow, he claimed. The associations would spread to all Kwangtung, for no matter how perfect the Haifeng association, the future would demand that peasant organization expand to all China and indeed the entire world.

It was an image to conjure with, however feebly based on evidence. But as though to fulfill a prophecy, within two days a greeting came from Ch'en Chiung-ming's military aide addressed to P'eng P'ai, the "chairman of the Haifeng Peasant Association." The commander had explicitly recognized its existence in writing. He also announced that the magistrate had agreed to release the jailed cadres. With great elation, P'eng sent someone to bail them out and prepared a welcome.

He had nearly forgotten his promise to go to Huichow. Now a telegram that made him even happier came from that quarter: Ch'en cancelled the invitation because of the death of his younger brother Ch'en Chiung-kuang. That Chiung-kuang, the most effective of Ch'en's military subordinates, was gone might have given P'eng pause. It meant one more chink in the armor of the knight whose steed he still rode. But P'eng continued to throw himself into village activities, propaganda, administration of underground associations, and the establishment of a temporary central office for the county organizers in a villa overlooking the Haifeng floodplain.

A few days later came another of Ch'en's telegrams. He was coming to Haifeng to bury his brother. P'eng hastened to prepare a welcome for him. If he could not produce peasants for this occasion, his reputation would be at stake. The task was not easy. First he needed a resolution of his association comrades to make the demonstration legal in their eyes. Then he spread the word. When the appointed day arrived, a scant dozen farmers turned out at the proper place. P'eng stuck more than a thousand little red flags he had prepared for the demonstration in the ground and scurried off. In the neighborhood of his staging place, a small bridge about three miles outside the walled town in the direction of Ch'en's home village, P'eng found around thirty odd-job hired laborers at work on the paddy dikes. He paid each of them a cent apiece to come hold the flags. Still, only fifty men would bring ridicule on such a great association, so P'eng began to sing songs, light firecrackers, and lecture in a loud voice. His skills as an entertainer did not fail him. Within an hour five or six hundred curious peasants turned out to listen. Given the flags at the proper moment, they made a deep impression on the funeral cortege by doffing their hats spontaneously in proper peasant fashion.

Ch'en stopped briefly to review the crowd. Yang Ch'i-shan, freshly released from jail, spoke only to say that the people in the crowd were all delegates of the Haifeng associations assembled to welcome Ch'en personally and to request that he permit them to restore their association. Ch'en uttered an enigmatic one-sentence reply: "Workers, merchants and students all have their own associations. Why not the peasants?"

P'eng decided that with this approval he could begin work, but starting at the bottom and building upward. The first to come back to life was the small association in Chiehsheng, the rich coastal fishing district near Swabue. P'eng and Li Lao-kung personally chaired the congress of two hundred, representing one or two thousand claimed members of the organization. P'eng's message had a curiously traditional sound: the steady drain on tenant finances caused by oppressive rent arrangements would make the proper observance of filial piety impossible; families would no longer be able to support the aged and infirm. Hence, Haifeng needed peasant associations. The very day after he returned from this meeting on March 12, 1924, P'eng was ordered to a meeting at Ch'en Chiung-ming's private villa.

It was a pure confrontation. Ch'en, who sat in the second-story room beneath a great window overlooking the plain, had assembled all the men whom P'eng hated most deeply. There was Wang Tso-hsin, the magistrate; Ch'en Chan-lin, the geomancer who labored to restore the boundaries of land disrupted by irate tenants; Ch'en K'ai-t'ing, the "Sixth Uncle" who ran the military government; and Li Cho-ts'un, the chief of the Protection Corps. Though he did not say so, Ch'en Chiung-ming was holding a hearing to decide what attitude to take on the objections all these men had to further peasant movement growth. He began abruptly, without the usual civilities, by asking if it were true that P'eng was putting on opera performances without permission.

It was not exactly true, though P'eng had in fact planned to do so in the near future. The gentry were obviously still most concerned about crowd behavior, and this had been one of their most potent arguing points with Ch'en. When P'eng denied it, Wang Tso-hsin launched into his more general charge. "Master P'eng"—he studiedly used the familiar honorific reserved for close scholar friends—was a fine young man, but his actions were extremist ones like proposing rent reduction and advocating violence. His charge was brief and without substantiating evidence, as though the mere statement of it would suffice to convince the others in the room.[20]

P'eng saw the challenge and accepted it. "The question of my character, good or bad, does not arise here," he said. "What is at stake is the charge of extremism." If anything we have been too moderate, he said. It is the gentry who have been extreme in their treatment of the peasantry in a disaster year. Had not the association volunteered a moderate slogan of 30 percent payment? The general does not believe your silly charges about peasant rebellion, he asserted hopefully. He will believe that true extremism lay in breaking up our association and throwing our leaders in jail. Ch'en Chiung-ming murmured his approval.

"But this is not all," P'eng continued. "There is something more that the general should know." He went on to cite instances in which the county magistrate had himself received money taken as fines from farmers who refused to pay their rents, how his cousin and chief of his personal police had pocketed moneys sent into the prison for the comfort of the prisoners. P'eng flourished in the air a list of the farmers he claimed had been forced to pay money to the officials of the county, the district, or the garrison command. "Here is your evidence. It would take me three days to get through it all. You tell me is all this evidence of extremism, or is it pure and simple stupidity!"[21]

Ch'en Chiung-ming appeared indignant. If these charges were true, there would have to be an investigation. The gentry had been put on the defensive. They sought again to press the charge of buying weapons, but P'eng shrugged it off as an act of self-defense. They attempted to appeal to him by referring to their mutual family connections, but P'eng's anger was aroused. "Even if you were my own father or mother," he spat out truthfully, "I could not forgive you such monstrous crimes against the interests of the majority of the people." Gradually the meeting began to dissipate as each man tired of the argument and descended the stairs. Ch'en Chiung-ming retired and the room was left entirely to P'eng P'ai, watched only by one of Ch'en's personal bodyguards. We have no independent account of the meeting, but P'eng assures us without any attempt at modesty that this bodyguard turned to him before he left and signed up with the peasant association whose right to exist he had for the moment at least managed to preserve.[22]

Fresh from what he thought to be his victory over the gentry, P'eng set March 17, 1924, as the date for his reopening congress of the county association. He announced his plans to stage a three-day festival to attract customers. March 16 arrived. The stands for the audience were ready and the operatic troupes had arrived when a new message from Ch'en Chiung-ming arrived. The old general seemed to plead with him. P'eng's proposed opera was causing Ch'en to "lose face." Either cancel it or move it outside the walls of the town where it would no longer be seen as a threat to the urban order, Ch'en requested. But P'eng was determined to have his show and felt the tide was moving in his direction.

He could not have been more wrong. While he had been busy planning the festival, the gentry had worked hard to regain Ch'en's confidence. Though unable to refute P'eng's charges against them, they did succeed in gaining the ear of Ch'en's octagenarian mother, whom they convinced to persuade her son to allow them to block the coming congress. Further, for the first time they alluded to P'eng P'ai's probable membership in the Chinese Communist party and hinted that he might even be tied up with the Kuomintang, which had just closed its reorganized first congress in Canton. The last charge was probably false.[23] But Ch'en reluctantly agreed to allow Wang another chance to disband the association.

The next morning the walls of the brick buildings lining the main streets of Haifeng were covered with bulletins issued in the magistracy. "The Peasant Association," they declared in bold letters, "favors common property and wives. It manufactures lies to befuddle the masses. This magistrate has already once ordered it dissolved. If this order is disobeyed, the punishment will be severe. Let all villagers be fully aware . . ."[24] The signature was Wang Tso-hsin's.

P'eng quickly called a conference of the delegates. This time there would be no risk of a massacre, no public humiliation of the movement. The group resolved to dismantle their public organization and go underground entirely. P'eng P'ai and Li Lao-kung were ordered to escape from Haifeng as quickly as possible in order to grow externally and make contacts. All the important documents and the name lists of the Haifeng associations were secreted away for the day when the association could once again come into the open. The first chapter in the Haifeng peasant movement was at an end, and P'eng and Li headed for Canton where the movement might still be kept alive.

The peasant reactions of indifference and suspicion that P'eng met on his first sortie into the villages would plague Communist rural agitators for decades. His early discussions among his own small group of adherents reflected ways of thinking that would crop up over and over again. The successful techniques for gaining the positive support of the peasantry provided a basis for later peasant movement expansion into hundreds of countries. But on the other hand, Haifeng was, for the 1920s and for later, a misleading example of Communist rural success. P'eng P'ai's special relationship with local power holders, the experimentalist approach of his policies, his relative independence from insensitive, heavy-handed party direction, and the advantage of surprise that naturally accrued to a pioneer all rendered the early Haifeng experience a dangerous, if appealing, example of how to capture peasant support for the Chinese Communist party.

8

THE POLITICS
OF DEPENDENCY:
KWANGNING,
1924-1925

By early 1924, when Ch'en Chiung ming returned to his native county, P'eng P'ai's early efforts in Haifeng had failed. Collaboration with Sun Yat-sen's party, however, opened the prospect of renewing a peasant movement effort near Canton. The logical place to begin building a Communist rural base would have been in the rich Pearl River delta under the protection of the new local Kuomintang branches. As it turned out, virtually all the peasant associations formed in the summer of 1924 were within thirty miles of Canton.

There was one exception to this pattern, an exception that surprised and pleased the activists as much as it puzzles us, the observers. By mid-1925 the most successful locale for the peasant movement in all Kwangtung province was a tiny, backward county on the northwestern edge of the province, Kwangning. As in Haifeng, the Kwangning peasant organization preceded the Kuomintang and grew despite the determined opposition of local gentry and officials. Like P'eng P'ai in Haifeng, the Kwangning peasant leaders combined agitation with skillful negotiation to keep their movement alive. But in contrast with P'eng's experience, the West River movement was able to fall back, at least for a while, on Canton's support,

albeit against a different and more formidable enemy. These parallels and subtle differences make the Kwangning case worth examining in some detail.

Why the movement settled in Kwangning and achieved much
success there remains a puzzle. The county was medium sized (four
hundred thousand in 1920), of middling agricultural wealth (a half-
million *tan* in 1937), with no more than average commercial contacts with the outside world (largely pine, cryptomeria, and tea).
Though the farm population subsisted reasonably well on the 10
percent of land that could be cultivated, their diet had to be supplemented with low-quality yams. Yet there was enough grain to export
regularly a 20 percent surplus.[1]

Internal transport was poor and mountain paths were the only
substitute for small wooden public boats that plied the tiny Suichiang from northwest to southeast. Human ambulation, including
the carrying of heavy burdens by shoulder-pole, remained the chief
form of transportation throughout most of Kwangtung beyond the
major river systems. It took three days to reach the county from
Canton, but that is no longer than it took to reach many other places
where Communist organizers failed to penetrate.[2]

Peasant movement sources mentioned as a matter of ritual the
degree of exploitation in Kwangning. The tenancy rate, that portion of the population that rented rather than owned land, may
have been around 60 percent as these sources claim, a figure slightly
higher than the Kwangtung averages.[3] Yet a more important claim
concerned the quality of landlord-tenant relations.[4] In some parts of
the West River area (for example in certain districts in Kaoyao
county) legal serfdom was still openly practiced. Kwangning landlords traditionally felt free to demand services from their tenants at
any time, and as in Haifeng rent payments had to include a number
of small but expensive gifts to the lord. It is probably significant that
the movement regarded Kwangning as among the most feudal
counties in this respect. Yet their detailed studies, unlike those of
Haifeng, fail to mention any concrete cases of tenant-landlord hostility.

Movement sources further stressed a history of agricultural im-
poverishment and tenant rebelliousness.[5] Hundreds if not thousands
of Kwangning villagers emigrated after 1900 to Canton, where they
entered such growing industries as food processing—much as the

Haifengese became rickshamen. In 1898 some tenants demanded a reduction in rising rents, and the unrest that followed landlord recalcitrance ended only in 1905 with a brutal purge of the villages (a *ch'ing-hsiang* in the bloody old tradition). But of course people from all of central Kwangtung migrated to the cities. The 1905 suppression was aimed at remnants of a secret society that had attempted to seize the county seat, and not against tenants.

Indeed Kwangning's out-of-the-way location did not prevent it from being a battleground for the forces struggling for control of Kwangtung after the 1911 revolution. When in 1916, during the war against Yüan Shih-k'ai, the local *tuchun* in Canton switched allegiances, anti-Yüan troops from Kiangsi to the west swept into the province to bring him down. The entire West River region was isolated for three months and Kwangning city was ravaged by the marching and counter marching armies.[6] In the early 1920s armies swept across Kwangning from every direction, but particularly from Kwangsi in the west, where powerful militarists such as Chu P'ei-te, Yang Hsi-min, and Liu Chen-huan, ambitious to rule Canton, made their headquarters. As recently as mid-1923 Kwangning had been the scene of a fierce battle in which local militia and gentry armies had helped drive out the most recent Kwangsi invasion, that of Shen Hung-ying. Little wonder that the leaders of the peasant movement felt that Kwangning was a sensitive, strategic area.[7]

Commercial pressures, class cleavages, economic hardship, underdeveloped communications, a recent history of unrest — any one of these factors or a combination of them might have been decisive in producing a Communist peasant movement in remote Kwangning. They would have had equal impact, however, on any of dozens of counties in central Kwangtung. A closer look suggests the overriding importance of an accident, one of the facts that persistently force students of politics to look beyond social and economic conditions to relations between men. Kwangning came first for the simple reason that a small core of revolutionaries who hailed from Kwangning and studied together in Canton had coalesced in early 1924 and were ready to return to their home villages. As in Haifeng, the place of origin of an externally educated elite was the random but decisive factor.

The core of the revolutionary leadership in Kwangning, as was so often the case in twentieth-century China, originated with a small

group of middle-school students. In 1921 the Kwangtung Provincial
Superior Industrial School (Kwangtung sheng-li i-teng kung-yeh
hsueh-hsiao) had among its student body a number of young men
from Kwangning. Chou Ch'i-chien, T'an Hung-ch'i, and his brother, T'an Hung-shan, were in their third year. Studying at nearby
Kwangtung First Provincial Middle School (ti-i sheng-li chung-
hsueh) as a freshman was Ch'en Po-chung, an orphan who had been
raised by relatives and attended a Confucian school. As was the way
with out-of-town students, these young men all came to share a
room together along with fellow villagers Chou Ch'i-po (Chou Ch'i-
chien's younger brother) and Wang Shih-lu.

These Kwangning students in Canton spent most of their spare
time together, plunging into the intellectual wake left behind by the
May Fourth movement. Their talks about domestic and foreign
affairs and ancient and modern social theories lasted far into the
night. Lacking P'eng P'ai's wealthy friends and his foreign travel
experience, too young to have joined in the glorious days of protest
of 1919, and too little educated to enjoy the polemic scholasticism
into which that protest had declined, these boys craved some outlet
for action.

They chose the tumultuous world of Canton workingmen's organizations. In the spring of 1922 Chou Ch'i-chien, who was to
become the mainspring of the West River peasant movement, along
with Lo Kuo-chieh and T'an Hung-ch'i, graduated from vocational
school and threw himself into the Canton workers' movement. At
the first occasion, Lo Kuo-chieh returned home to Kwangning to
help organize a paper workers' union; Ch'en Po-chung spent his
summer vacation collecting funds in his home village and among his
fellow students for a planned strike in the paper industry.

In the summer of 1923 Chou Ch'i-chien, through his labor union
connections, went to work in the propaganda committee at Sun
Yat-sen's general headquarters (*ta pen-ying*). The committee was
headed by the Communists T'an P'ing-shan and Feng Chü-p'o. It is
not clear when Chou joined the Communist party, but it must have
been around this time. During this summer, Ch'en Po-chung organized a dozen-man propaganda brigade of his Kwangning fellow
provincials to go back to their villages to work secretly for the extension of revolutionary power into the West River region. They established a pattern for peasant movement work in other areas, much of

which would be carried on by young men home on brief vacations. Their stay was a relatively prolonged two months, after which the entire team returned to Canton to study. They left behind only plans, no personnel.[8]

During the early winter of 1923-1924 the Kwangning students rested. Chou Ch'i-chien fell ill with an annoying skin disease. Lo Kuo-chieh was also unwell, and Ch'en Po-chung was attending his last year at middle school. Ch'en continued to take an interest in student movement activities and before the First KMT Congress he joined the Kuomintang. He even became a member of the executive committee of one of the district suboffices in the Canton party organization.[9] There he struggled with right-wing district party members at every meeting and brought the majority of them over to his side.

At the time of the First KMT Congress, Chou Ch'i-chien, his illness healed, returned to Canton. He reentered the workers' movement by joining the oil workers' association, promptly becoming its secretary. Curiously, the employees in the edible oil industry in Canton were almost to a man peasants who had recently come to the city from the neighboring counties to the north and west. The oil workers' association, like the rickshamen's for Haifengese, was a natural constituency for Kwangning natives. The industry was plagued by massive unemployment due to recently introduced automation, and nearly half the union members had joined the Kuomintang. Within a few weeks Chou and his comrades had brought over two thousand oil workers into the Kuomintang. A canvass of these oil workers and a fund collection drive by Ch'en Po-chung among the Kwangning students raised enough money to send the first team of peasant movement organizers to Kwangning.[10]

The first trio of organizers set out from Canton on April 8, 1924. All of them came from a large market district in the northeast part of the county. The region served by the town of Chiangt'un was a natural marketing area of paddy fields. Its watershed emptied not into the Suichiang near Kwangning's county seat but into the North River across the Ssuhui border. The central market of three thousand residents had been a ripe plum for bandit raids in the past because it was several hours' fast march away from the administrative seat.[11] The remoteness of their home from the administrative seat would ease the students' entry into county politics just as it would

make difficult their later work. The officer of the county administration in Chiangt'un district, Huang O-t'ang, at first refused even
to see them; but Chou Ch'i-chien, the senior of the three, gave
Huang an account of his family connections and a statement of the
new Kuomintang peasant policy. It would not be wise, Huang must
have thought, to offend the new administration in Canton by insult-
ing its emissaries. Finally persuaded by the official KMT party seal
on Chou's letter of introduction, Huang granted the students permission to enter and live in Chiangt'un.

On the next day the rest of the team of organizers arrived in
Chiangt'un, and after breakfast a conference of the preparatory
officials was held to discuss the immediate strategy. In what was to
become standard procedure for such discussions, the deliberations
centered around three basic questions: what slogans to use, what
methods — meaning activities — to engage in, and what kind of organizational structure to create. These problems were discussed item
by item and a work plan based on decisions made in Canton before
departure was adopted.

The slogans to be used at the beginning had no local referent.
They included only appeals to fight the alien foreigners (*lao-fan*),
bad armies, illegal landlords, bandits, and evil gentry. Peasants
were to rise up quickly and unite.[12] These were obviously a safe set
of appeals to begin with, in the absence of specific definitions of the
terms, no one could take immediate offense against this general
program.

Likewise there was nothing elaborate or objectionable about the
meeting's plans for disseminating these appeals. On market days
speeches would greet shoppers from the villages. The visitors from
Canton would take the name preparatory officials and travel from
village to village, and especially to their home hamlets, making
speeches and spreading propaganda. They would also canvass from
household to household, concentrating especially on villages that
were related by blood or friendship to those in which movement
officials resided. Finally, the main leaders, Chou, Lo, and Hu Shao,
were to travel personally on lecture tours of some of the main northeastern towns — Chiangt'un, T'anpu, Shekang, Kuloying, K'omutsui, and Lokang, the seats of the ineffectual district-level administration.

The new preparatory office would have Chou Ch'i-chien and Hu Shao as cochairmen, Lo Kuo-chieh as secretary, and would include more than thirty preparatory officials (*ch'ou-pan-yuan*). Chou and his friends decided to announce the founding of the office as soon as four hundred families had been brought into the organization. Whenever ten families in a village could be brought to join the association, they would be allowed to send one representative to the preparatory office. The lecturers and officials would go to the villages with a notebook and request signatures. Those who signed would receive a stamped document saying their household approved of the peasant association.[13]

This initial meeting also decided that the funds for the operation would continue to be collected in Canton: fifty cents from each Kwangning resident in the city was the goal. There was also to be a levy on each official of the oil workers' association and of the Kwangning Students' Association. It was hoped that a rapid growth of peasant membership would soon supplant this source of income.

The final item decided by this first conference had to do with the steps necessary to legitimize the establishment of the associations. The decision was that the letter from the KMT Central Committee would have to be delivered personally to the magistrate, whose attitude was the key to the reactions of lower-level gentry and administrators. With this decision, the movement became involved in the intricacies of county revolutionary politics.

The magistrate, a local figure of some power named Li Chi-yuan, had made a name for himself in 1923 through a stout defense of the county against the Kwangsi invaders. Given the title of Kwangning joint garrison commander (*lien-fang ching-pei ssu-ling*), he commanded a personal force of over six hundred troops and was widely known and respected. Nine months earlier T'an P'ing-shan, the Communist who produced much of Sun Yat-sen's propaganda in 1923, had singled out Li's garrison for its special bravery in battle.[14]

On April 12 Chou Ch'i-chien and Hu Shao visited Li in his offices in the old yamen within the walled city. Chou made a formal appeal that Li grant official permission to establish a county peasant association. Li Chi-yuan may well have never heard the expression before and preferred to change the subject. He seemed to be paying most of his attention, Chou later recalled, to the game of mahjong his retainers were engaged in. As Chou tried to press him further with questions, supper arrived and the Communists were invited to join. Chou Ch'i-chien has described the rest of the conversation.

> At the table he turned to me and asked "You have only just graduated from industrial school and must be thinking of going on with your studies. Why are you fiddling with this kind of work? Isn't it all more or less in vain?"
>
> I knew that this man had been a muddlehead, and so I was not surprised that he would react this way about such a new thing as our peasant movement. So I repeated to him what I told Huang O-t'ang at the Chiangt'un Corps Office. I was unprepared for the way his apparent drunkenness turned to anger.
>
> "I don't understand a word of what you are saying!" he shouted.
>
> By this time the wine was exhausted and the guests had left the table, again to take up their mahjong game. I thought to myself, that perhaps he had not seen the letter from Central after all, and so I asked, "Magistrate Li, have you read the letter which our Central has sent you?"
>
> His reply was negative, but his secretary contradicted him: "I handed it to you last night."
>
> By this time Hu Shao had moved into Li's seat at the mahjong table — the magistrate having tired of the game. He, — Li, that is — then rammed his favorite, long opium pipe into the floor and shouted angrily "In this office I only receive orders from the Provincial Governor, not from the Central!"
>
> The coterie of mahjong playing evil gentry and flunkies just stood there with faint smiles on their faces. By this time I too was unable to hold back my irritation:
>
> "Mr. Li, you aren't any petty officer in Kwangsi. Neither are you a counterrevolutionary. Today you are within the sphere of power of the party government. You are also a party member. How is it then that you do not obey a public letter from the party Central? Central has the authority to send this letter to you, and I have the authority to pass it on to you."
>
> "Are you trying to threaten me with the name of Central" Li began to say, but the evil gentry and flunkies rose to hold us apart. "I am not refusing to permit you to file your request — so long as you make it an official affair of the province."
>
> "Well, why didn't you say so earlier. You might have avoided spoiling the atmosphere." Hu Shao and I took our leave.[15]

This report of their meeting suggests how deep was the contempt of the young radicals for the soporific, pettifogging atmosphere of the county yamen, as well as the incomprehension of the elder generation for this new breed of professional peasant organizers. The anger and mistrust that broke to the surface in this first conversation were to become guiding forces in the struggles to follow.

From this point the gentry leaders suffered from a major misconception about their adversaries: namely, that the young peasant movement leaders were interested only in obtaining money. One of the most persistent rumors the local elders spread in the following weeks was that Chou and his friends were collecting contributions and recruiting men only with the intention of pulling out and leaving the peasants to bear the burden of punishment. Such, apparently, had been the history of the earlier rent reduction struggles. And this time the leaders were "all oil workers, with one leg deep in cow's urine and not a drop of ink in their veins."[16] And besides, where else did such a thing as a peasant association exist?

Despite the coolness of the first reception, Chou and his colleagues decided that the time had not come to attack Li directly, beyond dropping hints in propaganda that the magistrate was not working actively for the peasants' interests. The proper approach would have to be through Li's superiors in Canton, and Chou and Hu Shao decided to travel back to the capital.

On departing Chou left behind a plan of action to be executed in his absence. His men should make it clear that the peasant movement was a permanent feature in the county. They should prepare reliable lists of the district associations' members and get ready to elect delegates to the larger countywide organization he planned.[17] Chou left two younger men behind in Kwangning in charge of this work. For six weeks in April and May these two men represented the Communist party in Kwangning while Chou Ch'i-chien worked in Canton. One of them, Lo Kuo-chieh, spent most of this time outside the county seat organizing support in the outlying villages. His comrade, Ch'en Ch'uan-hsi, manned the mimeograph machine and made the lecture circuit around the county. When Lo decided to settle for several weeks and teach in a middle school on the southern border, Ch'en took charge of all movement activities.

This was an unfortunate move. Ch'en, though a loyal worker, was a poor public speaker. He could not refrain from cursing landlords and gentry, even in their presence. When challenged in public, he would ruthlessly seek out the name and address of the heckler, find him, and give him a verbal lashing. Chou Ch'i-chien later admitted that even the progressive peasants regarded this kind of speech and behavior as excessive. The opposition found that Ch'en's behavior gave them excellent ammunition.

The secretary of the central peasant bureau, P'eng P'ai, arrived in the midst of this tense situation sometime during the middle ten days of May. P'eng was little more than a month from his unfortunate 'showdown with Ch'en Chiung-ming and the Haifeng gentry, though he had in the interim risen to his new Canton post. During the dozen-odd days he stayed in Kwangning county on his first trip P'eng engaged in familiar activities and spread familiar nostrums: agriculture is no longer a profitable occupation; the peasants have to sell sons and daughters to pay debts; they must begin economic struggle; the majority cannot be defeated by a minority, and so on. We are told that in the places he gave these lectures the response was remarkable: in Hots'unt'ung, K'omutsui, Shihtsui, Chiangt'un, and T'anpu the total number of association members jumped from four thousand to seven thousand in two weeks. In view of the man's renown and charisma, the simplicity of the recruitment procedure, and the lack of active opposition, we have little reason to doubt these figures.[18]

But just as in Haifeng, the vision of swelling ranks of hostile commoners and the presence of the magnetic P'eng P'ai alarmed many of the Kwangning landowners. Most agitated were the elders in the Chiangt'un area, whose interests had been the first target of the movement. An informal meeting of some of these men with the commander of the Northeastern Kwangning Joint Corps on June 7 produced no results, so the Chiangt'un elders turned to their own town Popular Corps commander. They offered him three hundred men from their private clan armies. Fifty of these men might feign a popular demonstration in front of the county magistrate's office in the walled city while the remainder ransacked the peasant association offices at Chiangt'un. In fact, the association leaders learned of this plan in advance but refused to believe that the landlords would dare take such bold action. So the Chiangt'un association was completely unprepared for the onslaught.

On the morning of June 10 fifty men claiming to be Popular Corpsmen descended on the Chiangt'un office, fired a hundred-odd rounds, and moved in on the quarters. Most of the local peasant association officials escaped over the back wall. Two of them were beaten badly. The attackers also seized Hu Shao's younger brother, who was carrying a bucket of liquid manure. Young Hu was forced to the ground and the contents of his bucket poured down his throat. After this the brigands forced their way into the offices, throwing out all the furniture and burning all documents. The next day the process was repeated with the association offices in T'anpu and the loot taken was auctioned off on the spot.

The Popular Corps would have gone further to liquidate all the associations, but on the afternoon of June 11 they learned that Canton had ordered Li Chi-yuan dismissed. This order, issued a week earlier by the provincial governor after repeated appeals by P'eng P'ai in Canton, had a sobering effect. The landlords decided to temper their tactics by using financial pressures instead of open violence: they decided to place a special five-yuan tax on each association member. These smaller associations were unable to shoulder this burden and disbanded voluntarily.

The reaction of the peasant movement leaders to the landlord violence was immediate but in view of their powerlessness hardly aggressive. Faced with a naked show of force, they had no choice but to seek outside help. Hu Shao and Ch'en Ch'uan-hsi were on the trail from Lokang to Chiangt'un bound for a lecture when they heard the news. They decided on the spot to go to Canton instead. In the provincial capital Chou Ch'i-chien, still occupied with the affairs of the oil workers' association, began to receive a steady stream of emigre erstwhile organizers. He gave them comfort and encouragement and set about drumming up support in Canton.

Fortunately Chou did not have to rely solely on these feeble propaganda efforts to save the situation. Important political changes were occurring at that moment in Canton that would make the job of protecting the movement easier. On June 13 Liao Chung-k'ai, whose financial skills and personal loyalty endeared him to Sun Yat-sen, had been elevated to governor of Kwangtung.[19] Liao's sympathies for the peasant movement were well known. Within a week Liao ordered the punishment of the town Popular Corps commander in Chiangt'un, and on July 4 he proclaimed that the peasant associations would henceforth enjoy the protection of the provincial government. He explicitly mentioned the Kwangning Peasant Association, thus giving it firm legal status.[20]

No longer would the county magistrate be able to hold back the association by claiming he had no authority from the governor. Liao's statement, which was soon distributed in the West River area by appreciative peasant movement cadres, momentarily helped the movement cause. But the damages wrought by gentry-landlord opposition would take more than a proclamation to redress. Meanwhile, for almost two months in the summer of 1924, the associations in Kwangning languished while Canton occupied itself with handling the Merchants' Corps incident.

The landlord attack of the first week of June put the peasant movement on the defensive for the next several months. Like P'eng P'ai in early 1923, Chou Ch'i-chien in mid-1924 enjoyed the right to organize and work openly to expand the movement's influence. He could claim public recognition of a government in Canton more powerful and healthy than was Ch'en Chiung-ming's the previous year. Yet he seemed no more able to put down his local opposition than P'eng had been before the boost of the 1923 typhoon.

One important difference lay in the position of the county magistrate, Li Chi-yuan. Li was a more powerful politician than the kindly old gentleman scholar who had faced P'eng P'ai. Li's continued refusal in May to grant legal status to the association had been based on a belief that the provincial authorities would not back the associations. Though his dismissal had proved him wrong, Li knew he could fall back on powerful support at home. The northeast commander of the Popular Corps had helped him with tax collection and shared some of the spoils of the magistrate's office. Li, like Ch'en Chiung-ming, maintained close contact with Kwangning merchants in Hong Kong.[21] These contacts, along with the natural resentment of many residents of the northeast corner of the county, helped Li hold out against rising Kuomintang and peasant movement pressure until well into the summer.

The movement focused its energies during this period on what it called the expel Li movement. The attack was two-pronged. First they agitated in Canton to discredit Li and prevent him from raising funds or support in the provincial capital. Li Chi-yuan's political friends (including many who were in the Merchants' Corps then mounting an antileftist drive) tried public demonstrations in Canton demanding his reinstatement. But cleverly planned disruptions on at least two occasions prevented his supporters from being heard. During one of these incidents Chou Ch'i-chien seized the podium and read out a long list of Li Chi-yuan's crimes. Chou's labor friends then blocked the passage of the demonstrators to the provincial office building. This incident in Canton on June 17 and another in Kwangning on June 21 convinced Li he would have to resort to arms to unseat the associations.

The movement's other strategy was to win over the potent garrison army assigned to keep the peace in the West River area. This force, the several thousand men of the Cantonese third division under Teng Jun-ch'i, had moved to Kwangning only a short time before and had clashed with Li Chi-yuan's native troops over foraging rights. Moreover, Canton's new appointee as magistrate in Kwangning to replace Li was a former third division officer. It was no great task to convince the third division that they should resist Li's attempts to remain in the stable. By contrast, Li Chi-yuan's military forces in mid-1924 were drawn, officers and men, exclusively from the three market towns in northeast Kwangning where the peasant movement had first taken root. When he attempted in the last week of June to stage an open attack with eight hundred soldiers on the walled town of Kwangning, he was easily repulsed.[22]

Although Li never succeeded in making his comeback, the forces he unleashed were potentially more threatening than was P'eng P'ai's opposition in Haifeng. The summer 1924 stalemate in Kwangning pitted the countryside against the city. But the countryside was controlled by the gentry or conservative side, not by the radicals, resulting in a dangerous polarization.

Chou Ch'i-chien's efforts in the autumn of 1924 went almost entirely into organization building. To be sure, he let few chances slip to prod Canton for support against what he called the forces of Li Chi-yuan. When in September an unknown body of bandits began hampering traffic up the Sui River, Chou called for more troops for the third division. He urged Canton to declare Li and his friends evil gentry and force the present magistrate to arrest them. He even privately requested that Li's successor as magistrate be in turn replaced by one more responsive to the masses. But he turned seriously to building his organization and training an effective leadership for his peasant movement, jobs P'eng P'ai had never directly faced in Haifeng.

The events of the summer led him to extract some lessons for the future. His analysis is striking in retrospect for its resemblance to later Chinese Communist efforts at self-criticism. Chou's remarks were divided into the errors committed by the movement leaders and the lessons that he thought they should draw from their experience.

In Chou's view the Communists' mistakes could be explained by inexperience. The movement's slogans had aimed too high — not the earlier, more cautious ones, but the ones that the aggressive P'eng P'ai had brought with him from Canton. Then the attacks on the gentry during the spring of 1924 had been too coarse — here he pointed indirectly to the hapless Ch'en Ch'uan-hsi. Infantilism on his own part had driven him to send Lo Kuo-chieh down into a middle-school teaching job when he was more needed in the county seat. Finally, an excessive stress on propaganda to the exclusion of organization had produced weaknesses in basic-level structures. Having committed these mistakes, Chou said, the movement leaders simply ducked and ran. During the June offensive against the association, even organizers in secure villages had left.[23]

The lessons Chou drew from these failings were to serve equally well for Communist organizers decades later. Workers among the peasantry had to be disciplined. Slogans should be raised only after careful review to be sure they matched the movement's needs. Calm and strength of conviction would help organizers through temporary defeats. Strict attention to basic-level work in the villages, the advance selection of good elements to become comrades, and proper announcement of the correct propaganda line were all essential preparations for political struggle. Finally, movement cadres had to be supple and adaptable in the face of adversity, as prepared for defeat as for victory, able to summarize past experiences in preparation for the future. These simple cardinal rules were elementary to Lenin's party workers in Russia, but in China they had to be discovered anew. P'eng P'ai had struggled for years in Haifeng without this kind of wisdom.

P'eng had also built an organization on his charisma alone. Haifeng had not suffered from Kwangning's geographical polarization. Chou would have to generate real organization and match it to the varied needs of Kwangning villages. Canton's new peasant association charter spelled out a useful step-by-step procedure, one that ensured no higher-level associations would be names without the reality. Chou recommended that the associations build rapidly in the peasant territory near the county seat, even moving quickly there to a rent reduction policy. In the other parts of the county, more caution should be exercised. To his comrades' demand that he guarantee them protection against the enemy and promise early rent reductions to win more peasant support he replied it was more important to convince peasants of their own strength through organization.

The new Kwangning County Peasant Association formally established at a congress on October 10 embodied many of Chou's recommendations. A total of fifty-seven villages reported establishing organizations. Seven districts (Cheshih, K'omutsui, Shekang, Kuloying, Chingch'u, Chiangt'ou, and Taitung) had district peasant associations; three (Chiangt'un, T'anpu, and Lokang) had no associations; two (Kuoyuan and Kutufan) were organizing associations; four (Chiangchi, Maots'un, Hsikan, and Shihchien) had one to three village peasant associations but had not yet had time to form district peasant associations; two (West and South Suburbs) were under complete control but still had to be organized to give protection to the county peasant associations; and one (Paisha) had yet to be broken through to for communication purposes. A contingent of thirty-two delegates from virtually all the districts of the county attended this congress, joined by a thousand interested onlookers. China's first county Peasant Self-Defense Army made its debut, a tiny crew borrowed from the Canton unit of the same name with Chou Ch'i-chien its commander.[24] Henceforth the Kwangning peasant movement would speak through Chou as chairman of the executive committee of this new county association. Where P'eng P'ai's organizations had been staffed by his old friends, Chou's new group in Kwangning drew upon cadres from the new Peasant Movement Institute in Canton and upon the Kuomintang and Communist parties. Despite these organizational strengths, the glaring weakness still remained. Only seven of the nearly thirty districts of the county had formed associations. The areas of early movement penetration were still under firm opposition control.[25]

The Rent Reduction Movement. The peasant movement approached the rent reduction question with great caution. In Kwangning this caution was evidenced by an early reluctance to raise the slogan at all and then later by an order that it be applied

only in certain geographic areas that were under firm movement
control. As late as the beginning of November 1924 rent reduction
remained only a slogan. What were the considerations that led to its
becoming a movement that lasted over three months and led ultimately to bloody armed conflict?

There are some hints that the reason behind the beginning of the
rent reduction was financial. A large majority of the forty-odd full-
time organizers of the county movement were from poor peasant
backgrounds. The closing of many associations in midsummer had
cut off the flow of funds and put these men deeply in debt. Moreover, the Peasant Army would have to have money to buy badly
needed weapons. Though Canton did supply a small sum (around a
hundred dollars) to pay for the county congress and a few guns as
well, Chou knew that a rent reduction drive might divert needed
cash into his hands.[26] Hence he elected to present a rent reduction
resolution to the founding congress of the county association.

The year 1924 had not produced a bumper crop and with the
devastations resulting from the midsummer disorders many farmers
were in difficult financial straits. They flocked eagerly to public
meetings in October to hear young graduates of the peasant institute
propose a way out of their difficulties.

District-level mass meetings in the secure areas in late October
decided on a reduction of 40 percent of the total rent, of which 30
percent was to go to the tenant and 10 percent to the peasant association. Each district issued notices that any deviation from the
standard 60 percent payment would be considered illegal and
warned the populace to anticipate threats and attacks from landowners. Violation of discipline would be adjudicated by a discipline
commission and punished severely. The peasant leaders felt these
determined demands would help build their base of support after
the poor harvest.

Another cause for the urgency of October was the behavior of the
new county magistrate, who had been appointed at Chou Ch'i-
chien's request but who had not used the office to favor Chou's
movement. Indeed, Ts'ai Huo-p'eng's first official act as magistrate
had been to call upon the hated Li Chi-yuan in his Chiangt'un mansion. Chou threatened to denounce the magistrate openly if he did
not come out for the reduction plan and temporarily secured Ts'ai's
neutrality in the third week of November.[27]

At the same time the movement issued the first of what was to be a long series of rent reduction manifestos. Read in retrospect, it is a curious document. It contained none of the fiery denunciations of landlord crimes with which P'eng P'ai had launched his first rent reduction drive. Instead, Chou Ch'i-chien stressed the landlords' moral obligations to their tenants, especially that of sharing tenant losses as well as profits. "We deeply hope," the manifesto concluded, that "our beloved landowners," all "benevolent Confucian gentlemen," would "open wide the lapels of their understanding" and welcome the association's rent reduction policy.[28] This unctuous plea must have sounded as strange to the revolutionary leadership in Canton as it does to us today. But Chou hoped that by proper caution and deference he could avoid the powerful and concerted reaction of the landed interests that had doomed P'eng P'ai's earliest efforts. For this misconception Chou later attracted much criticism from his comrades.[29]

He was mistaken. The landlord reaction was swift and well orchestrated. Only two days after Chou's first manifesto some elders in the villages most strongly organized by the movement met to form what they called a congress for the protection of property. This meeting drew up letters to all landowners who might be affected in the three- or four-village areas, posted long proclamations denouncing rent reduction on red paper, and swore they would send armed rent collectors at harvest time. They offered a 50 percent reduction in rent only to those farmers who would join them to fight Chou's association. Despite their soft words, Chou and his young friends were selfishly motivated, the congress asserted, and aimed to destroy the heavenly ordained relationships between owners and their tenants or serfs.

This congress for the protection of property was the prelude to the formation of an alliance of much wider proportions. On November 22 the landowners in Chiangt'un and Fuch'i inaugurated a county-wide association for the protection of landlords. The name clearly echoed the Haifeng Grain Protection Society's title, but it drew also on the tradition of the societies for the protection of commerce (*shang-yeh wei-ch'ih hui*) that had formed in many Pearl River delta counties during the autumn Merchants' Corps incident. Just as revolutionary pressure on merchants had created solidarity downriver, the government's support for an antilandlord association brought

owners together. By the last week in November landlord opposition
had put together a military force some eight hundred strong composed of the local Popular Corps and many members of Li Chi-
yuan's private army. This force, assembled in the northeast of the
county, let it be known it intended to march on the association
strongholds at Shekang and Cheshih as soon as possible. Chou Ch'i-
chien quickly moved his executive committee and his tiny Peasant
Army of two hundred men into the market town of Cheshih and
prepared for combat.[30]

The peasant movement leaders had brought about precisely the
situation they knew they were least prepared to handle. Despite the
confident talk about the crucial role of organization according to
the charter, the importance of solidarity, and the efficacy of propaganda, the Communists in charge of the Kwangning movement
found themselves thrown into a civil war in which the outcome
would be decided by bullets. But neither they nor their opponents
could be sure of a military victory, since both sides knew how feeble
Kwangning's armies were compared to those of Canton and the
Kuomintang.

The first target for both sides' blandishments was the county
magistrate. Although Ts'ai Huo-p'eng remained in touch with the
Kwangning gentry and entertained delegations of landlords protesting the rent reduction, he stood to gain little from open warfare in
his county. He feared the Communists' ability to amass unruly
crowds, but he had little real control over the landlord vigilantes.
His promises to police a ceasefire, often reiterated to Chou Ch'i-
chien, proved empty as the opposition raided association offices at
will. P'eng P'ai's arrival on the tense scene in early December if anything strengthened Ts'ai's natural aversion to involvement. P'eng,
ever eager to challenge administrative authority, urged Chou to discredit Ts'ai before the masses and particularly before the Canton
government.

But Chou's problem with his rank and file was to keep them calm
and unprovoked. The peasant movement military was hardly a
match for the private army of one village alone, let alone a combined force of well-paid soldiers. Chou urged his men even to yield
to the armed rent collectors, promising them that he would get the
money and grain back later. He had decided to place his faith in
salvation from outside the county and wrote secret letters requesting

Canton to intervene. His first request for a mere thirty armed men suggests his underestimation of the problem.[31] In mid-December Chou still believed that the landlord side could only see two or three days in advance and would flee at the slightest show of force from Canton.

Governor Liao Chung-k'ai's decision to send not just thirty men but the crack armored brigade, the pride of the Kuomintang's modern military, brought joy to the peasant movement camp. Indeed, even before the force arrived, Chou Ch'i-chien laid ambitious plans to step up the rent reduction demands, place new conditions for a negotiated solution, and whip up mass enthusiasm to participate in the coming victory. Chou and P'eng P'ai harangued the crowd and led a march to the county seat, where they once again extracted promises of action from an intimidated county magistrate.

The arrival of the armored brigade from Canton on December 11, 1924, boosted P'eng P'ai's spirits. Now he would have the chance he had been seeking since 1922, the chance to do real battle with the evil gentry he detested. Chou Ch'i-chien and his executive committee of peasant movement cadres were fine young men, but like his brother, Han-yuan, they lacked the stomach for confrontation. At P'eng's side now stood, in the uniform of a commander of troops in the brigade, one of the few Communists in the Kuomintang army, Liao Ch'ien-wu.[32] P'eng for the next month would lead the new military committee of the Kwangning Peasant Association, trying to build local confidence. Liao would stand by prepared to back up P'eng's peasant army with force.

It did not take long for the Peasant Army to prove itself no match for the landlord troops.[33] When on the next day P'eng marched on landlord-held T'anpu village with sixty men, Liao had to rescue him with three hundred. Far from destroying the opposition, the Communists merely drove them into one of the ancient walled fortresses for which this part of Kwangtung was famed. The seven-story blockhouse of the Chiang clan at T'anpu had stood for generations against bandit and official soldiers alike. The armored brigade, for all its modernity, had no artillery large enough to destroy the ancient walls, and the local cannon P'eng commanded soon exploded from overdoses of powder. The siege of T'anpu would take weeks to accomplish.

P'eng's move against the Chiang blockhouse brought immediate responses from opponents throughout the county. An attack on a clan as large as the Chiangs brought many relatives to its defense. Before the day was over, eighty Chiangs had moved into the block-house for protection and to defend the family fortunes. In a nearby village a second blockhouse owned by the Huang clan quickly filled with resisters and declared its alliance with the Chiang fortress. Throughout the county and even into neighboring Ssuhui, small bands of armed men, some paid, some unpaid, formed and pre-pared to march to T'anpu.

Into this charged siutation came a new element of uncertainty with the arrival of two new companies to reinforce the third divi-sion's garrison in Kwangning. These hundred and thirty-odd Can-tonese were less loyal to Sun's Kuomintang than they were to their commander, Teng Jun-ch'i. Teng, a veteran of several decades of civil warfare in Kwangtung, had risen in the ranks of the Kwang-tung army in the teens. While the Kwangtung army under generals Teng K'eng and Li Chi-shen changed its political allegiance from Sun Yat-sen to Ch'en Chiung-ming and back again, Teng had maintained close personal command over his troops and a certain independence from Canton. His two companies did not inspire peasant movement confidence when they paid first respects not to P'eng P'ai but to the chief of the opposing Popular Corps. The peas-ant movement learned that the corps had treated Teng's men to a sumptuous feast of roast pig and had offered them lavish pay to serve the county. P'eng quickly branded this contact a collusion be-tween landlords and counterrevolutionary warlords and moved to neutralize the third division's impact.[34]

Exploration revealed that the third division officers had already formed a poor opinion of the peasant movement. The word had spread in Canton that Chou Ch'i-chien was a vagabond without even a clan to call his own, that the peasant associations were confis-cating rent in violation of the law, and that the peasant movement was depriving the provincial government at Canton of tax income. To refute these misconceptions, P'eng assigned Hsu Ch'eng-chang, who could appeal to their sense of pride in the new national revolu-tion, commander of the armored brigade. The rank and file of the two units were more difficult to handle; they had to be persuaded by a more personal appeal. P'eng, drawing again on his Haifeng expe-rience, instructed some older association members in the village where the Cantonese were camped to greet them with banners and impressive smiling crowds. Chou Ch'i-chien spoke with passion to a large mass meeting in the marketplace at Shekang under the watchful eyes of the new troops. A giant peasant-soldier welcoming congress on December 19, with skits, songs, speeches, and cakes home-baked by farm girls from the peasant villages, climaxed the appeal.[35]

Chou and P'eng were hardly confident that they had won over the Cantonese soldiers. Again the Kuomintang government might have to intervene. P'eng assigned his comrade Liao Ch'ien-wu to the capital with instructions to persuade the peasant bureau to help. Liao's appearance in Canton on December 14 alarmed Communist secretaries of the bureau, who had assumed the movement was in no danger. Liao assured them that the peasants were winning in Kwangning but that unless the blockhouses could be smashed, the Left could not hope to hold Kwangning for very long. He insisted on an interview with Liao Chung-k'ai, recently appointed governor of the province as well as chief of the peasant bureau.

Governor Liao was preoccupied in December 1924 by Ch'en Chiung-ming's threat to march on Canton from Haifeng in the coming spring. Unless Sun's government could solve its domestic disagreements and stage an Eastern Expedition, it might face quick defeat from enemies such as Ch'en. The governor was disturbed to hear that Teng Jun-ch'i was wavering and ordered Teng to move his artillery to Kwangning to attack the blockhouses. Governor Liao also proposed that the Kwangning dispute be resolved quickly by a pacification commission that he would appoint.[36]

This last recommendation did not please the peasant leaders, especially when they learned who was to be on the commission. In addition to their own representatives, P'eng P'ai and Liao Ch'ien-wu, the governor named the county magistrate and another opponent suggested by Teng Jun-ch'i. P'eng P'ai's goal was not rehabilitation or pacification but defeat for the reactionaries. He had no faith in the magistrate, whom he regarded already as the tool of the local landowners, and little in Commander Teng Jun-ch'i. The commission was bound to fail.

Liao Ch'ien-wu made sure that P'eng P'ai learned of the governor's idea long before the county magistrate. P'eng swiftly painted signs and declared the pacification commission established at the peasant headquarters in Shekang. When the magistrate refused to attend a meeting there, P'eng used his refusal to turn the third division's new appointee against him. When P'eng, Liao, and this new appointee walked the eight miles to the magistrate's offices, the pathway was lined with cheering association members. Sustained by a much-impressed Cantonese army representative, P'eng and Liao wrote the rules for the new commission in the magistrate's presence and appointed two of their own cadres the secretaries, whose expenses were to be paid by the county.

At the commission's first meeting on December 26 P'eng voiced several demands closely resembling the association's rent reduction manifesto that had precipitated the violence three weeks earlier. The three-man majority voted to arrest certain reactionary leaders. But their deliberations were halted when a group of peasants, among whom could be recognized P'eng's comrade Hu Shao, entered the room and demanded seats on the commission. P'eng didactically explained that while the rules of the commission (which he had of course drafted) permitted their attendance, it did not permit their vote. When Hu Shao replied that peasants had their right to vote according to the new Kuomintang charter, P'eng had his excuse to cancel the meeting to wire for more instructions from Canton.[37]

For two days the commission rested as peasant movement leaders toured the countryside speaking in its name for rent reduction. On the third day, December 29, P'eng found the chance he needed to discredit the magistrate in the eyes of Canton. Ts'ai Huo-p'eng's messenger invited him personally to a banquet honoring the chief of the Kwangning Popular Corps Bureau. This local gentry leader had, P'eng asserted, consistently persecuted association members and negotiated for more antimovement support from the Popular Corps general command in Canton. For these acts the commission had posted his arrest. P'eng convinced a reluctant third division representative that the pacification commissioners should go to the banquet to arrest the corps chief. By eight-thirty that evening P'eng's men, backed up by the armored brigade, had surrounded the Confucian temple where the banquet was in progress, disarmed the Popular Corps sentries, kidnapped the corps chief, and taken him back to the peasant headquarters at Shekang. Ts'ai Huo-p'eng, his authority as magistrate openly challenged, departed for Canton to consult with his superiors and the pacification commission was dead.[38]

The bold stroke of the kidnapping of the Popular Corps chief bolstered the movement immensely. It restored the tiny Peasant Army's confidence and it began for the first time to interdict the landlords' rent collection patrols. The associations began to demand again that the armored brigade disarm the Popular Corps. The movement's leaders now dared to confiscate several hundred tons of rice warehoused in their area but owned by landlords in the enemy village of Fuch'i. In the first week of January 1925 P'eng P'ai relaxed briefly to commemorate the movement's dead.

P'eng remembered the ill fate of his burial association in Haifeng and took pains with the arrangements for this ceremony, often to be repeated as the Chinese Communist revolution continued. He set up the preparatory committee, distributed circulars, and collected contributions for a compensation fund. Then he herded a crowd of little Shekang children with bundles of rice and other gifts to the homes of the selected martyrs. At the funeral P'eng performed another of his shows for more than three thousand sober villagers. His speech recounting the days of combat and promising revenge for the dead ended with the solemn roar of a cannon salute. By bringing together the families of the fallen comrades he felt that he had welded together what he called the axis of the Kwangning peasant movement — the separate villages of Shekang and Cheshih.[39]

Yet a major obstacle remained. The fortified blockhouses of T'anpu were still a defiant challenge to the peasant movement's claim to countywide authority. An underpowered armored brigade could not raze them, nor would the third division move without its commander's explicit orders. P'eng P'ai again fell back on Canton for his solution. The breakup of the pacification commission gave him an excuse to send Chao Tzu-hsuan, a Whampoa-trained peasant Army officer, to politick for more Nationalist troops. Chao returned to Kwangning on January 8, 1925, armed with Generalissimo Hu Han-min's promise to send his own personal guard regiment to help break the siege.

Again the movement leaders greeted an uncertain ally. Unlike the third division there was no question about the guard regiment's loyalty to the Kuomintang and to Sun and Generalissimo Hu personally. Its commander, Lu Chen-liu, ranked high in the esteem of both men. But the Kuomintang was not the Communist party, and Communist members of the regiment, such as Political Commissar

Wang Han-chin, privately voiced their doubts about Lu's leftness. They soon put him to the test. Just as the new guard was to arrive armed with a powerful artillery piece and ammunition for the block- houses, the peasant association welcoming committee marched boldly toward T'anpu waving the peasant flag. The provocation at- tracted fire from the fortress. The brigade drew near, heard the shooting, and assumed hostilities were in progress. P'eng P'ai urged Lu Chen-liu to throw his men into the fray. But he did not reckon that the age-old stones of the clan fortresses would withstand even modern cannon shot. After firing a few times, Lu Chen-liu called off his bombardment, saying he intended to try his own methods. He unilaterally declared a five-day armistice to negotiate with the landlord lineages.[40]

The Communists suspected foul play, especially when they learned Lu had arrived with only twenty rounds of ammunition for the big weapon. The considered throwing the Peasant Army against the forts in defiance of the truce but demurred out of prudence. During the armistice new outbreaks against association members heightened the anxiety. When P'eng protested personally to Lu on January 14, the commander insisted that negotiations with the T'anpu gentry were under way. Two days later P'eng was shocked to learn that Lu had dined with local Popular Corps figures inside the Huang block- house, had toasted his new comrades in the fort, and had promised to pull back the Peasant Army sentries from the gates. On January 19 P'eng P'ai came out for the purge of Lu Chen-liu.

P'eng assembled all his verbal artillery for this attack. He sent vir- ulent telegrams to Hu Han-min, Liao Chung-k'ai, Chiang Kai-shek, and even dying Sun Yat-sen in Peking accusing Lu of colluding with counterrevolutionaries. He spread the word among the guard regiment and the armored brigade that their commander was the worst and most reactionary traitor to the Kuomintang.[41] Then along with Comissar Wang Han-chin he traveled to Canton to seek in- structions and plead for another act of grace. Once again Liao Chung-k'ai supplied the right decision: the guard regiment would henceforth be commanded by P'eng, Liao Ch'ien-wu, and Lu's former deputy commander.

The Haifeng peasant leader assumed his command with gusto. He appealed to the regiment's nine Whampoa Academy graduates not to begrudge his dismissal of their old commander. At yet another long banquet his organizers applied their persuasive skills. Chou Ch'i-chien reminisced and joked with the cadets about the times past in Canton, played party games, and discoursed with them on the national revolution. P'eng P'ai, ever the raconteur, related a narrative about a rent reduction fever that had swept Kwangning county nearly two decades earlier. Chao Tzu-hsuan flattered the soldiers with stories of the Whampoa Academy's reputation among the peasantry. The young cadets returned to their posts full of praise for the movement and convinced that Lu Chen-liu had been in fact an evil rightist. When the guard regiment returned to the peasant movement villages after a brief New Years' vacation, they needed only a warm welcome by the Shekang association to prepare them for the onslaught on the fortresses.[42]

This final offensive nonetheless took P'eng nearly two weeks. He tried a number of stratagems to crack the blockhouses, including one unsuccessful attempt to mine them from tunnels dug underneath. A premature explosion of a casket full of gunpowder very nearly cost P'eng his life. But faced with the firepower of the guard regiment and the troops of the armored brigade, the Chiang fortress surrendered on February 13 and the Huangs a day later. Within four days of this victory the Kuomintang soldiers departed for Canton to join the coming Eastern Expedition into Ch'en Chiung-ming's territory, leaving behind at least a few weapons for the Peasant Self-Defense Army.

THE DIVINE STRIKE CORPS (Shen-ta-t'uan) had been a fixture of the western Kwangtung landscape for decades. Without knowing the details of its ritual no observer could tell whether it partook of the Triad, the Great Sword, or the Green Gang versions of south Chinese mystical militarism. It was typical of all such societies in its arcane ritual, its fierce independence from other similar societies, and its dependence on autochthonous personal leadership. Like the other societies, its organization and doctrine blended religious and military elements. Every district in Kwangning had one regimental chief (*t'uan-tsung*) who commanded not squads but an altar (*chiao-t'an*) in each village — usually an inconspicuous shrine decorated with paper mottoes, censers, and ritual objects. The altar chiefs evangelized the countryside around their villages with a doctrine less of charity and enlightenment than of self-defense. Divine Strike sermons combined religious camp meetings with useful military drill. After an altar chief delivered his lecture or chanted his imprecations, an acolyte (*tung-tzu*) would put the spectators through a series of military calisthenics that often ended after several hours in competitive races.[43]

Canton journalists and the peasant movement people themselves compared the Divine Strike Society to the Boxers of north China who rose in rebellion in 1900 against first the Manchu monarchy and then the foreign powers. Like the Boxers, the Shen-ta relied more on noise than firepower in combat. The troops were armed with long knives, bamboo poles, and the belief that religion made them immune to the enemy's bullets. Casualties could always be blamed on the extravagance or sexual misconduct of the injured. What was different about the Divine Strike was not so much the elements of ritual or warlike behavior as their self-image as protectors of local order. In Kwangning the targets of the secret society were neither the foreign aggressors nor corrupt and marauding outside armies but local outlaws.

This secret society differed somewhat also from the many societies in the Canton delta that flourished in the middle of the preceding century. As Frederic Wakeman has shown, the resistance to the new foreign presence in Kwangtung after the opium war of the 1840s produced a tenuous alliance between the underworld societies and the orthodox local scholar-gentry.[44] Then during the Red Turban risings of the 1850s and 1860s this alliance dissolved into bitter warfare as the gentry rallied to the Manchu cause against increasingly rebellious societies, formed their Popular Corps defense groups, and suppressed the heterodox sects. Kwangning, along with several of the remote West River counties, had, however, avoided the gentry-society split and brought intact the old alliance between gentry and societies into the twentieth century. The Divine Strike's turn-of-the-century leader, a provincial graduate of the Ch'ing examination system, left his successors in 1914 an organization with tens of thousands of members and extensive official connections. Though the new leaders were less qualified as scholars, the Divine Strike continued to serve important functions for local notables well into the twenties, long after the gentry's monarchy had been overthrown.

Indeed the Kwangning society quickly filled an important need after the 1911 revolution. The collapse of the Ch'ing government at

Canton diminished the credibility of the orthodox local defense structures throughout the province and especially in Kwangning, where those structures had been weak.

The Divine Strike filled that need for a succession of governments in Canton. When in June and July of 1923 forces from Kwangsi under Shen Hung-ying attempted to march on Canton through Kwangning, the Divine Strike, raising an army of forty or fifty thousand spear-wielding soldiers, drove them out. In fact the titular leader of this vaunted divine army was none other than Magistrate Li Chi-yuan, who received lavish praise from Sun and his Communist friends in Canton. Local defense could, however, mean defense against Canton as well. In early 1924 the Divine Strike and Li Chi-yuan moved to block the entry of the third division into Kwangning and actually engaged the Cantonese in several skirmishes in April, just as the peasant movement agitators first entered the county. When Magistrate Li, dimissed from his post at peasant movement request, appealed to the Divine Strike to help him return to power, he was rebuffed. But the possibility of continued cooperation between the society and the former gentry in the name of self-defense against the Canton revolutionaries remained very real.

To block this occurrence the peasant movement made several overtures to the secret society in the summer and autumn of 1924. In October Chou Ch'i-chien personally wrote the divine chieftain Ch'en Chu-t'ing pleading for society neutrality in the coming rent reduction drive. When P'eng P'ai returned from his late November trip to Canton, he urged more efforts to contact the divine army and several delegations of executive committeemen made the trip up to the mountain lodge of the Shen-ta in remote Huangtung. P'eng even requested that Ch'en Chu-t'ing rename his force a peasant army and offered to receive him as an officer in the new revolutionary military. After all, P'eng said in one letter, 90 percent of the society's members are poor and suffering peasants.[45]

Lo Kuo-chieh bore P'eng's offer to Divine Strike. The young organizer took along a fellow student who had sworn himself into the society before joining the peasant movement. On his way Lo learned that the society was staging one of its frequent military exercises that very day. Landlords in nearby Chiangt'un, he discovered, had spread rumors that the peasant associations were preparing to attack not just the blockhouses but the secret society headquarters as well. Two thousand village males had assembled to drill for the coming hostilities. By the middle of the evening Lo and his guide had reached the camp. The rural people from the village training units had already returned home and only a dozen-odd leaders remained at the temple. Candles and tapers burned within. The roll of gongs reverberated through the valley. A rich banquet of vegetables and fruit filled the table before the assembled chieftains. Lo Kuo-chieh approached, imitated his guide's deep bow before the altar, and began what he called his special propaganda. The peasant association, he said, shared certain points in common with the society—opposition to taxes, largely peasant membership, the desire for justice. He explained why he thought rent reduction was necessary and summed up some facts about the oppression of the peasantry. He concluded his speech by appealing to the society to bring itself under the associations, which he promised would then fight the enemies of the Great Sword Society. He left unclear just who these enemies might be.[46]

For all its banality, Lo's propaganda appeared successful. Returning to Shekang, he insisted to P'eng P'ai that the Divine Strike leaders could not be bought off by the enemy. Their leaders, especially the present high chieftain, Ch'en Chu-t'ing, were coming gradually to understand the motives of the peasant movement. Lo asserted that if the society followed Ch'en's orders, it would absolutely to a man refuse to serve the landlords or even to help them out.[47]

The inaccuracy of Lo's prediction was to be regretted in the months ahead. There was one incident in the visit that stood out in hindsight. Lo reported a single exception to the unanimously satisfied reception the divine leaders gave him. An elderly man had shaken his head on nearly every point and several times explained that the peasant associations were the creatures of Sun Yat-sen. He had called Sun the spirit of a demon and the peasant movement men his demonic cohorts. Although Lo Kuo-chieh's visit held off the Divine Strike through the spring of 1925, the secret society did not take lightly the advice of the forthright old man. In the end the divine army turned on the demonic cohorts in 1926 and brought the peasant movement in Kwangning to a premature end.

THE STORY of Kwangning, which appealed strongly to the eager dozens of recruits to Mao Tse-tung's peasant institute in Canton, had heroes, villains, drama, and a happy ending. In 1926 as in 1925 Kwangning provided the second largest contingent to the May First Peasant Congress, a contribution consistent with its claim of nearly seventy-three thousand memebers.[48] But dramatic endings never are so final as they seem, however much millennialists might hope them to be. An important lesson that the Chinese Communists would painfully learn over the next thirty years was that victories had to be preserved with the same determination that won them. The next time Communist armies swept through Kwangning (in 1949) the suppression of the enemy would be swift, sweeping, and permanently patrolled. But not this time. Detailed peasant movement accounts of the Kwangning events invariably end with the fall of the T'anpu blockhouses. It was assumed that the February 1925 victory was decisive if not final. It was in fact only a brief breathing space before the counterattack. The government troops returned to Canton where they were needed in the preparations for the first Eastern Expedition against Ch'en Chiung-ming. The peasant movement leaders, after a brief flurry of propaganda activity to take advantage of the success, soon left for other counties, leaving the peasant associations in charge of their local comrades.[49]

The mutiny of the Kwangsi military leaders who had brought Sun to power in Canton gave the movement's opposition an opportunity to strike. The armored brigade, along with virtually every other element of the new Party Army, was caught away in eastern Kwangtung and would have to fight its way back to Canton. Teng Jun-ch'i, the Cantonese army leader, desperately needed troops to combat the Kwangsi rebels and sent his recruiting officer into Kwangning. His officer found a quick solution in the absorption of Li Chi-yuan's three-battalion-strong personal army that had retreated to the west of Kwangning city to Shentung to gather strength.[50] Teng's sergeant recognized the value of well-trained and well-armed troops, and Li Chi-yuan saw the benefits of an official commission in the Cantonese army. The magistrate, Ts'ai Huo-p'eng, remained aloof. The peasant associations naturally wished to put a stop to the rebellion, which had forced a premature end to the first Eastern Expedition. They got some further financial support from Canton to build their own self-defense army.

The stage was set for treachery. As the Kwangsi troops retreated from Canton in defeat before the returning Party Army, they passed up the valley to Chiangt'un, where Chou Ch'i-chien had arrayed his peasant troops. For five days (July 7-11, 1925) Chou's poorly armed peasant force held off the entire Kwangsi army at Chiangt'un and awaited relief from the Cantonese. Li Chi-yuan had his revenge. When Chou ran out of ammunition and surrendered, Li could pick up the pieces and once again rehabilitate the county.[51] In this way also, scarcely two years later, Chiang Kai-shek would liberate a Shanghai whose Communist movement had been decimated while he waited outside.

Yet the Kwangning Peasant Association held on through the summer of 1925, even after the August assassination of its protector, Liao Chung-k'ai. While Canton's attention was diverted to the second Eastern Expedition in October, Li Chi-yuan once again sought, but was denied, the post of county magistrate. There were some encouraging phenomena in late 1925. As elsewhere in Kwangtung, the old county leadership trimmed its sails to the new revolutionary winds. Many older, more conservative men joined the peasant associations and spouted their praise. The Kuomintang party, which at the fall of the Chiang blockhouses in February 1925 had not existed even as a tiny cell, began to grow. The county party office established in the fall of 1925 numbered thirty-one members by the end of the year; twenty-four of these were classed as peasants. The county began to pull together to keep down the threat of banditry; the old Popular Corps was allowed to reorganize itself under the name of Joint Corps (Lien-t'uan), apparently under new leadership.

But these phenomena were not in fact entirely favorable to the peasant movement. The rise of the association to its new position as an official mass organization increased its responsibility to the state. It was called upon many times to help fill the quota of national expedition funds being collected by the provincial government. The new Kuomintang in 1926 began to absorb more and more merchants and professionals who were better at raising funds than the peasant members. The new peace-keeping alliance of the Joint Corps did not view with favor Communist attempts to reduce rents in districts outside the central axis. Though the movement was able to hold its own through the winter and spring of 1926, it was not prepared for the effects of rising disorder in the villages, a disorder that fed on the basic uncertainty of the county's future.

In October 1925 the Divine Strike moved its headquarters from the northern hills into the lower Suichiang valley below the county seat where it began systematically to pirate river traffic. The cancer spread slowly, then more rapidly in the spring of 1926. It became clear that Canton would not be willing to intervene again in Kwangning to support the associations.[52] Encouraged by the government's inaction, the secret society leadership, including the same Ch'en Chu-t'ing who was purportedly won over to the peasant movement side in late 1924, forged a new alliance with Teng Jun-ch'i's garrison army. This new grouping, which called itself the general office for the West River, planned to storm the county seat in April 1926; and its military leader, declaring himself to be the true son of heaven in ancient rebellious style, swore publicly to destroy the movement's small army and the associations. Though this plan failed, the Divine Strike did manage to wipe out the Lokang Peasant Association.[53] Again in late May a number of villages to the south of the original peasant movement area were raided, one by one, and their leading cadres shot. The peasants down river began to leave their homes before the advancing terror. From June 15 to 19, 1926, the soldiers rampaged through the county, burning and pillaging in dozens of villages. By the end of June the society rebels, not very vigorously opposed by the garrison, occupied the entire west bank of the Suichiang for dozens of miles and raided across the river at will.

Chou Ch'i-chien reported candidly in late fall, after a concerted drive to win back lost territory for his peasant association that his men were able to operate in only twelve of Kwangning's twenty-six districts. Many of his associations in outlying districts had become bandit associations on his own admission — units that owed him no allegiance. He wrote that bandits had become the central problem for the peasant movement. Chou struggled desperately to develop his feeble armed force and to reregister his entire membership.

The Communist reaction was one that would be repeated many times in the future when crises, real or imagined, were at hand: Chou ordered all of his operatives to abandon their bureaucratic desks and get down into the countryside. He gave several cogent reasons for his order: the desire to stay out of the way of the military, then attempting to surround and exterminate the bandits; to bring the peasants to recognize them; to regenerate mass interest in the peasant associations. But more poignantly, this, perhaps the first *hsia-fang*[54] in Chinese Communist history, the move to the villages had an exhilarating effect. "This point is amusing," he wrote for the private consumption of his comrades in the central peasant bureau. "Two days after [T'an] Hung-shan went back to his home village, his chronic old illness virtually disappeared. [Lo] Kuo-chieh and [T'an] Hung-ch'i fattened up from their sallow urban states. The gloomy visage of P'an Yueh-fang brightened like a light . . . We seem to be competent again!"[55]

Despite the new confidence, however, the task was too great. Before Chou's report could be published, the associations had been crushed on orders of the Canton military commander Li Chi-shen, executed by his erstwhile ally Teng Jun-ch'i. The potent military force imported to suppress bandit disorder in Kwangning found it far easier to side with the local gentry, the local Kuomintang, and the local underworld to suppress the associations.

In spite of the outcome in 1926-1927, Kwangning, even more than Haifeng, was the showplace of the movement in the early years of the Communist-KMT collaboration. Starting with only the barest notions of how a mass organization should be built—largely on the lines of the craft labor unions of Canton to which many of the peasant organizers belonged—the Kwangning movement went through a process of trial and error toward a procedure they thought would be effective in other counties as well. Its experiences were written up in detail and distributed to students at the Peasant Movement Institute and elsewhere.

There are two notable facets to Chou Ch'i-chien's procedure: how to deal with the peasantry and their enemies in the home county and how to deal with the revolutionary authorities sent out from Canton. It was characteristic of the Kwangtung movement as a whole, and of Kwangning in particular, to consider the Canton problem more important than the local one.

Of course there were some guidelines for bringing the masses into the struggle. The principles of constant exposure through lectures, mass meetings, and circuit riding speech tours, which had been practiced in Haifeng, were brought to bear in Kwangning as well. Moreover there appeared an elaborate set of stratagems, often of the most obvious sort, to involve the ordinary peasant in struggle and to convince him against his well-conditioned judgment that he did in fact hold the strength of the majority in his hands. That any intelligent villager could have seen clearly that it was not in fact his own exercise of power that brought the blockhouses down and the landlords to their knees, but rather that of the soldiers from Canton, was not sufficient reason to neglect to make the claim. It was part of the mystique of the movement that the national revolution needed the masses and not vice versa. There was even an element of truth in the belief, since the impressively well staged demonstrations of comradeship for the arriving troops from the capital more than once helped to earn the support of the soldiers.

But the bulk of the Kwangning report is devoted not to the masses but to negotiations with the enemy and dealings with questionable friends. The movement made and rejected allies at an alarming rate, constantly accepting the support of figures on the basis of a common loyalty to the Kuomintang then denouncing them with the Canton authorities for failing to come up to movement standards of revolutionariness. Those standards shifted through time: Li Chi-yuan failed to permit the associations to make themselves independent of the provincial administration; Ts'ai Huo-p'eng refused to throw the county authority behind the new rent reduction campaign; Lu Chen-liu attempted to talk peace once the battle lines were drawn.

In each instance the peasant movement forced the revolutionary authorities in Canton to decide between them and the new opponent. The efforts of persuasion expended on Canton are not well documented, and the fact probably is that during the successful rise of the Kwangning movement little real persuasion was necessary. The big decisions were probably made by the movement's angel, Liao Chung-k'ai. Nevertheless on practically every issue it was felt necessary to send representatives back to ask for advice or help—the latter in the form of the essential dismissal or the dispatch of effective troops.

This dependence on the Canton government comes through most strongly in the Kwangning report. Thus it was that lessons drawn from the 1924 experiences were extremely dangerous in the latter phases of the movement since those lessons were reduced to the simple conclusion that victory depends ultimately on a favorable political situation. The thought that once the situation in Canton shifted the mass organizations would be at the mercy of the powerful local opposition forces they had generated appears to have been unthinkable. The possibility that the Divine Strike or the gentry-landlord paramilitary forces that appeared to collapse with the fall of the T'anpu blockhouses might stage a comeback at a time when Canton was unable or unwilling to supply the necessary suppression forces was not anticipated. In fact this is precisely what occurred in mid-1926 in Kwangning when what had been the most promising peasant movement in the province was brought to its knees.

What is astonishing about the movement's enemies in Kwangning is the extent of the development of informal paramilitary organization. Important gentry families such as the Chiangs or the Hwangs had private armies that numbered in the hundreds at their command. They could retreat in the face of adversity to elaborate fortifications in outlying villages. Should they require greater strength, they needed only to tour the surrounding villages where armed men were available for the asking. There was in addition a military religion, the Great Knives or Divine Strike, which spread its influence through a combination of Taoist mysticism and practical military self-defense training. The balance of local military might in the county ultimately had to rely on the preemption of one or more of these forces.

Having alienated the local military force—the gentry-controlled Popular Corps—the peasant movement had no alternative but to seek other military allies. P'eng P'ai's suggestion that the Divine Strike be won over to form a part of the peasant army was far-sighted. It foreshadowed the successful use of the secret society armies in some other counties in Kwangtung and particularly under Mao Tse-tung in Hunan. But in Kwangning, as in Kaoyao down the river and many other counties in China later, the societies proved to be totally unreliable allies.

Kwangning provides us with a lesson in the geography of Chinese rural politics. The movement got its start in the market town of Chiangt'un, well into the forbidding limestone terrain northeast of the county seat. The location was selected presumably both because it was the seat of the richest clans and was far from the county capital. Just as in Red Hills in Haifeng, one of the periodic market towns became the base from which to expand. Any larger population center would be difficult to control; any smaller one would provide no base. And the periodic market nature of the *hsu* (*yueh* in the East River area) meant that every week or ten days peasants from all the surrounding villages would make their way to the town occupied by the association.

The prominent landlord families in Chiangt'un and T'anpu later became a liability and those markets fell outside the safe peasant area. The movement fell back into the towns nearer to the county seat—Shekang and Kuloying—and left the distant hills to the control of opposing forces. This pattern of control over market towns took advantage of the natural regions of the peasant economy and tended to ignore the direct control of county administrative power. It was a pattern that lasted consistently throughout the peasant movement period and well into the early growth phase of the Chinese soviets in the late twenties.

But there was no conception at this point of independent territorial control for the movement. All activities focused on making the associations into a county-level power and ultimately on controlling the county government itself. In the absence of an independent peasant military force—Ch'en Po-chung's efforts to create a peasant army were tokens only—this concentration meant that the movement was at the mercy not of the masses but of their superiors. The failures of Kwangning taught that a peasant movement cannot succeed without disciplined, determined, and reliable military leadership. But it would be years before the Communists learned this important lesson in revolution.

9

THE FACE
OF THE ENEMY:
HUA COUNTY, 1926

By mid-1926 the rapidly moving forces of revolution had left Kwangtung a political backwater. Chiang Kai-shek, now Sun Yat-sen's unanointed heir, had turned his Whampoa army into a great northern expedition force well on its way to conquering the Yangtze valley to the north. The province around Canton, now unified by the success of the last great campaign against Ch'en Chiung-ming in late 1925, had been left to the leadership of largely Cantonese military forces and to a handful of left-behind recent converts to the Kuomintang cause. No longer the capital of the national revolution, Canton was becoming its great rear area.

The peasant movement's local fortunes in mid-1926 reflected this change in revolutionary politics. For a brief period in late 1925 many Communists hoped for a rapid consolidation of rural power under their leadership. The Haifeng movement resumed its past glories with P'eng P'ai's return to his East River home. The provincial peasant association continued to expand its roster of association members, and the Hunanese Mao Tse-tung as principal of the Peasant Movement Institute continued to train young Cantonese and his own fellow provincials for work as agitators.

But by summer 1926 the movement had lost its momentum in

Kwangtung. Its advocate and protector, Liao Chung-k'ai, had been assassinated; its pipeline into KMT politics, the central peasant bureau, had been purged of its top Communists after Chiang Kai-shek's March 20, 1926 coup; its local associations were increasingly the rivals, not the vanguard, of expanding KMT branches and local government authorities. Nowhere were these debilities more apparent or more damaging than in the suburban environs of Canton.

The peasant movement's crisis in Hua county, a commuter train ride from the city, thrilled readers of the Canton press for three months in the late summer and early autumn of 1926. That tiny county differed from two other centers of peasant movement activity—Haifeng and Kwangning—in several respects. The two previous cases, being isolated in the East and the West River regions, remained remote from revolutionary authority, but Hua county was a part of the Canton metropolitan region intimately linked to the provincial capital for which it was already a vegetable garden suburb. Alluvial rather than mountainous, producing paddy rice rather than fish, salt, or lumber, a day's walk from the city, Hua tested the peasant movement's ability to expand and flourish in densely populated lowland China.

Flourish it did in the heyday of expansion. Peasant associations in Hua blossomed after the rain of early interest in rural organization. In mid-August 1924 the central peasant bureau reported that of the forty-seven associations set up in the first six months, fourteen were located in Hua County.[1]

Organizers from Hua had attended the Peasant Movement Institute—the most prominent being Liang Po-yü of the second class—and returned in 1924 and 1925 to spread the associations into the villages near the county seat, much as had their fellow students in Kwangning at the same time. Not so surprisingly, the district where they penetrated first became the strongest source of later opposition. The market town of P'ingshan, rather like the Kwangning town of Chiangt'un, was by 1926 the major base of antimovement forces. An incident in mid-1926 that pitted the movement against its local enemies much resembled its predecessor. But the contrastingly indifferent response of the Canton military and political authorities revealed how much Communist influence in high circles had diminished.

The incident began with a confusing series of alarms in the Canton newspapers in the last week of August. On August 27 a front-page headline shouted "Corps bandits destroy peasant association in Hua county; situation worsening." A day later the Kwangtung Provincial Peasant Association published a telegram declaring an emergency and predicting the impending collapse of the county's association and all its mass movements. The local KMT party office in Hua county reported twenty-five hundred villagers homeless after three days of arson and shooting. Finally on August 30 a dozen bedraggled refugees marched into the Kuomintang's central headquarters and demanded action to stop the local violence.[2]

Clearly the peasant movement was in grave trouble. But what was the cause and who was at fault? The newspaper accounts and refugees invariably mentioned the Popular Corps and one of its local officers, Chiang Hsia-yen, as the major troublemakers. But beyond the charges that Chiang and his men had attacked peasant organizations, killed KMT members, and looted a dozen villages, there was little explanation.[3] As the newspaper drama unfolded it became apparent that Canton itself, with its multiplex of power centers and interests, remained unable to resolve this ultimate issue of causation.

The Kwangtung Provincial Peasant Association's sense of urgency was greater than that of any other revolutionary group in Canton. The defeat of peasant forces in Hua county so close to the capital by a Popular Corps with connections to more conservative Cantonese forces would mean the end of the peasant movement. Its general appeal to the peasant associations to rally to the cause, hold immediate meetings to discuss aid for the Hua peasant comrades, send telegrams to the government and the party offices, and contact the revolutionary masses so they could make a united response underlined the seriousness of its attitude. Only by standing together could the peasant movement guarantee that the national government would keep its promise to protect the peasant associations.

But where in early 1925 the association could count on the support of Liao Chung-k'ai and leftist armymen to support their request for military aid, it now had to deal with a caretaker central party office under Chiang Kai-shek's protégé, Ch'en Kuo-fu, and a general headquarters in Canton under the former Kwangsi warlord, Li Chi-shen.

The arrival of the refugees from Hua county into Canton coincided with the noisy celebration of an anniversary in the party head-quarters. Confronted by a band of weeping peasants, the party authorities passed a resolution protesting the behavior of the alleged villain, Chiang Hsia-yen, and demanding that the national government and the general headquarters send troops, including peasant self-defense units from other nearby counties, to quell the disorder.[4]

The general headquarters appeared somewhat less moved. When the peasant delegation first arrived, the general headquarters sent them to plead their case directly with the army corps responsible for the Hua county area (the Second Army, also under Li Chi-shen's command). After several days of discussion and some prodding from the county authorities, the headquarters decided to assign one of its own units, stationed a hundred miles north along the railway, to the locality. The affair had become one that affected the entire rear area. But unlike the party and the association, the general headquarters deliberately skirted the question of blame for the outbreak, omitted the name of Chiang Hsia-yen, and stressed the importance more of keeping the peace behind the front than of administering justice to the wronged peasants.

The reason for the general headquarters hesitation soon became obvious. Any firm position on the guilt of one of the parties would risk confrontation with their superiors in Canton—the peasant association on the one hand and the powerful Popular Corps command on the other. This latter organization, set up to bring order to the burgeoning provincial militia in 1925, was headed by a formidable Cantonese former warlord, the underworld chieftain Li Fu-lin, himself now tenuously tied to the military leader of Kwangtung, Li Chi-shen. The Hua county incident risked escalation into a major conflict between two main segments of the provincial bureaucracy.

To avoid this confrontation the party office demanded a meeting between the potential opponents. Significantly, the gathering took place in the corps command offices rather than in the association offices. The head of the provincial peasant association, Lo Ch'i-yuan, and the central peasant bureau secretary, Ch'en K'o-wen, were joined there by Wu Kuan-ch'i, who represented the corps command.

Wu was the headmaster of a small military school located between Canton and Hua county where he supplied training to future members of the Popular Corps. The descendant of one of the grand families of a part of Kwangtung famous for its scholarship in the former Manchu dynasty, he was a devout Buddhist and a strict military disciplinarian. Wu would soon become the peasant movement's major adversary as the incident unfolded.[5]

Wu greeted the peasant leaders in his spacious office inside the general headquarters building. He stressed the complexity of the Hua county incident, explaining that there were bandit connections on both sides of the dispute. The association chief, Lo Ch'i-yuan, pressed him for proof of peasant movement complicity with the underworld but could not obtain a reply. Lo urged Wu to send a government force to handle the situation, threatening to organize a posse of peasant self-defense armies from the surrounding counties if he did not. But Wu remained unmoved, insisting that the newspaper and refugee reports remained heavily biased and inaccurate.

With the facts in dispute, the only alternative was a thorough investigation, the results of which might be used to persuade Wu's superiors in the general headquarters and the KMT central authorities of the rightness of the peasant cause. The committee would have to include a member of the command, even Wu Kuan-ch'i himself, as well as representatives of the provincial peasant bureaucracy. Its chairman would be Teng Liang-sheng, a prominent member of the provincial peasant association. The case was important enough for the Communists to call in their most famous peasant leader, P'eng P'ai, from Haifeng to represent the movement.

P'eng P'ai instinctively distrusted the entire procedure. He was told to appear at eight o'clock on the morning of September 1, 1926, at the Kwangsi Hall to meet the other members of the committee and depart for the train station. The guard at the gate refused him entrance on the grounds that he did not look official. A half-hour later armed bodyguards escorted him into Wu Kuan-ch'i's presence. P'eng found three men in military dress in the room, accompanied by four civilian bodyguards with revolvers in their hands. Of the three officers, one was of higher rank, fiftyish, tall and lean, with a small face adorned with old-fashioned gold-rimmed spectacles. He wore an inch-long mustache and an ancient Ch'ing dynasty military uniform, minus the monarchical red collar and covered with greasy stains. P'eng, always a snappy dresser, instantaneously disliked Wu Kuan-ch'i for his attire, if not for his politics.[6]

His trust did not grow during the investigators' brief half-hour train ride from the north station in Canton to the stop in Hua county. Wu insisted that his sources proved the peasant associations in Hua were thoroughly bandit in nature. He needled P'eng to tell him more about the deeds of the "peasant corps" in the East River, over which P'eng was the acknowledged chieftain. When P'eng described how the Haifeng associations were now working on improving food grain production, education, and reforestation, Wu teasingly suggested P'eng should visit his own village near Canton and give them a few pointers. Arriving in Hua county station, Wu insisted that the investigating committee move immediately to P'ingshan, the main stronghold of the Popular Corps. Finally Wu presented P'eng a document, the draft of an edict to be issued in the name of Chiang Kai-shek, that blamed both the Popular Corps and the peasant forces for insubordination.

To allow the investigation to work out of P'ingshan, P'eng saw immediately, would repeat his tactical error in Kwangning a year earlier when he had permitted the government troops to make their first contact with the local militia instead of with the peasant forces. Moreover, allowing the edict to be issued risked grouping the peasant forces with its enemies as equally at fault in the popular mind. P'eng even bridled at the use of the term peasant corps instead of the preferred Peasant Self-Defense Army. Momentarily forgetting that the origins of the Canton peasant armies lay in Sun Yat-sen's 1924 policy of permitting workers, peasants, and merchants to form their own military units, P'eng wanted to demand that the term be corrected in future proclamations.[7]

On both these points P'eng won the support of the young military man assigned to lead the investigating committee's small armed contingent. This man, Lei Te, had been a squad leader in the bloody pacification of Hsiangshan county a few months earlier and boasted that he had summarily shot a number of unruly militiamen in that incident. Together Lei and P'eng insisted that, to be fair, the investigation would proceed from a neutral village halfway between the Popular Corps headquarters and that of the peasant association. Thus the team proceeded the next day to a spot halfway between P'ingsan and Chiuhu, in fact, a spot well within the area under Peasant Army control. The investigators sent messages to both sides in the dispute and to the county officials under the magistrate and proclaimed a cease-fire until some settlement could be reached.

The brief respite in the neutral village gave P'eng P'ai time to reflect on the novelty of the situation. He knew more about the alleged villain Chiang Hsia-yen than he admitted in public. Chiang Hsia-yen, like P'eng's Haifeng nemesis, Wang Tso-hsin, had once taught the classics to the unlettered warlord Ch'en Chiung-ming, now in disgrace and exile in Hong Kong. Since Ch'en was now thought to be raising funds for the enemy of the Northern Expedition, Wu P'ei-fu, P'eng might try to make him a target for establishing Chiang's guilt by association.

But unlike Wang Tso-hsin and unlike the movement's enemies in Kwangning county, Chiang had developed extensive contacts within the Kuomintang bureaucracy in Canton as well. When in mid-1924 Chiang organized a Hua County Landlord Protection Association to resist the first incursions of the peasant movement, he relied heavily on the financial support of the urban Merchants' Corps. When the Merchants' Corps was disarmed by Sun Yat-sen in late 1924 and after several assassination attempts (one of them successful) on leaders of the Hua County Peasant Association in early 1925, Chiang retreated to Canton and developed friends in the emerging provincial bureaucracy of the Popular Corps command under the underworld leader Li Fu-lin. The right-wing putsch of March 20, 1926, in Canton encouraged Chiang to return home and begin organizing what he called bandit suppression. On April 14 he staged an attempted coup against the Hua County Peasant Association and fled back to Canton after the failure. Only a few days before the latest incident Chiang returned to Hua county, bought the services of an additional four or five hundred recruits for his P'ingshan Popular Corps, and launched the August 27 attack on one of the weaker villages under Communist control. He simultaneously sought through his urban friends to prevent the dispatch of P'eng's group and to encourage the assignment of other Popular Corps units to Hua county. P'eng P'ai's problem thus was to discredit the behavior of a man with influential support among Canton military circles.[8]

The most obvious tactic was to defame Chiang by describing his troops' actrocities. P'eng described how Chiang's men burned and looted the villages they attacked, even wrecking the ceramic cookstoves and breaking the chopsticks. The villages attacked on August 27 belonged to the Hakka minority, and Chiang's Punti (Cantonese) men did not hesitate to rape and pillage the homes of the "foreigners," walking off with all the farming tools and livestock they could handle. Although P'eng had his own evidence, gained through peasant movement agents, of such military wantonness, he still needed proof that would convince the Canton authorities and his coinvestigators that Chiang's Popular Corps was the main group at fault in the incident.[9]

New evidence of the forces at work was not long in coming. On the morning of September 2, P'eng, Wu Kuan-ch'i, and the government troops broke camp to move into the disputed area east of the small town of P'ingshan. When they reached the region at midmorning, they learned that a Popular Corps force had only an hour before attacked the periodic market town of T'ienho and was on its way to the peasant association's stronghold, the village of Chiuhu. A company of government troops sent to T'ienho to reconnoiter was halted by a motley looking mob of three hundred combat-experienced men who had just finished looting the marketplace. Commander Lei Te marched the remainder of his force at double time to T'ienho and received a counterattack in waves of several hundred men supported by old-fashioned grapeshot cannons. When the government troops retook the market town and P'eng P'ai and his fellow investigators settled into the schoolhouse for the day, evidence of widespread looting in T'ienho quickly came to light. Moreover, eyewitnesses claimed that the looters had announced they were fighting the revolutionary army.

P'eng P'ai was convinced that the perpetrators were mercenaries of the Popular Corps leader Chiang Hsia-yen. But how could he prove it? Wu Kuan-ch'i insisted that the armed men were merely acting in their own self-defense, that three men who had been caught stealing were in fact removing their own cattle, and that the Popular Corps had not been involved. P'eng took up the challenge. The looting lasted four hours and thus required confederates within the market to prevent news from leaking out. The three men had been seen opening the village gates to the band of armed men earlier in the morning and were known to have gossiped maliciously about the Kuomintang and the peasant associations.

The investigators argued their points through the evening and again the following morning, with P'eng P'ai insisting on an immediate and public censure of the local Popular Corps and Wu Kuanch'i demanding that the looters, who were still in the vicinity, be disarmed before further action be taken. P'eng suspected that the mo-tive for Wu's delay was to give the Popular Corps time to regroup elsewhere, perhaps closer to their home villages, but the previous day's crimes could not go unpunished. By 10:30 in the morning the entire expeditionary force prepared to storm the looters' positions.

The lay of the land was not very different from Kwangning. The looters chose as their stronghold a blockhouse less than a mile from T'ienho that had been built centuries before to defend the interests of the Chiang clan against bandits and marauders. Though he had no proof, P'eng P'ai suspected that Chiang Hsia-yen had incited his clansmen to believe that the revolutionary troops were outside invaders like the English troops, who had roamed through Hua county in 1841 at the opening of the first opium war.[10] Before the expeditionary forces had moved a hundred meters out of T'ienho toward the blockhouse they were pinned down by fierce resisting fire.

P'eng, Wu, and Commander Lei ducked a crossfire as the Popular Corps from another nearby village entered the firefight. Government troops, braving oncoming bullets, charged the tower and threw grenades through the windows only to find that the enemy had climbed the stairs to fire on them from the upper stories of the blockhouse. They attempted to set fires but were frustrated by the sturdy stone construction and by the peasant defenders' uncanny ability to douse their fires with stored water. The defendants sent the women to the top of the tower to beat on gongs and cry for help from surrounding villages.

In just this way villagers had been summoned to fight the English a few miles to the south in 1841. But this time the enemy was a new Chinese government contending for imperial power. Soon peasants from all around had come and many were pleading with the defenders to surrender and throw down their guns. Only when Commander Lei managed to set a roaring fire did a peasant woman finally descend and unlock the gate. To P'eng P'ai's chagrin, there were no more than a dozen people in the blockhouse, more women than men. The fall of the blockhouse took seven hours and netted only a few weapons. On the one hand, P'eng had his evidence that the Popular Corps was willing to resist not only the peasant movement but the Canton government as well. But on the other, his enemy's tricks caused him and the government troops to appear overzealous and unconcerned about the hearts and minds of the local villagers who sent the women to fight.

It seemed apparent that P'eng P'ai's expedition had stepped into the middle of a small civil war raging in the county. The county magistrate, who happened onto the blockhouse scene late in the afternoon in his elegant sedan chair, tried to explain the background of the events and his efforts to bring peace. It was only his entreaties to both sides in late August, he claimed, that had produced the shaky cease-fire that preceded P'eng's arrival. The old man, a veteran of the 1911 revolution in Canton, took pride in his earlier works as the minister of finance of the provincial government. Reduced to a mere county chief, he found taming deep-seated local passions more difficult than high finance or social reform. His reputation as reformer of Canton's brothels hardly qualified him to solve Hua county's strife.[11] But he was determined to remain neutral, at least until he could learn what solution his superiors in Canton might prefer. P'eng P'ai could extract no more support from the magistrate than the assurance he had not yet made up his mind who were bandits and who were not.

Wu Kuan-ch'i, for his part, could not be pleased with the outcome of the fight for the blockhouse. His purpose in joining the commission was to demonstrate the righteousness of the local cause against the Communists, not to defeat them in battle. The looting and wanton behavior of his side and the government forces' open defiance at the blockhouse, however properly motivated, could only reflect badly on his cause. The following day he borrowed one of the prisoners taken at the blockhouse and walked to the Popular Corps headquarters in P'ingshan to explain his views.[12]

His prisoner guide preceded him by several minutes, instructed to tell the P'ingshan leaders not to shoot even though Wu was a member of the government investigation commission. On arriving safely, Wu found several hundred corpsmen preparing to do further battle with the official troops. He berated them for their errors of the previous day and urged them to disband lest they clash further with the government. He had been forced, he explained, to go along with the attack on the blockhouse, since otherwise he might have compromised his role as an intermediator. He had thought, he said, that the Popular Corps would realize it was fruitless to struggle against such great odds and would withdraw to their home villages. He recognized that once country people started a fight, they did not know how to stop it. Still, it had been a tactical mistake to lock the blockhouse up and sound the gongs.

Wu claimed credit with the corps leaders for having moderated the Canton officials' demands. He claimed he had prevented the intervention of three hundred Peasant Self-Defense Army troops from Nanhai county; he had prevented attacks on other blockhouses in Hua county; and he was now trying to convince the authorities that the Hua Popular Corps should not be disbanded but only disarmed. He would try to strike a bargain limiting the number of guns turned over and extending the time period for compliance. During his extended plea, Wu arranged to have the military commander of the expedition, Lei Te, invited to the meeting to listen to corps grievances, and the two men retired to T'ienho in the late afternoon, convinced they had won acquiescence in the cease-fire terms.

Overnight, however, hostilities continued. Corpsmen attacked and occupied the peasant association building in Hsiangshan village, and revolutionary government troops retaliated by attacking several more blockhouses near P'ingshan. This fresh violence heightened emotions at the next morning's meeting (September 5). It was hard for the corps to claim it owned only a few dozen guns when there had been firefights extending over many kilometers. How could the Canton side be credible when only yesterday Wu Kuan-ch'i had promised no further attacks on blockhouses? The meeting resolved that the corps would turn over ninety weapons over a twenty-four-hour period after the cease-fire, during which both sides would inspect the disputed area between P'ingshan and T'ienho.

On this inspection trip P'eng P'ai made his only convert in Hua county. Wu Kuan-ch'i's aide-de-camp, Wei Jao-ch'in, who had joined the group back in Canton, volunteered to serve as P'eng's personal bodyguard, the peasant leader being as usual unarmed. While they walked along toward Yuant'ien village they discussed revolution, the people's interest, and the behavior of Wei's erstwhile superior. The simple soldier, admitting that he was willing to go along with the revolution, asked P'eng to enlighten him. P'eng's reply, truncated and unimpressive in the telling, was that the corps was after all set up by a small number of landlords and gentry who hoped to use it to obtain their own private advantage. Wei Jao-ch'in admitted that he had always been uneasy about the way Wu Kuan-ch'i incessantly praised the Popular Corps and cursed the peasant movement. He then confessed that when he heard Wu Kuan-ch'i's ingratiating appeal to the corps leaders of the day before (it was in fact Wei who made the essence of Wu's speech available to the peasant movement leaders), he had become convinced that Wu was a double-dealer who was betraying the revolution.

When the two arrived at Yuant'ien and surveyed the desolate scene, Wei's conviction was confirmed and he dutifully recorded in his notebook all the sad details. The poverty of the village, the complaints about high taxes, the starvation on the faces of the peasant children, and the suffering of the feeble and elderly in the scene of rural violence affected him deeply. They apparently had some effect on the peasant revolutionary too, for P'eng P'ai soon complained that he had not eaten or slept sufficiently for several days, excused himself, and returned to the base camp at T'ienho.

As it had been in his Kwangning experience, luck was with the Haifeng agitator. Shortly after P'eng left, Wei Jao-ch'in, proceeding toward corps-occupied territory, was surrounded near Loch'ang by a band of thirty armed corpsmen and told to drop his weapon. He started to tell them he was there with Wu Kuan-ch'i to help them but was summarily shot in the stomach. His chronicler adds that he lived long enough to reach P'eng P'ai's side and dictate a will.

The other party of inspectors, which included Wu Kuan-ch'i and his other aide-de-camp, Kuan Yuan-chuang, was more fortunate.[13] At five in the afternoon on their way back to P'ingshan, this second team heard the shooting from Loch'ang. Wu Kuan-ch'i hurriedly decided that he was needed in the county seat, if not in the provincial capital, and sped away. His aide, Kuan, was left behind to return through the no-man's land to T'ienho. Passing through Loch'-ang, he too was captured by corpsmen. He attempted to explain that he was one of Wu Kuan-ch'i's men, but this seemed to anger the corpsmen even more. They searched him, took his money and other possessions, and lined him up facing south against a firing squad. Kuan thought for a moment and decided that his only chance was to drop not Wu's but Chiang Hsia-yen's name: the local corps leader had not been implicated in the efforts to disarm the Popular Corps. Only by presenting the corps squad with two of Chiang Hsia-yen's calling cards did Kuan secure his release. His escape was the cause of much mirth in Peasant Corps headquarters on his return. On an earlier visit to P'ingshan, Kuan had absentmindedly picked up a handful of the corps leader's greeting cards and stuffed them in his kit.[14]

That evening, Lei Te's report to Canton sounded an ominous

note.[15] He said that the commissar of the general headquarters had
been seriously wounded; Wu Kuan-ch'i had gone to the county seat
and it was clear that Wu was shielding the counterrevolutionaries.
Chiang Hsia-yen had seven hundred to eight hundred corps troops
in P'ingshan and T'iehshan alone, he reported, another two hundred
in Hsiangshan, and roughly a thousand in Kaot'ing and Chiangts'un.
They had been forced to delay to get full scouting reports, and Canton might have to send an extra battalion of troops to outflank them
from Hsinchieh.

Meanwhile Wu Kuan-ch'i, in the county seat, had heard of the
shooting of his aide-de-camp. His fears were not for Wei, however,
but that the incident would bring retaliation from Lei Te's battalion,
against which the corps would be no match. He sent an attendant
to fetch his briefcase, which contained a secret weapon: he had
brought along with him a number of letterheads with the imprima-
tur of the central command and Chiang Kai-shek's personal seal already engraved on them. He wrote his own ticket, ordering the battalion commander to hold his troops in T'ienho and await further
orders. Wu ordered him not to do anything on his own and signed
the general commander's name. The letter went out at 6:30 A.M. on
the sixth and prevented Lei from taking any action that day. Wu
Kuan-ch'i, Lei Te must have thought, was in sufficiently high favor
with Chiang Kai-shek so that to disobey him might bring serious difficulties.

Forced to temporize until new orders from Canton arrived, the
revolutionary leaders turned to mass activity. They organized another meeting, a grand celebratory congress of peasants, workers,
merchants, and students. Soldiers, needless to say, joined in as well.
Held in the open marketplace at T'ienho, the proceedings attracted
a number of farmers from the surrounding villages and all the merchants, all of whom openly aired their grievances. Lei Te gave an
impassioned speech. This was no armed conflict, he said, but a
counterrevolutionary attack on the peaceful Peasant Army. There
was concrete evidence that the corps were in collusion with bandits.
The bandits had an ulterior political purpose: Ch'en Chiung-ming
was seeking to stage a comeback. We revolutionary troops, he said,
are determined to stand firm to prevent this occurrence. The audience applauded wildly and filled the air with cheers.[16]

AFTER THE BREAKDOWN of the cease-fire, Wu Kuan-ch'i made his way back to Canton from Hua county. He was accompanied by the county magistrate and more than twenty corps bodyguards. Passing him on the rails of the Canton-Shaokuan railway was a trainload of soldiers, a battalion of the sixtieth regiment, twentieth division of the First Army under the command of Regimental Commander Li Kao. By the evening of the ninth the new battalion was safely lodged in the train station at Hsinchieh.

The afternoon of the next day P'eng P'ai traveled to Hsinchieh to consult with the new arrivals. He learned from the chief of staff that the battalion commander was empowered to negotiate an agreement with the corps based on a six-point memorandum. The six points were to be communicated to the corps leadership by a presumably neutral Hua county figure, Wang Ching-fang.[17] Wang was instructed to bring back the corps' answer by eight o'clock the following morning. P'eng P'ai gave his approval to the six points but attempted, unsuccessfully, to add three of his own. The revolutionaries waited until the next morning at eleven when Wang Ching-fang returned. His answer was to temporize: the corps would accept the conditions provided the revolutionary troops would once again meet them peacefully at P'ingshan, their home base.

When P'eng and his friends arrived at P'ingshan at three in the afternoon on September 11 they found that the corps had prepared a welcome for them. Banners had been painted and bore the slogans "Welcome to the Army of the Revolution." P'eng learned that the main force of the corps had disbanded into the surrounding settlements and in Hsiaopu and Lianglung. Those who had remained behind in P'ingshan market were disguised in civilian clothing and carried no weapons. He decided to call the negotiating meeting for the next day, and the troops settled down for the night.

Meanwhile during the two days that the negotiations were under way the Popular Corps had continued to be active in the outlying villages. In Ch'inglung village an eighty-year-old man was worshipping at a temple when he was approached by several corpsmen. He was not a member of the peasant association, but when he mentioned his discontent with the current wave of violence, he was taken from the temple and summarily executed—shot with eight bullets.

Chu T'ang, a high-ranking officer in Li Chi-shen's entourage and chief of staff of the newly arrived troops, presided over the meeting. But his chairmanship was hardly nonpartisan. After the ritual incantation of the will of Sun Yat-sen, Chu began the meeting by berating the corps representatives. The Popular Corps, he said, had been vicious and brutal. It dared to resist soldiers of the revolutionary government. It brutally murdered a special emissary, Wei Jaoch'in, who was clad in military dress and who explained that he was on a mission for the central government.

> You cannot excuse yourself by pretending this was a misunderstanding. You must realize that the government is not afraid of you. Ask yourselves just how much strength you have? How do you compare with the Kwangsi warlords Yang and Liu whom we defeated easily. Can you top Wu Pe'i-fu in strength? All these were smashed by the government. Do you mean to say you think your little "popular corps" is its match?

But Chu relented:

> For the sake of reconciliation we will not punish this crime too severely. We are not here to negotiate the terms. These conditions have come to us from the national government and are unalterable. There was not in fact much reason to hold this meeting, except that since there might be some misunderstanding about the contents on either side we felt it necessary to discuss them at a meeting.[18]

Regimental Commander Li Kao rose to speak. Reiterating Chu's accusation that the attack on the army and the murder of Wei must have been premeditated, Li added the revealing comment that the way he had determined that the Popular Corps were bandits was that the Popular Corps alone would not have gone so far as to attack his men at T'ienho. He asserted that he had come to the meeting to discuss matters with the corps rather than simply to exterminate them in order to avoid embarrassing the government and because the honorable Mr. Wang Ching-fang was acting as the go-between. He urged the corps leaders to submit without question and threatened, if they failed to do so, to destroy their villages.

Even the county magistrate entered the chorus. Berating the corps for misbehaving during the Northern Expedititon, he likewise urged the representatives of what he called the "Peasant Corps" to accept the imposed terms. He said that he had never had any authority over them and they had never listened to his orders. They created their own mess and must take the responsibility for it.

The six conditions were undeniably harsh. The Popular Corps

would have to compensate the owners of all the houses destroyed before the arrival of the government troops—from $200 to $500 per house. All villages that opened fire on the troops had to surrender 60 percent of their weapons. The corps was required to compensate the family of Mr. Wei Jao-ch'in ($5000) and the families of other injured troops ($500). Between five and ten thousand dollars had to be provided for a school or a library in memory of Wei Jao-ch'in. The murderers and bandit chiefs had to be given into custody or rewards for their capture would have to be raised. Both sides had to agree to terminate the affair on the government's terms. The corps was to be cleaned up and undesirable members expelled. Both sides were to withdraw their sentries. No massing of troops would be permitted unless there was a clear alarm that the villages were being raided by bandits.

Not satisfied with this list of conditions, P'eng P'ai rose to speak. He said that a number of them in the visiting delegation and in their peasant association had investigated this matter. In view of the vicious and criminal behavior of the corpsmen, there was no reason from a truly revolutionary viewpoint not to liquidate them totally. Mr. Wang Ching-fang's assistance in these negotiations had been invaluable, but the would have to insist on adding the following three conditions to the settlement: the Popular Corps should be required to support the families of the peasants they had killed. The losses sustained by the merchants in T'ienho should be reimbursed. And the Popular Corps in the market town of P'ingshan, the center of counterrevolutionary activity, should be dissolved. There was no debate on P'eng's motion so he assumed it passed without debate.

With careful coordination Teng Liang-sheng, representative of the central peasant bureau, rose to amend these recommendations: the corps would have to take care of all refugees and homeless in the incident and would have to turn in *all* their weapons and clear deadlines for the performance of all these stipulations would have to be laid down. Lei Te rose to second and to suggest that the deadlines be strictly enforced in light of the corps' earlier failure to abide by imposed time restraints. With this instruction the county magistrate turned to the corps leaders and asked if they were willing to accept the various points. Given the situation, they could hardly refuse. P'eng P'ai's account is obscure about what happened next. He alleges that when the time came to write down the points of the agreement, only the conditions set out by the central command were actually written. His own stipulations and those of Teng Liang-sheng were somehow forgotten. He protested loudly but only managed to get two of the peasant movement proposals passed. They were included only as an appendix to the general agreement: the compensation for the merchants' losses in T'ienho and the payments to the bereaved families. Clearly the central command was not willing to support peasant movement demands that the corps be emasculated by having its main center destroyed and its weapons wrested away. It did, however, draft a list of the major criminals in the Hua incident with the infamous Chiang Hsia-yen at the head. The P'ingshan conference purported to settle the Hua incident and received a press to this effect in Canton.[19]

But P'eng P'ai, writing to Canton only two days later, saw how tenuous the arrangement with the corps was. There had been no provisions for enforcement of the deal and no time limit set. Within twenty-four hours the revolutionary army units had begun to withdraw to Canton. The corps turned in fifty-four guns, mostly damaged beyond repair, and returned to their old defense lines.

LEFTISTS IN CANTON tried for days to convince themselves the Hua county incident had ended in a victory for the revolution. A great welcoming party held at one o'clock in the afternoon of September 14, for example, brought together more than sixty mass organizations to celebrate the pretended triumph. Red banners proclaimed the virtues of the expeditionary force into Hua county and the evils of the local Popular Corps criminals. Peasant movement politicians from Kuomintang peasant bureau chief Kan Nai-kuang to P'eng P'ai spoke and led the chanting slogans well into the evening.[20] At the center of the banners quietly hung Sun Yat-sen's epitaph: "Until the revolution is won, our comrades must still struggle."

Meanwhile in Hua county on the very same day the second massacre began. Less than two hours after the troops left, a peasant association member named Chiang Chin-i was shot and killed on his way to the periodic market at Shihchiao. Several other peasants going to other markets were accosted, stabbed, and robbed. That evening, as the slogans were being shouted thirty miles to the south in Canton, the houses of several peasant association members in T'aot'-ang village were burned to the ground. Bandits stormed the peasant corps villages of Tach'engchuang and Lingch'ü, but they were repulsed. The local Popular Corps began to spread rumors that Ch'en

Chiung-ming was returning to Kwangtung, that all the labor unions were going to be disbanded, and that all peasant association members would be shot.

September 16 the Hsiangshan market festival was held and the Popular Corps appeared in force. They searched out and arrested persons who had represented the peasant associations—including those who had attended the September 14 party in Canton, men such as Wang Ch'ih, Ju Ping, and K'ung Jung. Ju was the first to be summarily executed. On September 21 over a hundred bandits from the Li-ch'i Popular Corps surrounded and attacked T'uhukang village and abducted an association member named Ch'en, among others. There were numerous such incidents. After the revolutionary army departed, the Hua county corps burned, looted, and kidnapped everywhere. Worst of all, their weapons shipments continued to arrive in preparation for an even greater massacre.

The key to the September situation was the attitude of Li Ssu-yuan, the county magistrate. Without his authority and his commitment of peace-keeping troops, the shaky mid-September truce would not have been possible. Li's attitude in September had been affected in turn by his shock at the brutality of Popular Corps combat, and particularly at their murder of Wei Jao-ch'in.[21] But the movement's influence over Li was only temporary. What was more long lasting was the growth of the Popular Corps in Hua into a far more powerful force. Liang Po-yü, the peasant institute student turned organizer, reported secretly in late September that a number of corps had expanded quickly during the preceding weeks of strain. They soon had disagreements among themselves, which Liang blamed on their absorption of bandit elements, though it may have been simply the pangs of growth; but their internecine struggles fanned the flames of discontent. Not only did the growth of the corps quickly swamp the weak forces of the peasant associations, but the rising level of violence reduced the flow of commerce and trade and thus cut directly into the income of the county offices. Already by October 1926 the localistic forces of Chiang Hsia-yen had won over the magistrate to their side and were on their way to total extermination of the peasant movement's local base.[22]

HUA COUNTY in 1926 was a key test area for the peasant movement strategy. Failure in the Pearl River delta would imply that the movement stood little chance in the countryside near the cities where the majority of the peasant population lived. It would indicate that the threat of leftist government-military intervention would not intimidate local opposition. It would suggest to the centrist and rightist members of the ruling junta that they had little to fear from Communist peasant organizations. Thus the futility of P'eng P'ai's efforts in autumn 1926 drove him toward his revised strategy of insurrection in his native Haifeng in 1927.

P'eng and his comrades drew a number of lessons from the failure. Communists would have to win over to their ranks purely military figures such as Lei Te, who were not members of the party. Mere membership in the National Revolutionary Army would not guarantee the loyalty of armymen to the Communist cause. The peasant movement could no longer assume that the pre-1926 coalition of leftist Kuomintang politicians and Communist organizers had a sympathetic ear in Nationalist military circles. Wu Kuan-ch'i, it appears, had more support in Canton than P'eng P'ai dared publicly admit. At the village level, the peasant movement would be in conflict with the new administrations imposed from above by the provincial authorities. County magistrates and Kuomintang officers had interests in peace keeping and fund raising that conflicted with the aims of the peasant organizers. Finally, Communists would have to arrange it so that the forces of localism and resistance to outside penetration worked in their favor, not against them as in Hua county.

The events of September 1926 in Hua county marked one of the last times the Kuomintang-Communist alliance could agree to take harsh measures against local paramilitary forces in Kwangtung. The reason for the decline of collaboration had little to do with the alleged capitulation of Ch'en Tu-hsiu, the Russian advisers, or the provincial peasant leaders to Chiang Kai-shek. It was not related to any concerted policy of restraint on the peasant movement. The new political alignments in large part drew their strength from the vitality of local Cantonese anti-Communist political forces in the counties and the countryside. There are no signs in Hua county that P'eng P'ai attempted to restrain the associations. There are many, however, that the Popular Corps and other informal and formal police and vigilante groups had sustained a powerful impetus of their own. Knowledge that such groups existed and were fully as capable of accepting leadership and expanding military capabilities as were the radicals spread easily to Canton (and to Hong Kong). The anti-Communist purges of 1927 were based squarely on village peace-keeping forces such as those with which P'eng's delegation did battle in Hua county in the fall of 1926.

10

THE BIRTH OF
A PEOPLE'S WAR:
HAIFENG, 1927

Lin Piao's famous 1965 account of the origins of what he called
people's war gives scant attention to the years before 1928. According to his story, the revolution strategy employed against the Japanese and the Chinese Nationalists was worked out in practice after
1927. Its essential features, the Communist armies, the territorial
bases in remote regions, the battle without lines for the minds of the
rural population, and the united front that abandoned little of
Communist autonomy, were all developed under the brilliant leadership of Mao Tse-tung after he reached the safe haven of Chingkangshan. Although Lin's description of Communist strategies and
work styles is by and large accurate, he is mistaken in dating the origins of these important elements of CCP victory after the rise of
Chairman Mao. In fact it can be argued that the first full practi-
tioner of people's war in the Maoist sense was not Mao or Lin, but
P'eng P'ai of Haifeng.

During the peasant movement period the Communist party came
to accept the importance of involving the peasantry in their revolution, the need for going to the countryside, and the value of fitting
local tactics to national politics. They gradually learned how to
form and maintain independent bases of power. A concept of insur-

rection that did not require urban-based organizations or entangling alliances with non-Communist forces emerged in mid-1927 only to be challenged by the disastrous defeat of Mao Tse-tung's Autumn Harvest Insurrection that same year. But there was one tiny corner of China where all these lessons were drawn briefly together to produce something like people's war in late 1927 and early 1928. The parallels between P'eng P'ai's Haifeng soviet and the militarized insurrectionary communism of Yenan and Hanoi of later decades deserve a moment's attention.

The eastern seacoast of Kwangtung had been more than just the cradle of the peasant movement. Throughout 1925 and 1926 the two counties of Haifeng and Lufeng remained an eastern paradise in the minds of Cantonese revolutionaries. These counties supplied more cadres than any other to the central schools and staff of the peasant movement. They welcomed more warmly annexation by the national government. They went further in distributing the land than any other counties in China during the period. By early 1927 Haifeng was the jewel of the peasant movement and had earned the title of "little Moscow." These accomplishments attested to the vigor of peasant movement organizers in general and P'eng P'ai in particular.

After General Ch'en Chiung-ming forced P'eng out of Haifeng in early 1924, the strength of revolutionary influence in the East River area depended entirely on the ascendency of the Kuomintang's star. P'eng P'ai worked in 1924 on peasant movements like Kwangning's near Canton and on running the central peasant bureau for Sun Yat-sen's party. But his eyes remained on his home county, which he learned of often through an elaborate network of informers, many of the Haifengese in the ricksha and coolie trades in Canton. Back in Haifeng, his comrades from 1923, led by his brother, Han-yuan, continued their work underground. They collected weapons and ammunition to prepare for the military expeditions P'eng repeatedly predicted would be arriving from Canton.

These preparations paid off twice: one in February and March 1925, when Chiang Kai-shek's Party Army, including the armored brigade and guard regiment of Kwangning fame, marched eastward to Swatow through Haifeng. Then once again in October of the same year came a repeat performance of the same campaign. On both occasions the peasant movement supplied informers, mes-

sengers, and porters for the invading armies, and the retreating
troops of Ch'eng Chiung-ming suffered harassment and sabotage at
the hands of movement agents.

After both these successful Eastern Expeditions P'eng P'ai restored the earlier vehicles of his peasant movement. The new mass
organizations of 1925 differed somewhat from the advocacy groups
P'eng had assembled in 1922. They were called by the new four-
character appellation approved by the association charter, instead
of P'eng's archaic sounding *nung hui.* They obtained a potent military force, a militia trained by P'eng's old friend, the Whampoa
graduate Li Lao-kung.[1] The peasant associations also found new
urban allies in labor unions among dye factory workers and black-
smiths in the county town.

Under P'eng's urging in 1925, the social policy of the Kuomintang
government in Haifeng moved far to the left of that in other counties. It was not that the county magistrate, the police or militia officers, or even the Kuomintang county cell secretary were Communists. Rather, the Haifeng prerevolutionary elite was far easier to
discredit in Canton's eyes because of their connection with Ch'en
Chiung-ming. P'eng's policies permitted association levies and con-
fiscations to slide easily from political punishment to economic. The
mass exodus of old scholarly families, businessmen, Christians, and
most bureaucrats connected with Ch'en's regime left their lands un-
managed; so many associations moved easily into land confiscation
and deed burning. P'eng openly used the hunger for land in turn to
attract more peasants into his associations.[2] In these ways Haifeng
bore more resemblance to central Hunan during the Northern Expedition than it did to the central Kwangtung counties where P'eng
also worked during this period.

In some respects P'eng P'ai's success at building mass organizations in 1926 was a mixed blessing. To be sure, P'eng generated
much support by building a student movement out of the few hundred high school students and teachers, by assembling twenty thousand village children into a workers' boys' army modeled on Lenin's
Young Pioneers, and above all by recruiting a Communist party of
several hundred — the largest county organization in China at the
time. But when the split with the Kuomintang came to Kwangtung
in April 1927, many Haifeng Communists clung tenaciously to the
cities and eschewed rural work. Even the tiny city of Haifeng

thought of itself as "little Moscow," the urban center of revolutionary authority, and not as part of Bukharin's world village, where the battle would have to be fought.

P'eng P'ai was in Hankow hundreds of miles away when Haifeng heard of Li Chi-shen's anti-Communist putsch of April 16, 1927. The Haifeng Communists, unlike Mao Tse-tung four months later, had little chance to debate the merits of insurrection. P'eng's brother, the moderate Han-yuan, tried briefly to play for time, even promising Li Chi-shen to arrest his younger brother and deliver him in chains to Canton. But Han-yuan quickly took his movement underground and prepared a coup d'état against the Kuomintang county authorities. He recruited villagers into forty-man units in each village and selected a four-hundred-man Dare to Die Corps to lead them. When munitions sources in Canton dried up, Han-yuan armed his men with bird guns and spears. He set May Day as the target; after that date his failure to contribute the county grain tax due to Canton would reveal a mutinous intent. By two in the morning of May 1 P'eng Han-yuan's force had disarmed the magistrate's police, the salt gabelle guards, and the county police and arrested most of the non-Communist county officials.

In retrospect it was an ideal putsch. The police were disarmed and replaced by a new urban armed force. All taxes were abolished —safely, since the year's revenues were already at hand. Within three days of the seizure, people's courts were operating; within six days several dozen criminals met their ultimate fate, some for no more specific crimes than being bullies, gentry, or officials. Indeed the long list of public enemies of the first government illustrates something of the pervasiveness of non-Communist influence even in "little Moscow" in early 1927: the rebels executed the chief administrative officer, the bailiff, the first district chief, the Swabue city manager, and the salt monopoly chairman in the first round of trials. These men had little to do with Ch'en Chiung-ming's regime of earlier years. They were Kuomintangists first, Cantonese second, and Haifengese third. Their executions marked the cutting of the knot that both bound the Communists to the Kuomintang and Haifeng to the provincial capital.

Despite its swift ruthlessness, the first seizure of Haifeng obeyed the old rules of the collaboration period. The mass meeting of the morning of May Day 1927 was the biggest yet seen in the county of

Haifeng, perhaps inflated by the large and curious crowds of farmers from the surrounding fields. But what was there to say? The only
slogans the Communists felt authorized to issue were the commonplace nostrums of Wuhan: "Wipe out the counterrevolutionaries."
"Support the KMT central party office and the national government." The rest of the Wuhan laundry list was all old reading matter in Haifeng: eliminating the supernumerary taxes, reducing rent
by 25 percent as recommended in the joint conference resolutions of
1926 — these ideas had long since become reality in Haifeng. "Insurrection was for the revolution. But what will we get after it? For that
we had no clear answer," P'eng P'ai later admitted.[3]

P'eng P'ai's later criticism of his comrades' policies during this period focused on their failure to understand the prerequisites of revolutionary political power. First, the government had failed to make
clear what it promised to the peasantry; second, it had failed systematically to decimate the counterrevolution within Haifeng borders. Those who argued against extermination of internal opposition felt that such drastic measures should be taken only as a final
act to prevent the fall of Haifeng from within while under siege from
without. Since the enemy's attack came quickly, there was no time
and not enough people were killed. Third, financial matters were
very poorly handled. When the Communists had to retreat from the
county seat, they took nothing with them. The party had failed to
collect backup funds, so the army would have to live off the land,
P'eng complained.

It is difficult to agree wholly with P'eng's reflection, penned in a
sulphurous anger in early 1928. Radical slogans, political murders,
and heavy extractions, though they later became orthodox dogma
for the soviet, would also become part of its liabilities. Perhaps after
the Communists established their rual independence, terror might
have become a fruitful policy; but in their state of weakness and disarray of May 1927 the escalation of violence would simply have hastened the discrediting of their regime, the growing resistance from
within, and the invasion from outside.

However well Haifeng's domestic crisis had been handled, the
central fact was that the Communists controlled only two of Kwangtung's ninety-odd counties and had virtually declared war on all the
rest. P'eng Han-yuan fell out of touch with the Communist movements in neighboring counties. His party comrades in Canton issued

and revised ill-considered plans for insurrections, plans that usually depended on unreliable left Kuomintang majors and colonels. Haifeng Peasant Army leader Wu Chen-min nearly staged an insurrection in neighboring Huiyang county but halted when a supposedly friendly garrison commander turned on the Communists on May 7 and executed several left-leaning battalion commanders. Unable to expand outward, could the Communists even hold their position in Haifeng?

The debate among the Communists over how to handle the inevitable retaliation from Canton revealed the uncertainty of leadership. Most of the non-Haifeng Communists appointed by the Canton region favored abandoning the county and heading for Wuhan. Local Communists, among them the P'engs' old comrades Lin Tao-wen and Wu Chen-min, argued for defense of the people's government. It was a classic dispute, one that would occur again among Chinese Communists when the Nationalists threatened to surround the Kiangsi base in 1934 and in 1947 as Chiang Kai-shek again prepared to invade the Communist capital at Yenan. Haifeng decided, unfortunately, to make a stand. When the Nationalist general Liu Ping-ts'ui marched on Haifeng for the third time since 1924, Lin Tao-wen's Peasant Army tried to check him at a mountain pass called Fenshui west of Haifeng. Lin's three hundred peasant troops, hampered by homemade ammunition and poor timing, were quickly overrun during a tropical rainstorm on the night of May 9 and Liu Ping-ts'ui easily recaptured Haifeng. In the future Haifeng's leaders would have little faith in the conventional defenses of their territory. The alternative, already broached in these discussions of early May 1927, was to station professional troops in specially protected bases, engage the enemy only when he entered a trap, and rely on well-prepared local populations for information, supplies, and manpower. The strategy of people's war was beginning to take shape.

FROM THE MIDDLE of May to the middle of September 1927 Haifeng county resembled central Vietnam in the early 1960s. Too remote from the capital to arouse immediate metropolitan response, the county suffered from what in normal times had been the advantage of distance. After his April anti-Communist coup Li Chi-shen built up his base in Canton, purged the Communist mass organizations in the Pearl delta, and negotiated with Chiang Kai-shek against the Wuhan regime. Although he, like the Saigon generals, had little interest in seeing his eastern reaches fall to the Communist enemy, he wanted to prevent other rival military politicians from enhancing their power at his expense. Like the I Corps area in the narrow neck of central Annam, Hai-Lufeng was too remote to invade, yet too close to abandon.

In Hunan after May 21 the anti-Communist generals who ran the province systematically swept every county and purged it of radical elements. But Canton's half-hearted commitment to the eastern reaches of its province offered room for the Communist party to continue to operate. Here again, Kwangtung's relatively high degree of development — the clear articulation of competing interests in Canton, the elaborateness of the metropolitan political game, the preoccupation of the elite with the central, primate city — made it less likely that a military challenge would be met. Canton's inaction would continue so long as major defeats were not imminent. Where in Vietnam the fall of a provincial capital was the only event that could trigger a massive response from Saigon, it would take the loss of the county seat to attract Canton's retaliation. So long as that threshhold was not crossed, the Communists would be free to develop their rural base in the villages. In the summer of 1927, in the aftermath of the abortive May putsch, this essential prerequisite of people's war — the implicit agreement to divide the contested area into hostile rural and urban armed camps — emerged in Haifeng county.

After the defeat at Fenshui, several weeks elapsed before the Communists gave up hope of recapturing the cities. They staged three unsuccessful attempts before May 16. The first, a day after Liu Ping-ts'ui's entry into Haifeng, employed villagers armed with spears and was called off before it could begin. The second, planned for May 10, depended on Wu Chen-min's Party Salvation Army, which accidentally encountered an enemy patrol en route and turned back. The last attempt, planned for May 15, broke up in confusion when Wu learned of fresh enemy reinforcements. In each instance Wu Chen-min was blamed for the failure, at least in part one suspects because he was a native not of Haifeng but of Chekiang. But by the middle of the month the Communists were asking themselves the rhetorical question "Now how are we to exterminate the enemy?"

How indeed? The only weak spot seemed to be Wuhua county, where there were only two companies of anti-Communist troops. On

May 21 Wu Chen-min took his regular Peasant Army from Haifeng across the border to the north toward Wuhua city. There, on the same day as the disastrous Day of the Horse anti-Communist pogrom in Ch'angsha to the north, Wu's army fell prey to one of the oldest of Chinese military stratagems: the empty city ruse. A sizable garrison army, whose existence was unknown to Communist intelligence, fell in behind the unsuspecting Haifengese and very nearly destroyed them to a man. Wu Chen-min was launched on his own fatal Long March toward Wuhan, never again to be seen in Haifeng.[4]

With the Reds out of the city and their largest unit out of the county, the Whites began to return. Steamship service was restored connecting Haifeng with Hong Kong and Swatow. On the boats came the refugees, the politicians, and the military figures who had fled the "Red holocaust." Many who had only a few months earlier been reviled in their exile as traitors, mutineers, or cohorts of Ch'en Chiung-ming were returning as loyal KMT comrades, wearing the proper Sun Yat-sen suits (the high-collared tunic later known as Lenin garb and then as the Mao suit) and decorated with the white-sun-blue-sky emblem. The new slogans of May in Canton sounded fierce enough: the Kuomintang was to be purified of all rebellious taint; all Communist bandits were to be stamped out. Instead of enjoying the benefits of rent reduction, the villages were to be mopped up and the countryside rehabilitated. Although the posture of the new county rulers seemed determined enough, in practice they permitted the Communists free rein in the countryside.

Liu Ping-ts'ui's new government avoided all contact in the first few weeks of his rule. Instead he formed reorganization committees within the moribund Kuomintang and its mass organizations. He relied largely on the feeble Popular Corps to investigate the villages (largely those within a few kilometers of the county seat). Though a number of villagers were arrested and tried for complicity in the rebellion or even for being kin to a known Communist bandit, the punishments were light. Liu seemed more eager to get a confession and a declaration of pious respect for his new government from the captives than he was to remove them from society.[5]

The unspoken rule of mutual avoidance and toleration that became a part of the people's war stalemate allowed the Communists to maintain their influence in the paddy villages outside the towns throughout the summer. The Haifeng peasant armies continued to collect provisions openly, to train new units, and to stage occasional public executions of counterrevolutionaries. Through the summer these bands remained intact, dodging pacification raids, darting into villages to hang posters and collect rice or to destroy a Popular Corps communications post. The Peasant Army quickly supplanted the Communist party organization as the skeleton of village political authority. The party ceased holding cell meetings and limited itself to issuing propaganda outlines that extolled the virtue of courage in adversity.

To be sure, the balance of forces of summer 1927 was not based on love and affection so much as on mutual fear and uncertainty. Liu feared to send his patrols abroad at night because of the known hostility of certain villages to his government. Without military protection, landlords dared not collect their rents, and association coffers continued to grow. Liu Ping-ts'ui might have made certain inroads in the peasant associations, which he permitted to exist through the summer, by declaring that meetings were no longer compulsory. But his reorganization commissioners refused to visit the villages since they were the announced targets of Communist assassination squads. On the other side, when the Communist party asked for volunteers to infiltrate the Kuomintang urban apparatus, it found none. The insurgents were pleased enough that they were still alive and functioning.

Another important element in the stalemate was the nature of peasant support for the insurgency. Many villagers felt a stronger attachment to the associations than to the party or the Communist Army.[6] They were happy to live without the pressures of rent and taxes. The welcomed the idea of a new government that worked for their interests and were willing, if necessary, to fight for them. But they conceived their interests narrowly. Peasant troops, P'eng P'ai later averred, were much better at the defense of their home villages than outside. They were more reckless than determined, but in the heat of battle the peasantry was much fiercer than the urban working class. The problem in the summer was that without a main force army such as Wu Chen-min's most villagers felt recklessness would be suicidal. The promise at least of professional military support from outside the village, if not victory, is an essential element in sustaining people's war.

So also is a commitment from the insurgents to remain at least temporarily happy with a village existence. The Communist party in Haifeng debated the alternative ways to maintain their support. As in Hunan and Hupeh, there were counsels of radicalism urging immediate land confiscation and those of moderation urging promises of rent relief. The radicals tended to favor, as did Mao Tse-tung later in Hunan, immediate attack on the county seats. The Kwangtung Regional Committee would not permit the county to go beyond Sun Yat-sen's slogan of "all land to the tiller." The Haifeng Communists further agreed that insurrection could not be produced by merely ordering it and that a failure in the attempt to seize the walled city would be disastrous. They decided for the duration of the summer to support "stirring up trouble in the villages," and thus by their decision confirmed the de facto division between town and country.[7]

Here lay a crucial difference between P'eng P'ai's Haifeng and Mao Tse-tung's Hunan: the village enemy in many parts of Haifeng had been destroyed long before the attempt to recover the cities. A strategy of people's war that pitted the villages against the city in a protracted conflict and took advantage of the reluctance of Canton and the local military to travel outside its own urban world made much sense in late summer Haifeng. But when a new central Politburo appeared in August, the Haifeng Communists, like Mao Tsetung, learned they would have to justify their village-based strategy by quick urban victories. Fortunately for that purpose, though perhaps disastrously for the strategy of protracted rural warfare, an opportunity to seize the city swiftly and cheaply came in September 1927.

Had the party resolved in summer on a strategy of retreat to the mountains to build powerful armies, it might have avoided the sudden defeat of February 1928. Mao's Chingkangshan strategy of balancing provincial authorities against one another in the classic excision strategy (*ko-chü*) could conceivably have been applied in the hills of the East River watershed, just as the Chingkangshan base was carved out along the Hunan-Kiangsi border in 1928. But to have done so would have required preserving a sizable military force from the beginning. The Peasant Army, however, was undermanned and badly outgunned and its Communist party leadership determined on urban victory, so the opportunity never really arose.

The Haifeng party's plans for early September closely resemble the Central Committee's strategy for Hupeh and Hunan at the same time. If cities were to be taken, they should strike a number of places simultaneously to throw the military into psychological confusion. But in Haifeng the devices for creating confusion were more plentiful: there were enough peasant organizations left to step up alarmingly the scale of rural marauding. The main military blow in the plan would be struck at the weaker of the two county seats, Lufeng, which would be isolated from Haifeng by an insurrection planned for the districts in between.[8] The plan would not have succeeded had there not been a turn of good fortune for the Communist party.

The stroke of luck came late at night on September 7 when a squad of government troops posted in Kungp'ing mutinied over a matter of pay and declared themselves Communists. This contingent of only sixty men was a pivot in Liu Ping-ts'ui's strategy of controlling the main towns of the county with his Peace Preservation Corps. Indeed the mutineers had turned back several Communist attacks in late August before their defection. Lin Tao-wen happily regrouped these men and distributed their weapons among his own Peasant Army.

The mutiny upset the delicate balance of forces in Haifeng. The government had deliberately left the villages to the Reds, counting on control of certain key towns, of which Kungp'ing was the most important. Communist raids on villages, especially on those with prominent government ties, was now stepped up, and the Peasant Army marched easily into the capital of Lufeng and into Swabue on September 8. By the twelfth Haifeng was surrounded by people's governments in each of its satellite market towns. Though the Communist general Lin Tao-wen led five or six hundred men, of which only half bore arms, several times into an attack on Haifeng, he did not capture the city for three days. By that time the garrison commander and the newly appointed county magistrate had fled, taking with them dozens of men from the Popular Corps and their commanders. Forty years later the commander might have escaped by mounting a helicopter. But without a technological skyhook, the evacuees marched through the hostile countryside into the neighboring county to recoup their losses.

Lin Tao-wen's new governments, which he set up both in Haifeng and Lufeng on September 17, called themselves worker-peasant dictatorships instead of people's governments. Only two days later would the CCP Central Committee authorize the use of the name soviet, too late for word to reach Kwangtung. In Haifeng city Lin Tao-wen, who had been one of P'eng P'ai's first converts in 1922, set up his headquarters again in the familiar Lin family temple in Ch'iao-tung. His quartermasters quickly emptied pawnshops to re-stock provisions—a fact that did not escape the town leaders, who could use it on returning to demonstrate how the Communists disregarded the belongings of the common people. Wherever offices and residences of municipal bureaucrats could be identified, they were burned to the ground.[9]

On their second return to urban control, the Communist party knew what to do. Devastation had become, in fact, the main goal of social policy. Suppression of the counterrevolution was the euphenism for widespread executions, many carried out without orders and without discipline.[10] There were, of course, central instructions that could have been quoted to justify the policy, though we have no proof that even the August 7 emergency conference's resolutions were available in Haifeng. A special party conference in Haifeng on the eighteenth laid down lines, however, that would be later praised in the same November Communist central Politburo resolution that criticized Mao Tse-tung for his Autumn Harvest errors. Rather than attempt to hold the city and draw the inevitable reprisals, the Communists would, according to these decisions, kill a number of their most virulent opponents (called counterrevolutionary obstacles), plunder the larger merchant houses to replenish military stores, and quickly retreat to a remote mountain base on the borders of the four East River counties. At this meeting the strategy of extra-rural base building—finding a safe camp in mountains remote from the paddy countryside—toward which Lin Tao-wen had been groping during the summer gained explicit recognition. The same strategy had been proposed, though not yet practiced, in Hupeh and Hunan.

So in the few days of their occupation of the city the Communists focused on wiping out small anti-Communist groups that had emerged since their last departure. Many members of the rehabilitation and pacification committees set up by Wan Ping-ch'en had been unable to escape with him and had gone back to their home villages to hide among relatives. The infrastructure of the Communist government—the Red Defense Corps (Ch'ih-wei-tui) and the Boys'

Army—formed posses to locate such persons. Later accounts assure us that their searches yielded only those "illegal landlords, native bullies (*t'u-pa*), evil gentry, and local hooligans (*ti-p'i*)" who were "guilty of the most heinous, bloody crimes."[11] But the several hundred who were put to death were given little opportunity to defend themselves agains the charges.

Amid the bloodshed, Lin Tao-wen prepared for a quick retreat. A team systematically dismantled the Nanfeng textile factory, the one modern plant in town, and transported its machinery on poles and back-packs to the mountainous northwest where it would be reassembled to produce military uniforms. The town pawn shops yielded cotton quilt blankets and bedrolls as well as easily marketable gold ornaments. Further funds came from the sales of confiscated property. Lin's propaganda men even took the flatbed press from Ch'en Chiung-ming's now defunct private newspaper, the *Lu An Daily*, whose editors P'eng P'ai had confronted in 1922, and transported it by boat and overland into the Communist mountain base at Chungtung. By the time the press issued its first copy of a new newspaper called *Red Flag*—the first of a long series of the title in Chinese Communist history—Haifeng was already back in the hands of the enemy. It had been held all of nine days.

Should the city have been seized at all? Until as late as August 1930 the Chinese Communust party would continue to raid county seats and even provincial capitals on the theory that seizure of the administrative capital was the best way to further the revolution. The capture of needed weapons, provisions, machinery, and money would justify brief urban occupation. To others, as in the case of the Tet offensive in South Vietnam in 1968, it would seem a useful if costly device to display military capability. But the costs of urban conquest and control would continue to outweigh the benefits long after the collapse of the Haifeng movement. Those costs were already apparent in the short September raid: urban populations, even in towns that were as strongly pro-Communist as Haifeng, did not enjoy urban warfare; the psychological boost of an urban victory would be minimized by its brevity; local notables could use the threat to urban authority to appeal for wider support outside. The continued existence of rural Communist forces depended in Haifeng as elsewhere on the disinclination, for whatever reason, of urban central authority to exert itself in the villages. The September raid, as later the November Communist city government, increased the likelihood of a mobilized opposition.

Abandoning the cities for the mountain base on Maanshan took a great deal of courage. It meant abandoning the prized "little Moscow" and surrendering even the most thoroughly communized districts in the plains. Wu Chen-min had already made his decision to flee from Kwangtung altogether, though Haifeng did not realize that this decision brought his unit to quick disaster. Mao Tse-tung had already made such a decision and was marching toward Chingkangshan, with contrasting success. By this time in late September, Mao probably realized better than the Haifeng leaders the military hopelessness of the insurrectionary plans and had determined on survival as his primary objective. Mao's answer to the problem of survival as it emerged in the next three years would be insulation from outside attack by the selection of strategically defensible bases in remote areas. Yet even as late as 1934 Mao would be reluctant to leave the Kiangsi base because he wished to be near the valley of the Hsiang where his peasant movement had first grown.

Protection is the essence of people's war. No group that seeks to turn country against town, tenant against owner, people against police can do so without some form of protection that draws upon forces that the country, the tenant, and the people do not themselves possess. During the peasant movement period protection for the movement came, or was at least expected, from the Nationalist armies. During Mao's Kiangsi efforts, protection came in the immediate instance from his own Red Army troops, which in turn relied even more on geographic insulation and their own high mobility. In the anti-Japanese war period, when the Communist armies built their governments behind enemy lines in the north China plain, protection came largely from the mutual annihilation or self-neutralization of anti-Communist forces. None of these types of protection were available to the Haifeng leadership in 1927. So they did the only thing they could do: they waited for help from Nanch'ang.

Chinese Communist tradition now dates the founding of the Red Army from a mutiny of Communist officers and their Cantonese troops against the Kuomintang at Nanch'ang, Kiangsi, on August 1, 1927. The rebels acted more from military than from political motives, since their move defied the Communist Central Committee policy of sending all hands into the Autumn Harvest Insurrection.

Chou En-lai, the Communist political commissar to the Nationalist armies, argued along with strategist T'an P'ing-shan that it would be folly to disband the only Communist force of division size in the name of scattered peasant risings. Haifeng's P'eng P'ai agreed with them, largely because their plans called for a forced march back to Kwangtung, where he thought the peasantry was inherently more reliable than in the Yangtse valley. Indeed, he virtually promised them that their path, like those of progressive armies in Kwangning and the East River counties earlier, would be lined by joyous rural supporters dutifully mustered by eager peasant organizers.

His expectations were dashed. The path of the Communist army ran through territory in Kiangsi where the peasant movement had little base, but P'eng and Chou scarcely expected the open hostility they met in the villages and along the roads. The word had spread before them that they were another northern warlord army bent upon communizing wives and property. Further, the reception did not improve much when the troops crossed into Kwangtung and entered the East River watershed. Communist Peasant Army units in the mountain market towns had dwindled to a fraction of their former size. The lack of peasant enthusiasm for the Communist cause drove the commanders to reject P'eng P'ai's suggestion that they head for Haifeng. Instead the Nanch'ang insurrectionaries attempted to capture the two major cities of eastern Kwangtung, Swatow and Ch'aochou, and fell victims on September 27 to an anti-Communist force three times their size. One group of stragglers under Chu Teh and Lin Piao, then a nineteen-year-old junior officer, marched several hundred miles back into southeastern Hunan, where early the next year they joined Mao Tse-tung in retreat on Chingkangshan. Another group, including Chou En-lai and P'eng P'ai, escaped by sampan to Hong Kong. In the end only a few more than a thousand ragtag remnants without even their straw peasant hats stumbled into the Maanshan base in Haifeng on October 19, 1927. There would be no further help from Nanch'ang.[12]

In place of his deeply desired main force army Lin Tao-wen had to forge a new unit out of demoralized troops. Here he drew on the Peasant Army tradition. Comfort teams brought the troops peanuts, radishes, and pork delicacies. The party allotted them a half-ton of polished rice, confiscated from landlord stores, and new hats and sandals, each carefully marked with Communist labels. Lin eased them into combat with an easy victory or two, and by the fourth week of October he was ready with a pincer plan that threw his new division against the city of Haifeng.

His opposition was not made of the sternest stuff. The new garrison commander of Haifeng after the last Communist government was no more inclined to patrol beyond the city walls than was his predecessor. Moreover, he had gotten wind of an impending coup d'état in Canton that would have affected his future in the provincial government. When on October 25 he heard of Lin Tao-wen's preliminary move into the plains near Huangchiang, he overreacted strongly. A "pacification" force of three thousand streamed up the valley to Huangchiang, burning villages along the way. Lin traced the enemy's arrival by the smoke and ambushed him. The commander organized yet another evacuation of the city. On November 1 Lin Tao-wen walked unopposed into Haifeng for the third time and set up the first Chinese soviet government.

Strictly speaking, the first soviet government in China was not one government but fourteen. Soviets ruled over the five districts of Haifeng and the nine of Lufeng, but the two counties lacked formal governmental administrations. The Communist party organization, however, easily filled the gap. The East River Special Committee, soon headed by P'eng P'ai, supervised work in both counties from the old Lin family temple in the Haifeng suburb of Ch'iaotung—the location of P'eng P'ai's early successes. Party committees also substituted for county administration. The Haifeng party, under the future renegade Ch'en Shun-i, set up quarters in an aristocratic mansion within the city walls. Interlocking appointments among these committees and the district governments further confirmed the central role of the party in administration of the soviets.

P'eng P'ai's personal influence on the Haifeng soviets was, we suspect, more important than their formal structure. It is true that the founder of the peasant movement had not set foot in Eastern Kwangtung since late 1926 when he joined the Northern Expedition.[13] Moreover, P'eng was not among the stragglers of the Nanch'ang revolt who limped into Lin Tao-wen's mountain base in October. He preferred to stay close to the Communist leadership and reestablish his connections with the Central Committee after the confusion of military defeat.[14] For two months he worked underground in Hong Kong, raising funds and support among the refugee population. He therefore played no role in the early November provisional revolutionary government. But as soon as he arrived in Haifeng around November 15 P'eng reassumed his position of personal authority over the newly established soviet and over the East River Special Committee of the party.

We have only one eyewitness to P'eng's leadership style, a young Korean Communist who worshipped the Japanese-educated Haifeng leader. Kim San's portrait, as told to Nym Wales, is full of paradoxes. P'eng was a man with many loyal followers and a revolutionary dictator with plenary powers. He had a large staff that followed his directives without question, but he spoke often of mass democracy, without which all the centralization of powers would, he said, "be no firmer than a bean curd." P'eng's conception of democracy has since became very familiar in China—in one form, indeed, the informing ideology of Mao Tse-tung's Cultural Revolution of the 1960s. In this conception ideal revolutionary government dispenses with bureaucracy and formal centralization of authority in favor of free discussions, mass meetings, and persuasion. But of course, as in the case of Mao Tse-tung forty years later, the authority of the revolutionary center itself could never be questioned. Kim San summed up the neat Rousseaunian antinomy that underlay P'eng's concept: "If ever one man was in control, P'eng was in control of the Soviets. Yet he never thought of himself in this light at all, but believed in and jealously guarded the majority decision.[15]

Time has left us little record of mass meeting life in Haifeng. Of early P'eng P'ai gatherings there is only one priceless photograph in the Kuomintang party archives in Taiwan. From the appearance of the buildings, it dates from around 1923. In fact, the slight mist that is falling suggests the occasion may well have been the eve of P'eng's showdown with Chung Ching-t'ang in autumn of that year. In any case the Lin family temple is undecorated by any slogan or official signs. The crowd is serious, even somber, as it peers at the camera from under umbrellas. Not a woman is in sight, but at the front stand many children, eager for a portrait, and a number of well-dressed student types. P'eng has staged the photograph so that he appears at the rear of the crowd, standing on a head-high table with his body partially turned away from the camera. He is about to turn toward us, his right hand raised as though on the upbeat of a march, his eyes piercing from beneath a shock of black hair. The magician was ready to perform.

Four years later the lone spellbinder had become the conductor of a well-trained orchestra. The Haifeng congress of November 18, 1927, exceeded any meeting before or for twenty years after in the extent of its preparations and the ardor of its festivities. Dancing, singing, and music accompanied the meeting. The last flyspeck of dust was swept clean from the place in front of the temple, which was decorated with pictures of Marx and Lenin. Cushions and pine boughs graced the mercifully dry dirt of the meeting ground. The conductor finally had his marching band all of Hunanese brass. At 10 A.M. a gong introduced the meeting and the Internationale. Since Sun Yat-sen's death KMT meetings had traditionally kowtowed to his portrait; now P'eng, unable to break completely with the past, led his presidium to bow three times to the saints of the Communist party.

There were speeches. The soviet's president, Ch'en Shun-i, the Ch'en who in 1928 was to betray the Communists after capture, welcomed the delegates. P'eng and others repeated similar greetings and the congress turned to serious business. A delegate from the seventh district, with some pretense of spontaneity, rose to make a long speech. A Min-t'uan force, he charged, had occupied the walled city of Chiehsheng. Though the peasant army had them surrounded, the city had not yet fallen. How nice it would be if the congress could deliver as a body the final blow. At two in the afternoon the second division under Tung Lang departed Haifeng for Chiehsheng, twenty miles away. P'eng P'ai delivered the departing speech. When they arrived, he said, they must show no mercy. "Kill all the counterrevolutionaries," he ordered, "and be back here by the twentieth." The crowd shouted its approval.[16]

P'eng's speech to this congress is his last utterance of which we have a record. The presently available text may be adulterated; it was certainly a longer speech than the twenty-page version of it handed down to us. But the attitudes expressed in it are typical of November 1927 and the mode of expression, with its terrible simplification, is clearly P'eng's. Like many Chinese Marxist-Leninist leaders before and after him, P'eng's personal persuasiveness and eloquence in small group, face-to-face discussion evaporated in formal public speech. Unlike native peasant leaders like Emiliano Zapata elsewhere, he often traded his role as spokesman of the local farmer for one of representative of central party authority. The vivid personal examples and images of his private speaking style yielded to

sweeping platitudes and dubious generalities. But there was nevertheless some relief in his speech. Like Mao Tse-tung and Lo Ch'i-
yuan, P'eng was never a mere sloganeer.

His first point would have been familiar to those who knew his
speeches of 1923. He neatly divided the entire world into two types
of people: the monied and the moneyless. Of the two, of course, the
latter were in the vast majority: for every one with money, there
were somewhere nine without. The majoritarian poor had begun to
object to the cheating of the minority rich. Many years ago there had
been an old teacher named Marx who saw the plight of the poor and
raised the slogan "Workers of the world unite." That was the significance of this congress in Haifeng.

The congress, he asserted, would cause the spirits of foreign devils
to turn in their graves. As an example he offered the English. The
English monied have great power. They own factories as well as land
extorted from the peasantry. They use a "thing like a putt-putt car"
to drag the plow and drive peasants to London. But Russia is different. There "teacher Marx's advanced student, Mr. Lenin" organized a Communist party. He conceived of the Communist parties of
the world as "a spider web with Russia as the center." Mr. Lenin was
the spider, P'eng declared proudly. He formed a Red Army just like
the one in China and "went out and shot reactionaries." Their job in
China was in part to support this new Russian worker-peasant government.

P'eng gave his audience an account of the dunce-cap ceremony he
had learned of from Mao Tse-tung's Hunan, ending with the execution of the landlord. There, he exaggerated, without counting the
far greater losses on the other side, more than ten thousand landlords had been killed in this way. He hoped the movement would do
better in Kwangtung; and in Haifeng the killing had begun. Now
the home county was Red and peasants would no longer have to
scrimp to pay their year-end debts. The peasant would pay rent only
to himself; the gentry and landowning bully would get the beatings.
And perhaps, he rhapsodized, the year after next they could buy
large machines from outside countries to till the land. And the year
after that perhaps every village would have electric lights, running
water, leisure places, schools, and libraries. New Year's would each
year be bigger and better. Yet all this, he concluded, depended on
how well they worked together.[17]

Unfortunately it depended on a great deal more than that. But there is reason to marvel at the persistence of his dream of rural reform and improvement even at the height of brutality. Mao Tsetung was never inclined to a lyrical praise of rural electrification. Had the Kwangtung peasant leaders come to dominate the Communist movement, might P'eng's dream have been realized earlier? We will never know, for the killing phase of P'eng's revolution lasted until he too was dead. But here in November 1927 his soviet still had several months to live, and Chiehsheng was about to fall.

Indeed, before P'eng could finish his two-day speech the news of victory had arrived. The congress greeted the news with cheers and moved en masse to the bus station to greet the returning heroes. As Lin Tao-wen reported his success, his men paraded some thirty hapless anti-Communist prisoners onto the ground in front of the station. P'eng's presidium rhetorically asked how the captives should be handled and were not surprised by the unanimous demands for the death penalty. Thirty ragged defenders of the walled town, probably as poor and hungry as any worker-peasant, fell to the ground, slain. A torrential rain had begun, and the crowd returned to what had been the Buddhist Temple of Everlasting Life to commemorate the death of the one Communist soldier lost at Chiehsheng.[18]

The discussions at this Haifeng Soviet Congress set the tone for county government in the next two months.[19] The fullest and most heated debate was over Ch'en Shun-i's resolution on the land question. All agreed that the question of land confiscation was central to the future of soviet rule in Haifeng. But discussion centered about the recommendation that all boundaries between plots of land be obliterated. The avowed purpose of Ch'en's recommendation was to confuse the landlords about where their land was located and thus to blunt their objections to total confiscation. But its effect was equally serious on the many small holders who retained an interest in their own land. Ch'en and the Communist leadership additionally recommended that confiscated land be redistributed after a thorough investigation. Delegates raised a number of questions about these provisions. Some spoke in favor of immediate special treatment of those who had given ardent political support to the peasant associations and yet had no land to till. Others suggested that only land that a farmer was clearly unable to till on his own be allocated as excess to another cultivator. Some raised questions about what to do when families grow or diminish in size—should there be constant redistribution or not? Finally, after the terms and the relative permanency of the distribution were determined, how much, if any, of the year's harvest should be taken by the district and village governments to pay the salaries of officials? These were issues that were to plague Communist rural governments that rose to power on land platforms in the future. Haifeng came up with compromise solutions.

The congress decided that only those land boundaries that were clearly hindering efficient farming should be eliminated, at least in the short run. Apparently even in the heat of civil war the strength of small-holder opinion could not be resisted. They also decided to mix the criteria for redistribution to include a large number of factors: the number of persons in the family, the relative labor power of the household (whether young or old, weak or strong, male or female), the economic situation of each family (whether they have other outside income or not), and finally the fertility of the land. The length of time during which the redistribution would be valid could be decided by the district governments, who would take in 10 percent of the total harvest each year as a fixed levy in lieu of taxes. This last provision was shoved into the future, where of course it became irrelevant, by the stipulation that the tax would not be collected until June 1928. But the congress tacked a trailer onto their confiscation resolution that was designed to ensure that the masses would remain loyal and productive members of soviet society: the slogans "no work, no land" and "no revolution, no land" were to become part of the propaganda that accompanied any redistribution.

The rest of the resolution on land confiscation passed without discussion. The measures, although mild toward the small holder, were undebatably draconian toward the landlord. All land deeds were to be burned in public if they had not already been destroyed. Any person who secreted a land contract of any kind, who signed a deed after the resolution passed, or who protected or knew of any such person would be punished by death. Land-use certificates would be issued henceforth by the soviet government. Copies of certificates now on display in the revolutionary museum show a simple statement of the name of the plot and the present tiller. We have no way of knowing how many of them were issued, but we can believe reports that these certificates, worn proudly on villagers' clothing, became safe conduct passes in thoroughly Red villages.

The evidence is that the Haifeng Communists put far more energy and conviction into the ruthless suppression of the opposition than into the niceties of proprietorship and taxation. The resolution on the thorough killing of reactionaries began with the list: "all persons aiding the enemy and all reactionaries, such as corrupt officials, greedy bureaucrats, bully landowners, evil gentry, spies, propagandists, policemen, Peace Preservation corpsmen, messengers and tax collectors for the enemy, and all those who work in their offices must be seized and executed."[20] In the villages the houses of such people must be burned to the ground and all their personal and family possessions seized. Their wives must be returned to their parental homes unless they themselves have engaged in counterrevolutionary activities, in which case they too must be shot. Widows and other bereaved enemy women may be married off to someone else at the discretion of the district government. Needless to say, the congress was equally harsh in its penalties for those aiding the enemy and other criminals. In no case was a village to release any suspect. A man found not guilty was to be turned over to higher authorities for further investigation. There were, to be sure, other more positive measures. Labor conditions were to be improved by the standard provision for an eight-hour day, controls on foremen, restrictions against child labor, and hedges against wage inflation. But since Haifeng had under a thousand wage laborers in a total population of nearly half a million, these stipulations were there largely for effect.

More important was the attempt to improve the conditions of the revolutionary army soldier. As later in the Communist movement, the leadership in Haifeng fully realized the importance of maintaining morale, loyalty, and efficiency in the fighting corps. The congress ordered immediate provisions and the issuance of cotton, new uniforms, and felt for the coming winter months. It recommended armymen's clubs and schools to improve the military's cultural level — not to say its morale. It forbade the mistreatment of rank-and-file soldiers and demanded an accountant's offices in each unit to prevent graft and corruption. It ordered the improvement of medical facilities and the gift of land to soldiers' families. In a clearly preferential move, it allowed army families to hire labor to till land while the fighting men were away at the front. A separate set of regulations stipulated that the families of the injured or killed should be given extra land and special treatment by their local governments.

The choice of delegates to the November 18 congress was not random. The county of Haifeng was divided into nine districts for the purpose of electing delegates. The number of delegates for each district appears to have been decided more on the basis of contribution to the Communist cause than on that of total population size. The three districts of Haifeng, Kungp'ing, and Meilung, the largest producers of Communist support, received favored treatment. Chiehsheng, just at that moment fiercely resisting Communist attack, received far less representation. That the three Communist districts were favored for their contribution to the cause can be surmised from the fact that twenty-eight of the thirty soldier delegates to the congress came from these districts. The category of worker in Haifeng is as confused as it later became in the Kiangsi period. The working class in a county such as Haifeng was not easy to discover; it is suspicious that highly agricultural districts such as Meilung and Kungp'ing should produce the majority of worker delegates. It is reasonable, however, to expect that Swabue, probably the only true commercial entrepôt in the county, would have some worker representation, and that Chiehshih and Ch'iehsheng, the two walled-town centers of gentry reaction, should have none.

It is tempting to explain the difference between the Communist and non-Communist districts of Haifeng in terms of social and economic distinctions. Several sources have commented that Haifeng was divided nicely between a rich southeastern coastal plain and a poor northwestern mountain plateau. Certainly, with this distinction, Communist strength was in the poorer geographic regions of the county, particularly if we consider the location of the mountain bases. But there are other distinctions as well that must enter in: the southeastern districts were in large part nonagricultural, with fishing, trading, and salt-producing interests and occupations. The northwestern districts, especially those settlements above a hundred meters in altitude, tended to have a higher proportion of the Hakka minority. We know Meilung to have been a district of sharp landlord-tenant conflict, but this may not have been characteristic of the equally Communist Kungp'ing district. There is no indication that the ratio of villages to markets, which in one theory might reveal the degree of market orientation or commercialization of the district, bears any relationship to Communist success in the district.[21] A better fit seems to be the average size of the village, with the districts with large villages producing fewer peasant movement successes. We could speculate about possible mechanisms, including the probability of single-clan domination, the greater average wealth, or connections with the market economy, but without further evidence such speculation would not be fruitful.

Just as important as considerations of the social background were the political backgrounds of the various Haifeng districts. That Kungp'ing should be assigned far more soldier delegates than any other district underlines its importance in supplying military people to the movement: not only the mutineer regiment of Kuo Ch'i-kuan, but many other recruits to the original and later peasant armies came from Kungp'ing district, as did many of Tai K'o-hsiung's Popular Corps. Meilung had from the beginning produced more socially motivated Communists. Chiehsheng, Ch'ingts'ao, and K'ot'ang with their large fishing populations had never been good movement recruiting areas, and indeed Chiehsheng was still in strong anti-Communist hands when the delegates were assembled. Although we have suggested reasons why Meilung and perhaps Kungp'ing were early successes in peasant movement history, the important fact about them in 1927 was rather that they had such a history. P'eng P'ai's earliest 1922 successes were achieved in the three districts of Haifeng, Kungp'ing, and Meilung, in that chronological order. As with any political force, in peasant movements and in people's war, the importance of background causes tends to fade with time as the conscious elements of memory and loyalty play a greater and greater role.

A BACKGROUND of loyalty and new departures in local policy were not enough to sustain long-term government. One of the advantages of maintaining the bipolar equilibrium of people's war is that both sides can shirk the responsibilities of rule. Justice, instead of a difficult but redemptive process of value building, becomes a mere tool against the enemy. Taxation, instead of the source of regenerative investment, becomes an optional pressure to penalize neutrality as well as a direct input into war-making capability. The public interest, rather than uniting all citizens in a common cause or restraining the unpopular interests of a few in the interest of many, becomes a form of special pleading used to divide society into adversaries. Though the Ch'en Chiung-ming county government was guilty of each of these political derelictions, the soviet government proved also unable to avoid them. The generation of legitimacy for a revolutionary regime is at least in part a function of its ability to perform the basic functions of government. The requirements of prolonged urban rule in Haifeng were enormous, just as they would later be when Communists established their more or less permanent rule in north China or north Vietnam. The soviet would need manpower, money, and weapons to continue to exist.

One intriguing solution to the problem of manpower was the use of womanpower. Western observers of the Chinese Revolution have remarked many times about the energies that the Chinese version of women's liberation has released.[22] It is not surprising that the Haifeng Communists placed great stress on the creative role of women in their revolution. Chu Teh remarked to Agnes Smedley that when he arrived in the East River area with the Nanch'ang armies, he had marveled at the large number of women working in the fields.[23] The Haifeng region's women had taken over agricultural work since the imperialists had siphoned off all the men as coolies for overseas labor, he said. Emigration doubtless played an important role in raising the status of Ch'aochou women, but local customs of female ownership and other rights also contributed to Haifeng's physically strong and emancipated women.

P'eng P'ai, who in youth had startled Haifeng residents by strolling hand in hand with Ts'ai Su-p'ing in the marketplace, had great success in organizing the Haifeng female population. He gave the keynote address at a woman's congress held outside the east gate in January 1928, devoting his attention to the advantages that would accrue to women who joined the women's associations. He received the most applause, we are told, when he broached what he called the love question. The women's association, with the particularly active leadership of six young women popularly called movie stars, met regularly to demand freedom of divorce, a freedom already granted by the soviet government. But the encouragement of divorce without the processes of mediation later developed to go along with it probably caused more problems than it solved—particularly since the departure of many rural women from their collateral households sharply reduced many small farmers' labor supply. The stress on female military participation may have also backfired. The most spectacular of the women's guerrilla teams that P'eng's men organized was that of the Ch'ihk'ang district. This brigade of three hundred well-drilled female soldiers was impressive in parades, but even in P'eng P'ai's account it tended to be bloodthirsty when called in to one of Haifeng's many public executions. Anti-Communists later collected much sympathy with tales of ballet-cum-decapitation exhibitions on the famous Red Field of Haifeng city.[24]

But however fierce onstage, the women could not carry the battle to the enemy. And no matter how enthusiastic many young men were about joining the Communist military and paramilitary during the height of the soviet, mounting losses made membership in Red Guards or the Worker-Peasant Army less desirable. Training schools, the well-tried institution of the peasant movement period, could produce only so many men. The Workers' Army Training Institute set up in January 1928 produced around six hundred men, all groomed to be lower-level officers. The Red Guards, known to be poorly led and disciplined, were provided with a Model Brigade Finishing School. But rank-and-file expansion of the new Red Army depended mostly on conscription. On February 10 the East River Special Committee government passed the first conscription order of an Asian Communist regime. According to the order, thirty-five hundred men would be drafted, following quotas that would distribute the burden among all villages, large and small. Families of conscripted men were given special privileges, and conscripts were paid two dollars a month wages. A series of rules issued in late February foreshadowed much more elaborate legislation later in the 1930s and 1940s that ensured special treatment for the families of Red Army soldiers. The dependents of soldiers killed or injured in action were by these regulations guaranteed the money needed to bury their dead. In 1923 funeral guarantees had failed because of a rash of deaths. Not that in 1928 any fewer people died, but now their burial was, on paper at least, guaranteed by the people's government. The new rules promised education to sons and daughters of those who made the supreme sacrifice. Later regulations for preferential treatment would be more detailed, but the essence of privilege for military men would be maintained under Communist rule into the 1970s.[25]

With the rights of membership in the Communist Army went responsibilities. By February the major problem was desertion from the ranks. Rumors of the impending arrival of suppressing troops from Canton or Swatow were rife (and accurate) in February. Some men silently harbored doubts about whether the Reds could hold out against the provincial authorities. Those caught speaking about the rumors were shot. More prevalent than open dismay was stealthy desertion. To prevent escapes the Communists had to assign sentries along the Huiyang border. By late February so many had escaped that the people's committee issued notices to district governments authorizing sharp punitive measures.[26] The myth that because people's wars are fought in the name of the people they are willingly supported by young men of fighting age would nevertheless not be easily dispelled.

The Labor Bank of Haifeng would have printed its own money if it had possessed the facilities. As it was without a printing press, the bank fell back on the one considerable capitalist institution of the county, the Nanfeng textile mill, for its currency. In the years after the 1911 revolution the mill issued its own silver certificates as a hedge against inflation. The new government simply added its stamp to these bills when it confiscated the factory. By the end of February, the government had raised over one hundred thousand yuan in this fashion.[27]

But printing money was not the way out of Haifeng's financial dilemma. The Canton and Swatow authorities had tried on and off to bottle up Haifeng trade with the outside. There was of course no arsenal in the East River area, so all ammunition and military material not seized from the enemy or exhumed from private caches had to be purchased in external ports. The revolutionaries debated how to raise cash for external purposes and decided finally to take advantage of Haifeng's one major raw material export: salt. Produced by the ton in large brine fields at the edge of the sea, salt from Haifeng flowed in normal times to the major urban markets. The problem now that the outflow had been cut off was how to revive this source of hard cash.

The answer was bribery. P'eng P'ai sometime in January 1928 sent one of his close cadres, Ch'en Yun-fu, to the Pearl delta to line up bottoms for salt transport. Ch'en found thirteen large vessels whose captains were willing, for a price, to carry the salt. Ch'en then interviewed the chairman of the provincial salt monopoly to request a permit. The undercover fee for his services was two hundred thousand yuan. Salt boats began to deliver their goods from the tiny coastal ports of Haifeng and Lufeng, and the infusion of cash permitted the East River Special Committee to continue to build up their powers of resistance.[28] Thus did communism flourish, as later in north China and Vietnam, on the venality of its opposition.

More important than salt for the domestic well being of Haifeng was the supply of rice and other foodstuffs. Haifeng and Lufeng were rich rice-producing counties whose per capita production in normal years was higher than that of many Kwangtung counties. But the disruptions of 1926 and 1927 had drastically reduced the winter's supply. Since imports were impossible, some other means of padding the supply had to be found. Meetings in February discussed the alternatives, but the only real solution was complete confiscation of all foodgrains for redistribution. Large storehouses of grain, such as the granary (*i-tsang*) of Chiehsheng, the Liangsheng in Shakang, and the Chingli in Nant'u, along with the private larders of many wealthy families, remained intact well into December. A foodgrain management committee took charge of the redistribution, which was done in response to requests from military or civilian groups. Naturally there was a strong tendency to favor groups with greater revolutionary fervor. The clamor for foodstuffs followed the Communists' arrival in Haifeng—as it did in other Asian countries— instead of preceding it as in Russia a decade earlier. Much of the confiscated grain found its way into the Red mountain strongholds of Yenshih and Chungtung.[29]

Haifeng demonstrated many of the problems and but few of the solutions that the Chinese Communists would develop in their approach to the problem of establishing legitimate rule. It showed how difficult it would be to extract the large surpluses needed for full-scale military operations from a nonindustrial population. The salt problem alone, if Edgar Snow's report is correct, would have brought about the fall of the Kiangsi soviet seven years later. The strategy of cooperative organization, military participation in production, special privileges to army recruits, and carefully thought out social change that would release constructive instead of destructive energies would take years to develop and would be essential ingredients to protracted people's war. But Haifeng was at least a beginning.

11

THE DEATH OF
A REVOLUTION:
HAIFENG, 1928

Arguments about how to defeat as much as those about how to win a people's war have raged for decades. Before the collapse of the peasant movement in China there were few who openly faced the question of how to exterminate the Communists. But with the Nationalist and Communist wings of the Great Revolution at war, many had to deal consciously with the issue. The options were as many and varied as in Vietnam. Compromise, neutralization, political reconstruction, military suppression, and foreign intervention were proposed and to some extent tried, though of course without the costly, long, and indecisive experimentation of the Vietnamese case. Within less than a quarter of a year after the formation of the Haifeng and Lufeng soviets the Communist movement had been routed permanently, or so it seemed, from the eastern seaboard of China. What was the nature of the process of defeat and can we draw any lessons from it?

It is surprising today to realize how disinterested the Western powers were in suppressing the first Asian Communist government. To be sure, the Americans, English, and Japanese were intensely concerned about the expansion of Russian influence over the Kuomintang and in the threats to the persons and property of foreigners

in the treaty ports. Chiang Kai-shek's about-face at Shanghai in
April had received praise and rewards from all the outside interests.
English and Japanese vessels helped Li Chi-shen and Li Fu-lin crush
the brief Canton insurrection in December.[1] But Haifeng never
triggered the emotional anti-Communist reaction among the Western powers that by the 1960s was thought to be axiomatic.

Diplomatic and refugee accounts conflicted on the amount of
anti-Western activity in Haifeng and Lufeng. British missionaries
had been driven out of Swabue as early as 1925, at the beginning of
the Hong Kong-Canton strike. But church property had not been
touched and many Westerners had left Haifeng safely before the
Communist governments were formed in 1927. A number of Chinese Christians, including doctors trained in Western medicine,
chose to stay on even after the soviet government was formed. It was
only in mid-December 1927, after the crushing of the Canton uprising, that acts of violence against foreigners and Christians began to
be reported. Some stragglers spread the word that large-scale mas-
sacres of Christians were staged for Christmas Day, and in fact on
that day soviet authorities arrested several Italian priests and nuns
for holding outlawed worship services. On the same day two of the
sixteen Presbyterian chapels in Haifeng burned and Red soldiers
occupied the rest. Foreigners, taken from their homes, found themselves held prisoner in the only hotel, which they superciliously
called a "native inn," in Swabue.[2]

This Christmas Day incident produced the only brief encounter
between the new Haifeng soviet government and imperialism.
Answering an anonymous call for help, the British gunboat H. M. S.
Seraph entered Swabue harbor on December 27 with the mission of
rescuing the captured Catholics. It anchored a mile from the dock
and disembarked thirty armed sailors, a dozen marines, and one
priest aboard a battery-powered dinghy. A brigade of the Haifeng
Worker-Peasant Revolutionary Army, armed to the teeth, lined the
shore. The English paused and instructed the priest to deliver his
letter without going ashore. His letter employed the most polite diplomatic jargon of the day. We understand, it said, that you have
Chinese and Western, male and female missionaries "under your
honorable control" who have been arrested and would like to be
freed. Please release them and return them in the "public interest."
It closed with a list of the names with three "Western females" un-
identified.[3]

The Haifeng government clearly wanted to avoid an incident with the English; yet they wished to make clear their own legal rights in controlling the activities of foreigners in Communist-held territory. Their reply was conciliatory:

> To whom it may concern: We have your letter. The persons you mention, with the exception of Huang Tzu-lien, who has been arrested for crimes against our humble government, are residing in the Chung-hsing Hotel in our city. Since the case of Huang Tzu-lien has not yet been resolved, he must be detained, but the rest of the missionaries resident in Chung-hsing Hotel have been informed that your boat waits.[4]

The British were becoming impatient with the politesse. "Our humble ship," they said, "is here solely to transport male and female missionaries to Hongkong." It has no other purpose, they asserted, somewhat unconvincingly. "As long as your honorable army has not mishandled missionaries and churches," the Englishmen shook their fingers, everything will be fine. But "we shall return to determine whether such harassment occurs in the future." The captain announced his intention of picking up *all* the missionaries, including Huang Tzu-lien.[5]

The soviet government yielded gracefully but reiterated its principles. They said that Huang was without question a Chinese subject, not an Englishman. The soviet had every right to try him without interference from any foreign government. But in the interest of friendly intercourse between nations, it would release him.

> But there is one word we must add: The Hai-Lufeng masses have been conscious for some time of religion and are unanimously opposed to it. There is no reason for you to return to our part of the country to spread religious propaganda any more. Finally, there is little reason for the "empty threat" to return here to check up on "such harassment." We have behind us the full strength of the entire world's proletariat which is entirely united and will not be deterred by evil forces.[6]

After stating this essentially metaphysical position, the Communist government closed with a threat to "not stop at mere words" should the English ship return. But they released Huang Tzu-lien and seven other missionaries, who returned with the *Seraph* to Hong Kong without further incident.[7] There would be no further attempt at foreign military intervention, though some Western residents of China would continue to recommend it.

In fact the chief of the Presbyterian mission, the Reverend Douglas James, had some words of praise for the Communist government. There had been no consistent attack, despite the strength of the feminist movement, on family life under the soviet, he reported. The government favored monogamous marriage. Though many had fled, some of James's Chinese pastors had gone off to work for the Communists.[8]

The missionary's account was disputed by the American consul at Canton, Mr. Jay Calvin Huston, who had not been to Haifeng. Huston stressed tales of submission to free unions forced upon young Christian girls abducted to the Communist headquarters. He noted that famine lies in wait for Haifeng since few believed that private stores of grain would be allowed by the soviet, which in any case was confiscating all surplus foodstuffs. Farmers, their land communalized, had refused to plant the next year's crop. A large number of refugees would make the problem of relief, for whatever government controlled the county, insurmountable. Indeed Mr. Huston in his despair arrived at a solution for the Haifeng problem that sounds depressingly modern:

> From these facts it will be clear that nothing will rid Hoifung and Lukfung [sic] from Bolshevism, and from being a centre of communistic trouble in South China, except the occupation of the district by a strong Nationalist force, and the occupation must be a prolonged one. The Communists have so affected the masses, their doctrines have so taken hold of many of the younger generation, and their terrible reprisals have so frightened the others that nothing except the security arising from the presence of a strong force, on which the Nationalists can securely and permanently rely, will end the trouble.[9]

Huston's view that only a strong Nationalist force could save Kwangtung from chaos led him to propose to Ambassador Mac-Murray in Peking that American banks give Li Chi-shen a massive loan. Huston offered to negotiate the loan directly with the National City Bank of New York late in December. But the U.S. embassy in Peking sternly refused. "It would obviously be contrary to American policy," the ambassador chided him, "for diplomatic or consular officers to associate themselves in the financing of factional strife in China."[10]

If Huston thus appears as the first hawk to urge American intervention in an Asian peasant war, his nearest State Department colleague to the east may have been the first dove. The American consul at Swatow, David C. Berger, was of a different opinion than the Reverend Mr. James about the extent of religious persecution. He reported in one letter that he had received reports that at least one very large Catholic village in Huilai county had been wiped out by the Reds. Several thousand had been murdered in the raid.[11] But his sense of outrage nonetheless did not drive him to embrace the anti-Communist cause or to argue for foreign intervention. He reported candidly that

> The radicals are at present the only really unified and purposeful politi-
> cal group in this section of Kwangtung, and it would seem to be certain
> that, without a radical change of heart and a considerable increase in
> political sagacity and honesty of the moderates, the radicals must in the
> end triumph. This is not meant as a tribute to the radicals, who are also
> remarkably stupid, but as a reflection upon the political ability of the
> group which at present constitutes the government of this district.[12]

Unswayed by Berger's perception, the American ambassador at Peking, largely on the basis of Huston's ill-informed reports, continued to support the view that the East River soviet was organized and supported by the Russians. The nearest the Russians had come to Haifeng and Lufeng, so far as can be gathered, had been when seven of them, who had accompanied Ho Lung and Yeh T'ing southward from Nanch'ang, were left stranded in Swatow, nearly a hundred miles east, in late September. The seven, six men and one woman, had attempted to stow away on an English steamer bound for Hong Kong but had been discovered and forced to await transport to Amoy. The only non-Chinese present during the soviet period were several Koreans, one of whom was Kim San. Nevertheless it became the fashion in the West to speak of P'eng's soviet as a spearhead of Russian penetration into China. The lesson that civil wars in largely peasant societies cannot depend solely on external support or ideas would take many years to learn, if it has yet been learned. But even so, the distance to southeast China in days of mere steamship transportation, the insignificance of American economic interests in the vicinity, and the feebleness of our sense of "face" in the Orient at the time all combined to make the idea of American intervention uninteresting to Washington. Our disinterest, and London's and Tokyo's, was strengthened by the fact that other forces were rapidly destroying the "Bolshevik menace" in China.

THE MOST POTENT of Mr. Huston's Nationalist forces with any capacity to act in the East River area was Li Chi-shen's Canton army. In an important sense the Haifeng soviet received its fatal blow in Li's suppression of the attempted Communist coup d'état in Canton from December 11 to 13, 1927. Though the Haifeng Communists did not know about the planned rising, its failure made an invasion from the direction of Canton only a matter of time.

The tragedy of Stalin's last attempt to play at insurrection in Canton has already been spelled out by many historians. Although Li Chi-shen had since April applied severe pressure to the Communist party in Canton, there had been no full-scale pogrom of party members such as had decimated the left wing in Shanghai as well as other cities. But the very availability of real Communists, however covered by the reaction, was enought to tempt Moscow, through the Communist Central Committee and the Kwangtung Regional Committees, to try to turn back the tide. As in the Hunan case of three months earlier, the insurrectionary planners claimed to have great confidence in peasant uprisings. They could hardly have expected as much help from Haifeng's "worker-peasant-soldier mass proletarian regime" as they claimed. Haifeng had in fact sent a delegate to Canton before the rising, but his job was to seek $20,000 in weapons for the defense of his own embattled county.[13]

Later apologists insisted that the provincial committee had tried to involve the suburban peasantry in their insurrection. But the list of their accomplishments on this front is brief indeed. A few of the usual training classes, a few propaganda pamphlets spread along the railway, and a peasant news column in the underground Canton paper were hardly activities likely to surround the city from the countryside.

The insurrection itself was utterly and purely urban. It was a classic coup d'état: a swift, surgical strike at the headquarters of the city garrison; the seizure by Red Guards of the public security apparatus and of the transport fleet of the Canadian consulate; the turning of well-stocked arsenals and embattlements against their original commanders. There were, to be sure, left-wing overtones to the strike that began at 3:30 A.M. on the eleventh. Political prisoners had been released on the spot and recruited immediately into the Communist Army. Some of the Red labor union members who had managed to remain organized after Li Chi-shen's bloody suppression in April and then again in October moved into their old offices and began to function again. In fact, later propaganda made much of a group of suburban peasants being the first to enter the unarmed Canton-Hankow railway station. To give the soviet government some external significance, P'eng P'ai was even appointed, in absentia, its agricultural commissar.

The post mortems admitted that the soviet was largely a military operation. The major failures were neglecting to wipe out Li Fu-lin's armed fortress at Honam across the river and permitting the anti-Communist garrison to keep a foothold on the bund opposite Honam. Ostensibly there were those who argued how important it was to get support from insurrectionary peasants outside Canton, but others insisted that Haifeng was at least six days' march away. At least as much criticism was leveled against the comrade who went too slowly on orders to invade and destroy the aristocratic sector of Canton (Tungshan) that housed the city's non-Communist politicians. As in Hunan and Hupeh in the summer, the peasant movement was blamed for having already lost the battle for the countryside some months before. But perhaps at least as important in the disastrous defeat of the soviet within seventy-two hours was the fact that the Red Army, in its drive to exterminate diehard resisters, had set fire to the currency vault of the central bank building and thus deprived itself of the means to purchase the allegiance of non-Communist troops.[14]

The bloody purge of the Reds in Canton has been described in sordid detail in a number of accounts. Where the Communist leadership had restrained the insurrectionists from systematic destruction of the upper-class districts of the city, the anti-Bolsheviks offered no such leniency. Even as the confused and defeated Communist armies retreated from the city, Li Fu-lin's men were moving into the workers' quarter. Members of the Communist Picket Corps had, during the seventy-two-hour insurrection, worn red scarves about their necks as their badges of identification. Many had put on the scarves simply to avoid being singled out for attack. Li Fu-lin's men thus found it easy to track down the sympathizers of the insurrection: they searched houses for red cloth and not finding that examined closely the necks of suspicious (lower-class) people for the telltale scarlet stains left by the poorly dyed kerchiefs. Jay Huston, the American consul, permitted himself the callous observation that had the working masses of Canton "been less immune to the use of soap," many of their sons and daughters might still have been alive in 1928.[15]

Soap and water would not, however, wipe out the birthmark of accent or the accident of residence. The soldiers of Li Fu-lin, largely recruited from the Pearl delta countryside, turned easily on the outsiders from the East River area, whom they could identify by their flat, sibilant dialect. Rickshamen were automatically suspect, since such a large portion of them came from Haifeng. The more so since on the last day of the insurrection it was the rickshamen who, as the Red soldiers retreated, had seized the private standard of the anti-Communist Haifeng Local Association and charged the police station. The next day, the Haifeng rickshamen were massed together in several movie theaters within the southern gate quarter where the poorest classes lived and paraded out in groups of fifty beyond the eastern gates, where they were machine-gunned down.[16]

Haifeng received news of the defeat at Canton only two or three days after the fact. In the uprising over a thousand Haifengese residents had been slain fighting with the Communists. The vast majority of them were impoverished ricksha drivers, sons of farmers from poorer agricultural areas of the county.[17] Many of these men and other manual laborers had seen and fired a weapon for the first time on December 11. Little wonder that in retreat the Canton insurrectionist army should fall into rapid disarray. As it passed northward into Hua county, the scene of earlier peasant movement drama the year before, it broke up into smaller and smaller units. The main unit, led by Yeh Yung, numbered only slightly over a thousand men by the time it reached Haifeng on December 19.[18] Some were armed with modern weapons like revolvers and some even had that eternal badge of the higher political cadre, the fountain pen. But even the great mass meeting of the twentieth attended by seventy thousand in the Red Field, at which Yeh·Yung was introduced as the new commander of the new fourth division of the Worker-Peasant Revolutionary Army could not hide the fact that these were all that remained of the military and political arms of the Communist movement in Kwangtung. The failure of the last urban rising in Chinese Communist history, though it seems so predictable in hindsight, left Haifeng in perfect isolation.

IN HUA and Kwangning counties the domestic counterforce alone was never enough to stop the peasant movement, but it did require delicate treatment and in the end helped speed the movement's downfall. In Haifeng, native opposition also performed a similar function; though since Haifeng had reached the stage of people's war, its importance for a time seemed negligible. In other counties there were three different types of interest opposed to the peasant movement. The resistance of the gentry always came first, since the masters of the older statecraft were most sensitive to the unsettling influence of outside agitation. Landowners, as soon as the movement touched the vital economic issues of rent, interest, and land ownership, were the next to become involved. The third type of interest, which emerged only after the peasant movement obtained a foothold in a county, was the administrative interest in tax payment, in economic growth, and in law and order. It was this last interest that the new antiradical military elsewhere in Kwangtung found most to its liking. The peculiar conditions of the takeover of Haifeng and the ease of identifying these three interests as counter-revolutionary made the consolidation of revolutionary power in the county in 1925-1926 simple. But in 1927, although the open expression of antiradical interests had become impossible, there remained a number of organized antiradical political groups.

In other counties these interests could be expressed through a number of types of antiradical associations. The most obvious and least effective of these was the landed interest pressure group. The grain protection association of Haifeng, which quickly found imitations in every county of Kwangtung after 1923, could not survive the clear enunciation of socialist goals and the imposition of Kuomintang power. In other counties, such as Hua, the modern Chinese militia — a type of paramilitary transvillage armed self-defense organization — could be turned to antiradical causes by the proper conditions. But Haifeng had never, even at the height of gentry vigor during the T'aip'ing and Red Turban rebellions of the previous century, produced a strong *t'uan-lien* organization, perhaps because those rebels were less interested in the impoverished eastern coast than they were in the rich delta counties. Again, elsewhere, the secret society — that association-party that mixed religious, political, and military pretentions — became as in Kwangning a potent antiradical force. In Haifeng, though the Triad Society had staged a rebellion as recently as 1898, it had been largely recruited from Huiyang to the west and in any case had been effectively crushed by the new Republican government of Ch'en Chiung-ming after 1911. That peculiar combination of social and economic backwardness and political modernity evident in Haifeng seemed to have made native opposition less formidable to the peasant movement.

The advantage of backwardness could be seen in the struggle for control of Meilung district, west of Haifeng, during 1927. Meilung had been ruled for three centuries by one powerful lineage, the Lin clan of Kueifeng hamlet. The Lins had been brought into Meilung by the imperial armies and given over a thousand acres to colonize and pacify (*t'un-ch'ing*). But though in this way their original power base resembled that of the Chiangt'un Huangs in Kwangning, the Lins did not follow the classic nineteenth-century model of gentry mobility. They concentrated on maintaining their legendarily despotic authority over their tenants and developed no special reputation as a stable of scholars.[19] They raised their own private armed forces, which protected them and the collection of their rents. But the highly developed particularism of the Lin clan was its undoing. Peasant movement leaders found it an easy target in 1923 when P'eng P'ai's youthful associate Yeh Tzu-hsin turned half of Meilung's tenant villages against the clan. In 1927 the Lin extended family of three thousand was virtually exterminated in a series of persecutions lasting from May to October. Familistic bodyguards were no match for even a small and poorly armed Peasant Army.[20]

Of course in more remote parts of the counties of Haifeng and Lufeng such old-fashioned clans could continue to exist, since the new Peasant Army was not yet a truly modern People's Army. Armed clans intervened to prevent the linking of Haifeng with the Swatow occupation. The Communist base at Maanshan fought off incursions by one of the largest clans in the watershed of the East River, the Chungs of Nanling. In both cases the Reds could defend themselves and retaliate, but could never successfully wipe out the military strength of the familistic armies. This was one reason why they resorted so often to the destruction of entire villages.[21]

A second result of the onset of people's war was the elimination of the gentry as an immanent force in Haifeng. Communist victory separated traditional leaders such as the relatives of Ch'en Chiung-ming from their natural constituency. The flight of the non-Communist elite made easier the job of controlling the non-Communist rank and file just as it did after 1949 in mainland China. Chinese exiles, perhaps more than those of other nations, have traditionally remained influential in their own counties, largely due to the cultural expectation that success earned abroad will be redistributed at home. Yet for several years the former ruling class of Haifeng seemed permanently exiled and not likely to rebuild its former influence.

Mao Tse-tung noted the phenomenon of voluntary exile in his famous Hunan report. He could rank the gentry of his home province according to how far from home they wandered to escape revolutionary unrest. But Haifeng exiles, like those from rural Vietnam, in fact were concentrated in one place. The British colony of Hong Kong, like the former colonial metropolis of Saigon, harbored a disproportionate number of refugees from Communist rule. In the 1925-1926 period the exiles cheered conservative resistance from the sidelines and aided British police with intelligence about radical activity in the colony. They began to raise large sums for the relief of the home counties in late 1927, drawing heavily on welfare organizations such as the China International Famine Relief Commission and the Tung Wah Hospital Group. They created a front called the Hai-Lufeng Association to speak out against Communist "atrocities" and to publish appeals and notices in the treaty port papers.[22]

The Hai-Lufeng Association was unable to interest Canton in invading Haifeng in 1927. The rivalries in the Kuomintang government ran too deep and its problems loomed too large. Therefore a number of members of the Hai-Lufeng Association resorted to military operations of their own in late 1927. Ch'en Yao-huan, a Hong Kong resident against his will since 1925 and a former associate of General Ch'en Chiung-ming, moved to Huilai county east of Lufeng and set up a small training camp for anti-Communist rangers in a small market town called Kueit'an. Unable credibly to threaten an invasion of the Red counties on his own, Ch'en resorted to spreading rumors of impending massive KMT troop movements. This boasting, much as South Vietnamese trading in American promises, bought some support within Haifeng and Lufeng but would produce real results only when the promises came true.

But even before the Kuomintang armies arrived in force, Ch'en Yao-huan found domestic friends. He discovered that certain large clans in the villages along the highway running east from Lufeng were prepared to support him with weapons and funds. Many of these clans had been aligned with one another in one of the ancient feuds that had divided the lowland Hai-Lufeng region for a century. An example was the Ch'en clan of Pomei hamlet, whose elder Ch'en Tzu-ho negotiated in December the formation of a White Flag Corps designed, in his words, to save the countryside. Another was the Lin clan of Shangp'u hamlet, a bulwark of the feuding group that had been called the Black Flags in the nineteenth century. A third was the Ma family, which called Kueit'an its home but which owned much paddy land across the border in Lufeng. By early January the Communists had massacred the inhabitants of Ch'ieh-shih, Huangt'ang, and Chienmenk'ang in Lufeng and it seemed clear that the large settlements along the highway had grim futures. Ch'en Tzu-ho's informal army grew rapidly as the clans of the Black Flag exhumed the ancient weapons they had buried long ago and smuggled them out of Communist territory into Kueit'an. He was joined by a secret society called the Long Goatee Party (Ch'ang-hsu-tang) whose very name lent a supernatural aura to his force. In mid-January he also welcomed the support of the native sheriff of the tiny coastal town of Chiatzu, the port through which the Communist front committee had escaped to Hong Kong the previous October.

On January 8, 1928, in one stroke Ch'en Tzu-ho's White Flag Army, as it had come to be called, seized control of three of the largest village settlements along the Lufeng-Ch'aoan highway. On the eleventh with only a hundred men they moved into Lufeng city virtually without opposition. The Communists took forty-eight hours to strike back, and after retaking Lufeng promptly walked into an ambush in Shangp'u hamlet, the home of the Lin clan. The White Flags recaptured Lufeng and for a few days in mid-January operated an anti-Communist county government there. Ch'en Yao-huan's preparations paid off as he marched unopposed from Kueit'an into Lufeng with three hundred of his rangers. The two Ch'en's, one an exile, the other an angry resident, held Lufeng until driven out by a Communist division under Tung Lang. They broke through the Communist lines with a terrifying clamor of gongs and shaking of secret society censers and escaped to Kueit'an to prepare for a later battle. Communist troops systematically destroyed the hamlets of Shangp'u and Pomei in retaliation. The White Flags, who in many ways resembled the dread Anti-Bolshevik Corps that mercilessly attacked the Communists of Kwangtung, Kiangsi, and Fukien from 1928 to 1931, had put together clan society and exiled gentry elements into a nearly successful combination.[23]

Under conditions of people's war the inherent capacity of localities to resist radical incursion may erode rapidly. The radical movement forgets about legitimate restraints and begins to depend on violence. As the radicals "go over into insurrection," open political activity in villages by supporters of the anti-Communist cause becomes unsafe. In villages that lack a standing tradition of self-defense (in Haifeng and in large parts of north China, for example), the inhibition of public political discussion may suppress the only source of native opposition. People's war, by raising the level of violence in villages, drives out the opposition's natural leaders. Refugees from civil war are seldom distributed randomly through the population; the first to leave are those who can afford it, who have contacts or even residences in the cities. It is just such people who, as in Kwangning and Hua, would be expected to mount an antiradical platform, and people's war drives them out. Finally, in those localities where the monopoly of force is in the hands of the radicals, ancient modes of control such as the narrowly political lineage demonstrate their impotence. The Lins of Kueifeng proved unable to hold out against the Communists in part because they could not make appeals to and generate contacts with other villages. People's war divides the countryside and will be able to conquer so long as the countryside does not find new ways to unite.

But these advantages are purchased at a certain risk, one of which was all too clear in the Haifeng case: that village opposition will manage to overcome past hostilities and feuds in the face of the new threat. The White Flag party, like the numerous parties of central and southern Hunan in 1927, was in large part a new amalgam of forces composed of former bitter enemies and produced by the rapid rise of the radical movement.

The success of people's war ultimately depends on protection. Victory for one side or another in such wars, as in those among nations, often depends on each side's ability to generate external support from its allies or at least to secure the neutrality of potential outside opponents. As long as the collaboration with the Kuomintang lasted, protection could be obtained through the political intervention of the central executive committee or through the military actions of the Party Army. Fifteen years later, during the anti-Japanese war, the Communist movement would be able to win protection by camouflaging itself as one of a number of nationalistic military forces fighting the invaders. Or it might find a form of protection by retreating into the no-man's land behind Japanese lines, where potentially anti-Communist Chinese forces could not penetrate because of the very presence of the Japanese. In the 1930s protection from the outside could be bought by settling in remote areas on the borders of provinces and on the periphery of central government concern. But none of these umbrellas—politics, nationalism, military or geographic insulation—was available to the Haifengese. After all hope for aid from Nanch'ang and Canton was lost in December 1927, Haifeng was protected from outside attack only by transportation time and the ponderosity of the enemy.

Anti-Communists in Canton had not yet agreed at the end of 1927 on a large expedition into the Hai-Lufeng region. The delicate balance of power in the provincial capital between the Cantonese under Chang Fa-k'uei and Li Chi-shen's Kwangsi friends kept the larger military units close to the city through most of January. Yet all agreed that the Communists would have to be confronted. The compromise worked out in the last week of January was to send a small Expeditionary Force to Exterminate the Reds. Li Chi-shen, slowly emerging as the leader of a new coalition that would rule Kwangtung for the next decade and more, agreed to appoint two Haifeng natives to head this force. One, Chung Hsiu-nan, was an older politician with Ch'en Chiung-ming connections whose home was in ravaged Meilung district. The other, Ts'ai T'eng-hui, a lean young general of the Whampoa stripe, was the Popular Corps leader who had served Canton loyally, if incompetently, during the first Communist rising in the preceding summer. The combination looked attractive, but it took scarcely a week to show that Haifeng would fall only to a larger and more professionally brutal force.

With only two thousand men, Chung and Ts'ai threw themselves at the toughest part of Haifeng: the western reaches. Though nearest to Canton and their own base at Huangfou in Huiyang county,

Meilung and Ch'ihshih had been organized for too long and were defended by Yeh Yung's determined veterans of the Canton uprising. Departing Huangfou on January 22, Chung and Ts'ai took Ch'ihshih easily two days later. Yeh Yung learned how feeble the invading force was and surrounded them on high ground with three thousand Communist troops on the night of January 28. Ts'ai roused his men to charge the hills in counterattack but was badly mauled in a two-hour firefight in which Chung Hsiu-nan narrowly escaped death. The dozen native guides, mostly members of the Lin clan of Kueifeng, were killed by the surrounding Reds.[24]

Chung Hsiu-nan reflected on his late January experience. He had spent several years in exile in Hong Kong as a member of the Haifeng Association waiting for the chance to return home and had not expected such a setback. He blamed the inadequate leadership of Ts'ai T'eng-hui, the unreliability of the Popular Corps on which both men had depended, and the fierce hostility of the peasantry in the vicinity of Meilung. Communism had been well entrenched in the villages around Ch'ihshih for a long time. His own men had been rendered immobile by anxiety as soon as they entered the county's borders. They were caught in a dilemma: if they behaved harshly and aggressively they would at the start lose the hearts and minds (*jen-hsin*) of the people.[25] If they failed to do so, then defeat, as at Ch'ihshih, was inevitable.[26]

He had no answers to the dilemma that would face government troops in other people's wars. Ordinary rural people in China and elsewhere will trust their own friends and their own defenders more than an outside force. Firepower used against civilians, no matter what their connection with the insurgents, will not help win their hearts and minds. Chung Hsiu-nan noted that the enemy was also making a few friends with its new tactics of assassination and arson, but it did demonstrate his courage. He urged fellow Haifengese to act quickly lest the "devilish theories" of the Communists sink in even more deeply and "all the killing in the world will not help."[27]

The solution was to do the killing sooner rather than later. For this Chung and Ts'ai were clearly unqualified, so the job fell to an older, more experienced soldier. Ch'en Chi-t'ang, the man chosen, represented more than symbolically the new Cantonese military that had helped crush the peasant movement in other counties. A native of the far west of the province, Ch'en had risen through the ranks of

Li Chi-shen's Kwangtung Army, attended the pre-Chiang Kai-shek military school at Whampoa, and sided with Li against Chang Fa-k'uei in December 1927.[28] By late February 1928 Ch'en, who had been sent east to combat the Nanch'ang armies, had his orders to march on Haifeng. More cautious than Chung and Ts'ai, he first contacted the White Flag partisans in their village base at Taan and moved against the weaker of the two Communist county governments. Yeh Yung's second division was no match for this division of nearly ten thousand well-armed men, and the capital of Lufeng fell after a four-hour battle a mile outside the northern gate. Two days later Ch'en delivered a similar defeat to the other Communist division, that of Tung Lang, at Kungp'ing. The county seats of Haifeng and Lufeng would not fall under Communist rule again for twenty years. Within a week, after bitter street fighting, the market towns were also in government hands.[29]

It is true that bringing the villages under government control was not easy. There are many stories of fierce resistance to the new conquerors, especially from villages with a longer history of Communist influence. Especially strong was the hostility in Ch'ihshan (Red Hills), the village where P'eng P'ai made his first peasant converts in 1922. When the new garrison commander's soldiers were attacked by an angry Ch'ihshan widow with a butcher knife, they responded by rounding up several hundred villagers and marching them to the county seat for trial. Several days later other villagers tried to break into the jail to free them. In the end more than a hundred Ch'ihshan natives were executed.

In other villages, however, non-Communist rule returned more easily. Especially in Lufeng the known military weakness of the Communists and the spectacular flourishing of the White Flags had led many to expect the soviet to be short lived. But also, even in Haifeng, the Communists had made many enemies, and a number of local commissars were betrayed to the new rulers in their village hideaways.

By early March the eleventh division had driven out all armed Communists from the two districts around the county seat of Haifeng. The only effective troops under the Reds' command had retreated to the hills to the northwest of Meilung. It would be some time before Chung Hsiu-nan, the new county magistrate, discovered their mountain camps in Chungtung and P'utzu. One reason for the delay was that the area of the remaining Communist military preserve was policed by the fabulously inept Ts'ai T'eng-hui. Unable to anticipate his enemy's moves, Ts'ai time and time again marched into well-set ambushes. But the overwhelming advantage of daytime control of the valleys, of support from the outside, and of arms and ammunition allowed him nonetheless inexorably to reduce the scope of Communist territorial control.[30]

The devastation of the two Communist mountain sanctuaries took several weeks. First Ch'en Chi-t'ang's subordinate Yü Han-mou, guided by local Popular Corpsmen, moved his three thousand men from Tzuchin county seat on March 18 to a position just northwest of the Yenshih stronghold. For three days, Yü's Communist-chasing army moved through the foothills of Chungtung and Yenshih, attempting to engage the Red main force. He succeeded only on the twentieth, when, breaking through a CP-held perimeter he found himself within the territory of the Communist fortress. Supported by Popular Corpsmen from as far away as Chienmenk'ang — the Lufeng village that had been ravaged by the Communists in January — Yü battled with the well-entrenched Reds for nearly two days. Finally at dawn on March 22 a drive from four sides broke through the last defenses, and Yü discovered an ingenious fortress carved into the mountainside well stocked with large amounts of vegetables, dried fish, salt, and rice. More than four hundred Communist troops were counted dead in this encounter, and a large supply of weapons and grain fell into Yü's hands. The victory, which cost Yü's army considerable losses, drove the remnants of the Communist Haifeng army across into Huilai county to the east. The second stronghold, in east Haifeng, fell less than a week later.

In midsummer 1928 Yu Han-mou captured Lin T'ieh-shih, chairman of the Lufeng soviet who had been educated at Keiō University in Japan. Lin's testimony to his interrogators revealed the extent of the anti-Communist victory. There were fewer than five hundred armed Reds by July, he said, less than a quarter of the combined second and fourth divisions only six months earlier. The peasant armies, he explained, had disappeared as organized units largely because of the great sacrifices that guerrilla warfare imposed upon them. Peasant troops, Lin avowed, knew that to fight on they would have to eat yams in the deep mountains, watch for marauding bandits, and suffer from unnamed illnesses, and many simply

returned to their fields. Yeh Yung, also captured in April, con-
curred. His men, defeated in an attempt to seize the capital of
Huilai county in March, had refused to keep fighting. "The peasant
bandits with us," Yeh complained, "insisted they would profit far
more from pillaging than from fighting serious battles." Lin T'ieh-
shih admitted that the various leading organs of the Chinese Communist party had lost touch with one another in the chaos of the
defeat.[31]

THERE ARE MANY objections that historians will raise against the
argument that Haifeng in 1927-1928 was the first prototypical example of the type of revolutionary warfare that Lin Piao in recent
years termed people's war and that has been practiced in South
Vietnam by the Vietnam Workers' party. First, the Haifeng soviet
government, for all its extensive mobilization efforts, did not benefit
from the mass line techniques of rule that Mao Tse-tung and Liu
Shao-ch'i developed during the anti-Japanese war. There were no
real cooperatives like the south ward cooperative, no army-run
farms like Nanniwan, no rectification campaigns, no arguments
about the proper style of leadership or work within the party.
Indeed anyone who might have suggested such innovations in the
brief life of the soviet would probably have been accused of treason-
ous diversion of revolutionary energy. Likewise, there was no external enemy like the Japanese in north China or the French and
Americans in Vietnam to focus mass nationalism and xenophobia.
The Haifeng government handled its only contact with the Western
world with great circumspection in the full knowledge that introduction of foreign forces into Haifeng would not strengthen revolutionary power. Finally, Haifeng, unlike the governments in north
China in the 1940s or in Vietnam in the 1960s, did not have the
geographic sanctuaries that protected Communist military and
political power. Lenin's spider web, centered on Moscow but
stretching around the globe to protect his revolutionary minions,
could not be compared to the security of an inviolable boundary or
of an impenetrable mountain fastness.

On all these points, to be sure, Haifeng differed from Hanoi and
Yenan. But for the history of rural revolution these differences are
not essential. They relate far more to the ultimate success or failure
of the greater movement than they do to the existence of people's

war as a phenomenon. Haifeng had, unlike any of the other peasant movement counties, produced by 1927 the four conditions for that type of revolutionary warfare.

First Haifeng possessed a rural-urban split of major proportions. The forces that produced this split are not entirely obvious. In some cases, for example in the Meilung district in western Haifeng, a long history of clan-landowner domination of the town produced deep-seated hostility in the nearby tenant population. In others, for example in the Chiehsheng-Swabue coastal area, the predominance of fishing interests over agriculture exacerbated the sense of alienation from town life shared by those who lived even just outside the walls of the towns. Hostility toward the towns was heightened after 1924 as landowners and other notables fled their home villages to seek safety in the market settlements, the county seat, and in Hong Kong and Swatow. Absenteeism, itself a product of the growing hostility in the villages, further increased the width of the split.

Second, Haifeng had a rural underground far better developed than any other Chinese county in the period. Anti-Communists are fond of using the sinister-sounding term infrastructure to refer to Communist basic-level organization. But while stressing the importance of this organization to movement growth, many are content to recite the tables of organization and the articles of party faith that refer to organized life. In Haifeng the phenomenon preceded the intellectualization and was therefore even more formidable. Communist party organization grew rapidly in many villages in the specially favorable conditions of Haifeng, where there was no need to accommodate local notables or militia powerholders. But the essence of that growth was the difficult job of political organization, a job that P'eng P'ai had begun already in 1922. If P'eng's earlier experience is any indication, that work involved great efforts to introduce the idea of organization, to overcome the opposition of ordinary people as well as of the powerful, to maintain enthusiasm, to extract contributions, and to enforce discipline. The contacts, the attention, and the involvement that kept the rural underground alive in Haifeng were indispensable elements of the people's war phenomenon.

Third, the Haifeng Communist party developed virtually independently a strategy of protracted warfare. Rural revolutions of the people's war type are never over in a few days or weeks or months.

The delicate balance of forces that makes them possible cannot produce rapid victories. The Haifeng Communists were pushed several
times into rash attempts to seize county power by an impatient
Central Committee. But in each case there were strong voices arguing for long-term protection of the rural base, for a retreat to defensible mountain strongholds, and for hit-and-run strategies designed
to preserve the movement. In rural revolution, protracted war
means being resigned to nonurban life for years on end. This resignation, despite the euphoric moments of urban occupation, most
Haifeng leaders shared.

Finally, the phenomenon of people's war has as a precondition,
perhaps the most important precondition, a paralyzing vacuum of
urban authority. Cities are, even in so-called underdeveloped societies, still powerful beacons of attraction and potent centers of
repression. Many ridicule the Kuomintang of the 1940s and the
Saigon regime of the 1960s for their urban orientation. The risk is
evident: cities have soft living standards, become easily demoralized
by urban problems, and depend heavily on the food-producing
countryside for their existence. But cities also are great sources of
wealth through taxation, of manpower through recruitment, and of
political support through education and communication. No political authority or government that controls urban centers will happily
relinquish them.

But what often happens, and did happen in the Haifeng case, is
that urban authorities become enfeebled through processes that are
beyond their control. In Haifeng the power deflation of urban
authority began with the baiting of P'eng P'ai's first association,
progressed through the defeat of Ch'en Chiung-ming's authoritarian
regime in the county, and culminated in the isolation of Haifeng
from the rest of the province for most of 1927. P'eng's early clashes
with the old magistrate Wang Tso-hsin had demonstrated the military feebleness of the local government already in 1923. When the
Kuomintang took over from Ch'en K'ai-t'ing in October 1925, P'eng
made certain that anyone connected with the old regime was removed from authority. He deliberately prevented the development
of magisterial police or Popular Corps forces and put more energy
into organizing the Communist party than the Kuomintang. When
his followers seized the county seat in 1927, they demonstrated
quickly that backing for county authority from Canton or Huiyang,
although it came in time, was not inclined to stay and sink deep

roots. The withdrawal of one anti-Communist force to participate in a minor coup in Canton produced at least one of the Communist county governments. There can be many causes for the paralysis of urban authority, of which the Haifeng case presents us with but a few. But without it the people's war phenomenon stands little chance of occurring.

These four conditions — the town-country split, the village underground, the rural commitment, and the urban paralysis — were all present in Haifeng and helped to produce Asia's first Communist government. And yet the Haifeng soviets were crushed. Does our study yield any wisdom about how peoples' wars, once started, can be defeated? Perhaps, but it is not very uplifting. We have already made several obvious points: that the Communists lacked a sanctuary into which to retreat, that they failed to involve enough of the population, and that they antagonized too many by their radical bloodthirstiness. All these may be true, but the brutal fact is that the Haifeng soviet was crushed by the overwhelming application of armed force.

This is not to say that those who applied the force did so without any political support. The White Flag parties in Lufeng, a number of large market towns such as Chiehsheng and Ch'iehshih, and an enormous number of refugees to Canton, Swatow, and Huiyang cheered the advances into Communist-occupied territory in 1928, though they could not have approved of the wholesale destruction that went along with the campaigns. All these demonstrated fierce resistance to the imposition of Communist power in Haifeng and Lufeng. And many others, less committed to a political position, contributed to the fall of the soviets by joining in the armies, by supplying information, or just by going about their daily business. Though the anti-Communists were not inclined to perceive it, the outcome of every kind of warfare, particularly revolutionary and counterrevolutionary warfare, depends in some degree on loyalty, the sense of justice, judgments of legitimacy, and perceptions of power — the core concerns of politics. Just as war among nations is an extension of international politics, so people's war represents the tragic end product of domestic political processes. Yet the final outcome of any peasant movement once it develops to the point of people's war is unavoidably military, just as in 1949 the Chinese Communists applied their own military solution to their conflict with Chiang Kai-shek.

12

THE LEGACY
OF CHINA'S
PEASANT
MOVEMENT

The Chinese Communists who took part in the peasant movement from 1922 to 1928 shared a set of common perceptions of the revolutionary struggle. These perceptions did not merit being called a strategy, since they were not consciously expressed in any body of doctrine. Although there was no well-worked-out blueprint for action, everyone connected with the movement possessed a set of axiomatic beliefs that gave his political actions form and content. Already in the mid-1920s the basic elements of an ideology of rural revolution had begun to take shape.

Movement ideology held that the huge rural population of China was the most powerful force in the nation. This conception took shape slowly, under some pressure from Moscow, with some support from traditional concepts of China's rural foundations. It was resisted by many in the Communist movement who for reasons of Marxist (though not perhaps of Leninist) orthodoxy insisted that the economic power of the industrialized cities would ultimately be decisive. Many Communists still felt constrained, as did Mao Tse-tung, to assign the peasantry slightly less weight in the national revolution than did more enthusiastic Kuomintangists. Mao's assessment in his Hunan report that the countryside contributed more to

the revolution than the cities by a factor of seven to three fell short
of the eight to two or nine to one proportion that some KMT peasant leaders espoused at the time. But he was squarely in the movement mainstream in considering the peasantry the main force army
of the Great Revolution.

A second article of peasant movement faith was that the key to
capitalizing on this force lay in penetrating the countryside. Empty
phrases about the strength of the peasant masses would never create
the needed influence. Remaining behind desks in safe, urban,
bureaucratic surroundings would not win the revolution. The party
that won the countryside would do so by expanding geographically
to parts of China never before touched by political organization.
The Communist party's most significant organizational contribution to the Kuomintang was to open up new, largely rural territory by
building local party cells. For the first time a political party in
China paid attention to maps, checked off counties, and counted
rural membership. The peasant associations spread to villages untouched even by the new rural party. Behind all this intense organizational activity lay the conviction that control of the countryside
would determine victory or defeat for the revolution.

A third peasant movement article of faith was that organization
could only be built on conflict. The neat, geometric pyramids of
structure envisaged in the peasant associations' charter were satisfying to the grand architects of the worker-peasant policy, notably
Sun Yat-sen and Liao Chung-k'ai. But their inferiors assigned to
build them soon learned that allegiance demanded something more
than mere membership. Villagers were all too ready to sign up a.
negligible cost and all too reluctant to remain involved when danger
threatened. Stronger, more permanent ties could be forged only by
aligning the associations with certain local groupings against others.
The variety of the cleavages that proved useful was dismaying.
Dialectical differences, intervillage hostilities, faiths and superstitions, clan rivalries, historical feuds, virtually any distinction that
separated one rural group from another might be useful in gaining
leverage. But the crucial element in the eyes of the movement in
building an organization was the existence of an identifiable local
enemy—whether he be called landlord or KMT rightist or warlord
or corps bandit. Time and again the movement would switch
enemies in midstream as a new situation unfolded or mass enthusi-

asm slackened, until the lasting impression remained that struggle itself was the essence of progress.

A fourth and final article of faith, one that proved the fatal weakness of the movement, was that its own rising influence and excitement would suffice to transform the less responsive, less progressive segments of the revolution. Peasant movement leaders thought of themselves, it seems clear, as the yeast of revolutionary growth. Once the mass organizations had grown to proper size, they felt, the revolution would quickly reach maturity. They assumed that the Kuomintang could not long remain untransformed when millions of peasants flocked to join the associations and, from below, the Nationalist party. Ch'en Tu-hsiu's belief in the existence of a KMT Left was based on this characteristic faith in the availability of support among the rural masses. The transformation of the Kuomintang would come not from a party purge but from a party flood, an inundation of the small elitist bureaucracy by wave upon wave of new peasant adherents.

Yet by 1928 any reasonable observer of China would have found these elements of a political creed incredible if not ludicrous. The sharp struggle in the villages that produced allegiance also produced disaffection. Local organizations, however well placed, were not capable without outside help of seizing real political power. The mass organization structure was a mere skeleton, a feeble assemblage of rigid shapes without substance to resist the direct armed onslaught of military power. The movement's final recourse to a broad armed uprising against the Kuomintang meant little more than voluntary self-immolation for all but a select few of the participants.

Why did the peasant movement fail? Our natural tendency in dealing with such a question is to search for scapegoats, for humans who can be shown to have committed mistakes or crimes. The impulsiveness of P'eng P'ai, the dependency of Chou Ch'i-chien, the vacillation of Ch'en Tu-hsiu, the naïveté of Mao Tse-tung, the treachery of Chiang Kai-shek, each of these character flaws has entered briefly into our analysis, but none enough to be convincing alone.

P'eng P'ai and other special delegates of the central peasant bureau did indeed often provoke the anger of powerful enemies and readily generated their own formidable opposition. But these failings in P'eng's case at least were in part a function of his youth. It is true that his earliest activities in Haifeng brought his association to the brink of violence more times than it could safely withdraw. P'eng was consistently restrained by the more cautious hand of his brother, Han-yuan.

His victories after 1925 in Haifeng, though obviously supported by some important segments of the local population, were clearly imposed from outside the county. Had Haifeng's external security been guaranteed after 1928, P'eng's aggressive posture would have been seen (as most observers now see that of the Chinese Communists between 1949 and 1953) as the product of a crafty assessment of the balance of social forces.

Dependency was of course another matter. The movement constantly reminded itself of the importance of building mass strength and of the mistake of relying on outside force. Why then were the Kwangning and the Hua county cases, which demonstrated clearly the leadership's reliance on troops from Canton when trouble arose, widely touted as examples of success? Our answer has been that first, the very concept of the peasant movement as a part of the Kuomintang's national revolution made reliance on outside authority a matter of course. Either Canton or Wuhan would come to the peasant's aid or there was no sense in attempting a peasant movement at all. And second, without Canton's or Wuhan's approval it would be impossible in most cases to construct an independent peasant armed force that could stand up against the native opposition. Those who might have urged Chou Ch'i-chien in Kwangning or Liang Po-yü in Hua to go it alone would have condemned their embryonic peasant armed forces to very short lives indeed. Except in Haifeng, and perhaps for a brief while some counties in Hunan where the enemy (the corps, the clan armies, the secret societies, the garrison armies) either did not exist or had been discredited and destroyed by the Nationalist armies for their connection with the warlord regimes, to begin civil warfare relying on the strength of the peasant masses would have been as suicidal as the final Autumn Harvest Insurrection. In any case, neither in the peasant movement period nor in the later history of the Chinese Communist revolutionary involvement with the peasantry did the slogan rely upon the masses ever mean abandon whatever military allies you might be able to use. Dependency on the KMT military was a symptom, not a cause, of the death of the peasant movement.

Chiang Kai-shek's turn to the Right in 1927 was not, we have sug-

gested, an arbitrary act of betrayal. There were many politicians—
including several chiefs of the central peasant bureau—who
applauded his act, as well as many who urged it before the fact. The
new military elite under Chiang after 1924, preoccupied as they
were with problems of strategy and security, quickly sensed the
insignificance of the peasant movement for their own goals. Prominent military politicians, such as Li Chi-shen in Kwangtung and
T'ang Sheng-chih in Hunan, were less willing than their subordinates to move against the Communists because of their ties with the
Kuomintang party. Chiang Kai-shek's final blow was telegraphed by
countless feints and jabs of anti-Communist local commanders—
men such as Teng Jun-ch'i in Kwangning, Wu Kuan-ch'i in Hua,
Hsu K'o-hsiang in Ch'angsha, and Chung Ching-t'ang in Haifeng.
In such men as these the peasant movement created powerful
enemies through its local-level work, enemies against whom their
feeble peasant armies were a pitiful match. Chiang Kai-shek's betrayal of the Communists was in fact an act required to reestablish
the trust of his antiradical supporters.

We have absolved Ch'en, Mao, and other Communist leaders of
the charge of restraint of the movement. To urge the movement to
control its excesses or to limit its infantilism, as the Communist
party leaders at times did, made perfect sense. Rural Communists
were by and large as radical as their local situations permitted them
to be. In Kwangtung they moved more rapidly than their superiors
wished to demanding comprehensive rent reduction. That they did
not go further to demand a solution to the land question was due
more to their judgment that land ownership mattered far less than
the movement's own well being. Where significant opposition evaporated, as during late 1926 in Hunan or early 1927 in Haifeng, peasant movement leaders easily began to confiscate land. The typical
peasant movement posture was not frustrated radicalism but prudent militance.

What about the Communist leadership? We have found Ch'en
Tu-hsiu to be a man battered about in the policy storms that en-
gulfed his entire party and the international movement. Not disinterested in the force of the peasantry from 1923 onward, he nonetheless was distracted by the imaginary success of the urban movement in 1925 and overwhelmed by the obvious potency of the non-
Communist national armies. After mid-1926 he, like Mao Tse-tung,

wavered between a compromising commitment to the KMT collaboration and a desperate hope that the peasantry would help him out of that collaboration. But though neither man arrived at a clear position on the peasant question until after the split, their confusion could not have been the major factor in the movement's collapse. Had both Mao and Ch'en decided for the radicalization of the movement (as Mao attempted briefly in early 1927, before the harsh realities of the Wuhan government became clear to him), the outcome of the insurrection would have been little different from what it was in late 1927. Had they both opted for permanent collaboration, as did Kan Nai-kuang and Ch'en Kung-po, the peasant movement would still have been at the mercy of their local enemies and the ineffectual KMT left politicians.

It is also difficult to place the blame squarely on the non-Communist Kuomintang. Even where the movement's KMT sympathizers were not, as was Liu Yueh-ch'ih and the Left Society in Hunan, undercut by impatient and impulsive Communists, their careers were limited by the powerlessness of the movements they fostered. Our examination of the central peasant bureau and the rest of the peasant movement apparatus pointed out that the bureau chiefs and other leftists operated in a no-man's land between the Bolshevik and the non-Bolshevik portions of the Nationalist movement. They were perfectly capable of helping the peasants or pursuing the worker-peasant policy when no matter of party power stood in the way. But their primary allegiance, both by personal preference and by the nature of the KMT bureaucratic-political system, was to the party center, not its periphery. That the Kuomintang did not as a matter of life or death need any of the mass movements was the clear lesson of the 1924-1927 period. It was even more obvious that, having made this decision, there would be many reasons to move against a Communist party that had in its actions and policy made clear it awaited a chance to stage the second revolution.

So from the various indictments of murder we must turn to more systemic explanations of the peasant movement's demise. This essay at each stage has pulled us toward the interpretation that the movement died of natural causes. The human inputs, the decisions, the efforts, the exercises of will and discipline that went into creating and then into killing the movement were essential in the unfolding of the tragedy. But we have argued that none of the actors, least of all the peasant movement leaders, could have averted the defeat, given the critical facts of Chinese politics of the day.

First of all, the Communist party was far too small and feeble in 1923 to expand rapidly without exceptionally favorable circumstances. The optimum circumstances for party growth were provided by the KMT alliance, much to the surprise of some Communist opponents of that collaboration. Yet the precondition of Communist growth under the wing of the KMT had to be the preeminence of the Nationalists. In fact after 1924 not only did Nationalist growth greatly exceed that of the Communist party but what was more important the growth of the non-Communist specialists in violence was greater still. This startling trend had already become discernible in 1925, though preoccupation on all sides with the expanding mass participation and geographic area of the national revolution obscured it. But even if the Communists had recognized that they were losing out to other forces, which they found difficult to admit after the May Thirtieth movement, the costs of dismantling a partially profitable alliance would have outweighed the advantages. The peasant movement, like other partially successful segments of the Communist effort, had already developed a stake in its own existence and constituted a powerful interest group in revolutionary politics.

Second, the Nationalist movement was not and could never become a Bolshevik party. Most Chinese Communists shared two fundamental misconceptions about Lenin's party that might have been corrected had they understood Russian history. First they assumed that Lenin's organizational principles could be separated from the group that was to practice them. The essence of Leninism is the centralization of all authority in one person or at most a handful of persons; its successful practitioners are *also* able to command a tightly knit, disciplined, and sizable following. But in Lenin's case the man and the leadership group existed long before the Bolshevik party expanded its influence. Sun Yat-sen's party also had a long existence, possessed a centralized authority figure, and seemed committed to total control and discipline. But Sun was never convinced of the value of using one segment of society against another unless that struggle demonstrably redounded to his personal benefit.

Sun's political heirs were hardly a unified coterie of loyal party functionaries. His death came scarcely a year after his controversial decision to introduce the Communists into his inner circle. Where Lenin's followers were united by a body of codified doctrine taken from the socialist movement in Europe, by a sense of organized living inherited from conspiratorial habits, and by the shared sweet taste of recent victory, Sun's followers had little to bind them other than their common respect for his person. After his death the Kuomintang underwent a succession crisis far more severe than that of Lenin's party, and in that crisis the KMT politicians who strove for power and influence had to treat the peasant movement as a pawn and not as the point of the game. The Kuomintang's succession struggle deprived the would-be Bolshevist peasant movement of its indispensable leadership.

Chinese Communists also misconceived Lenin's claims to mass support as his main *point d'appui*. In the Russian case the peasant and working-class masses had played a crucial role in bringing down the old state in stopping the Russian participation in the world war, and in supporting the new parliamentary assemblies that moved to reorganize Russia in 1917. But they were not groups that supported Lenin's Communist party; Lenin simply made brilliant strategic use of preexisting mass organizations. Chinese Communists accepted without question the notion that their revolution would have to have such groups and set about building them without calculating how they would contribute, if at all, to the power situation of either the Kuomintang or the Communist party. Like the Japanese copying imperial palaces at Nara or the Nigerians importing parliament, the Chinese simply assumed a lively peasant movement could be a powerful force. Their assumption was fortified, if not created, by the mystical belief in human numbers that the peasant movement leadership shared.

The third critical fact about Chinese politics in the 1920s was the immunity of much of the countryside to radical peasant movement tactics. Here the organic analogy of a natural death may be the most suited to our argument. In case after case we have seen how the new serum introduced by peasant movement organizers generated its own antibodies among the local population. The movement grew on the promise of future gain for people of low status, on the occasional payoffs of struggle with the wealthy, on the sense of solidarity, and particularly on the growing allegiance to a new revolutionary authority promising peace and justice. Yet this very growth produced jealous, smarting, outraged enemies virtually everywhere. Much of this opposition came from elements that had for a century been responsible for keeping the peace in the countryside in the absence of central authority. But there were also new alliances forged between long-standing enemies against the newest threat to village stability and tranquillity. In many counties, such as Kwangning and Hua, these forces emerged as a new antimovement in their own right. The promise of outside support and defense, from the start its highest card, became the peasant movement's only trick by the end. By that time outside support and defense were in the hands of the opposition.

What are the chances that a peasant movement of a type not envisaged by the Communists might have noticeably increased rural participation in Chinese progress? Other societies at other times have supported highly influential pressure groups organized around rural interests. To pick a single example, in Venezuela less than a decade after the destruction of the Haifeng soviet, Romulo Betancourt and other Marxist politicians allied themselves with rural leaders to form a bloc that within twenty years had captured national power and introduced substantial reforms. The Accion Democratica kept alive through two decades of repression a tradition of democratic practice in an oligarchical society. By its success it opened up the structure of politics to a new, reform-minded elite more responsive to rural and lower-class urban needs.[1] Though the Venezuelan model of peasant integration into the national polity may not have been perfect, it has so far been successful enough to permit us to ask why the Chinese movement could not have developed along similar lines.

Several of the explanations that leap to mind are attractive. The Chinese political tradition, so goes one, built a neat barrier between the farming and ruling segments of the population. The *shen,* or scholar-gentry, were literate practitioners of the fine art of government; the *nung,* or agriculturists, were not expected to understand affairs of state, though they might be aroused to rebellion by seditious notables. The Kuomintang inherited, in this view, the gentry's disdain for agricultural problems as well as their distrust of boorish peasants. Even Mao Tse-tung admitted he shared somethng of this view in his early years. But of course the Chinese political tradition was far more subtle than this stereotype allows. Rural reform has always been a central theme of Chinese statesmanship—whether through land distribution as in the latter Han dynasty, militia and mass organization as in the Sung, or irrigation and flood control as in virtually every period of Chinese history. The Kuomintang could have drawn, and to some degree did draw, upon this reservoir of agrarian reformism, even to the point of resuscitating the thousand-year-old *pao-chia* system of rural group responsibility.

All observers agree that after 1927 the Kuomintang, while trying to keep its mass base alive, never permitted autonomous growth of either labor unions or peasant associations. By 1937 Chiang Kai-shek's Nanking government claimed only three and a half million peasant association members in about a third of China's counties.[2] Party congresses argued about whether these associations should report to the KMT local party branch or directly to the central administration, but in either case no one doubted that the purpose of these organizations was to educate, control, and integrate the peasantry into the new national government. In this respect the new Chinese Communist government after 1949 was not wholly different. It too insisted on absolute control of its own recreated peasant associations.

An obvious second hypothesis, therefore, is this: the Kuomintang failed at rural reform because it could not recognize a legitimate plurality of interests. There is no denying the strong resistance to selfish expression of particular advantage that is shared by persons as disparate as the Ch'ing court conservatives and Mao Tse-tung. Sun Yat-sen's caution about peasant movement advances at the expense of other segments of society expressed not any prolandlord bias but rather his typically Chinese desire to avoid internal pluralistic conflict. Mao justified his support of peasant radicals in 1927, just as he did his backing for student Red Guards forty years later, by the belief that they were acting in the interest of the general will of the Chinese people. But when peasants began to speak up for their own particular interests in 1966, they were quickly silenced, just as during 1926 the real demands of the peasantry, for peace, protection, and relief, yielded to the leadership's own notion of the revolutionary purpose.

Convincing as this appeal to political culture seems, it cannot be the full story. In areas where the political system permits, as for example in present-day Singapore, Chinese populations readily organize themselves to exert political influence. Although pluralism in the context of Chinese national weakness and instability understandably could not be a cardinal principle of Kuomintang politics, interest articulation was hardly unknown in twentieth-century China. The question remains why the peasant movement idea, stripped of its insurrectionary guise, did not flourish under Nationalist auspices.

A third hypothesis, then, is that the Kuomintang after the split with the Communists was constitutionally incapable of social change because of its own class makeup. The Nationalist party, the argument goes, sprang from an alliance of landlord interests and new urban military capitalists committed to the continued exploitation of the peasantry. The continued pressure of wealthy rural interests supposedly explains Chiang Kai-shek's inability to carry out even Sun Yat-sen's moderate land reform program. Perhaps, but the landlord interest was not particularly well represented in the Kuomintang in the thirties. About a quarter of the Nationalist central executive committee could be called members by origin of the landowning classes. By 1940 virtually every one of these had spent twenty years as a full-time party professional without agrarian concerns. Even in provinces like Kwangtung, where urban commercial and banking interests dominated the party almost to the exclusion of agriculture, the Nationalists failed to reform the land situation. If the Communists, with as many representatives of the landlord class, could transcend their family backgrounds and act in the interest of the peasants, why could not the Kuomintang have done so? The answer lay in large measure in the bitter memories of the peasant movement period that non-Communist Kuomintang members carried with them into the Nanking decade after 1927. Politicians to the left of Chiang Kai-shek could never outlive the stigma of association with the Communist party. Mass movements with their threats of dissension, subordination, and rebellion could never again be allowed to threaten central Nationalist authority. The Kuomintang after 1927 was motivated far less by landlord representation or pressure than by a generalized distrust of mobilization. In this atmosphere of distrust the leftist politicians of the pre-1927 period were unable to function as brokers of mass interests in the fashion of Romulo Betancourt.

Consider the careers of the non-Communist peasant bureau chiefs of the twenties. Kan Nai-kuang left China in 1927 to study political science at the University of Chicago and returned to spend his days as a minor KMT functionary. Teng Yen-ta traveled briefly to Russia and returned to join former Communist T'an P'ing-shan in their short-lived third party. His life was cut short by a KMT secret police bullet in Nanking in 1930, not long after P'eng P'ai and his wife met a similar fate in Shanghai. Ch'en Kung-po, the former communist, kept his political career alive only by riding the coattails of Chiang Kai-shek's chief political rival, Wang Ching-wei. As a member of Wang's reorganization clique from 1927 to 1930, Ch'en wrote often about the need for mass work, but he had no government position in which to practice it. After 1931, as the chief of the Kuomintang's committee for mass movements, Ch'en sponsored countless empty resolutions to build centralized peasant organizations. The party's failure to respond and his close friendship with Wang Ching-wei drove him, by 1939, into the ill-fated Japanese puppet government in Nanking.

What distinguished these men from Romulo Betancourt or from the Japanese or Italian post-World War II rural radicals was not their lack of conviction so much as their lack of a legitimate arena in which to perform. The Kuomintang was not contesting elections, but civil wars. Soldiers may well vote with their feet, but they do not do so often or regularly every twenty-four months. Military victors, whether on the Northern Expedition or in anti-Communist extermination campaigns, seldom pause to take the pulse of the conquered. Betancourt's strategy could not work in China because China was not a single polity wherein the resolution of political conflict through nonmilitary solution was an accepted fact. Without a protected arena, however shabby and inadequate, for performing political acts, there could be no real opening for noncombat leftist politicians. Whatever its causes the disaster of 1927, by opening the wounds of civil war within the Kuomintang camp, helped make radical-reformist agrarian politics impossible.

If rigid disillusionment with mass action was the Kuomintang's inheritance from 1927, what about their opposition? Its record of failure from 1927 to 1928 would suggest that the Communist movement should have sought a different path to success in the future. Indeed, if we look for the descendants of the peasant movement, we discover a missing generation of leaders. Of the important peasant

movement figures of the 1922-1928 period, men of national reputation as peasant leaders, only Mao Tse-tung survived past 1935. P'eng
P'ai, betrayed by a former Hai-Lufeng comrade, was shot in Shanghai in 1929. Lo Ch'i-yuan, betrayed by a jealous rival in love, met
the same fate in 1931. Fang Chih-min, the Kiangsi peasant leader,
was killed by the Kuomintang in his home county of Iyang in 1935.
Most of the middle-level Kwangtung and Hunan provincial figures
perished in the 1927 suppression. By 1949 the few hundred men who
survived the Autumn Harvest debacle and the fall of the Hai-Lu-
feng soviets numbered only a few dozen.[3]

But human groups, especially those with a transcendental sense of
mission, have memories longer than those of individuals. The failures of the peasant movement period would have to be thrashed out,
since the party is never fallible, and blamed on someone. In the official histories Ch'en Tu-hsiu takes most of the blame for what so patently was a group transgression. But the minor successes and the
more important creeds and commitments would still be remembered even, in the trite Chinese phrase, "after the Autumn Harvest."

The emergence of Mao Tse-tung as a peasant movement figure
has been touched on at a number of places. He is generally taken, in
China and abroad, to be the most representative figure of the peasant movement. The premises of the Peasant Movement Institute in
Canton have been converted to a museum, but the address is that of
Mao's short-lived fifth class. Nowhere is P'eng P'ai's more substantial
contribution recognized.[4]

In fact Mao Tse-tung was not the dominant peasant movement
leader his Peking biographers would like us to believe. His first contact with village work came three years after P'eng P'ai set up his
lectern at the crossroads in Red Hills. Even then the evidence hints
he was more interested in rural intellectuals and antiimperialism
than in rice-bowl peasant issues. It was not until February 1926,
when he assumed the role of principal at the institute, that he began
a movement career in earnest. His experiences as a teacher there impressed him more with the idealized and promising aspects of rural
work than with the discouraging recent experiences of real Kwangtung organizers. He therefore failed to recognize, unlike many of
the Canton workers, the serious difficulties that plagued the movement at lower levels in 1926. Arriving in Hunan on assignment from
the Kuomintang (as the principal of the institute) and the Commu-

nist party (as its new peasant movement committee chairman), he was carried away by favorable reports from six of Hunan's eighty-odd counties. But the enthusiasm of his report of that visit was quickly submerged in the realities of Wuhan politics; and Mao resumed his responsible and to some extent repressive role as high-ranking Kuomintang politician until the beginnings of the Autumn Harvest Insurrection. When the balance of forces within the peasant apparatus in Wuhan collapsed in July 1927, Mao enthusiastically doffed his Kuomintang cloak and with what he thought to be a clear Comintern mandate allowed his sympathies for the shattered peasant movement to take full rein. Boosted to high position in the Communist party in the purge of Ch'en Tu-hsiu, Mao planned and executed the Autumn Harvest Insurrection in Hunan province. In the course of this tragic failure, Mao's second identity was shattered as his plans to subdue Ch'angsha by surrounding it from the countryside ended in defeat. Mao had come to the peasant movement with the enthusiasm of a newcomer, seen it with the dreamlike vision of a would-be radical, worked to control its excesses, and then led it personally down the final path to destruction. We are undoubtedly justified in assuming that this vivid experience would remain with him the rest of his life.

But what sort of legacy might such experiences have left with Mao and with the other Communists who remembered the period of the Great Revolution? From 1928 to 1949 the Chinese Communist movement shaped every decision in order to avoid the pitfalls while preserving the vision of the peasant movement period. It attempted to recreate what peasant bureau chief Teng Yen-ta used to call the golden age of the Chinese national revolution.

The years in south China from 1928 to 1935 did not produce a strong mass base. In sparsely populated Chingkangshan from 1927 to 1929 there were scarcely any peasants to organize. Mao engaged his tiny Red Army, the remnants of the Autumn Harvest Insurrection, in a desperate holding operation. Later in south Kiangsi province, where Mao built his Central Soviet Republic, a primitive economy and savage suppression attacks drove him to adopt harsh confiscation and political terror tactics.

But even during the nadir of this soviet period, the techniques of mass work were kept alive. Mao Tse-tung attempted to resist the demands of Moscow and the Shanghai Communist leadership for more divisive land policies. He created an extensive network of rural government in the Kiangsi base that rivaled in complexity the association structure before 1928. The Russian word "soviet" was used, but the committee format of the Kiangsi local governments closely resembled earlier peasant movement rule in Mao's Hunan. But what was more important about the period in Kiangsi was that it showed Mao and his fellow rural Communists how to provide villages with the kind of military security for political activity that had been lacking in many places during the peasant movement period. Although in 1927 and 1928 the Communist Central Committee, still lured by the autumn dream of a widespread jacquerie, ordered Mao to scatter his forces across south China, he resisted. The 1927 failure had taught him that preserving an organized, concentrated armed force was more important than mindless expansion across territory. Again from 1930 to 1933 a new Central Committee tried to force him to seize large cities, but he refused, remembering the disastrous attempts to take Ch'angsha against overwhelming odds. The lessons of the peasant movement experience had been well learned.

It was also during the Kiangsi period that the Red Army began to shoulder the burden of rural mass work. Deprived of its sources of eager young intellectuals, the party turned for its supply of village organizers to the political departments of the Communist armies. The techniques of village penetration were taught in the military schools, as in the peasant movement period military techniques had been drilled into peasant cadres. True, the old clichés of mass movement work remained and indeed ossified even further and the skills of village propaganda declined somewhat in the new military mold, but the tradition was kept alive. The Red Army became during the Kiangsi period the heir of the peasant movement vanguard and the political commissar became a latter-day special assignee.

The outbreak of the Sino-Japanese War in 1937 offered the Communists a chance to recreate the environment of the Great Revolution. The strategy worked out by Mao and Liu Shao-ch'i to overcome the resistance of the still powerful Russian-oriented wing of the party succeeded, and made use of the experience of Kiangsi in reproducing many of the features of the pre-1927 movement. The intimate collaboration between military and political work that had been the ideal of the peasant movement became a reality in the rapid expansion of Communist forces across north China from 1937 to

1941. An elaborate system of mass organizations, some calling themselves peasant associations, and rural governments increased the ordinary villager's level of participation. Thanks to the galling presence of Japanese troops on China's soil, a plentiful supply of highly motivated students and villagers with education once again made themselves available for work of sedan chair bearers for the movement. This time, thanks to the lessons learned from the peasant movement, there was no problem of the military betraying the revolution because the military, as in 1926 to 1927, had *become* the revolution. Also because of the elaborate precautions taken in the new united front with the Kuomintang, there was little chance that non-Communists would overturn by nonmilitary means the state and mass organization apparatus.

The parallels extended even down to the fine points of style. There was the same striving for understanding, research and study, the curiosity about local problems, and the tradition of "visiting the poor and asking of their bitterness" that had been the expressed ideal of peasant movement work. There was the same sense of the dramatic, the communal, the festive, a love of the public spectacle with its roots deep in Chinese character, which could be used by those willing to travel like itinerant entertainers into the villages. Finally there was the irrepressible penchant for organization, the desire to enlist men into rolls, hold meetings, elect (or rather select) officers, hear interminable speeches, and enforce the active participation of every member of the village community that characterized the peasant movement from its earliest days.

There were undeniably new elements, of course. Yenan communism was much bigger, more self-confident, better organized and led than its predecessor of the 1920s. The panoply of political techniques that we associate with the Japanese resistance period, the rectification campaigns, the model workers, and the military attacks on agriculture, all added a unique flavor and vitality. But none would deny that in essentials the peasant movement tradition—both in its vision of rural revolution and in its style of village work—was being continued. Historians may quibble about which was truly the most representative period in the Chinese Communist odyssey, but none can deny that the victory of 1949 had been dreamed of for more than a quarter-century.

Undoubtedly the successes of political work in the Yenan period

had a profound impact on Mao Tse-tung's and Lin Piao's perceptions of the world and of Chinese political realities. The often-
made claim that "China has a Yenan complex"[5] asserts that the now
elderly leadership of the Chinese party and army hearken back nos-
talgically to that period of the anti-Japanese war when their programs finally caught fire. But there is also much to suggest that even
earlier experiences of failure or spottier success have continued to
shape Peking's concerns for the present and the future. Barely beneath the consciousness of the present Chinese leaders we may dis-
cern four important conceptions of politics that emerged first in the
peasant movement period. Because these conceptions have longer
and deeper roots than the democratic and nationalistic experiences
of the Yenan period, we may expect them to be displayed at least as
persistently in the future.

First of all, the concept of the rural strategy itself has had wide-
reaching implications. The continued predominance of the rural
element in the Chinese population coincides nicely with the basic
prejudice. Rightly or wrongly, the judgment that China's development depends largely on rural agricultural and not on urban techni-
cal growth will be hard to resist. Further, the image of populations
that are rural by analogy, of peasant substitutes like the oppressed
races or even the entire Third World of nations will continue to
loom large in Chinese thinking. Bukharin's dream of the cities of
the world inundated in a rising sea of village protest was readily accepted in the peasant movement period. It continues to bemuse
Chinese thinking about the world, as Lin Piao's nearly verbatim
borrowing of Bukharin's phrase in 1965 suggests.[6]

Second, the peasant movement left a legacy of faith in what came
to be called mass work. We have observed the sometimes hallucina-
tory belief in the power of the aroused masses. The Chinese Communists diverged early from Lenin's classical practice of agitation and
propaganda. Lenin thought of mass action as a direct revolutionary
act, a well-placed booby trap, a Molotov cocktail, a well-stormed
barricade. For him and for other European Communists, the
people's allegiance was a fleeting fact that had to be seized and
turned quickly to one's purposes. The Chinese from the peasant
movement period onward, by contrast, placed far more faith in
membership as the sign of allegiance and in human numbers as the
measure of strength.

In part the Chinese Communist fascination with the strength of the masses in this numerical sense is a function of the central fact of Chinese village life: high density habitation. Peasant organizers such as P'eng P'ai delighted in the theatrical joys of mass meetings, partly because of the natural excitement, the heat and noise of Chinese gatherings, and partly because the very fact of assembly constituted a political act in Chinese culture. Throngs of people were ideal devices to evoke the ire and provoke the arbitrary power of authorities. Village powerholders, whether traditional or Communist, made liberal use of public demonstrations of their might. The spectacle of punishment, whether in the form of public executions of Communists in 1928 or of public humiliations of anti-Communists as described so vividly, for example, in William Hinton's *Fanshen,* is a standard part of the Chinese repertory of legitimacy building. In part the fascination with the masses in Chinese Communist tradition must come from this experience of the peasant movement period: he who is not afraid of producing crowds may find them useful political vehicles. Chairman Mao's daring use of new organizations of his own small generals — the student Red Guards in 1966 — drew upon a long tradition of the use of crowds and the counting of heads.

A third legacy of the peasant movement period that antedates the Yenan syndrome by two decades is the militarization of politics. Ch'en Tu-hsiu may well, as his critics claimed, have neglected the all-important problem of military defense of the mass organizations. But there were many Communists, and many of them in the peasant movement, who very early understood the movement's intimate link with armed force. P'eng P'ai's disdain for armed defense in Haifeng brought his early efforts to naught. His involvement in Kwangning and then in Hua county was tied ever more closely to military units. In Haifeng and in parts of Hunan in 1927 these armies for a time monopolized the use of force. The armies of Mao Tse-tung and in Haifeng of P'eng Kuei and Ku Ta-ts'un, which grew into sizable units during the early Kiangsi period, emerged directly from these self-defense units. Of course, the unspoken agreement of the collaboration period was that the Communist party and the mass organs would not vie with the national revolutionary army for weapons or recruits; but even so the peasant self-defense armies were an integral part of local movement life and drew their conscripts directly from association rolls. Despite the restraints imposed by the peculiar relationship to the Kuomintang, we cannot fail to recognize the prominent features of the later militarized political movement. Armed propaganda, the intimate ties between army and association chieftains, and the unquestioning reliance on force as the ultimate resort in political struggle all characterized earlier and later Chinese Communist village work. The local roots of the Peasant Army soldiery and the contrast between them and the mercenary or purely military non-Communist armies became in turn the hallmarks of the new Red Army and then the People's Liberation Army after 1945. An important legacy of the peasant movement period was the faith in an aroused and armed local population, a faith that to this day finds expression in the repeated commitment to build a people's militia in the Chinese countryside.

A final legacy of the peasant movement period was the commitment to total autonomy for the Communist movement. The peasant movement period exposed the Communist party to the threat of absorption from two opposite directions. First of all, the Communist party was in a permanently subordinate role in the 1924-1927 collaboration. Despite the assurance provided by ideology that in the long run the Communists would control China's future, the Kuomintang, by its size and strength, was destined to win in the first showdown. Never again would the Communists be willing to place their fate in the hands of another Chinese power center. The notion of a united front, which was entertained as late as the end of the anti-Japanese war in Yenan circles, irrevocably excluded the surrender of autonomy over military units or base areas. Mao Tse-tung exclaimed angrily to Americans who hoped to bring him back together with Chiang Kai-shek that "that turtle's egg" ought to have stepped down long ago — as long ago, he must have meant, as 1927.[7] Who is to say whether this utter distrust of shared power is not still an element in China's relationships with the outside world? Perhaps the resentment of the quasi-racist Russian adviser to the Autumn Harvest Insurrections, Comrade Ma, or of the high-handed disdain for Communist lives of Comrade Stalin in 1927 remains an element in Peking's hostility toward Moscow.

And yet it was also part of the peasant movement experience that made the Communist party resist becoming nothing more than a peasant party. The relationship with the Kuomintang had allowed the Communist party to enjoy at least vicariously the feeling of being a national movement with aspirations to central power, a feeling that mere representation of one class or area against another could not satisfy. During the peasant movement period even at the cost of entire provinces such as Kwangtung the party's higher interest in seizing power dictated disciplined acceptance of what the leadership required. The elite that won China in 1949, happily the beneficiary of massive peasant support, would conduct its desired transformation of China in the name of the workers and peasants and to a great degree in their interest. But never would it, any more than the Communist leaders of the peasant associations, permit itself to be merely the tool of their interests or the mouthpiece of their expressed demands. The Communist party, like the peasant movement that it led, was a device to impose solutions on and extract power from the countryside. They led the Hunanese peasantry into chaotic slaughter in 1927 by claiming to represent the demands of the farm population when by their own admission the escalation of those demands was a device to protect and increase their own influence within the greater revolutionary movement. They would continue after 1949 to direct the fate of a half-billion Chinese villagers without pausing long to ask their views.

Ruralism, militarization, the worship of numbers, a fierce autonomy—these are the chief traits inherited by the Maoist movement traumatically born more than five decades ago. The intervening years have done much to transform the movement, which must adapt to its environment as does any group. The responsibilities of total power, the advantages of urban and industrial life styles, the benefits of foreign contact, and the irrepressible demands of particular human interests will undoubtedly crowd out of the powerful psychic claims of past experience—an experience that was after all crowned with great success. But the attitudes that predetermined survival in one era may not help in the next. Is it possible that the future of China will be determined by how well these remnants of its peasant movement past can be forgotten?

If we are not mistaken, there are the lessons and the legacies of the peasant movement for China. But what of the rest of the world? During the height of Lin Piao's career in the mid-1960s it seemed that the Chinese Communist leadership expected many other nations to follow Chinese footsteps in waging people's war on its model. What does our analysis of the peasant movement portend for other societies?

On the most obvious level, the 1927-1928 defeat of the peasant movement proved that the rural strategy was only an idea. Even when a Communist party beats everyone else to the rural strategy, finds widespread sympathy among the rural population, and takes to armed insurrection in an attempt to seize political power, it can still be crushed, and without using a single foreign soldier. Those who despaired of stopping Lin Piao's "dominoes" from falling in 1965 might have taken heart from this brutal fact. Of course the cure for revolution, on the other hand, may be worse than the disease, which may, with the new lessons and fresh immunities gained from an earlier crisis, strike again and again. Many who gloated with Chiang Kai-shek in 1927 have lived to regret their overconfidence. So too the apparent success of American intervention in Vietnam has already been tested with time.

What is perfectly clear is that there is no such thing as peasant revolution considered in the abstract, even when that expression is qualified by the words Asian or modern Chinese. It is tempting to argue that the Maoist model of rural revolution is a well-adapted product of Asian society, though the differences between enormous, autonomous China and tiny, colonial Vietnam are overwhelming. It is appealing to suggest that communism grows best among rice-cultivating peasants, until one notes how weak the peasant associations were in Kwangtung's richest paddy areas. It makes sense to refer to Mandarinism or familism or centrism — the central patterns of Sinitic politics — as the root causes of the Chinese peasant revolution, until we find that these very characteristics contributed to the defeat of the Communists in 1927. The peasant movement may have certain parallels with the Indonesian Sarekat Radja of the 1950s, with the Viet Cong insurgency of the 1960s, or with the Bengali Marxist-Leninists of the 1970s, but its development and fate were part of Chinese social, military, and especially political realities.

The game that the Chinese Communists lost in 1927 and then won in 1949 can be played anywhere, for it is the game of politics, played for the allegiance of people. Anywhere a group of persons wishes to play the game, it can try. If its strategy appeals to others, it will grow; but its ultimate strength will depend on whether it can make good on its promises. Whether it is crushed or not depends on whom it turns into an enemy, what it does to him, and how strong he is or can grow to be. How long it can hold out against or prevail over its enemies will depend ultimately on its leaders wits, flexibility, and strength of will. Cultural preconceptions, social structures, or economic forces are merely preconditions for political action and not their determinants. Peasant movements, whether of the now discredited Lin Piao stripe or not, ignore this fact at their peril.

The Communist-led peasant movement was crushed in 1927-1928 by an enemy with superior political assets and skills as much as by superior combat firepower. To the extent that the movement misjudged its own strength, misapplied its appeals, and underestimated its enemies, its defeat was less a military loss than a political tragedy. Only wisdom and prudence will assure that other peasant movements in other times, however exalted their ideals, will not share a similar fate.

APPENDIXES
NOTES
BIBLIOGRAPHY
INDEX

APPENDIX A

Chiefs and Secretaries
of the Central Peasant Bureau

CHIEFS	DATES
Lin Tsu-han	January-April 1924
P'eng Su-min	April-August 1924
Li Chang-ta	September (?) 1924
Huang Chü-su	October (?) 1924
Liao Chung-k'ai	November 1924-August 20, 1925
Ch'en Kung-po	September 18, 1925-January 1926
Lin Tsu-han	January-May 15 (?) 1926
Kan Nai-kuang	May 28-December (?) 1926
Ten Yen-ta	March-June 1927

SECRETARIES	
P'eng P'ai	March (?)-November (?) 1924
Lo Ch'i-yuan	November (?) 1924-May 15 (?), 1926
Ch'en K'o-wen	May 15 (?) 1926-July (?) 1927

Source: Roy Hofheinz, "Peasant Movement and Rural Revolution: Chinese Communists in the Countryside, 1923-1927 (Ph.D. dissertation, Harvard University, 1966), p. 19.

(?) Indicates no precise terminal dates available.

APPENDIX B

A Bibliographic Note
on Mao Tse-tung's "Report
on an Investigation of
the Hunan Peasant Movement"

Since there are a number of conflicting versions of Mao's report, both in Chinese and English, the reader should be aware of which version he is using. The report, signed on February 28, 1927, first appeared in incomplete form in the weekly magazine of the Hunan Communist Provincial Committee, *The Militant* (*Chan-shih chou-pao*), on March 5, 1927. A week later the Central Committee's *Guide weekly* (*Hsiang-tao*), no. 191, pp. 2061-2066, published presumably the same excerpt, comprising parts one and two of the three-part report. On March 28 the Kuomintang's official Hankow newspaper, the *Central Daily News* (*Chung-yang jih-pao*) reproduced parts one and two in its *Supplement* (*Chung-yang fu-k'an*). This last source was the only one available to the editors of the earliest version of the *Selected Works of Mao Tse-tung* (*Mao Tse-tung Hsuan-chi*), Chin-ch'a-chi Jih-pao She, 1944, pp. 115 ff. The third chapter, a long section now entitled "Fourteen Great Achievements" in the official *Selected Works* (Peking, 1951), I, 34-65, originally appeared in *The Militant* on March 28 but was never printed elsewhere during the peasant movement period. The first post-1927 Chinese version of this section appeared in the *Supplement* to the December 1947 Chin-ch'a-chi edition of the *Selected Works* with the note that it was taken from a manuscript copy and might therefore contain mistakes. This statement was repeated in the July 1949 Shanghai edition, and there has never been any further publication of the undoctored text. The present version of the report in the *Selected Works* first appeared in the official ideological magazine *Study* (*Hsueh-hsi*) IV: (January 1951) pp. 3-14, and differs from the original report in a number of significant respects.

Though we have no pre-1944 Chinese source for part three of the report, there is an independent earlier source — including all three chapters and a statistical appendix — that was printed in 1929. It is in a Japanese translation of a book titled *Peasant Movement in Hunan* (*Hunan nung-min yun-tung*), apparently published in Wuhan in April 1927, Research Office, South Manchurian Railway, Dairen, (Tōyō Bunkō 0929). This Japanese version agrees with the Shanghai 1949 text on every significant point at which the latter disagrees with the *Selected Works* version. Furthermore, the first two parts of the Shanghai version are faithful reproductions of the presently available 1927 text. The conclusion must be that the official version of 1944-1949 is an accurate as well as an authoritative version of Mao's report.

The differences between the presently authorized and the original texts are worth noting. The original included a statistical chart of peasant association membership by county, broken down into the various social classes. This chart has been omitted from the present version. Curiously enough, however, Peking has published it faithfully elsewhere without mentioning that it was the work of Mao. *Ti-i-tz'u kuo-nei ko-ming chan-cheng shih-ch'i-te nung-min yun-tung* (The peasant movement in the first revolutionary civil war), pp. 258-262. But more important than this omission are the systematic omissions and alterations of the original text.

As a result of these changes, Mao Tse-tung was made to appear less offensive to taste, less exhuberant about peasant excesses, and more outspokenly Communist than in fact he was. Certain vulgarisms (for example his "when the man from the peasant association lets a fart it is immediately ratified") have been expurgated, presumably because they were unbecoming to the Chairman of the People's Republic. Statements extolling the importance of the peasant movement (for example the famous remark giving it credit for 70 percent of the national revolution) have been dropped, perhaps because the new Communist government hoped in 1951 to turn quickly to the leadership of urban China and so hoped to forget its rural past. Finally, the new official version makes it appear that Mao Tse-tung was far more explicit about Communist leadership of the peasant movement than he allowed himself to be (a claim made explicitly on pages 32 and 49 of the Peking version). In the new version the reader is steered away from the implication that the peasant movement was an autonomous force that had developed under the Kuomintang banner. These changes may have served Peking's purposes in the early fifties, but they do not increase our understanding of Mao's role in the peasant movement.

NOTES

1. The Birth of the Rural Strategy

1. In fact this "Letter to the Peasantry" was widely circulated only after October 1926. It never appeared in the official Communist *Hsiang-tao chou-pao* (Guide weekly; hereafter *Hsiang-tao*) and was omitted from early published collections of Communist programmatic documents. The most accessible recent text is in *Chūgoku Kyōsantō gonenrai no seiji shuchō* (Five years of CCP political programs), pp. 114-123. See Ichiko Chūzō's review of this Japanese translation in *Kindai Chūgoku Kenkyū Sentaa Ihō* (Reports of the seminar on twentieth-century China), no. 5, pp. 5-15 (1964).

2. "The Reader's Voice," *Hsiang-tao,* no. 34 (Aug. 1, 1923), p. 258. Ch'en later expressed similar doubts when he lamented the defeat of P'eng P'ai's first efforts in Haifeng, "The Kwangtung and Hunan Peasant," *Hsiang-tao,* no. 48 (Oct. 17, 1923), pp. 367-368.

3. Ch'en Tu-hsiu, "The peasant question," *Ch'ien-feng* (Vanguard), no. 1 (July 1, 1923), pp. 51-57.

4. For accounts of early comintern peasant policies, see George D. Jackson, Jr., *Comintern and Peasant in Eastern Europe 1919-1930* (New York: Columbia University Press, 1966).

5. Bukharin's report was translated into Chinese and published under the title *Nung-min wen-t'i* (The peasant question) by Hsin Ch'ing-nien she (Wuhan [?], 1927), p. 59.

6. Secret documents of the period suggest a rationale for this policy: to ensure that Communist purpose and organizational strength was not diluted by the

infusion of poorly trained elements. "Resolution on KMT work and attitudes," presumably passed by a CCP Central Expanded Plenum in May 1924. Cited in Hsieh Ch'ih and Chang Chi, *Pao-lu Chung-kuo Kung-ch'an-tang te yin-mou* (An exposé of the Chinese Communist party plot; Shanghai, September 1924).

7. In March T'an and Feng visited Shunte county, a rich silk-producing district in the delta south of Canton, where they personally set up fourteen village cells with party membership of eight hundred. They classed five hundred of the members as peasant. By May 1924 Shunte had four KMT district offices, thanks to Communist efforts. Feng Chü-p'o, "Report of an Inspection of the Shunte Party Office," *Chung-kuo Kuo-min-tang chou-k'an* (hereafter *CKKMTCK*), no. 16, p. 4.

8. T'an P'ing-shan and Feng Chü-p'o, *Kuo-min ko-ming chung chih min-t'uan wen-t'i* (Canton, 1923).

9. Several speeches of early 1924, including many glowing references to "trainer" Borodin, may be found in *CKKMTCK*, e.g., no. 2, pp. 1-2, no. 27, pp. 1-3.

10. "The Tiller Must Have His Own Land" and "The Great Union of the Peasantry," in *Tsung-li ch'uan-chi* (Complete works of the premier), II, 296-500, 505-512. Sun's original penciled sketch of the peasant flag with notes about the colors and dimensions is found in the Institute of Party History archive, Ts'aot'un, Taiwan.

11. *CKKMTCK*, no. 40, p. 7.

12. For peasant movement claims in these incidents, see the Kwangtung Communist Party Peasant Movement Committee's "Report on the Kwangtung Peasant Movement" in *Kwang-tung nung-min yun-tung pao-kao* (Report on the Kwangtung peasant movement; Canton, 1926), pp. 55-60.

13. A Soldier, "Letter from the Kwangtung Front," *Hsiang-tao*, no. 110 (April 12, 1925), p. 1014. A. I. Cherepanov, *Zapiski Voennovo Sovetnika v Kitae*, gives a Russian view of the expedition. Liu Ping-ts'ui, *Kuo-min ko-ming chün tung-cheng chi* (A history of the National Revolutionary Army's Eastern Expedition), a Chinese view.

14. "Report on the Kwangtung Peasant Movement," in *Nung-min ts'ung-k'an* (Hankow, 1927; hereafter *NMTK*), II, 171.

15. "Communique of the Fourth National Congress," in *Chūgoku Kyōsantō gonenrai no seiji shuchō* (Five years of Chinese Communist party political programs), tr. Mikami Taichō, et al. (Kansai University Institute of Oriental and Occidental Studies, Osaka, 1963), pp. 65-71.

16. T'an P'ing-shan, *Entwicklungswege der Chinesischen Revolution* (Hamburg, 1927), cites the percentage figure.

17. "Letter to the Peasantry," in *Chūgoku Kyōsantō gonenrai no seiji shuchō*, pp. 187-190. "Resolutions on the question of organization," CCP Enlarged Plenum, October 1925, translated in C. M. Wilbur and Julie How, *Documents on Communism, Nationalism, and Soviet Advisers in China, 1918-1927*, pp. 100-103.

18. Central Committee, Chinese Communist party, "Resolution on the Peasant Movement," July 1926, in Wang Chien-min, ed., *Chung-kuo kung-ch'an-tang shih-kao* (Taipei, 1965), I, 133-137. Wilbur and How, pp. 297-302.

19. The Northern Expedition as an element in KMT-Communist politics has

been exhaustively treated. See especially Wilbur and How; Conrad Brandt, *Stalin's Failure in China, 1924-1927* (Cambridge, 1958). The point that peasant participation in this expedition, as in eastern Kwangtung in 1925, was more a myth than a reality is amply documented in Donald Jordan, "The Northern Expedition: A Military Victory" (Ph.D. dissertation, University of Wisconsin, 1967; University Microfilms UM 67-12, 132).

20. See Chang Kuo-t'ao, "Memoirs," *Ming pao yueh-k'an,* no. 18 (June 1967), p. 94.

21. Lo Ch'i-yuan, "The Events and Results of the Second Kwangtung Peasant Congress," *Chung-kuo nung-min* (The Chinese peasant). *Li-t'ou chou-pao* (Plough-share weekly) devoted a special issue to the expanded conference of August 1926, which heard detailed reports of local peasant movement needs (no. 15, Sept. 23, 1926).

22. Chang Kuo-t'ao, "Memoirs," pp. 92, 94.

23. Ibid., p. 92.

24. Anna Louise Strong, *China's Millions* (New York, 1928), p. 38.

25. Harold Isaacs, *The Tragedy of the Chinese Revolution* (Stanford, 1938), p. 197.

26. Chu Ch'i-hua, "Kokumin kakumei ni okeru nōmin undō," *Mantetsu Shina Gesshi,* vol. 9, no. 1 (January 1932), pp. 1-27.

27. The joint conference program embodied a large portion of the suggestions made in Ch'en's recommended nationwide program of July 1926, including the 25 percent rent reduction and village-committee government. It did not mention the Popular Corps question but rather proposed a special government inquiry committee to look into charges of mistreatment of peasant associations. But these matters concerned Ch'en less than the Kuomintang's positive response to his own program. The joint conference even volunteered that the government might give uncultivated or otherwise barren land to peasants. "Report on the Peasant Movement for October and November," *Hsiao k'an* (The school publication). Signed *"chung-chü"* or central (political) bureau.

28. Shu Chien, dispatches of November 10 and December 20, 1926. *Hsiang-tao,* no. 183 (Jan. 17, 1927), pp. 1940-1942, no. 185 (Jan. 27, 1927), pp. 1972-1974.

29. *Hsiao k'an,* found in Keiō University Library, Tokyo, is in fact issue number three of the central Politburo's secret bulletin *Chiao-yü Tsa-chih,* published December 1, 1926. See Ōtsuka Reizō, "Nenshi kō" (Draft chronology) in Hatano Ken'ichi, *Chūgoku Kyōsantō Shi* (History of the CCP), III, 886, which cites a partial table of contents of that issue corresponding to our mimeographed copy. *Hsiao* is "school." The educational sounding titles were standard code for party in the 1920s.

30. The text is in *Hsiao k'an.* It is at least conceivable that the comintern delegates were Nassonov, Fokine, and Albrecht, who wrote the Trotskyist "letter from Shanghai." An independent text, garbled by Japanese censors, may be found in a Japanese translation from "B. Freier" in *Shina ni okeru saikin no nōmin undō to nōgyō mondai* (The most recent peasant movement and agrarian question in China), p. 32.

31. *Hsiao k'an,* table of contents.

32. Communist International, seventh enlarged executive, *Puti Mirovoi Revoliutsi* (Pathways of world revolution; Gosudarstvennoe Izdatelstvo, Moscow and Leningrad: 1926), I, 415-416. That they engineered the substitution is obvious though I have no proof beyond M. N. Roy's recollection that T'an had been won over by the "big guns in Moscow" to a more conservative Borodin-like position. Robert North and Xenia Endin, *M. N. Roy's Mission to China* (Berkeley, 1963), p. 35. To be sure, T'an did squeeze in his view that the KMT land plank was an "arid phrase" (*pustaya fraza*) and could raise the issue of preparation for armed insurrection. But on both counts Stalin won the day.

33. Brandt, p. 100, from T'an P'ing-shan, *Entwicklungswege der Chinesischen Revolution.*

34. Wang Chien-min, I, 336.

35. Nassonov, et al., "Letter from Shanghai," in Leon Trotsky, *Problems of the Chinese Revolution* (New York, 1932), p. 398.

2. Mao Tse-tung as a Rural Strategist

1. The article appeared in no. 8 of the publication *Nung-min yun-tung* (Canton, Sept. 21, 1926). The compendium was *NMTK*, which he sponsored at the institute. The Wuhan edition of this set of volumes does not include Mao's preface.

2. The details of publication of the article in its various versions can be found in appendix B.

3. See K. A. Wittfogel, "The Legend of 'Maoism'," *The China Quarterly*, no. 2 (April-June 1960), p. 21. Wittfogel belabors this point to demonstrate how closely Mao hewed to Moscow's line when in fact many Chinese Communists assumed him to be following his Kuomintang lights.

4. Jun-chih (Mao Tse-tung), "Chiang-che nung-min-te t'ung-k'u fan-k'ang yun-tung" (The sufferings of the peasantry of Kiangsu-Chekiang and their movement to resist), *Hsiang-tao*, no. 179 (Oct. 25, 1926), pp. 1869-1871.

5. See Mr. Ōtsuka Reizō's "Bibliography" in Hatano Ken'ichi, *Chūgoku Kyōsanto-shi* (Tokyo, 1961), I, 667 and *Hsiao-k'an*, p. 1, which refers to a draft program on armed insurrection.

6. *Mō Taku-tō Shu*, I, 249.

7. *Ti-i-tz'u kuo-nei ko-ming chan-cheng shih-ch'i te nung-min yun-tung* (The peasant movement in the first revolutionary civil war: Peking, 1953; hereafter *Ti-i-tz'u*), p. 358. Mao's speech on December 20 to that congress (the First Hunan Worker-Peasant Congress) also stressed the young vanguard. *Hunan li-shih tzu-liao 1958:* no. 3 (July 1958), p. 53.

8. This table, which appears in *Ti-i-tz'u*, pp. 258-262, has been omitted from all the English translations, perhaps only for reasons of space. Its contents did not help to confirm Mao's theory of the new vanguard, but the point is that Mao tried to make use of the latest quantitative information to strengthen his case that there could be no revolution without the poor peasants.

9. *Selected Works of Mao Tse-tung* (Lawrence and Wishart edition), p. 27.

10. Ibid., p. 22.

11. He had proposed one in May 1925 to a central conference of the Kuomin-

tang in Canton, according to Hua Kang, *Chung-kuo ta ko-ming shih* (*Shanghai,* 1932), p. 237.

12. Chiang's speeches are in *pai-hua* or plain talk, but his diary is written in pure classical Chinese, a duality shared by other Chinese of his generation — perhaps even by Mao Tse-tung. The expression was "a settling of land accounts" (*t'u-ti chang-pen*). Mao Ssu-ch'eng, *Min-kuo 15 nien i-ch'ien chih Chiang Chieh-shih hsien sheng* (Mr. Chiang Kai-shek before 1926; Hong Kong, 1965 reprint of 1936 ed. [diary entry for Dec. 7, 1926]), p. 949. In December Chiang also told Borodin that "if the peasant question can be solved, the workers' question will be taken care of simultaneously." Surely his conception of the problem, not to speak of the solution, were different from his hearer's.

13. V. V. Vishnyakova-Akimova, *Dva Goda v Vosstavshem Kitae, 1925-1927 — Vospominaniia* (Moscow, 1965), p. 222.

14. Chiang Yung-ching, *Pao-lo-t'ing yü Wu-han cheng-ch'üan* (Borodin and the Wuhan regime; hereafter *Borodin*), says the document was "fabricated" by the same committee that wrote Mao's theses. But only Tarkhanov seems to have been familiar with the content at the meetings.

15. "Minutes of the Central Land Committee Meeting," April 23, 1927. Courtesy C. M. Wilbur.

16. Ibid.

17. Edgar Snow, *Red Star Over China* (New York, 1938), p. 160. Snow must have confused this resolution draft with the Hunan report itself in this paragraph.

18. The best works on Mao's various land laws are Chao Kuo-chun, *The Agrarian Policy of the Chinese Communist Party, 1921-1959* (Bombay: Asia Publishing House, 1960), and Hsiao Tso-liang, *The Land Revolution in China, 1930-1934* (Seattle: University of Washington Press, 1969). A compendium of later land laws under communist governments is found in *Chung-hua Jen-min Kung-ho-kuo t'u-ti fa ts'an-k'ao tzu-liao hui-pien* (A collection of reference materials on the land laws of the Chinese People's Republic; Peking, 1957). None of these mentions the Wuhan antecedents to later laws.

19. Chiang, *Borodin,* p. 286.

20. "Minutes of the Central Land Committee Meeting." Courtesy C. M. Wilbur.

21. T'an, in Chiang, *Borodin,* p. 28.

22. "In Hunan the present financial policies are bringing in only ten million yuan a year. In 1925 the province had a revenue of 15-20 million in taxes alone. If the land problem were solved, a land tax of 10 percent would bring in 56 million yuan, and the rate could even be increased to 15 percent if more were needed. In this way financial difficulties can be immediately solved" (Third Expanded Conference of the central land committee, April 22, 1927). He and Takhanov must have developed these figures together, since Takhanov cited similar statistics for Kuangtung and other provinces the next day.

23. Chiang, *Borodin,* p. 284.

24. "Minutes of the Central Land Committee Meeting." Courtesy C. M. Wilbur.

25. Chiang, *Borodin,* p. 297. *Ni-ch'an* is the expression. There had been

resolutions at the Hunan First Peasant Congress on the confiscation of such property. *Ti-i-tz'u,* p. 373.

26. There were seven regimental commanders: Lu Te-ming, Chou Shih-ti, Hsu Chi-hsin, Fan Lu, Liu Ming-hsia, Chou I-ch'ün, Liang Pin-shu. Chu Ch'i-hua, *1927-nien ti hui-i-lu* (Shanghai, 1933), p. 266.

27. T'ang Leang-li, *The Inner History of the Chinese Revolution,* (London, 1930). Taken from North and Eudin, p. 120.

28. Chiang, *Borodin,* p. 296, and "Minutes of the Central Land Committee Meeting."

29. Pavel Mif, *Chin-chi shih-ch'i chung te Chung-kuo Kung-ch'an-tang,* p. 20.

30. Chiang, *Borodin,* p. 299.

31. Ibid., pp. 301-302.

32. "Theses on the political situation," May 9, 1927, in North and Eudin, p. 250. Hsu Ch'ien had in fact spoken up for just that theory. North and Eudin, p. 76.

33. Yeh personally led a band of fifteen hundred military school cadets in their first exposure to combat and was forced to shoot several deserters with his own revolver. Chiang, *Borodin,* p. 319.

34. Wang Chien-min, p. 445.

35. The telegraphic code ideograph for the twenty-first day of a month is the one for horse.

36. *Kuo-kung ho-tso ch'ing-tang yun-tung chi kung-nung yun-tung wen-ch'ao* (A collection of writings and documents on the cooperation and split between the Kuomintang and the Communist party and on the workers and peasants' movements), III/O (Ichang), and III/P (Hsiangt'an), both dated May 19, 1927 (Hoover Library 2980/6482). Liu Chih-sun, a top official in the provincial peasant association, reported later that there was indeed a plan to attack Ch'angsha on May 31. *Ti-i-tz'u,* p. 383. The acting governor of the province later reported that two days before Hsu's action there had been large groups in the streets bearing red flags demanding that Hsu K'o-hsiang be disarmed. On the twentieth Hsu's crack guide regiment was surrounded by an angry crowd. On the twenty-first several soldiers and officers of Hsu's unit were taken into custody by unknown persons and then released. Chiang, *Borodin,* p. 328. He alleged that the Communists had suspected Hsu would be moving against them shortly, since associations in a number of counties had suffered sharp blows from their garrisons in the preceding several days.

37. Chiang, *Borodin,* p. 271.

38. Ibid., p. 344. From a speech of July 15, 1927.

39. Li Jui, "The Peasant Movement in Hunan," in *Ti-i-tz'u,* p. 285.

40. Ibid., pp. 286-287.

41. Ibid., p. 381. Liu was a peasant association director. See his wife's reminiscences of their parting on the Day of the Horse. *Hunan ko-ming lieh-shih chuan* (Biographies of Hunanese martyrs; Ch'angsha, 1952), pp. 96-97.

42. Another report from Yanghsin county down the Yangtze mentioned ten gentry, leaders of dissatisfied old-style policemen, and secret societies angry at the desecration of "superstitious" temples. Isaacs collection, III/21 (Hoover Library 2980/6482).

43. March 2, 1927. Tanaka Tadao summarizes them. *Kakumei shina Nōson no jisshoteki kenkyū* (Tokyo, 1930), p. 349.

44. January 4, 1927. The regulations presumably passed on this day. Li Jui, "The Peasant Movement in Hunan," in *Ti-i-tz'u,* p. 276.

45. Chiang, *Borodin,* p. 263. Chiang dates the killing in earnest in Hunan from a visit by M. N. Roy and T'an P'ing-shan to Ch'angsha on April 1 but gives no evidence.

46. *The People's Tribune* (Hankow), July 30, 1927. Miss Strong was not an eyewitness, having arrived in Shanghai only on May 18. Her observations were based on interviews with missionaries who were largely outraged at anti-Christian vandalism and the forcible occupation of church property. She could find no one who had actually witnessed an execution. She quoted one "well-informed" man as saying two hundred had been executed by the unions, as against twice that number in the retaliation by the military. Strong, p. 183.

47. If the isolated copies of clippings in the Isaacs collection (Hoover Library 2980/6482) are any indication. Vol. III.

48. Anti-Communists later reported bloody-minded speeches favoring terror by Communists in the Hunan party office. Chiang, *Borodin,* p. 264. (speech of Tai Shu-jen). To qualify for Hsia Hsi's praise (March 12, 1927), a county had to have executed some political enemies recently. Chiang, *Borodin,* p. 263.

49. "The True Situation of the Hunan Peasant Movement," report of the delegation of various groups in Hunan and the provincial peasant association. Brush copy of text in *Hankow Min-kuo Jih-pao* in Isaacs Collection. Also printed in *Kung-fei huo-kuo shih-liao hui-pien* (Taipei [?], 1964), I, 152-162.

50. Chiang, *Borodin,* p. 258 (speech of Jan. 31, 1927).

51. Ibid., p. 259.

52. Ibid., p. 348 and Li Yun-han, *To the Party Purge,* pp. 707-708.

53. Hsu, May 30 speech to Political Conference, Chiang, *Borodin,* p. 257.

54. Liu Chih-hsun, *Ti-i-tz'u,* p. 381.

55. Compare with difficulties in the People's Liberation Army in 1960-1961 when there were rumors of unrest and malnutrition affecting the soldiers' families. John W. Lewis, "China's Secret Military Papers: 'Continuities' and 'Revelations'," *The China Quarterly,* no. 18 (April-June 1964), pp. 76-77.

56. Lo Jung-huan, "Early Days of the Chinese Red Army," *Peking Review,* vol. 5, 31 (Aug. 3, 1962), p. 9.

57. Mao Tse-tung in fact personally transmitted the refusal, thus once again appearing to stand opposed to his Hunanese radical comrades. The Peasant Army attack actually did occur, belatedly, on March 31 and was repulsed with enormous loss of life.

58. Snow, *Red Star Over China,* p. 151.

59. Letter of August 30, 1927, *Chung-yang t'ung-hsun* (Central newsletter) no. 5. Cited in Roy Hofheinz, Jr., "The Autumn Harvest Insurrection," *The China Quarterly,* no. 32 (1967), p. 66.

60. For a more detailed account of the military order of battle and the relative performance of these units, see Hofheinz, "Autumn Harvest," pp. 67-76.

61. Ibid., p. 77.

62. Ibid., pp. 78-79.

63. The Hupeh Provincial Committee admitted later that they had only around four hundred Communists to assign to the nearly one hundred counties of the province. Of these fewer than half actually took up their assignments.

64. See his account in Snow, p. 150.

65. Ts'ai Ho-shen later admitted that some Chinese Communists made the claim in 1927.

66. Isaacs, *The Tragedy of the Chinese Revolution,* p. 292.

67. Letter of August 30, 1927, to the Central Committee. *Chung-yang t'ung-hsun* (Central newsletter), no. 5.

68. In fact there were complaints against Mao's units that they were treated by the masses as just another army passing through by local peasants who had never seen them before.

69. On the P'ing-liu-li rising, which occurred in the same counties with remarkable tactical parallels, see Jerome Ch'en, "Modernization of local protest: A study of the P'ing-liu-li rebellion 1906," paper presented to the conference on local control and social protest during The Ch'ing period, Honolulu, 1971.

70. For example, the leading Communist operative in south Hupeh, a few dozen miles to Mao's north, had led his remaining militia troops into a mountain hideout in the first week of September. See Hofheinz, "Autumn Harvest," p. 56.

71. For concrete examples of these ideas, see Hofheinz, "Autumn Harvest," pp. 57-60.

3. Staffing the Revolution: The Kuomintang Peasant Bureaucracy

1. V. I. Lenin, *What Is to Be Done?* (Moscow: Progress Publishers, 1964), p. 95.

2. For example, Li Yun-han, *Tsung jung-kung tao ch'ing-tang* (To the party purge; Taipei, 1966), p. 277.

3. T'an P'ing-shan, "Report on Organization Work" to the Second KMT Congress in January 1926. Manuscript in Yokota collection, Tōyō Bunko, Tokyo.

4. Chronicled in great detail in Li Yun-han.

5. The attribution of left characteristics to American educated Sun Fo, son of the party founder and the youth bureau chief in Wuhan, requires a stretch of the imagination. His reasons for toying with the Wuhan Communists were anything but a strong sympathy for the mass movements. But in early 1927 the Communists considered anyone willing to remain allied with them a "leftist." For a thoughtful piece on the nature and definition of the left Kuomintang, see Jerome Ch'en, "The Left-wing Kuomintang—a Definition," *Bulletin of the School of Oriental and African Studies,* vol. 25, pt. 3 (1962), pp. 557-576.

6. Harry Franck, *Roving Through Southern China* (New York, 1925), p. 263.

7. The KMT central executive committee declared it established at its first session on January 31, 1924. Formal powers were bestowed on February 9.

8. There were only three workers—the chief, the secretary, and a clerk as late as August 1924. Lo Ch'i-yuan, "Outline of a Report on the last year's work of our Bureau," *Chung-kuo nung-min,* no. 2, p. 155.

9. Ibid., pp. 162-163; "Detailed Regulations on the work of special assignees" (dated Sept. 5, 1924), *Chung-kuo nung-min,* no. 2, (Feb. 1, 1926), p. 166.

10. The members of the Communist *nung-wei,* as this committee was called, in mid-1924 were P'eng P'ai, Lo Ch'i-yuan, Juan Hsiao-hsien (later a prominent propagandist), and Chou Ch'i-chien, who was at the time agitating in his home county of Kwangning (see chapter 8). A secret report of summer 1926 described the work of this committee as including the supervision of the Kuomintang peasant bureaucracy, research on rural conditions, and publication in the name of the Kuomintang peasant bureau. Every Communist worker in the villages was required to present both oral and written reports to the *nung-wei* and to accept only oral orders. This same report admits the operatives of the central peasant bureau were virtually 100 percent Communist. *Kwang-tung nung-min yun-tung pao-kao,* p. 124. This report (Harvard-Yenching microfilm FC764) is reprinted in *NMTK* with references to the Communist party excised.

11. The dates were May 1924 and February 1926. In both cases the memberships of these committees had Communist majorities. The 1924 members were Liao Chung-k'ai, Lo Ch'i-yuan, and a Krestintern adviser named Franke. In the second the prominent Communists included Lin Tsu-han, Juan Hsiao-hsien, and Mao Tse-tung, recently appointed principal of the Peasant Movement Institute. The second committee met last on March 30, 1926, in the confusion after Chiang's coup. "Resolution on forming the Peasant Movement Committee," *CKKMTCK,* no. 22, p. 4. "Organizational Outline of the Peasant Movement Committee," *Chung-kuo nung-min,* pp. 448-449.

12. This last secretary of the bureau, Ch'en K'o-wen, whose name has been dropped from both the Communist and the Kuomintang histories of the era, survived the move to Wuhan, performed well for several months as the movement's coordinator, but turned anti-Communist in June 1927 just in time to help purge his former subordinates from KMT ranks. In Canton Ch'en's bureau for the first time began to hold regular bureau affairs conferences and to represent the peasant movement position forcefully in central party office meetings. *Kuang-chou Min-kuo Jih-pao* (Canton republican daily; hereafter *KCMKJP*), July 3, August 7, 1926. After the move to Wuhan Ch'en spoke eloquently for increased lower-level propaganda, greater fraternization between soldiers and the peasantry, and a stepped-up level of rural struggle. Speech to the expanded conference of the peasant movement committee, April 26, 1927. Courtesy C. M. Wilbur. For his turn against the Communists see Li Yun-han, p. 560, who cites Ch'en's July 9, 1927, speech attacking the Shensi Communists for driving the local peasantry into their party instead of into the kuomintang.

13. Lin's resignation was tendered to the central executive committee in late April. *CKKMTCK,* no. 20, p. 5. Chiang Kai-shek later accused him of trying by his move to distract loyal KMT members from the presence of so many Communists in Canton. In fact several Communists voluntarily retired in mid-1924 from prominent KMT positions—but always to jobs where they could work more directly on expanding the Kuomintang's organization. *Su-O Tsai Chung-kuo* (The Soviet Union in China; Taipei, 1957), p. 32.

14. Gaimushō Jōhōbu, *Gendai Chūka Minkoku Manshūkoku jinmeikan* (A

name list of modern China and Manchukuo; Tokyo, 1932), p. 128. Huang later became chief secretary of the Kwangtung provincial government. He published several speeches in *Chien-she Hsin-Chung-shan Yen-lun Chi* (Speeches on constructing the new Chungshan; Hoover Library). Huang's predecessor, Li Chang-ta, was a large landlord of wealthy Tungkuan county and later the director of Kwangtung's secret police apparatus. After 1949 his peasant movement connections helped him to win the election for vice-governor of the province.

15. See Liao's November 1924 "Letter to Wang T'ien-jen," in *Liao Chung-k'ai Chi* (Peking, 1963), p. 191, and his January 1925 "Letter to Teng Jun-ch'i," p. 228. Other of his personal interventions are noted in T. C. Chang, *Farmers' Movement in Kwangtung*, pp. 6-7.

16. His mid-1924 speech to the Peasant Movement Institute (*Liao Chung-k'ai Chi*, pp. 169-174) stressed China's need to industrialize and not any specific rural problem.

17. *Kwang-tung sheng nung-min hsieh-jui ch'eng-li ta-hui hui-ch'ang jih-k'an* (Journal of the founding congress of the Kwangtung Provincial Peasant Association), no. 4, p. 2.

18. See his "Shei shih kuo-min ko-ming-te chu-li chün?" (Who is the main force army of the national revolution?) in *Chung-kuo nung-min*, no. 8 (Nov. 1926), pp. 1-11. V. V. Vishnyakova-Akimova, a young Soviet adviser in Canton at the time, noted Kan's cooling attitude toward the Russians during the summer. Vishnyakova-Akimova, p. 358. Ch'en's private views of Kan were published in the secret Politburo journal *Hsiao-k'an* (The school publication) as well as in his "Political Report" of July 1926. Wilbur and How, p. 275.

19. On December 5 Kan announced his departure for Wuhan to join the central peasant bureau. The next week he reappeared in Canton with the mysterious announcement that he was not and never had been a member of the Chinese Communist party. On the same day as this announcement, Borodin and the KMT Left announced the formation of their new joint council in Wuhan, thus initiating the break with Chiang Kai-shek. Kan Nai-kuang never arrived in Wuhan and instead appeared in Chiang's camp. *KCMKJP*, Dec. 7 and 13, 1926.

20. Chang Kuo-t'ao remembers Teng as the "second most powerful man in Wuhan." "Memoirs," *Ming-pao yueh-k'an*, no. 18 (June 1967), p. 94. T'ang Sheng-chih, the warlord, was number one.

4. Education for Revolution: The Peasant Movement Institute

1. A list of the courses taught at this institute is found in mimeographed form in the Yokota Collection in Tōyō Bunko, Tokyo. In view of the similarity of course offerings it seems likely that many of the instructors at this institute also taught at the peasant school. That Liao Chung-k'ai lectured at both is an established fact. *CKKMTCK*, no. 28, p. 6.

2. "Plan for a first step in the peasant movement," proposed by the peasant bureau, thirty-ninth session of the Central Executive Committee, *CKKMTCK*, no. 29, p. 4.

3. Li Ching-ch'uan, the highest-ranking living alumnus, submerged during the Cultural Revolution of 1966 only to reappear with reduced power in 1972.

4. See, for example, Kao-pu-tse-po, "More Than Ten Mongolian Youths Visit Canton: Memories of Study Life at the Peasant Training Institute," *Min-tsu t'uan-chieh* (Nationality solidarity), 50:7-10 (July 1962).

5. Quoted in Kuwajima Kazue, *Chū-nan-shi chihō kyōsantō oyobi kyōsanhi no kōdō jōkyō ni kansuru chōsa hōkokusho* (Report on local Communist parties and activities in south central China; Tokyo, 1930), pp. 86-87. Chou arrived in Canton only in May 1924 and according to his own account left the Communist party the following winter, allegedly because he disapproved of Borodin's influence. Howard Boorman, ed., *Biographical Dictionary of Republican China* (New York, 1967), I, 406.

6. See the list of the sixth term teachers in Etō Shinkichi, "Hai-Lu-Feng," *The China Quarterly,* no. 8, p. 182, which estimates conservatively that seven of the fifteen teachers were CP members.

7. The second class was, of course, bolstered in midcourse by the introduction of peasant soldiers who belonged to a Min-t'uan unit outside Canton.

8. See the appendix to *Huang-p'u t'ung-hsueh tsung ming-t'se* (Nanking [?], 1933), I, 8.

9. *Chung-kuo nung-min,* no. 2 (Feb. 1, 1926), p. 168.

10. "Notice number two of the Peasant Bureau," *Chung-kuo nung-min,* no. 4 (April 1, 1926), p. 449.

11. Advertisement for the late February exams in Wuhan, printed in *KCMKJP,* March 4, 1926, p. 5.

12. See, for example, the obituaries of Ch'en Po-chung and Li Min-chih in *Chung-kuo nung-min,* no. 10 (December 1926), frontispiece.

13. "Outline of a report on the work of the Bureau during the last year," in *Chung-kuo nung-min,* no. 2 (Feb. 1, 1926), p. 168.

14. *Ti-i-tz'u,* p. 23.

15. *KCMKJP,* August 20, 1926, p. 11.

16. "Simple regulations for the peasant movement training institute," *CKKMTCK,* no. 29, p. 4.

17. "Charter of the Peasant Movement Institute," *Chung-kuo nung-min,* no. 2 (Feb. 1, 1966), pp. 169ff.

18. July resolution on the Kwangtung peasant movement, *Kwang-tung nung-min yun-tung pao-kao* (Report on the Kwangtung peasant movement; Canton, 1926), pp. 165-189.

19. *Kwang-tung nung-min yun-tung pao-kao,* p. 164.

20. *KCMKJP,* October 21, 1926, p. 11.

21. *KCMKJP,* October 18, 1926.

22. *Ti-i-tz'u,* pp. 21-22.

23. These textbooks were published in a series called Nung-min wen-t'i ts'ung-k'an (Peasant questions series).

24. *Ti-i-tz'u,* pp. 25-26. The similarities of this with certain present-day Chinese Communist study techniques is obvious.

25. The language was Lo Ch'i-yuan's. *Chung-kuo nung-min,* no. 2 (Feb. 1, 1926), pp. 168-169.

26. This figure is generous and includes all "peasant Communists," perhaps even untrained ones. *Kwang-tung nung-min yun-tung pao-kao,* p. 188.

27. Tanaka Tadao, p. 328.

28. Ibid. Mao's thought was quickly approved at the November 15, 1926, CCP Politburo meeting. "Plan for the peasant movement at present," *Hsiao-k'an,* p. 20-22.

29. Nine Kiangsi students were accused of rightism and jailed and ten others were expelled. Chou I-li's discussion of the work of the Central Peasant Movement Institute, "Minutes of the Expanded Conference of the (Wuhan) Central Peasant Movement Committee," April 26, 1927. Courtesy C. M. Wilbur.

5. Organizing the Masses: The Peasant Associations

1. An exception is Sydney Tarrow, *Peasant Communism in Southern Italy* (New Haven: Yale University Press, 1967), p. 248.

2. Edward Banfield, *Moral Basis of a Backward Society* (Glencoe: Free Press, 1958).

3. E.g., P. A. Sorokin, *Systematic Sourcebook in Rural Sociology* (Minneapolis: University of Minnesota Press, 1932), part 2, chapter 16.

4. This is Myron Weiner's analysis of why the agrarian movements of India have been so weak in the present century. *The Politics of Scarcity;* Public Pressure and Political Response in India (Chicago: University of Chicago Press, 1962), chapter 6. Barrington Moore's *Social Origins of Dictatorship and Democracy:* Lord and Peasant in the Making of the Modern World (Boston: Beacon Press, 1966) makes a similar argument for several other societies.

5. On the different constitutions of these two terms see Maurice Freedman, *Lineage Organization in Southeastern China* (London, 1958), who shows that the southern Chinese lineage was much more than simply an inflated family.

6. James B. March and H. A. Simon, *Organizations* (New York: Wiley, 1959), p. 84.

7. On village organization in north China, the most provocative recent work is Ramon Myers, *The Chinese Peasant Economy* (Cambridge: Harvard University Press, 1970). Myers demonstrates from Japanese investigations into village histories that local political organizations were growing rapidly and performing a widening set of functions during the 1920-1940 period. On the crop-watching societies, see also Sidney D. Gamble, *North China Villages; Social, Political and Economic Activities Before 1933* (Berkeley: University of California Press, 1963), chapter 5.

8. For a detailed account of Red Spears' contributions to these battles see Tanaka Tadao, pp. 252-263.

9. Soviet documents captured in Peking in early 1927 contained depressing reports of a Communist agent overwhelmed by the Red Spears' demands for money and high office. Chang Kuo-ch'en, tr., *Su-lien yin-mou wen-cheng hui-pien* (Collected documents on Soviet plots; Peking, 1928), III: 13b-20b. Chu Ch'i-hua (Li Ang) told a similar tale of failure with hopelessly illiterate and superstitious leaders in south Honan.

10. A fascinating recent account of British colonial government's losing battle against Chinese societies in Singapore is in Wilfred Blythe, *The Impact of Chinese Secret Societies in Malaya* (New York: Oxford University Press, 1969).

11. "Resolution to draw up a plan for the peasant movement," March 19, 1924. *CKKMTCK,* no. 16, p. 4.

12. There were two versions of the peasant association charter. The first was proposed by the peasant movement committee at the thirty-fifth session of the CEC (June 9, 1924) and passed on to the peasant bureau for revision. Passed in substance on June 12 by the CEC (thirty-sixth session), it was sent once again to the peasant bureau for the writing of a preamble. The June 16 version includes the preamble stating that the purpose of the association is to strive for the self-defense of the peasantry, to improve rural organization, and to better the livelihood of the peasantry.

The text of the first charter is found in *CKKMTCK,* no. 27, pp. 5-7, and in a pamphlet entitled *Nung-min hsieh-hui chang-ch'eng* (Canton [?], 1924). It contained in addition to the preamble fifteen chapters including eighty-three articles.

The second charter was apparently passed by the Second Kwangtung Peasant (Association) Congress in May 1926. A text of it is found in the pamphlet *Nung-min hsieh-hui chang-ch'eng shih-i* (Shanghai, 1927). A Japanese translation is in Suzue Gen ichi, *Chūgoku Kaihō Tōsō Shi* (Tokyo, 1953), pp. 520-531. A separate charter for the Kwangtung Provincial Peasant Association, which followed the main provisions of this revised charter, was passed by the May 1926 Kwangtung Peasant Congress. See its text in *NMTK,* I, 30-40. The charter in Wang Chien-min, I, 195-203 is the 1926 version.

13. *CKKMTCK,* no. 28. Thirty-eighth session of CEC.

14. Their dates were First Kwangtung Peasant Congress, May 1-8, 1925; Second Kwangtung Peasant Congress, May 1-15, 1926; All-Hunan Peasant Congress, December 1-28, 1926; Kiangsi Peasant Congress, February 20-28, 1927; Hupeh Peasant Congress, March 1-10(?), 1927.

15. First Kwangtung Peasant Congress, *Hui-ch'ang jih-k'an* (Daily gazette), no. 4 (May 3, 1925), p. 3.

16. See the case of the Ch'üchiang delegate to the Second Kuangtung Congress, *Chung-kuo nung-min,* no. 6/7 (July 1926), p. 684.

17. Second Congress *Hui-ch'ang jih-k'an* and Tanaka Tadao, pp. 335-336.

18. Li Jui, " . . . Hunan nung-min yun-tung," in *Ti-i-tz'u,* pp. 276-277.

19. The date established in the May 30 "Plan for a first step in the peasant movement," *Chung-kuo nung-min,* no. 1 (Jan. 1, 1926), p. 118.

20. By early September 1924 more than the five required county associations existed. *CKKMTCK,* no. 42, p. 4.

21. On this meeting Jean Chesneaux, *Le Mouvement Ouvrier Chinois de 1919 à 1927* (Paris, 1962), pp. 368-369. The Second All-China Labor Congress met from May 1-7 in Canton. There were some 281 delegates representing 166 unions and 540,000 workers. Teng Chung-hsia, *Chung-kuo chih-kung yun-tung chien-shih, 1919-1926* (A concise history of the Chinese labor movement, 1919-1926), p. 130. The groundwork was laid by the CCP workers' movement committee. Its work included the establishment of the National General Labor Union (Ch'üan-kuo

Tsung-kung-hui) and the passing of thirty-odd resolutions. It was later criticized for having excluded non-Communist unions (see the introduction to the reprint of Teng Chung-hsia, *Chung-kuo chih-kung yun-tung chien-shih,* [Yenan, 1942], p. 2) and for being mechanical in its attitude to class struggle.

22. *Hui-ch'ang jih-k'an,* no. 3 (May 3, 1925) and no. 4 (May 5, 1925).

23. See, for example, Kuo Chien-hua's speech on the women silk workers' strike in Shunte. *Hui-ch'ang jih-k'an,* no. 2 (May 2, 1925), p. 4.

24. "What county delegates should take note of in their reports," *Hui-ch'ang jih-k'an,* no. 2 (May 2, 1925), pp. 1-2.

25. *Hui-ch'ang jih-k'an,* no. 4 (May 5, 1925), p. 3.

26. Kwangtung had seven jurisdictions: North, East, and West Rivers, the Southern and Central "routes," and Hainan Island—with the favored East River divided into two districts. Yü Yen-Kuang, "The Kwangtung Peasant Movement during the First Revolutionary Civil War," in *Li-shih yen-chiu* (Historical studies), no. 9 (September 1958), p. 37.

27. *KCMKJP,* July 1, 1926.

28. *KCMKJP,* July 5, 1926.

29. *KCMKJP,* July 6, 1926.

30. *KCMKJP,* July 13, 1926.

31. T. C. Chang, *The Farmers' Movement in Kwangtung,* pp. 22-23.

32. At the February 1926 Expanded Conference of the Provincial Association Executive. As late as April 20 the CCP Central Committee was able to refer to the Canton meeting as a national congress. See also Wilbur and How, p. 258.

33. Speech by Mao to the Expanded Conference of the Central Peasant Committee, April 26, 1927. Courtesy C. M. Wilbur.

34. Lo Ch'i-yuan, "General Report on Association Affairs," *Chung-kuo nung-min,* no. 6/7 (July 1926), pp. 654-655.

35. "Kuo-min ko-ming yu nung-min yun-tung" (The peasant movement and the national revolution), in *Nung-min yun-tung,* no. 8 (Sept. 21, 1926), pp. 170-172.

36. As though to *be* a peasant one had to join the association.

37. Expanded Conference of the Peasant Movement Committee. Courtesy C. M. Wilbur.

38. T'an P'ing-shan and Feng Chü-p'o, *Kuo-min ko-ming chung chih min-t'uan wen-t'i* (The national revolution and the Min-t'uan problem; Canton, 1923).

39. *CKKMTCK,* July 17, 1924.

40. A copy is found in *Nung-min hsieh-hui chang-ch'eng shih-i,* pp. 79-83.

41. See chapter 10.

42. Kung Ch'u, who was attached to this unit, refers to it in *Wo yü hung-chün* (Hong Kong, 1954), pp. 34-36.

43. See chapter 1.

44. Lo Ch'i-yuan, "General report on association affairs in the last three months," *Li t'ou* (The ploughshare), no. 19/20, p. 27.

45. Mehmet Beqiraj, *Peasantry in Revolution* (Ithaca, N.Y., 1966), pp. 14-20.

46. William Hinton, *Fanshen* (New York, 1966), p. 187.

6. The Social Background: Explanations of Success and Failure

1. Rudolf Heberle, *From Democracy to Nazism: A Regional Case Study on Political Parties in Germany* (Baton Rouge: Louisiana State University Press, 1945). Eric Hobsbawm, *Bandits* (London: Weidenfeld and Nicholson, 1969). R. V. Burks, *The Dynamics of Communism in Eastern Europe* (Princeton: Princeton University Press, 1961). Eugen Weber, "The Men of the Archangel," *Journal of Contemporary History,* 1:1 (1966), 101-126.

2. Donald S. Zagoria, "The Ecology of Peasant Communism in India," *American Political Science Review* 50:144-160 (1971). Jeffery M. Paige, "Inequality and Insurgency in Vietnam: A Re-Analysis," *World Politics* 23:24-37 (1970). Edward J. Mitchell, "Inequality and Insurgency: A Statistical Study of South Vietnam," *World Politics* 20:421-438 (1968).

3. Ch'en Han-seng is perhaps the best example of such a theorist. See his *Kwang-tung nung-ts'un chih sheng-ch'an kuan-hsi chi sheng-ch'an li* (The relations and forces of production in the Kwang-tung countryside; Shanghai, 1936). For the evidence, see Dwight H. Perkins, *Agricultural Development in China, 1368-1968* (Chicago: Aldine, 1969). The anthropologist Fei Hsiao-t'ung adopted much of the theory of agrarian decline in his work on the decline of the gentry class. See his *China's Gentry: Essays in Rural-Urban Relations* (Chicago: University Press of Chicago, 1953), as well as his article on "Peasantry and Gentry" in the *American Sociological Review.* Jack Potter, *Capitalism and the Chinese Peasant: Social and Economic Change in a Hong Kong Village* (Berkeley: University of California Press, 1968), presents a convincing argument that the market economy emanating from the cities enriched rather than debased peasant families in an urbanizing environment. For an excellent summary and critique of the tenancy-based explanations of Chinese village society, see Ramon Myers, *The Chinese Peasant Economy* (Cambridge: Harvard University Press, 1970). Chalmers Johnson, *Peasant Nationalism and Communist Power* (Stanford, 1962) and Frederic Wakeman, *Strangers at the Gate: Social Disorder in South China, 1839-1861* (Berkeley: University of California Press, 1966), both stress the importance of foreign invasion in mobilizing Chinese responses a century apart in time.

4. See Roy Hofheinz, Jr., "The Ecology of Chinese Communist Success," in A. D. Barnett, ed., *Chinese Communist Politics in Action* (Seattle: University of Washington Press, 1969).

5. These variables are derived from an ongoing effort at Harvard to develop an atlas and handbook of Republican China county-level statistics. See Roy Hofheinz, Jr., "A Preliminary Atlas of Chinese County Development," a paper prepared for the New England Regional China Seminar, spring 1972. Republican period statistics require cautious examination, but they are of considerable potential importance for research and are too seldom used. We have selected the most reliable and verifiable measures for use here.

6. Curiously, this expression, which formed part of the Ch'ing dynasty vocabulary of peace keeping, was adopted by the National Revolutionary Army around the time of the Northern Expedition to mean "rangers" connected with the army and ultimately became the Communist word for "guerrilla."

7. "Resolution on solving the disputes between the Peasant Army and the Popular Corps," *KCMKJP,* September 1, 1926, pp. 10-11.

8. See Philip A. Kuhn, "Local Self-government under the Republic," in Frederic Wakeman, Jr., and Carolyn Grant, eds., *Conflict and Control in Imperial China,* pp. 287-295.

9. Nagano Akira, *Shinahei, tohi, kosōkai* (China—soldiers, bandits, and Red Spears; Tokyo, 1938), p. 278.

10. Ibid., p. 279.

11. Nagano Akira cites one national government study of Kwangtung in 1926 that lists fifty-two separate bandit lodges (*t'ang-k'ou*) numbering from twenty to two hundred men in each and another recording a total of twenty-six thousand bandits in only thirteen counties. Ibid., pp. 280-282.

12. Winston Hsieh, "The Revolution of 1911 in Kwangtung," (Ph.D. dissertation, Harvard University, 1970).

13. See Laai Yi-faai, Franz Michael, and John C. Sherman, "The Use of Maps in Social Research: A Case Study in South China," *Geographical Review,* 52:1 (January 1962), pp. 92-111, for a description of the areas of Triad operation in the last century.

14. Post-1949 accounts of the Kwangtung economy now readily admit that cash crops in the province reached an all time peak in the 1922-1928 period. See Liang Jen-ts'ai, *Economic Geography of Kwangtung* (Peking, 1956), translated in Joint Publications Research Service no. DC-389, p. 55.

15. See Maurice Freedman, *Lineage Organization in Southeastern China,* chapter 1.

16. On interethnic disputes in Kwangtung, see Myron Cohen, "The Hakka or 'Guest people': Dialect as a Sociocultural Variable in Southern China," *Ethnohistory* 15:3 (Summer 1968), pp. 237-292.

17. The report on the peasant movement in Kwangtung shows signs of having been compiled on the basis of reports following Lo's format.

18. *NMTK,* II, 132. This practice is mentioned in peasant movement sources.

19. See Juan Hsiao-hsien, "Hui-yang hsien nung-min-hsieh-hui ch'eng-li chih ching-kuo" (The founding of the Huiyang county peasant association), *Chung-kuo nung-min,* pp. 270-292, and "P'u-ning nung-min fan-k'ang ti-chu shih-mo chi" (The full story of the P'uning peasants' fight against landlords), *Ti-i-tz'u,* pp. 158-170.

20. *NMTK,* II, 144.

21. Lo Ch'i-yuan, "Chung-shan hsien shih-pien chih ching-kuo chi hsien-tsai" (The events and present situation of the Chungshan county incident), *Chung-kuo nung-min,* pp. 39-58.

22. See also "Kao-yao nung-min yun-tung te ching-kuo," (The events of the peasant movement in Kaoyao), *Ti-i-tz'u,* pp. 148-157 and "P'u-ning nung-min fan-k'ang ti-chu shih-mo chi," *Ti-i-tz'u,* pp. 158-170.

23. In October 1925, 1185 of the 1877 KMT members in Hupeh were students and 274 were teachers. "Report of the Hupeh KMT Tangpu" to the Second KMT Congress in *Chung-kuo kuo-min-tang ti-erh-tz'u ch'üan-kuo tai-piao ta-hui jih-k'an,* no. 3.

24. Li Jui, *Mao Tse-tung T'ung-chih-te ch'u-ch'i ko-ming huo-tung* (Peking, 1957), p. 243.

25. One interesting fact about references to Mao's stay in Shaoshan is the large number of people named Mao with whom he dealt: Mao Yuan-yao, Mao Fu-hsuan, Mao Hsin-hai, Mao Yueh-ch'iu, etc. See Mao Yuan-yao, "Tsai Mao Chu-hsi Ch'in-tzu chiao-yü hsia-te Shao-shun nung-min," in *Chung-kuo kung-ch'an-tang ling-tao hu-nan jen-min ying-yung tou-cheng-te san-shih-nien (Hsin Hu-nan Pao;* Ch'angsha, 1951), p. 66ff. In a Hunanese village this fact could only indicate that he relied heavily on his clan connections—people with whom he could safely have "close relations of friendship."

26. The timing of Mao's departure for Canton remains something of a mystery. He told Edgar Snow he arrived in Canton "about the time the Whampoa students [Chiang Kai-shek] had defeated Yang Hsi-min." Since the exact date of the fall of Yang in Canton was June 13, this would have given Mao two or three days at best to organize a revenge association among the peasant in Shaoshan. Visitors to Mao's birthplace in Shaoshan are now told that Mao was in his home village from January to August 1925 (see *Wen Hui Pao* [Shanghai] April 11, 1966, p. 2. Reference courtesy of Sydney Liu), a somewhat more reasonable dating. But even so, Mao's last few weeks were probably spent hiding from Chao's police.

27. *Hu-nan chin-pai-nien ta-shih chi-shu,* p. 494ff.

28. Li Jui, p. 266.

29. The secondary Communist sources provide many lists of these services. For some contemporary claims, see *KCMKJP,* July-August 1926 and Hsiang Nung (pseud.), "Hu-nan-te nung-min" (Hunan's peasantry), *Hsiang-tao,* no. 181 (Jan. 6, 1927), p. 1903.

30. *Chan-shih chou-pao* (The Militant), Sept. 19, 1926, reprinted in *Ti-i-tz'u,* pp. 239-240.

31. The first KMT congress for Hunan elected a nine-man executive committee, of which five were Communist party members.

32. There may be argument about the actual figures in Mao's report. In the text *(Mō Taku-tō shū,* I, 209) he claims a total membership of two million, but the statistical table that was originally published with it gives only one and one-third million. *Ti-i-tz'u,* p. 262.

33. Philip A. Kuhn, *Rebellion and Its Enemies in Late Imperial China* (Cambridge: Harvard University Press, 1970), pp. 135-152 on the militarization of this area in the nineteenth century; Jerome Chen, "Modernization of local protest: The P'ing-liu-li rebellion 1906," paper presented to the conference on local control and social protest during the Ch'ing period, Honolulu, 1971; Roy Hofheinz Jr., "The Autumn Harvest Insurrection," *The China Quarterly,* no. 32 (October-December 1967), pp. 37-38.

34. See Nagano Akira, *Shinahei, tohi, kōsōkai,* p. 300. Mao Tse-tung, *Selected Works* (Peking, 1964), I, 35. Interestingly, it was this area of south and west Liling county that was to produce so many Communist guerrillas after the Autumn Harvest Insurrection. See *Hu-nan Nien-chien* (Hunan yearbook; Ch'angsha, 1930), p. 510.

35. Chiang Yung-ching, *Pao-lo-t'ing yu Wu-han cheng-ch'üan* (Borodin and

the Wuhan regime; Taipei, 1963), p. 347.

36. *Selected Works,* I, 41.

37. Ibid.

38. December 1—*Ichang:* opponents "faked the insignia of the peasant association," "organized bandits," "colluded with the *t'uan-fang-chü,*" "tricked hooligans (*p'i-t'u*) and other backward peasants into a demonstration against the revolution," wrecked the peasant association and tortured its cadres in a certain district.

December 3—*Juch'eng:* the chief of the commerce protection force and the *t'uan-fang-chü* attacked the KMT county office, interrupted the postal system, and declared martial law.

December 28— *Yuehyang:* the chief of the *t'uan-fang-chü* set fire to a village. *Li:* the *t'uan-fang-chü* wrecked the county association, arrested and shot a number of peasants.

December 31 — *Yu:* the *t'uan-fang-chü* chief argued with peasants over his gambling, shot a movement leader.

January 14—*Hsiangyin:* a "*t'u-hao* colluded with the *t'uan-fang*" to dissolve the association by armed force. *Yu:* the east Hunan pacification commander (garrison commander) executed the chairman of a district association.

January 28—*Anhua:* "traitor merchants and *hao-lieh*" unite with *t'uan-fang* to dissolve the labor unions and "other revolutionary organs" in a district.

Compiled from Li Jui, in *Ti-i-tz'u,* p. 282, and *Hu-nan chin-pai-nien ta-shih chi-shu,* p. 522.

7. Origins of a Revolution: P'eng P'ai in Haifeng, 1922-1924

1. Winston Hsieh, "The Idea and Ideals of a Warlord; Ch'en Chiung-ming (1878-1933)," in *Papers on China* (East Asian Research Center, Cambridge, December 1961), XVI, 198-252.

2. The main source for this study is P'eng's "Hai-feng Nung-min Yun-tung" (The Haifeng peasant movement), published in pamphlet and article form in Canton in 1926 and also in Mao Tse-tung's *NMTK,* III. A more accessible copy may be found in *Ti-i-tz'u,* pp. 40-138. The article has recently been translated by Donald Holoch in *Seeds of Peasant Revolution: Report on the Haifeng Peasant Movement* (Ithaca, N.Y.: Cornell University Press, 1973), which includes a partial list of variations in the text, but does not cite the *NMTK* version.

3. Forty years later P'eng's followers would erect another statue on the sacred hill of Wen T'ien-hsiang: that of P'eng himself. Hai Feng (pseud.), *Hai-feng wen-hua ko-ming kai-shu* (An overview of Haifeng's Cultural Revolution; Hong Kong, 1969).

4. Etō Shinkichi, "Hai-lu-feng—The First Chinese Soviet Government," part 1, *The China Quarterly,* no. 8, (October-December 1961), pp. 160-183. See also Yong-pil Pang, "Peng Pai [sic]: from landlord to revolutionary," *Modern China* 1:297-322 (July 1975).

5. *Ti-i-tz'u,* pp. 49-50.

6. Ibid., p. 50.

7. Ibid., p. 52.

8. Ibid., p. 54.

9. Ibid., p. 56.

10. Ibid.

11. In the nineteenth century entire villages had taken sides in incessant bloody feuds.

12. These associations, like the traditional credit and crop-watching societies that they often resembled, have been neglected in the literature on rural China, largely because of the antipluralist bias of gentry writings. For example. Kung-chuan Hsiao's massive *Rural China* (Seattle, 1960) fails to mention them.

13. *Ti-i-tz'u,* p. 72.

14. Mehmet Beqiraj, pp. 96-97.

15. *Ti-i-tz'u,* p. 96.

16. The term is identical with the one Mao Tse-tung used in the 1930s to describe Communist partisan units. It has become the standard translation of the European word "guerrilla."

17. Wang Tso-hsin's telegrams of alarm to Ch'en Chiung-ming claimed P'eng had secreted weapons.

18. New calendar. The lunar date was July 7 and so the incident became publicized as the "7-7 Tide."

19. *Ti-i-tz'u,* p. 119.

20. Ibid., p. 128.

21. Ibid., p. 129.

22. Ibid., p. 130.

23. Interestingly, this reference to the Kuomintang constitutes the only mention of either of the revolutionary parties in P'eng P'ai's entire memoir. He clearly arrived at his peasant movement ideas independent of party pressures.

24. *Ti-i-tz'u,* p. 132.

8. The Politics of Dependency: Kwangning, 1924-1925

1. National Economic Planning Commission, Kwangtung Subcommission, *Kuang-tung-sheng chi-pen kung-yeh t'e-shu nung-yeh nung-ts'un fu-yeh tiao-ch'a pao-kao shu* (Report on basic industry, special agricultural products, and village subsidiary production in Kwangtung; April 1934, Hong Kong University Library).

2. In 1970 it still took a day's travel by steamboat and automobile.

3. Ts'ai Ho-sen, "The Kwangtung Peasant Movement at this year's Mayday," *Hsiang-tao,* no. 112 (April 28, 1925), p. 1034.

4. There was, for example, a custom called *sung-tsu* (presentation of the rent) in which the tenant was required to perform humiliating acts when bringing his year's payment. Instead of bringing the sacks of rice by wagon, he could be forced to carry them on his shoulders running all the way to his landlord's domicile.

5. Ts'ai Ho-sen calculated that the net loss per *mou* of land in Kwangning was around six yuan per year. According to his statistics this would amount to a gross expenditure rate of 70 percent above gross income. "Mayday," p. 1034.

6. *NMTK,* III, 82.

7. Ibid.

8. We are told that it was at this period that Ch'en Po-chung "made the decision to become a revolutionary and to go down among the masses." Presumably this means he became a Communist party member about this time. "Biography of the martyr Ch'en Po-chung," *Nung-min yun-tung*, no. 17 (November 1926). This obituary is the source of much of the above account of the early formation of the Kwangning peasant movement groups.

9. The seventh, under Feng Po-wan. *Chung-kuo Kuo-min-tang ti-i-tz'u tai-piao ta-hui t'e-hao* (Bulletin of the First KMT Congress), no. 2 (Jan. 23, 1924), p. 1.

10. See the unsigned article "Today's May Day" in the *Jih-k'an* (Daily gazette), no. 1 (May 1, 1925) of the first Kwangtung Provincial Peasant Association, pp. 3-4. The four main counties that contributed to this industry were Kwangning, Hua, Tech'ing, and Ch'ingyuan. By early 1927 the union, which had been formed in 1921, had 13,400 members, over 6000 of whom belonged to the Kuomintang. But 7000 were out of work because of new automated machinery. One source declares that the union members were 100 percent literate, a far higher ratio than found in other Canton unions. Canton Municipal Bureau of Social Research, *Kuang-chou-shih kung-hui tiao-ch'a t'ung-chi piao* (Statistics of an investigation of labor unions in Canton; Canton, 1926), p. 13.

11. In one raid by bandits in 1922 over a hundred merchants and their families were captured and held until the Ssuhui garrison could come to the rescue. *Hua-tzu jih-pao* (Chinese mail), March 14, 1922.

12. *NMTK*, III, 84.

13. Later this device was found to be too provocative and was abandoned.

14. T'an P'ing-shan and Feng Chü-po, *Kuo-min ko-ming chung chih min-t'uan wen-t'i* (National revolution and the Popular Corps question; Canton, 1923), p. 4. T'an declared that in the battle of July 1-7, 1923, Li commanded seventeen thousand troops. Many of these must have been secret society soldiers.

15. *NMTK*, III, 85-86.

16. This last bit of slander, implying that the peasant movement men were illiterate, was patently false.

17. By this time there were already associations in the following ch'ü: Chiang-t'un, T'anpu, Cheshih, Lokang, and K'omutsui. *NMTK*, III, 88.

18. *NMTK*, III, 91.

19. He replaced Yang Shu-k'an, a T'ung Meng Hui associate of Sun's from Szechwan who had closer connections to the older provincial politics than Liao. Tahara, Tennan, ed., *Chugōku kanshin jimmei roku* (A record of gentry and officials in China; Peking, 1918), p. 594.

20. Thirty-seventh Session of CEC. *Chung-kuo Kuo-min-tang chou-k'an*, no. 27, p. 7.

21. *Hua-tzu jih-pao*, July 25, 1924.

22. The first raid noted in the Hong Kong papers occurred on June 28, 1924. "Bandits" shot up the main street of Kwangning city doing $200,000 damage. They were driven out by ten thousand village corpsmen but not without sacking neighboring Tunghsiang in the process. They escaped by hijacking a steamboat. *Hua-tzu jih-pao*, July 10, 1924.

23. See Hofheinz, "Peasant Movement and Rural Revolution: Chinese Com-

munists in the Countryside, 1923-1927" (Ph.D. dissertation, Harvard University, 1966), p. 109-111.

24. The second class of the Peasant Movement Institute was in fact the source of the Kwangtung Peasant Self-Defense Army. These ten students must have come from the class that included T'an Hung-shan, his three brothers, and fifteen others whose home was Kwangning.

25. For a description of the First Kwangning Congress, see Hofheinz, "Peasant Movement," pp. 117-125.

26. *NMTK,* III, 106. Canton refused his request in October for several hundred yuan and a hundred weapons.

27. Hofheinz, "Peasant Movement," p. 127.

28. *NMTK,* III, 111.

29. *NMTK,* III, 110-111 has the texts.

30. Estimates of the size of the landlord forces range from 360 (Ts'ai Ho-sen, "May day," p. 18) to over 2000 [Ch'en] k'o-wen, "The death of Ch'en Po-chung, Ch'eng Keng Li Min-chih and Huang Shao-fan," *Nung-min Yun-tung,* no. 17 (Nov. 23, 1926), p. 371. This variety justified the Communists' uncertainty about the strength of the opposition.

31. *NMTK,* III, 126.

32. See Li Yun-han, *Ts'ung jung-kung tao ch'ing-tang* (From admitting the Communists to the party purge), 263, 282, 283, 286, 746 for Liao's Communist affiliations.

33. See note 30. A brief chart of the armaments available to T'anpu and to Cheshih-Shekang is instructive:

Weapon type	T'anpu (landlord)	Cheshih-Shekang (peasant association)
Borke (Luger-type)	6	1
Revolver	3	4
Local Single-shot	20	21
Bird guns	100	270
"Needleguns"	80	-
Local cannon	3	5
"Long dragons"	10	10

This balance of arms was sufficiently close to make the outcome uncertain. *NMTK,* III, 119.

34. *NMTK,* III, 131.

35. Hofheinz, "Peasant Movement," pp. 146-147, describes this occasion.

36. The text of Hu Shao's December 22 telegram for help is found in *NMTK,* III, 142-143. Liao Chung-k'ai's original response ordering the commission to intercede is reproduced in brush manuscript form in *Li-t'ou* (Ploughshare), no. 13, p. 9.

37. *NMTK,* III, 146.

38. The Hong Kong newspaper account of the incident says the chief was seized in his own offices "as a result of some unexplained misunderstanding" with the peasant association. *Hua-tzu jih-pao,* Jan. 9, 1925.

39. Hofheinz, "Peasant Movement," pp. 162-163.

40. Ibid., pp. 165-166.

41. Telegram of January 21. *NMTK*, III, 173.

42. Hofheinz, "Peasant Movement," pp. 169-170.

43. Ibid., pp. 156-158. We have no information about how it was related historically to the San-ho-hui (Triad Society) that flourished in the region in the nineteenth century, but it may be assumed that there was considerable overlap. For areas under Triad influence in the early 1800s, see Laai Yi-faai, Franz Michael, and John C. Sherman, "The Use of Maps in Social Research: A Case Study in South China," *The Geographical Review*, 52:108 (1962). One 1923 source claimed there were forty to fifty thousand society bandits in the North and West River basins. T'an P'ing-shan and Feng Chü-p'o, *Kuo-min ko-ming chung chih min-tuan wen-t'i*, p. 2.

44. Frederic Wakeman, *Strangers at the gate: Social Disorder in South China, 1839-1861* (Berkeley: University of California Press, 1966).

45. *NMTK*, III, 150.

46. Hofheinz, "Peasant Movement," pp. 159-161.

47. *NMTK*, III, 154.

48. T. C. Chang, *The Farmers' Movement in Kwangtung*, p. 15.

49. The county peasant association was reorganizing and given a roster of officials that does not reveal any mainstream movement figures. See "Biography of the martyr Ch'en Po-chung," *Nung-min Yun-tung*, no. 17.

50. *Hua-tzu jih-pao*, April 8 and 10, 1925.

51. Harold Isaacs records this "brief but sharp engagement" victory for the peasants but fails to note that the adversaries were *local* forces. *The Tragedy of the Chinese Revolution*, p. 69.

52. *KCMKJP*, July 13, 1926, p. 10.

53. *KCMKJP*, July 14, 1926, p. 10.

54. Literally "assignment downward" but often used in post-1949 China to indicate campaigns to transfer personnel to the countryside.

55. "Kwangning tsui-chin chih nung-min yün-tung" (The Kwangning peasant movement at present), in *Nung-min yun-tung chih kung-tso* (Practical peasant movement work; Hankow, July 1927). Pamphlet found in Kuomintang Ts'-aot'un archive, no. 484/147).

9. The Face of the Enemy: Hua County, 1926

1. "Achievements of the peasant bureau," in *CKKMTCK*, no. 42, p. 4.

2. *KCMKJP*, August 27 and September 1, 1926.

3. *KCMKJP*, September 2, 1926. *Li-t'ou chou-pao* (Ploughshare), no. 15 (Sept. 23, 1926), p. 23.

4. *KCMKJP*, September 1, 1926, p. 11. P'eng P'ai, "How corps bandits massacred peasants in Hua county," *Li-t'ou chou-pao*, no. 17/18 (Oct. 8, 1926), p. 5. This article, written by P'eng as a detailed report on the Hua county events to his peasant bureau, is the major source for the descriptions of events in this chapter. It will be referred to as "Hua Report."

5. Lo Ch'i-yuan, "Casquettes — A Preface [to P'eng P'ai's 'Hua Report']," *Li-t'ou Chou-pao*, no. 17/18 (Oct. 8, 1926), p. 2.

6. P'eng later noticed that Wu, on entering the countryside, changed to the scholar's long robes. Perhaps Wu, like Mao Tse-tung in his visits to Hunan in 1925, understood the continuing rural deference to education and status.

7. P'eng P'ai, "Hua Report," p. 7.

8. "Report on the Yangts'un Incident," August 22, 1926. Reprinted in mimeograph form for internal bureau circulation by Ch'en K'o-wen, the central peasant bureau secretary. Kuomintang Ts'aot'un Archive (Ch'ien-wu-pu [Former Five Bureaus], 8283).

9. Peasant movement archives contained records from two years earlier of "atrocities" against the Hua county association committed by one of Chiang's alleged coconspirators. But this incident of September 1924, was already ancient history.

10. See Frederic Wakeman *Strangers at the Gate: Social Disorder in South China, 1839-1861* (Berkeley: University of California Press, 1966), chapter 1.

11. *Hua-tzu Jih-pao* (Chinese mail), April 20, 1922.

12. This captive, Chiang Shih, who had been seized with a carbine in his hand, was a long-time subordinate associate of Wu Kuan-ch'i's.

13. Kuan was the official of the corps affairs committee in charge of direct dealings with the corps. *KCMKJP*, August 31, 1926, p. 7.

14. Wei is referred to in Lei Te's report as "Tsung-pu Wei-yuan" (delegate of the general headquarters). P'eng P'ai suggests that he felt Wu Kuan-ch'i had sent him knowingly to Loch'ang to be shot. P'eng P'ai, "Hua Report," p. 31.

15. Dated September 5, 9:00 P.M., P'eng P'ai, "Hua Report," p. 32.

16. The Hua County Peasant Association delegate to the meeting was Liang Po-yü, who at age twenty had been a member of the second class of the Peasant Movement Institute in mid-1924. *Chung-kuo nung-min*, p. 186.

17. There is no information on Wang Ching-fang, but we are probably not wrong to assume him to be a local notable resident in Canton who had taken a standoff position on the Min-t'uan issue. He was brought back to Hua by Wu Kuan-ch'i. P'eng P'ai, "Hua Report," p. 35.

18. Ibid., p. 36.

19. The final text of the contract is found in ibid., pp. 39-40.

20. Among those testifying were Juan Hsiao-hsien of the provincial peasant association and Ou Meng-chüeh of the women's association. Ou became, after 1949, a leading figure in the Kwangtung Communist party.

21. On this personal reaction see Liang Po-yü's September 23, 1926, report to the central peasant bureau. Kuomintang Ts'aot'un Archive (Ch'ien-wu-pu, 8293).

22. Reports of October 5 and 16 from Liang Po-yu to the central peasant bureau. Kuomintang Ts'aot'un Archive (Ch'ien-wu-pu, 8296).

10. Birth of People's War: Haifeng, 1927

1. Li graduated with the second class in June 1925. A communist, he was one of four Haifeng students at the academy. Another Haifeng student was P'eng P'ai's later arch enemy, Tai K'o-hsiung, the Popular Corps leader. Li was killed in action in October 1925 and Wu Chen-min assumed his duties. In retaliation, peasant association assassins shot Ch'en Yueh-po, P'eng P'ai's 1923 gentry opponent, who

was assumed to be connected with Li's death. Chung I-mou, *Hai-lu-feng nung-min yun-tung* (Canton, 1957), p. 41.

2. In some villages in 1925 the associations issued rent reduction certificates, which were honored by the new government, only to their own members, thus offering a major financial reward for joining the association. See Chung I-mou, "Hai-Lu-feng nung-min te pa-nien chan-tou" (The eight-year struggle of the Hai-Lufeng peasantry), in *Chin-tai-shih tzu-liao* (Materials on modern history; Peking, 1955), no. 4, p. 186.

3. We assume that P'eng was the author of the anonymous work *Hai-lu-feng Su-wei-ai* (Hai-Lu-feng Soviet — hereafter *SWA*). This book, ninety-five pages of leadprint, may have been printed in Shanghai where he lived underground in 1928. Its publication was announced on February 20, 1928, in the Communist Central Committee organ *Pu-erh-sai-wei-k'o* (Bolshevik), no. 18. The contents are in the form of a long report intended to justify the decisions of local Communists to Ch'ü Ch'iu-pai's Central Committee, probably written before the December 1927 Plenum of the CCP Politburo. The report's frank defense of Haifeng Communists against criticism by their regional committee suggests P'eng P'ai was the author.

4. Chung I-mou, p. 59.

5. Ibid., p. 60.

6. P'eng P'ai's post mortem admitted that some worker-peasant comrades were far cooler to the party than to their own mass organizations. *SWA*, p. 26.

7. *SWA*, p. 31.

8. *SWA*, p. 33.

9. Ch'en Hsiao-pai, *Hai-Lu feng ch'ih-huo chi* (Canton, 1932), p. 17. *SWA*, p. 35.

10. P'eng P'ai later admitted that "we constantly warned party officers and comrades at all levels that we would rather kill in error than allow anyone to escape our net." The burning of whole villages also got explicit approval. *SWA*, p. 35.

11. Chung I-mou, "Hai-Lu-feng nung-min te pa-nien chan-tou," p. 204.

12. C. Martin Wilbur, "The Ashes of Defeat: Accounts of the Nanchang Revolt and Southern Expedition, August 1 — October 1, 1927, by Chinese Communists who took part." *The China Quarterly*, no. 18 (April-June 1964), pp. 16, 20.

13. P'eng expressed his concern for his native Kwangtung in an article written just before he plunged into the crisis in Hua county. "Departing for the Northern expedition and the Hong Kong-Canton Strike," *Jen-min chou-k'an* (People's weekly), no. 18 (Aug. 12, 1926), pp. 8-10.

14. He left Lufeng for Hong Kong, bypassing his home county, sometime after October 7. Wilbur, "Ashes," p. 31.

15. Kim San (as told to Nym Wales), *Song of Ariran: A Korean Communist in the Chinese Revolution* (San Francisco: Ramparts, 1972 [?]), p. 207. Kim asserted that P'eng, had he lived, "would surely have become one of the greatest mass leaders China has ever known," since he shared with Mao Tse-tung that "rare quality of inborn leadership" (p. 206).

16. *SWA*, pp. 56-58.

17. *SWA*, pp. 70-79.

18. *SWA*, p. 62.

19. *SWA*, pp. 80-87.

20. "Resolution on killing all reactionaries," *SWA*, pp. 82-83. Where missionaries and anti-Communists reported tens of thousands dead, Lo Ch'i-yuan insisted in February 1928 that only 1822 "landlords and evil gentry" had been killed (*SWA*, p. 93). Kim San, the Korean Communist who witnessed P'eng P'ai's rule in early 1928, admitted the brutality of many such executions and noted P'eng personally favored killing more, not fewer, enemies. *Song of Ariran*, p. 186.

21. G. W. Skinner has suggested that high village market ratios relative to surrounding areas of the same basic social structure represent areas of transition between traditional and modern market economies. See "Marketing and Social Structure in Rural China," *Journal of Asian Studies* 24:3-43, 195-228, 363-399 (November 1964, February and May 1965). Interestingly, at the county level the East River region had the highest Skinner ratio of the province of Kwangtung and so on this measure would seem to be more rapidly modernizing than other regions. Within Haifeng the district with the highest Skinner ratio is Ch'ihshih, not a highly successful or unsuccessful county for Communist development. Kungp'ing and Meilung are in the middle of the scale.

22. See, for example, Jack Belden, *China Shakes the World* (New York: Harper, 1949).

23. Agnes Smedley, *The Great Road: The Life and Times of Chu Teh* (New York, 1956), p. 206.

24. Ch'en Hsiao-pai, pp. 58-60.

25. Ibid., p. 71. Chinese Communist army policies toward family members (*chia-shu*) have not yet been examined in historical perspective. See Davis B. Bobrow, "Political and Economic Role of The Military in the Chinese Communist Movement" (Ph.D. dissertation, M.I.T., 1962), and Thomas Jay Mathews, "The Military Exemplar in Communist China" (senior honors thesis, Harvard University, 1967).

26. An example: a bulletin of the East River Special Committee, dated February 28, admitted that one company of Tung Lang's second division had lost an entire squad of twenty-five men with eighteen precious weapons to desertion one night near Kueit'an. The committee urged its subordinates to arrest these men, since "there is no end to these stories of defections."

27. Ch'en Hsiao-pai, p. 66.

28. Ibid., p. 67.

29. Ibid.

11. Death of a Revolution: Haifeng, 1928

1. Harold Isaacs, *The Tragedy of the Chinese Revolution*, p. 289.

2. Presbyterian missionary Douglas James, letter to U.S. Consul J. C. Huston, February 7, 1928. United States Department of State Archive, 893.00/9871 (hereafter USDA).

3. Chung I-mou, p. 88.

4. Ibid.

5. Ibid.

6. Ibid.

7. Ibid., p. 89.

8. James, February 7, 1928, letter. USDA (record group RG-59;, State De-partment records relating to internal affairs of China, 1910-1929.

9. USDS, 893.00/9701.

10. USDS, 893.00/9668 (Oct. 31, 1927), 9764 (Dec. 31, 1927), 9701 (Jan. 9, 1928).

11. Berger had no proof that the raiders were Communists. He admitted that such raids had become "the custom of late in this consular district" and cited other examples of village raids by unknown forces. USDS, 893.00/9672 (Nov. 15, 1927).

12. Berger to MacMurray, February 14, 1928.

13. Chinese Communist party central provisional politburo, "Kuang-chou pao-tung chih i-i chi ch'i chiao-hsun" (The significance and lessons of the Canton Insurrection), January 3, 1928. (Koizumi Collection, Keiō University, Tokyo).

14. Ibid.

15. USDS, 893.00/9749 (Dec. 30, 1927).

16. Chung I-mou, p. 103. Huston, USDS, 893.00/9749 (Dec. 30, 1927) esti-mated that three to four thousand persons were massacred in this pogrom.

17. Chung I-mou, "Hai-Lu-feng nung-min te pa-nien chan-tou" (The eight-year struggle of the Hai-Lufeng peasantry) in *Chih-tai-shih tzu-liao* (Materials on modern history; 1955), no. 4, p. 209.

18. Ibid. Professor Etō Shinkichi accepts per contra Kim San's recollection that Yeh did not arrive until the first week of January. "Hai-Lufeng—The First Chinese Soviet Government," part 2, *The China Quarterly,* no. 9 (January-March 1962), p. 174.

19. The local gazetteer lists very few with the surname among noted manda-rins but a considerable number in the sections on pacification. We cannot, of course, be certain that these Lins were of the Kueifeng clan, but it seems likely. *Hai-feng hsien-chih,* pp. 82-84, 90-91.

20. For a list of the Lin elders executed, see *Hai-Lu-feng p'ing-Kung-chi* (printed by Political Training Office, sixteenth division, National Revolutionary Army [1928?]), pp. 95-96.

21. Nanling was finally broken by Lin Tao-wen in December 1927 after he resorted to the casket-bomb technique used by P'eng P'ai in Kwangning. Chung I-mou, pp. 100-101. Reactionary hamlets such as Huangt'ang and Chienmenk'ang in northwest Lufeng were raided and burned as early as 1925 but continued to con-tribute to anti-Communist efforts. Ch'en Hsiao-pai, pp. 1-2.

22. Ch'en Hsiao-pai, pp. 112-119. We need not accept the claim that seventy thousand Haifengese fled to Hong Kong in the last half of 1927, but the numbers were substantial.

23. Chung I-mou, pp. 46-48, 107-109.

24. Ch'en Hsiao-pai, pp. 49-50.

25. The expression is classical Chinese, from the millennial tradition of Con-fucian statecraft. The thought is universal.

26. Ch'en Hsiao-pai, p. 52. He cited an example from his own experience. His men had found a stockade, freshly constructed and resembling the ancient gun

towers of the Canton delta, near the market town of Ch'ihshih. The residents had refused to open the gates and Chung, justly frightened at the military potential of the enclosure, ordered it destroyed. Ten civilians were killed in the onslaught, including one cadre in the Ch'ihshih Peasant Association. "This incident made me very unhappy," Chung wrote, "as I was concerned that good citizens not be put to undue suffering." His concern was more than merely moral: the very next day, as his men staggered away in defeat, they were jeered and spat upon by hostile villagers who had sought shelter in the stockade.

27. Ibid., p. 52.

28. Howard Boorman, I, 161-163.

29. Chung I-mou, pp. 116-117. Chen Hsiao-pai, pp. 90-102.

30. Chen Hsiao-pai, p. 99.

31. *Hai-Lu-feng p'ing-Kung-chi*, pp. 89-92.

12. The Legacy of China's Peasant Movement

1. See John D. Powell, "Venezuela: The Peasant Union Movement," in Henry A. Landsberger, ed., *Latin American Peasant Movements* (Ithaca, N.Y.: 1969), pp. 62-100.

2. Jurgen Domes, *Die Vertagte Revolution; Die Politik der Kuomintang in China, 1923-1937* (Berlin: Walter de Gruyter, 1969), p. 539. There were 2 province-level associations and 715 county-level associations in early 1927.

3. Liu Hsing, "Some desultory recollections of the Autumn Harvest Insurrection," in *Chung-kuo Kung-ch'ang-tang ling-tao Hu-nan jen-min ying-yung tou-cheng-te san-shih-nien*, (Ch'angsha, 1951), p. 38. They included, however, such important leaders as T'an Cheng and T'an Chin-lin.

4. Visitors to Canton during the Cultural Revolution of the 1960s say that no other figure except Mao and Hsiao Ch'u-nü was represented in the exhibits at the Peasant Movement Museum, located on the site of the old Confucian temple where Mao's class met. P'eng P'ai, though his picture reappeared before my visit there in October 1974, was treated as one of a large group of peasant organizers.

5. See Mark Gayn, "China has a Yenan Complex," *New York Times Sunday Magazine,* January 30, 1966, p. 10. A more scholarly attempt to draw the parallel between Yenan communism and post-liberation China can be found in Mark Selden, *The Yenan Way in Revolutionary China* (Cambridge: Harvard University Press, 1971).

6. See Lin Piao, "Long Live the Victory of People's War," *Peking Review,* Sept. 3, 1965, pp. 9-30.

7. See David Barrett's *Dixie Mission: The United States Army Observer Group in Yenan, 1944* (Berkeley: Center for Chinese Studies, 1970) for an account of the abortive negotiations of late 1944.

BIBLIOGRAPHY

Andrews, Carol C. "The Relationship between the Chinese Communist Party and the Peasantry." M. A. dissertation, Columbia University, 1964.

Barnett, David D. *Dixie Mission: The United States Army Observer Group in Yenan, 1944.* Berkeley, Center for Chinese Studies, 1970.

Beqiraj, Mehmet. *Peasantry in Revolution.* Ithaca, N.Y., Center for International Studies, Cornell University, 1966.

Boorman, Howard L., ed. *Biographical Dictionary of Republican China.* New York, Columbia University Press, 1967.

Brandt, Conrad. *Stalin's Failure in China 1924–1927.* Cambridge, Harvard University Press, 1958.

Browder, Earl. *Civil War in Nationalist China.* Chicago, Labor Unity Publishing Association, 1927.

Bukharin, N. I. 佈哈林. *Nung-min wen-t'i* 農民問題 (The peasant question) tr. Hsin Ch'ing-nien Wuhan (?), 1926.

Chang, T. C. [Chang Tzu-ch'iang 張自强]. *The Farmer's Movement in Kwangtung.* Tr. Committee on Christianizing Economic Relations. Shanghai, National Christian Council of China, 1928.

Chao Kuo-chün. *The Agrarian Policy of the Chinese Communist Party, 1921–1959.* Bombay, Asia Publications House, 1960.

Chen Han-seng. *Agrarian Problems in Southernmost China.* Shanghai, 1936.

Ch'en Hsiao-pai 陳小白, comp. *Hai-lu-feng ch'ih-huo chi* 海陸豐赤禍記 (Record of the red holocaust in Hai-Lufeng). Canton, 1932.

Ch'en, Jerome. *Mao and the Chinese Revolution.* London, Oxford University Press, 1965.

Cherepanov, A. I. *Zapiski Voennovo Sovetnika v Kitae* (Notes of a military adviser in China: From the history of the first civil revolutionary war, 1924–1927). Moscow, Science Publishing House, 1964.

Chesneaux, Jean. *Le Mouvement Ouvrier Chinois de 1919 à 1927.* Paris, Mouton, 1962.

Chiang Kai-shek 蔣中正. *Su O tsai Chung-kuo* 蘇俄在中國 (Soviet Russia in China). Taipei, 1957.

Chiang Yung-ching 蔣永敬. *Pao-lo-t'ing yü Wu-han cheng-ch'üan* 鮑羅廷與武漢政權 (Borodin and the Wuhan regime). Taipei, 1963.

Chu Ch'i-hua 朱其華 [a.k.a.: Chu P'ei-wo 朱佩我, Chu Hsin-fan 朱新繁, Li Ang 李昂]. *I-chiu-erh-ch'i nien ti hui-i-lu* 一九二七年低回憶錄 (A memoir of 1927). Shanghai, 1935.

Chung I-mou 鍾貽謀. *Hai-lu-feng nung-min yun-tung* 海陸豐農民運動 (The peasant movement in Hai-feng and Lu-feng). Canton, 1957.

Chung-kuo kung-ch'an-tang ling-tao Hunan jen-min ying-yung fen-tou ti san-shih-nien 中國共產黨領導湖南人民英勇奮鬥的三十年 (Thirty years of the Hunan people's courageous struggles led by the Chinese Communist party). Ch'angsha, 1951.

Chung-kuo kung-ch'an-tang tsai chung-nan ti-ch'ü ling-tao ko-ming tou-cheng li-shih tzu-liao 中國共產黨在中南地区領導革命鬥爭歷史資料 (Historical materials on the revolutionary struggles led by the Chinese Communist party in central and south China), Vol. I, ed. The Marxism-Leninism Night School of the Wuhan Municipality. Hankow, 1951.

Chung-kuo Kuo-min-tang chou-k'an 中國國民黨周刊 (Chinese Kuomintang weekly), 1–42 (January–September 1924).

Chung-kuo Kuo-min-tang ch'uan-kuo tai-piao ta-hui hui-i lu 中國國民黨全國代表大會會議錄 (Minutes of the first KMT National Congress; Canton, January 1924).

Chung-kuo Kuo-min-tang ch'uan-kuo tai-piao ta-hui t'e-hao 中國國民黨全國代表大會特號 (Special publication on the National Congress of the Kuomintang), 1–3 (Jan. 20–30, 1924).

Chung-kuo Kuo-min-tang hsuan-yen hui-k'an 中國國民黨宣言彙刊 (Collected manifestos of the Chinese Kuomintang), ed. KMT CEC Propaganda Bureau. Shanghai.

Chung-kuo Kuo-min-tang kao t'ung-chih shu 中國國民黨告同志書 (A letter of the Kuomintang to all comrades), ed. Kuomintang Central Peking Executive Office (Western Hills). Shanghai, 1926.

Chung-kuo Kuo-min-tang ti-erh-tz'u ch'uan-kuo tai-piao ta-hui hui-i chi-lu 中國國民黨第二次全國代表大會會議記錄 (Minutes of the meeting of the second Kuomintang National Congress), ed. Kuomintang Secretariat. Canton, April, 1926.

Chung-kuo Kuo-min-tang ti-erh-tz'u ch'uan-kuo tai-piao ta-hui jih-k'an 中國國民黨第二次全國代表大會日刊 (Journal of the Second National Congress of the Kuomintang), 3–6, 8, 10–12, 14–16 (Canton, January 1926).

Chung-kuo nung-min yun-tung chin-k'uang 中國農民運動近況 (Recent state of the Chinese peasant movement), ed. Kuomintang Central Peasant Bureau. Canton (?), 1926.

Chung-kuo nung-min 中國農民 (The Chinese peasant). Official monthly of the KMT Central Peasant Bureau, 1–6/7, 8, 10 (January–December 1926). (Issues 1–7 reprinted by Daian, Tokyo, 1963).

Etō Shinkichi 衞藤瀋吉. "Chūkyōshi kenkyū nōto" 中共史研究ノート (A note on the study of Chinese Communist history), Tōyō gakuhō 東洋學報 (Reports of the Oriental Society) 43: 2, 63–87.

Feng Ho-fa 馮和法. *Chung-kuo nung-ts'un ching-chi tzu-liao* 中國農村經濟資料 (Materials on the Chinese rural economy). Shanghai, 1933.

Freedman, Maurice. *Lineage Organization in Southeastern China.* London, Athlone Press, 1957.

———— *Chinese Lineage and Society: Fukien and Kuangtung.* London, Athlone Press, 1966.

Fujita, Masanori 藤田正典. "Fang Chin-min to Min-Che-Kan sobieto ku" 方志敏と閩浙贛ソヴェト區 (Fang Chih-min and the Fukien-Chekiang-Kiangsi soviet district), *Ajia Kenkyū* (Asia studies) 6: 1–38 (1960).

Hai Feng 海楓 (pseud.). *Hai-feng wen-hua ko-ming kai-shu* 海豐文化革命概述 (An overview of Haifeng's cultural revolution). Hong Kong, 1969.

Hai-lu-feng p'ing-kung chi 海陸豐平共記 (A record of pacifying the Communists in Hai-Lufeng). N.p., n.d. Colophon dated December 1928.

Hai-lu-feng Su-wei-ai 海陸豐蘇維埃 (The Hai-Lufeng Soviet). N.p., n.d. Colophon dated Feb. 16 [1928].

Hatano, Kenichi 波多野乾一. *Chūgoku kyōsantō shi* 中國共產黨史 (A history of the Chinese Communist party), Vol. I. Reprinted Tokyo, 1961.

Hinton, William. *Fanshen.* New York, Monthly Reveiw Press, 1966.

Ho Chien 何鍵. *Hu-nan ch'an kung hui-pien* 湖南劻共彙編 (Collection on the suppression of communism in Hunan). Changsha (?), 1928.

Ho Kan-chih 何幹之. *Chung-kuo hsien-tai ko-ming shih* 中國現代革命史 (A history of the contemporary Chinese Revolution). Hong Kong, 1958.

Hou Feng 侯楓. *P'eng P'ai lieh-shih chuan-lüeh* 彭湃烈士傳略 (An outline biography of martyr P'eng P'ai). Canton, 1959.

Hsiang-tao chou-pao 嚮導周報 (Guide weekly). 1–201 (Sept. 13, 1922–July 18, 1927). Reprinted Tokyo, 1963.

Hsiao, Kung-chuan. *Rural China: Imperial Control in the Nineteenth Century.* Seattle, University of Washington Press, 1960.

Hsiao Tso-liang. *The Land Revolution in China, 1930–1934, a study of documents.* Seattle, University of Washington Press, 1969.

Hsu, Leonard Shihlien. *Sun Yat-sen: His Political and Social Ideas.* Los Angeles, University of Southern California Press, 1933.

Hsüeh Nung-shan 薛農山. *Chung-kuo nung-min chan-cheng chih shih te yen-chiu* 中國農民戰爭之史的研究 (An investigation into the history of the peasant wars in China). Shanghai, 1935.

Hu Hua 胡華, ed. *Chung-kuo hsin-min-chu chu-i ko-ming shih ts'an k'ao tzu-liao* 中國新民主主義革命史參考資料 (Reference materials on the history of China's new democratic revolution). Peking, 1951.

Hu Hua 胡華. *Chung-kuo hsin min-chu chu-i ko-ming shih ch'u kao* 中國新民主主義革命史初稿 (A history of China's new democratic revolution, first draft, rev. ed.). Peking, 1952.

——— *Chung-kuo ko-ming shih chiang-i* 中國革命史講義 (Lectures on the history of the Chinese Revolution). Peking, 1959.

Hua Kang 華崗. *Chung-kuo ta ko-ming shih* 中國大革命史 (A history of the great Chinese Revolution 1925–1927). Shanghai, 1932.

Hua Ying-shen 華應申. *Chung-kuo kung-ch'an-tang lieh-shih chuan* 中國共產黨烈士傳 (Biographies of the Chinese Communist martyrs). Hong Kong, 1947.

Huang-kang Team of the Party History Investigation Group, Wuhan University. "The Tempest of the peasant movement in Huang-kang," *Union Research Service* 25: 12–13 (Nov. 10 and 14, 1961).

Huang-p'u t'ung-hsueh tsung ming-ts'e 黃埔同學總名冊 (Whampoa student directory), Vol. I. Ed. Central Military Academy, Alumni Office. Nanking(?), 1933.

Hunan Chinese Communist Party Provincial Propaganda Bureau, ed. *Hu-nan ko-ming lieh-shih chuan* 湖南革命烈士傳 (Biographies of Hunanese revolutionary martyrs). Ch'angsha, 1952.

Hu-nan chin-pai-nien ta-shih chi-shu 湖南近百年大事紀述 (Chronology of important events in Hunan in the last century). Vol. I of *Hu-nan sheng chih* 湖南省志 (Gazetteer of Hunan province). Ch'angsha, 1959.

Hu-nan sheng hsien-cheng pao-kao 湖南省縣政報告 (Hunan province county government reports). Ch'angsha, 1931.

Hupei hsien-cheng kai-k'uang 湖北縣政概況 (Survey of Hupei county government). 3 vols. Hankow, 1934.

Hu-pei nung-min pao-tung ching-kuo chih pao-kao 湖北農民暴動經過之報告 (Report on the events of the peasant insurrection in Hupeh). Shanghai(?), 1927. In Keio University Library, Tokyo.

Isaacs, Harold R. *Five Years of Kuomintang Reaction.* Shanghai, 1932.

———— *The Tragedy of the Chinese Revolution.* Stanford, Stanford University Press, 1938.

Jen-min chou-k'an 人民周刊 (People's weekly), 17–19 (Aug. 1–20, 1926).

Johnson, Chalmers A. *Peasant Nationalism and Communist Power.* Stanford, Stanford University Press, 1962.

Kao Yin-tsu 高蔭祖, ed. *Chung-hua min-kuo ta shih-chi* 中華民國大事記 (Important records of the Republic of China). Taipei, 1957.

Kuang-tung nung-min yun-tung pao-kao 廣東農民運動報告 (Report on the Kwangtung peasant movement). Np., n.d.

Kuang-tung sheng nung-min hsieh-hui ch'eng-li ta-hui hui-ch'ang jih-k'an 廣東省農民協會成立大會會場日刊 (Journal of the founding congress of the Kwangtung Provincial Peasant Association) 1–5 (May 1–8, 1925).

Kuang-tung ti-erh-tz'u ch'uan-sheng nung-min tai-piao ta-hui hui-ch'ang jih-k'an 廣東第二次全省農民代表大會會場日刊 (Journal of the Second Kwagtung Peasant Congress) 3–6 (May 4–7, 1926).

Kung-ch'an-tang yin-mou ta pao-lu 共產黨陰謀大暴露 (Great revelation of the Communist party plot). Canton, 1924.

Kung Ch'u 龔楚. *Wo yü hung chün* 我與紅軍 (The Red Army and I). Hong Kong, 1954.

Kung-fei huo-kuo shih-liao hui-pien 共匪禍國史料彙編 (A collection of historical materials on the Communist disaster). 3 vols. Taipei(?), 1964.

Kuwajima Kazue 桑島主計. *Chū-nan-shi chihō kyōsantō oyobi kyōsanhi no kōdō jōkyō ni kansuru chōsa hōkokusho* 中南支地方共產黨及共產匪行動狀況に關する調査報告書 (Report on local Communist parties and rebel activities in south central China). Tokyo, 1930.

Landsberger, Henry A., ed. *Latin American Peasant Movements.* Ithaca, N.Y., Cornell University Press, 1969.

Li Chien-nung. *The Political History of China 1840–1928*, tr. and ed. Ssu-yu Teng and Jeremy Ingalls. New York, Van Nostrand, 1956.

Li Jui 李銳. *Mao Tse-tung T'ung-chih-te ch'u-ch'i ko-ming huo-tung* 毛澤東同志的初期革命活動 (The early revolutionary activities of Comrade Mao Tse-tung). Peking, 1957.

Li T'ien-min 李天民. *Chung-kung yü nung-min* 中共與農民 (Chinese communism and the peasantry). Hong Kong, 1958.

Li-t'ou chou-pao 犁頭周報 (Ploughshare weekly). Kwangtung Provincial Peasant Association, Canton, June 1926–January 1927.

Li Wei 李偉. *Ching-kang-shan* 井崗山 (The Chingkang mountains). Shanghai, 1956.

Li Yun-han 李雲漢. *Ts'ung jung-kung tao ch'ing-tang* 從容共到清黨 (From admitting the Communists to the party purge), China Scholarly

Works Prize Committee Series No. 15, Taipei(?), preface dated October 1965. 2 vols.

Liao Chung-k'ai chi 廖仲愷集 (A collection of the writings of Liao Chung-k'ai). Peking, 1963.

Lien-hsi hui-i hsüan-yen chi chueh-i-an 聯席會議宣言及決議案 (The manifesto and resolutions of the joint conference, November 1926). Second Kuomintang Central Executive Committee. Peking(?), 1926.

Liu, F. F. *A Military History of Modern China 1924–1949.* Princeton, Princeton University Press, 1956.

Liu Ping-ts'ui 劉秉粹. *Ko-ming ti-i-tz'u tung-cheng shih-chan chi* 革命第一次東征實戰記 (Factual battle reports of the first eastern expedition of the revolutionary army). Washington, D.C., Center for Chinese Research Materials, 1971.

Lo I-nung 羅亦農. *Wu-ch'an chieh-chi cheng-tang chih chien-she* 無產階級政黨之建設 (The building of a proletarian political party). Canton, 1926.

McVey, Ruth T. *The Rise of Indonesian Communism.* Ithaca, N.Y., Cornell University Press, 1965.

Mao Tse-tung hsuan-chi hsu-chi 毛澤東選集續集 (Supplement to the selected works of Mao Tse-tung). Chin-ch'a-chi, 1947.

Mao Tse-tung 毛澤東. *Hu-nan nung-min yün-tung k'ao-ch'a pao-kao* 湖南農民運動考察報告 (Report on an investigation into the Hunan peasant movement). Shanghai, 1949.

——— *Mō Taku-tō shū* 毛澤東集 (Collected works of Mao Tse-tung). Takeuchi Yoshimi, 竹內好 ed. Kokubōsha, Tokyo, 1972.

Mif, Pavel. *Chin-chi shih-ch'i-chung te Chung-kuo Kung-ch'an-tang* 緊急時期中的中國共產黨 (The Chinese Communist party in its critical days). Moscow, 1928.

Min-kuo shih-chiu-nien Hu-nan sheng cheng-chih nien-chien 民國十九年湖南省政治年鑑 (The political year book of Hunan province, 1930). Ch'angsha, 1931.

Mitrany, David. *Marx against the Peasant: A Study in Social Dogmatism.* London, Weidenfeld and Nicolson, 1951.

Muramatsu Yūji 村松祐次. "Shoki no Chūgoku Kyōsantō to Nōmin" 初期の中國共產黨と農民 (The Chinese Communist party and the agrarian movement during the early period). In Kazan Club, ed., *Ajia kako to genzai* アジア過去と現在 (Asia past and present). Tokyo, 1955.

Nagano Akira 長野朗. Shina nōmin undō kan 支那農民運動觀 (A view of the Chinese peasant movement). Tokyo, 1933.

North, Robert C. *Moscow and Chinese Communists.* Stanford, Stanford University Press, 1953.

—— and Xenia J. Eudin. *M. N. Roy's Mission to China: The Communist-Kuomintang Split of 1927.* Berkeley, University of California Press, 1963.

Nung-min hsieh-hui chang-ch'eng 農民協會章程 (The peasant association charter). Canton(?), 1924.

Nung-min hsieh-hui chang-ch'eng shih-i 農民協會章程釋義 (An explanation of the charter of the peasant association). Shanghai, 1927.

Nung-min ts'ung-k'an 農民叢刊 (Peasant collectanea), 4 vols. Shanghai, 1927.

Nung-min yun-tung 農民運動 (The peasant movement). 7–19/20 (Sept. 14–Dec. 7, 1926).

Ōtsuka Reizō 大塚令三. "Nenshi kō" 年志考 (Draft chronology), in Hatano Ken'ichi, *Chūgoku Kyōsantō Shi* (History of the Chinese Communist Party). III, 820–891.

The People's Tribune. Hankow, March 12–July 30, 1927.

Powell, John D. *Political Mobilization of the Venezuelan Peasant.* Cambridge, Harvard University Press, 1971.

Roy, M. N. *Revolution and Counter-Revolution in China.* Calcutta, Renaissance Publishers, 1946.

Schram, Stuart R. *The Political Thought of Mao Tse-tung.* New York, Frederick A. Praeger, 1963.

—— *Mao Tse-tung: A Political Biography.* New York, Simon and Schuster, 1966.

Schwartz, Benjamin I. *Chinese Communism and the Rise of Mao.* Cambridge, Harvard University Press, 1951.

—— "The Legend of the 'Legend of Maoism'," *The China Quarterly* no. 2, 35–42 (1960).

Seng Sin Fu. *China: A Survey of the Historical and Economic Forces Behind the Nationalist Revolution.* London, Communist Party of Great Britain, 1927.

Shina ni okeru saikin no nōmin undō to nōgyō mondai 支那に於ける最近の農民運動と農業問題 (The recent peasant movement and agricultural problems in China). Tr., Sangyō Rōdō Chōsajo'(Industrial Labor Research Center). Tokyo, 1929.

Shirley, James. "Control of the Kuomintang after Sun Yat-sen's Death," *Journal of Asian Studies* 25.1: 69–82c (1965).

—— "Political Conflict in the Kuomintang: The Career of Wang Ching-wei to 1932." Ph.D. dissertation, University of California, Berkeley, 1962.

Skinner, G. William. "Marketing and Social Structure in Rural China, part 1." *Journal of Asian Studies* 24.1: 3–43 (1964).

———— "Marketing and Social Structure in Rural China, part 2."
Journal of Asian Studies 24.2: 195–228 (1965).

———— "Marketing and Social Structure in Rural China, part 3."
Journal of Asian Studies 24.3: 363–399 (1965).

Smedley, Agnes. *The Great Road: The Life and Times of Chu Teh*. New
York, Monthly Review Press, 1956.

Snow, Edgar. *Red Star over China*. New York, Random House, 1938.

Spence, Jonathan. *To Change China: Western Advisers in China 1620–
1960*. Boston, Little Brown, 1969.

Strong, Anna Louise. *China's Millions*. New York, Coward-McCann,
1928.

Sun Yat-sen 孫文. *Tsung-li ch'üan chi* 總理全集 (Complete collected works
of the director-general), ed. Hu Han-min 胡漢民. Shanghai, 1930.

Suzue Gen'ichi 鈴江言一. *Chūgoku kaihō tōsō shi* 中國解放鬪爭史 (A history
of the Chinese liberation struggle). Tokyo, 1953.

Takayama Kensuke 高山謙介, ed. *Shina kokumin kakumei ni okeru nōmin
undō* 支那國民革命に於ける農民運動. Dairen, 1929.

Tanaka Tadao 田中忠夫. *Kakumei Shina nōson no jisshōteki kenkyū* 革命支那
農村の實證的研究 (A factual study of the Chinese countryside in
revolution). Tokyo, 1930.

T'an P'ing-shan 譚平山. *Chung-kuo ko-ming yü Kuo-min-tang* 中國革命與國民
黨 (The Chinese Revolution and the Kuomintang). Canton, 1923.

———— and Feng Chü-p'o 馮菊坡. *Kuo-min ko-ming chung-chih
min-t'uan wen-t'i* 國民革命中之民團問題 (The Min-t'uan problem
in the national revolution). Canton, 1923.

Tawney, R. H. *Land and Labour in China*. New York, Octagon, 1964.

T'ang Leang-li. *The Inner History of the Chinese Revolution*. London,
George Routledge, 1930.

T'an-ho kung-ch'an-tang liang ta yao-an 彈劾共產黨兩大要案 (Two
important documents in the case against the Chinese Communist
party). Ed. Kuomintang Central Supervisory Committee. 1930.

Teng Chung-hsia 鄧中夏. *Chung-kuo chih-kung yun-tung chien-shih, 1919–
1926* 中國職功運動簡史 (A concise history of the Chinese labor
movement 1919–1926). Peking, 1953.

Teng Yen-ta 鄧演達. *Teng Yen-ta Hsien-sheng i-chu* 鄧演達先生遺著
(Posthumous works of Teng Yen-ta), compiled by Huang
Ch'i-hsiang and distributed by Yang I-t'ang. Hong Kong, preface
dated 1949.

Ti-i-tz'u kuo-nei ko-ming chan-cheng shih-ch'i ti chi-chien shih-shih 第一次國內
革命戰爭時期的幾件史實 (Some historical facts concerning the first
revolutionary civil war). Shanghai, 1956.

Ti-i-tz'u kuo-nei ko-ming chan-cheng shih-ch'i ti kung-jen yun-tung 第一次國內
革命戰爭時期的工人運動 (The labor movement in the period of the
first revolutionary civil war). Peking, 1954.

Ti-i-tz'u kuo-nei ko-ming chan-cheng shih-ch'i ti nung-min yun-tung 第一次國內
革命戰爭時期的農民運動 (The peasant movement during the period
of the first revolutionary civil war). Peking, 1953.

Trotsky, Leon. *Problems of the Chinese Revolution.* Tr. and introduction
by Max Shachtman. New York, Pioneer Publishers, 1932.

Tsou Lu 鄒魯. *Chung-kuo Kuo-min-tang shih-kao* 中國國民黨史稿 (Draft
history of the Chinese Kuomintang). Shanghai, 1929.

Vishnyakova-Akimova, V. V. *Dva Goda v Vosstavshem Kitae 1925–*
1927—Vospominaniia (Two years in revolutionary China 1925–
1927: Reminiscences). Moscow, 1965.

Wales, Nym. *Red Dust: Autobiographies of Chinese Communists.* Stanford,
Stanford University Press, 1952.

Wang Chien-min 王健民, ed. *Chung-kuo kung-ch'an-tang shih-kao* 中國共產
黨史稿 (Draft history of the Chinese Communist party). Vol. I.
Taipei, 1965.

Whiting, Allen S. *Soviet Policies in China 1917–1924.* New York,
Columbia University Press, 1953.

Wilbur, C. Martin, and Julie Lien-ying Howe, eds. *Documents on*
Communism, Nationalism, and Soviet Advisers in China 1918–1927:
Papers Seized in the 1927 Peking Raid. New York, Columbia University
Press, 1956.

Wittfogel, Karl A. "The Legend of 'Maoism'," *China Quarterly* no. 1,
pp. 29–34 (1960).

——— "The Legend of 'Maoism' (Concluded)," *China Quarterly*
no. 2, pp. 16–34 (1960).

Woo, T. C. *The Kuomintang and the Future of the Chinese Revolution.*
London, George Allen and Unwin, 1928.

Wright, Mary C. "The Chinese Peasant and Communism," *Pacific*
Affairs 24.3: 256–265 (1951).

INDEX

HARVARD EAST ASIAN SERIES